A Condition Called Love ♥

Megumi Morino

2

CONTENTS

A Condition
Called Love

CHARACTERS

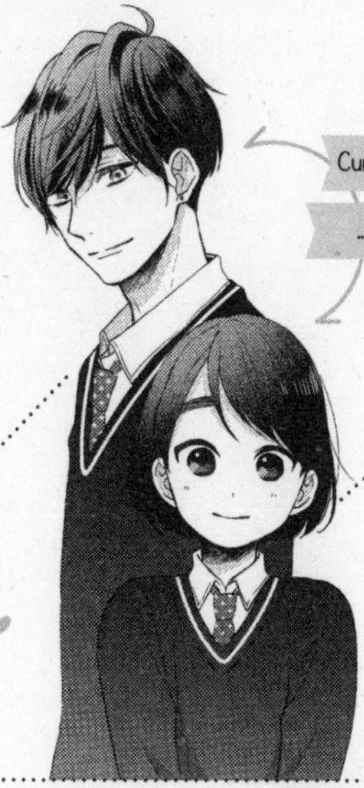

Currently going out...

...on a trial basis.

Hananoi-kun

The hot boy from the class down the hall. Rumor has it his grades are eight standard deviations over the norm. He is excessively romantic.

Hotaru Hinase

A first-year high-school girl who loves to eat. She thought she'd never love as long as she lived, but here we are...

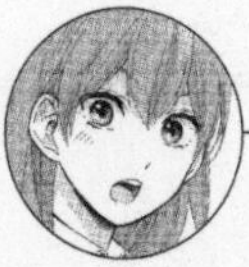

Hibiki Asami (Kyo-chan)

Hotaru's classmate. They've been friends since middle school.

♥ Currently going out!

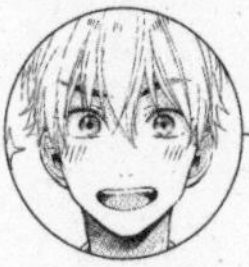

Keigo Kurata

Hananoi-kun's classmate.

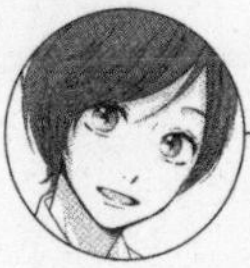

Tsukiha Shibamura (Shibamu)

Hotaru's classmate.

The Hinase Family

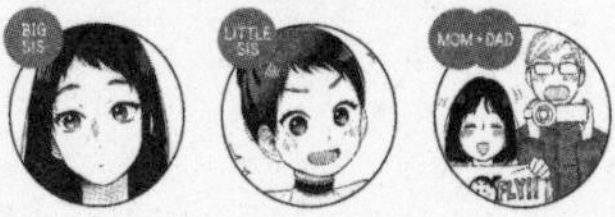
BIG SIS
LITTLE SIS
MOM + DAD

THE STORY SO FAR

One fateful winter day, Hotaru happened to run into Hananoi-kun, the boy from the class down the hall—just as he was getting dumped. As he sat out in the snow alone, she offered him her umbrella. Little did she know, that small gesture would change her life forever. Hananoi-kun asked her out the very next day, and though she turned him down at first, he eventually convinced her to go out with him on a trial basis until Christmas.

Hananoi-kun is overzealous in his affections...but he's sweet. And in their time together, Hotaru feels all sorts of emotions she's never felt before. Finally Christmas has come, and with it, the end of their relationship. But Hananoi-kun has one last surprise for Hotaru: he somehow found out that Christmas Eve is her birthday! He treats her to an enchanting date, and for the first time in her life, Hotaru feels special on her birthday. Now, can she really bear to say goodbye to Hananoi-kun?

Special thanks to... ♡

My editor, Y-san
Kyonko-san
Takematsu-san
Shiiya-san
Yuu Sugimoto-san
Everybody at the Sanseido
Bookstore in Omiya

Idenaga-san
Sato-san
Takahashi-san
The Dessert editorial staff

Nawata Kohei Design

And my friends, family and
former colleagues, who are
always there for me

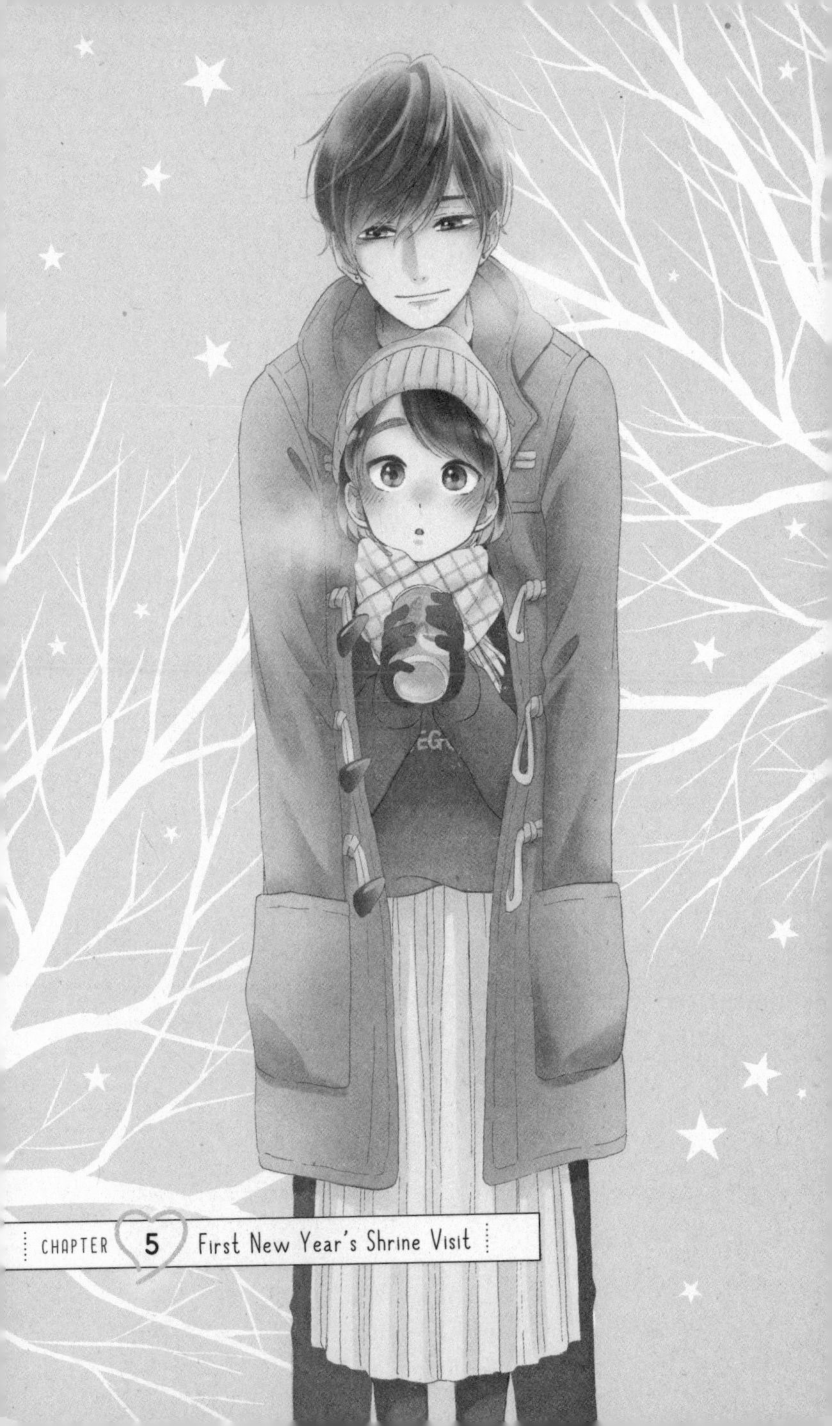

CHAPTER 5 First New Year's Shrine Visit

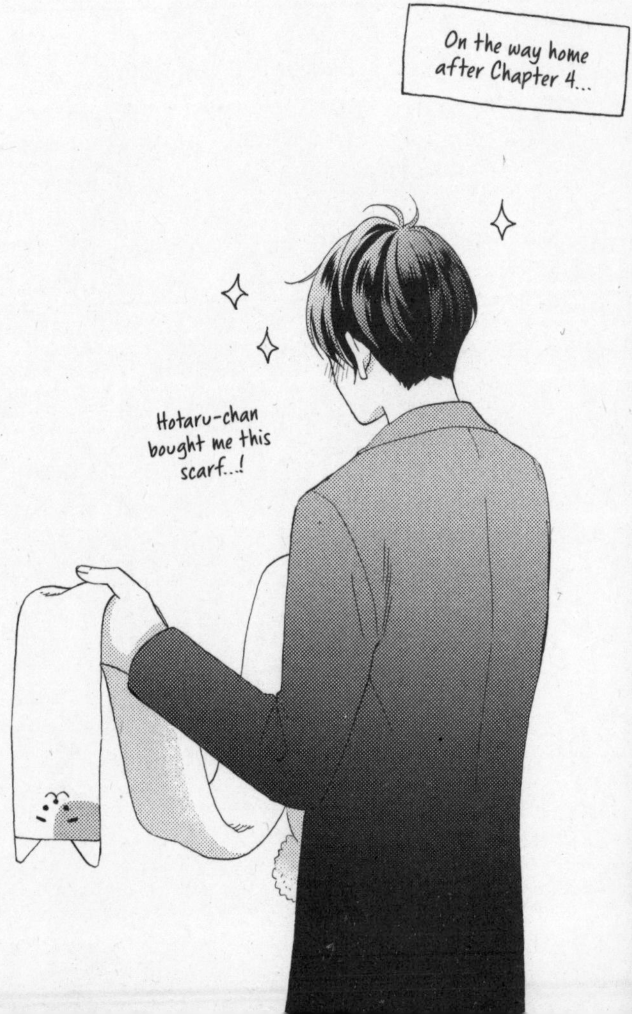
On the way home after Chapter 4...
Hotaru-chan bought me this scarf...!

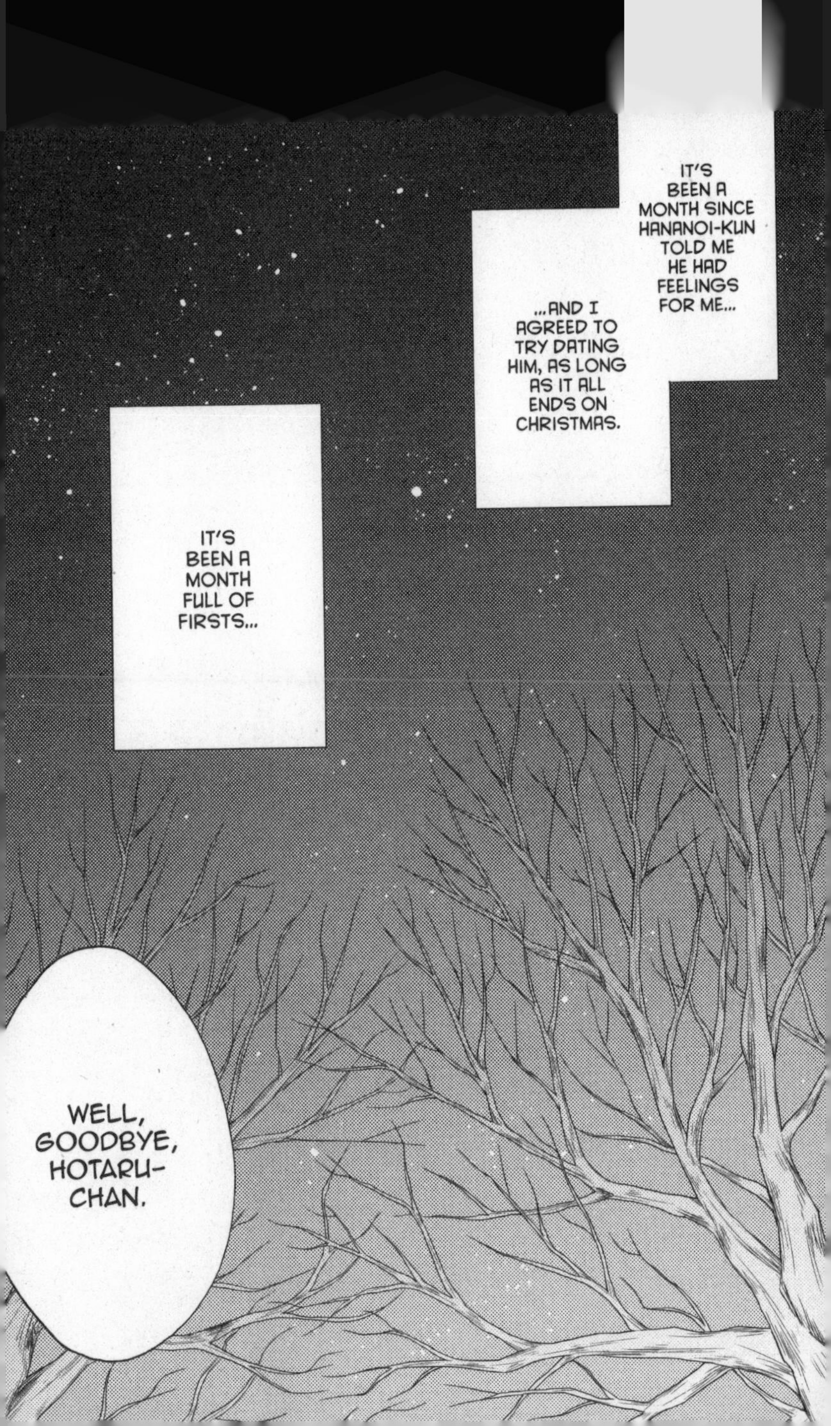
IT'S BEEN A MONTH SINCE HANANOI-KUN TOLD ME HE HAD FEELINGS FOR ME...
...AND I AGREED TO TRY DATING HIM, AS LONG AS IT ALL ENDS ON CHRISTMAS.
IT'S BEEN A MONTH FULL OF FIRSTS...
WELL, GOODBYE, HOTARU-CHAN.

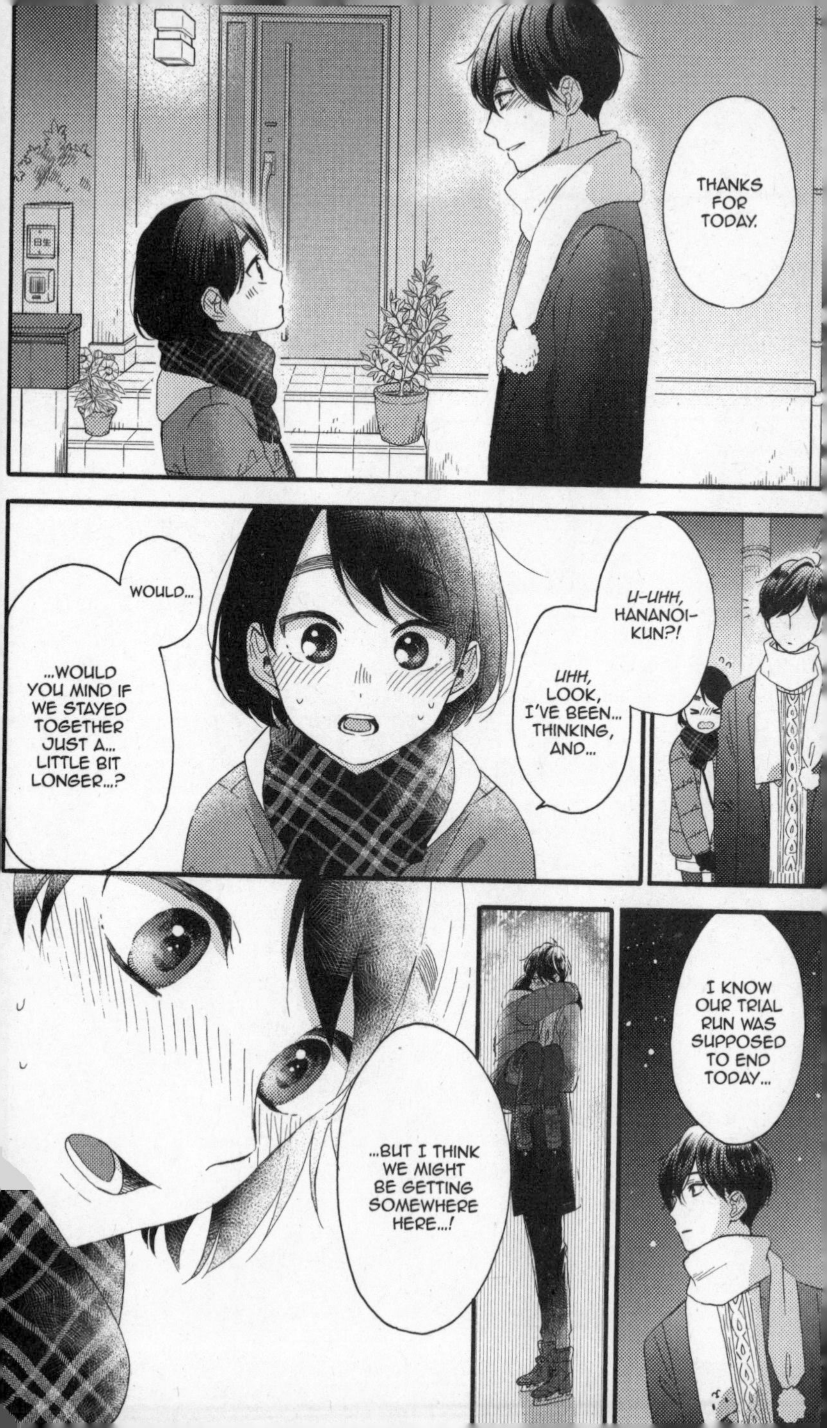
THANKS FOR TODAY.
U-UHH, HANANOI-KUN?!
UHH, LOOK, I'VE BEEN... THINKING, AND...
WOULD...
...WOULD YOU MIND IF WE STAYED TOGETHER JUST A... LITTLE BIT LONGER...?
I KNOW OUR TRIAL RUN WAS SUPPOSED TO END TODAY...
...BUT I THINK WE MIGHT BE GETTING SOMEWHERE HERE...!

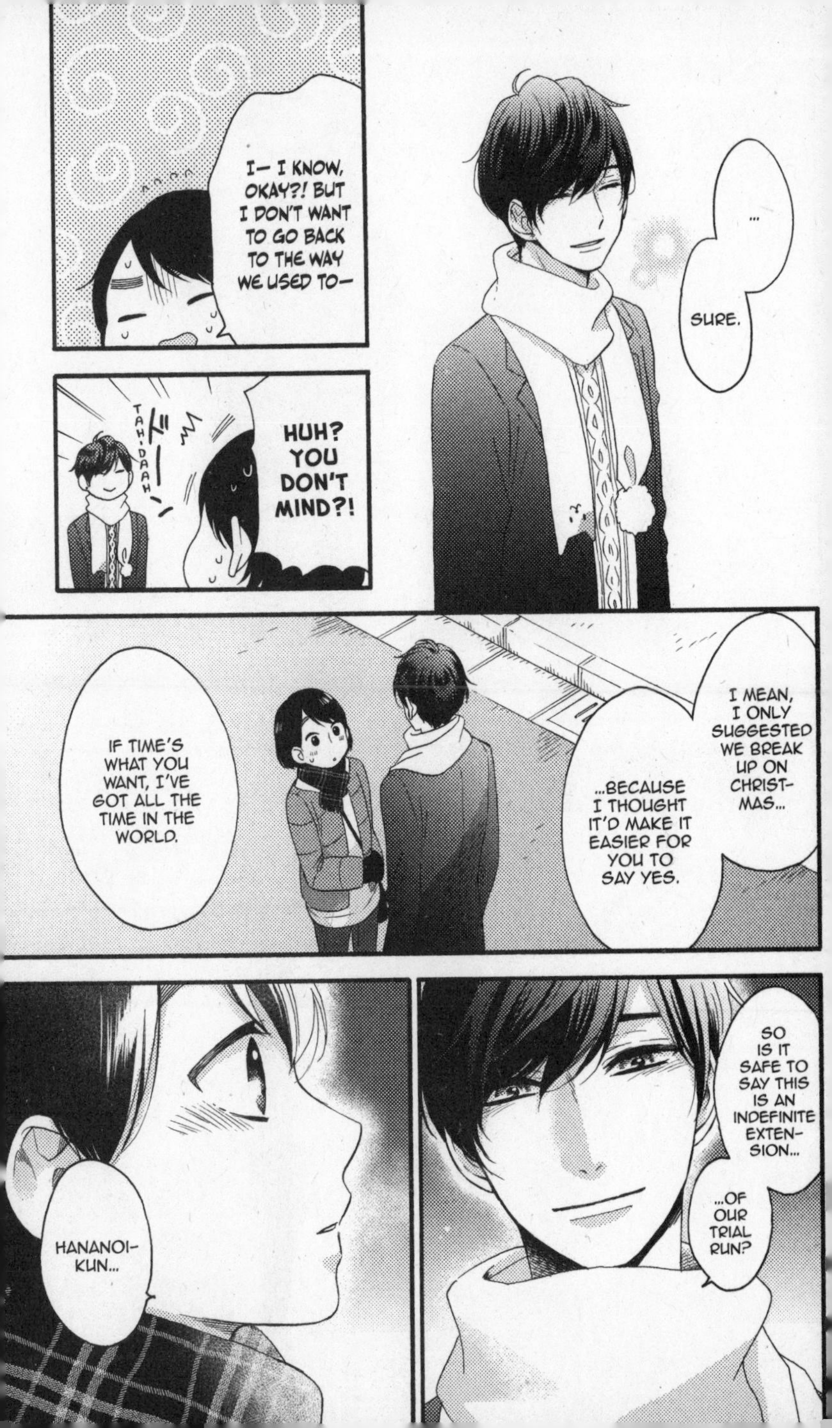
...
SURE.
I— I KNOW, OKAY?! BUT I DON'T WANT TO GO BACK TO THE WAY WE USED TO—
HUH? YOU DON'T MIND?!
TAH-DAAH
I MEAN, I ONLY SUGGESTED WE BREAK UP ON CHRIST-MAS...
...BECAUSE I THOUGHT IT'D MAKE IT EASIER FOR YOU TO SAY YES.
IF TIME'S WHAT YOU WANT, I'VE GOT ALL THE TIME IN THE WORLD.
SO IS IT SAFE TO SAY THIS IS AN INDEFINITE EXTEN-SION...
...OF OUR TRIAL RUN?
HANANOI-KUN...

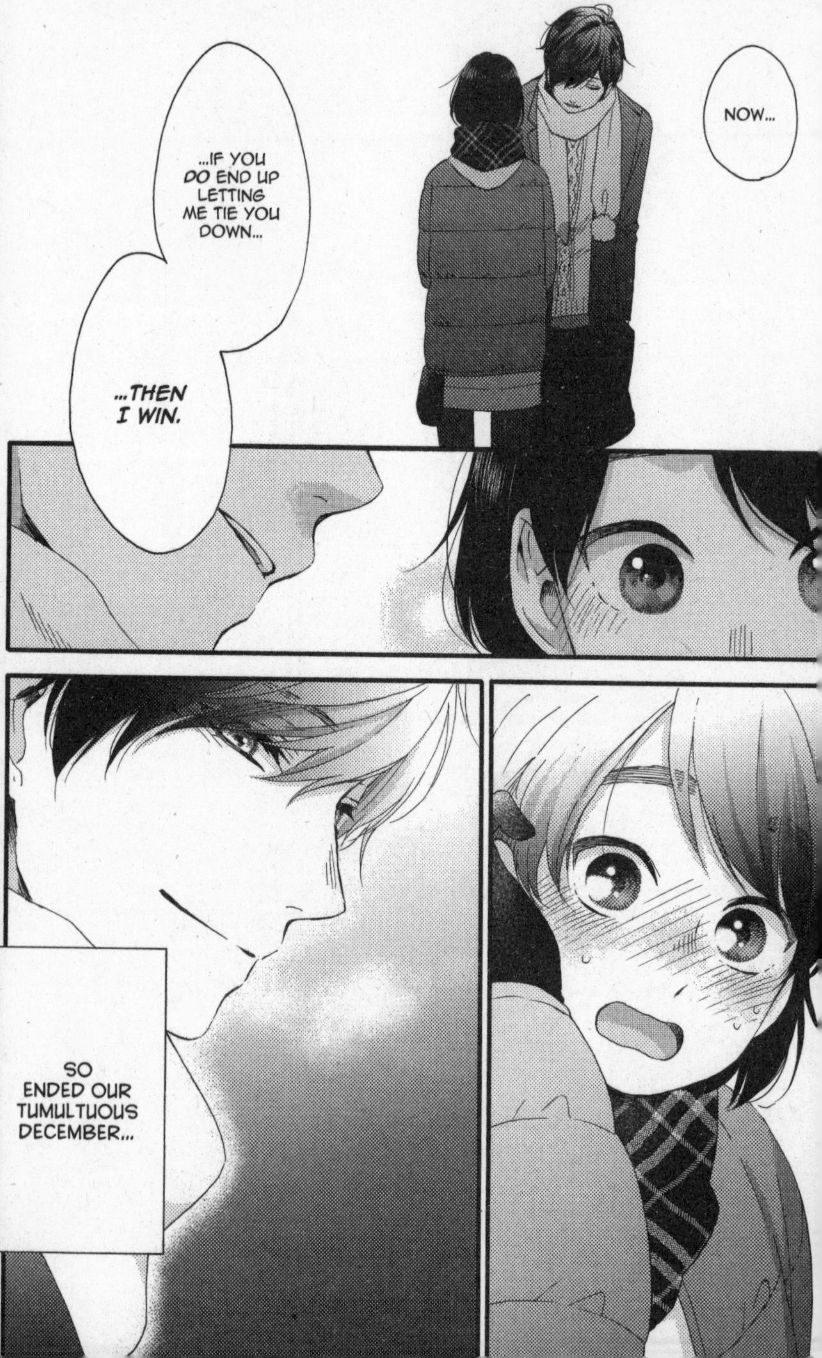
NOW...
...IF YOU DO END UP LETTING ME TIE YOU DOWN...
...THEN I WIN.
SO ENDED OUR TUMULTUOUS DECEMBER...

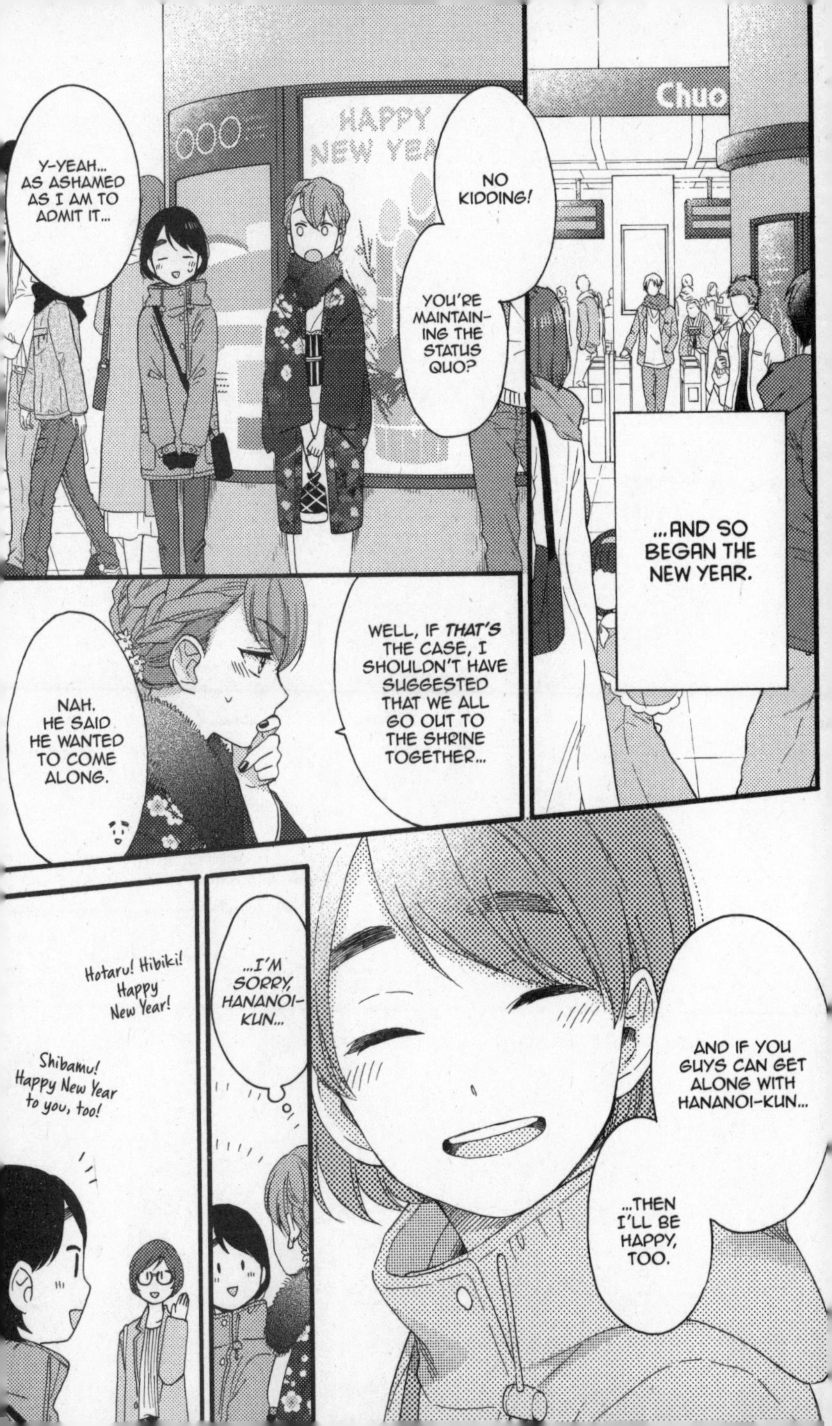
Chuo
...AND SO BEGAN THE NEW YEAR.
HAPPY NEW YEA
NO KIDDING!
YOU'RE MAINTAINING THE STATUS QUO?
Y-YEAH... AS ASHAMED AS I AM TO ADMIT IT...
WELL, IF *THAT'S* THE CASE, I SHOULDN'T HAVE SUGGESTED THAT WE ALL GO OUT TO THE SHRINE TOGETHER...
NAH. HE SAID HE WANTED TO COME ALONG.
AND IF YOU GUYS CAN GET ALONG WITH HANANOI-KUN...
...THEN I'LL BE HAPPY, TOO.
...I'M SORRY, HANANOI-KUN...
Hotaru! Hibiki! Happy New Year!
Shibamu! Happy New Year to you, too!

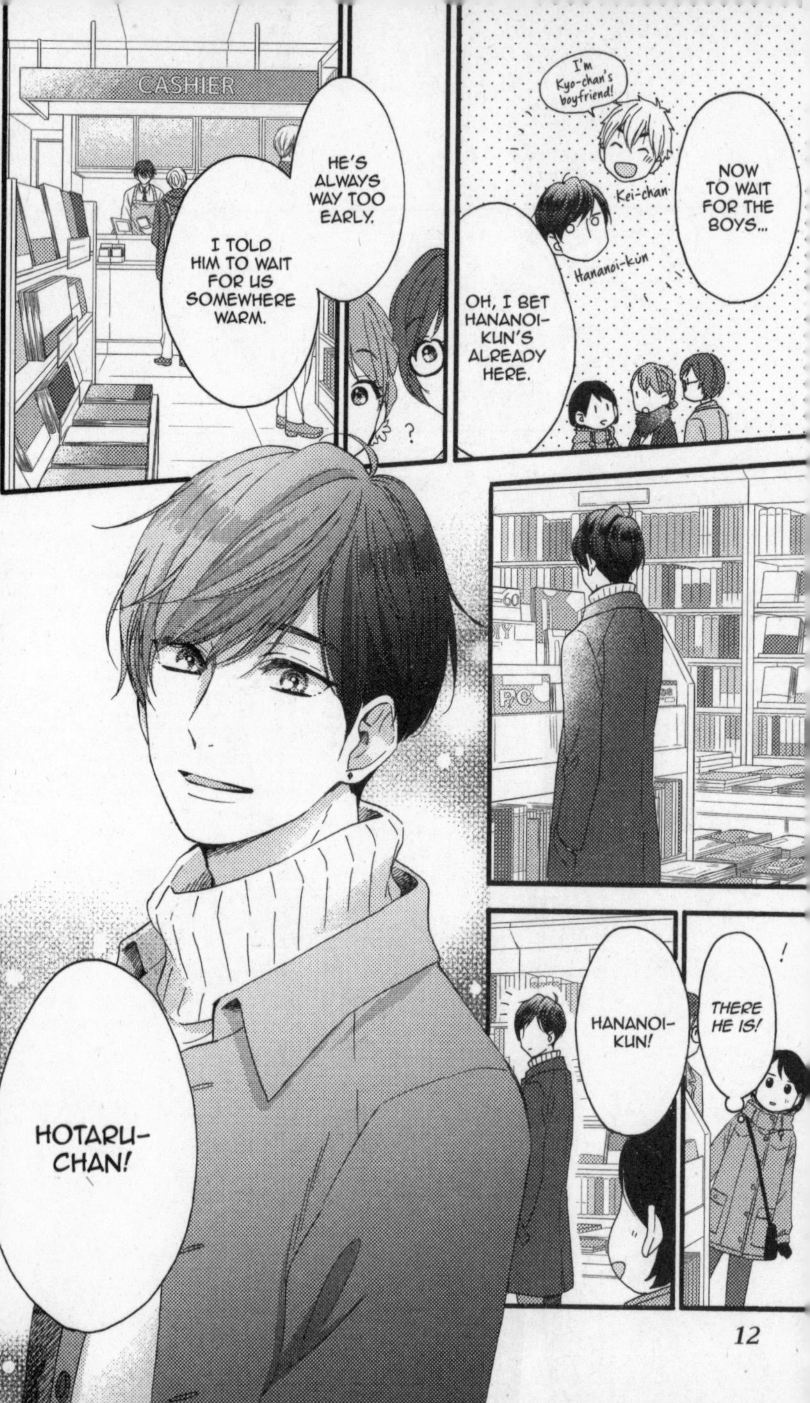
NOW TO WAIT FOR THE BOYS...
I'm Kyo-chan's boyfriend!
Kei-chan
Hananoi-kun
OH, I BET HANANOI-KUN'S ALREADY HERE.
HE'S ALWAYS WAY TOO EARLY.
I TOLD HIM TO WAIT FOR US SOMEWHERE WARM.
CASHIER
!
THERE HE IS!
HANANOI-KUN!
HOTARU-CHAN!

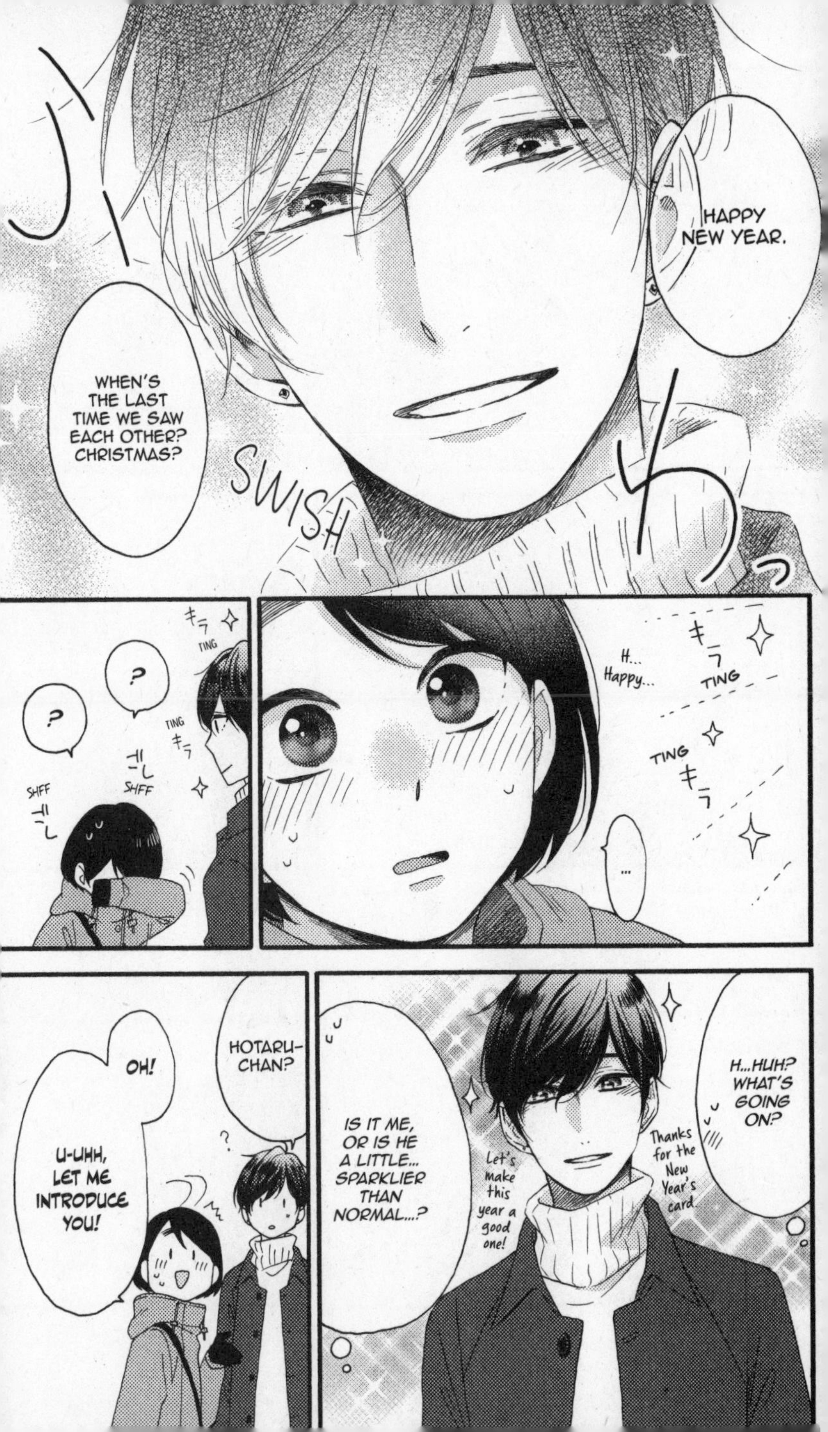
HAPPY NEW YEAR.
WHEN'S THE LAST TIME WE SAW EACH OTHER? CHRISTMAS?
SWISH
H... Happy...
TING
TING
...
?
?
TING
TING
SHFF
SHFF
H...HUH? WHAT'S GOING ON?
Thanks for the New Year's card
Let's make this year a good one!
IS IT ME, OR IS HE A LITTLE... SPARKLIER THAN NORMAL...?
HOTARU-CHAN?
OH!
U-UHH, LET ME INTRODUCE YOU!

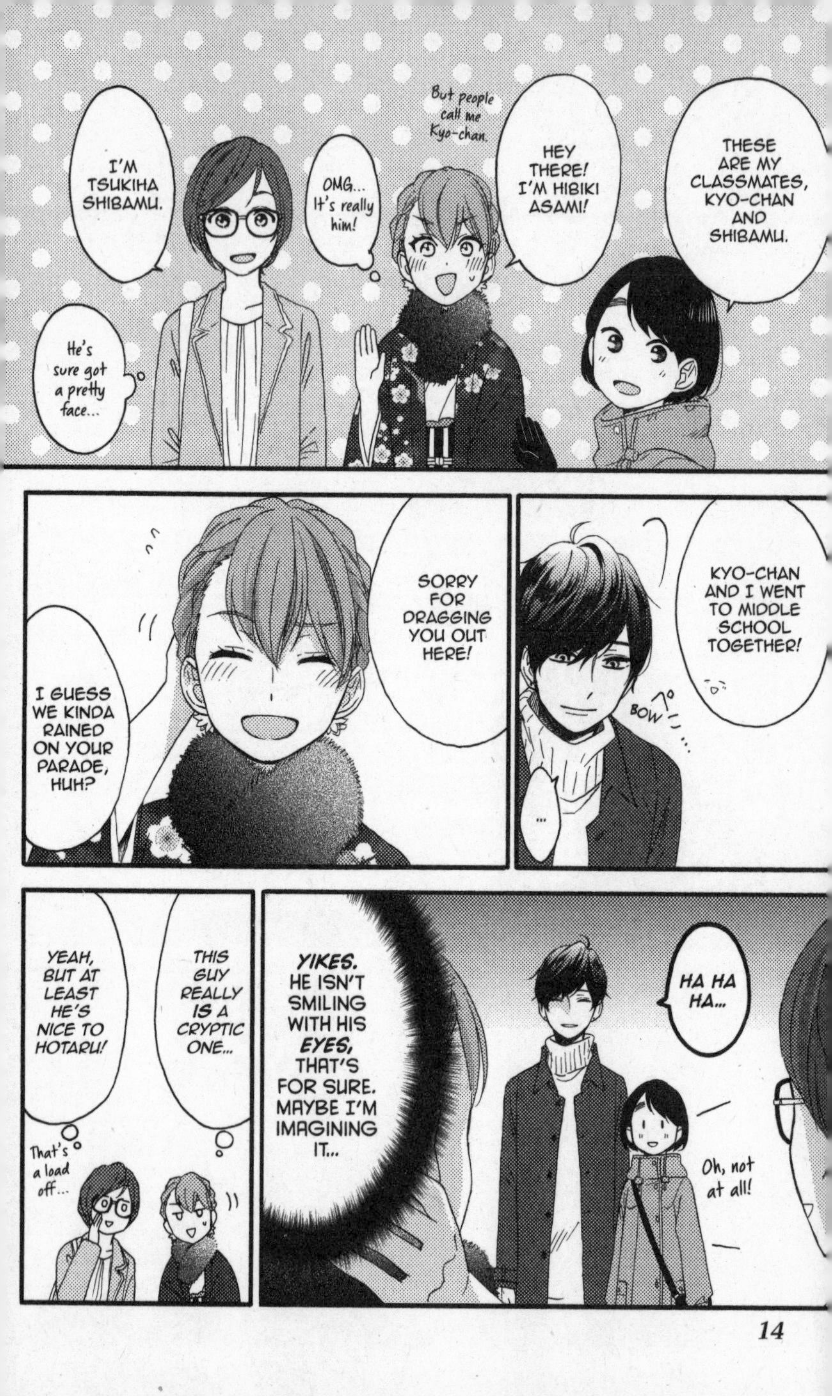
THESE ARE MY CLASSMATES, KYO-CHAN AND SHIBAMU.
HEY THERE! I'M HIBIKI ASAMI!
But people call me Kyo-chan.
OMG... It's really him!
I'M TSUKIHA SHIBAMU.
He's sure got a pretty face...
KYO-CHAN AND I WENT TO MIDDLE SCHOOL TOGETHER!
BOW
...
SORRY FOR DRAGGING YOU OUT HERE!
I GUESS WE KINDA RAINED ON YOUR PARADE, HUH?
HA HA HA...
Oh, not at all!
YIKES. HE ISN'T SMILING WITH HIS EYES, THAT'S FOR SURE. MAYBE I'M IMAGINING IT...
THIS GUY REALLY IS A CRYPTIC ONE...
YEAH, BUT AT LEAST HE'S NICE TO HOTARU!
That's a load off...

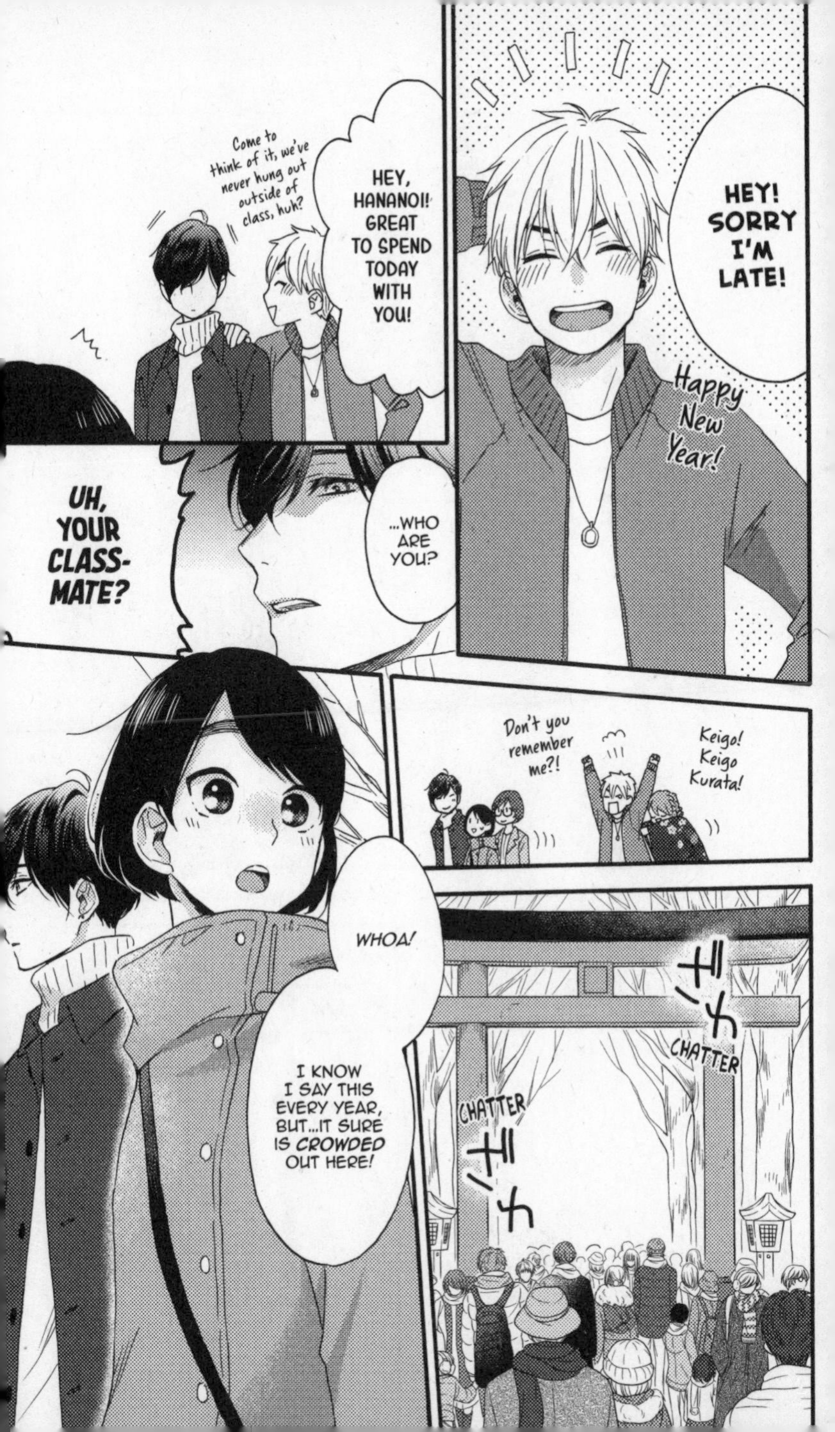
HEY! SORRY I'M LATE!
Happy New Year!
HEY, HANANOI! GREAT TO SPEND TODAY WITH YOU!
Come to think of it, we've never hung out outside of class, huh?
...WHO ARE YOU?
UH, YOUR CLASS-MATE?
Keigo! Keigo Kurata!
Don't you remember me?!
CHATTER
CHATTER
WHOA!
I KNOW I SAY THIS EVERY YEAR, BUT...IT SURE IS CROWDED OUT HERE!

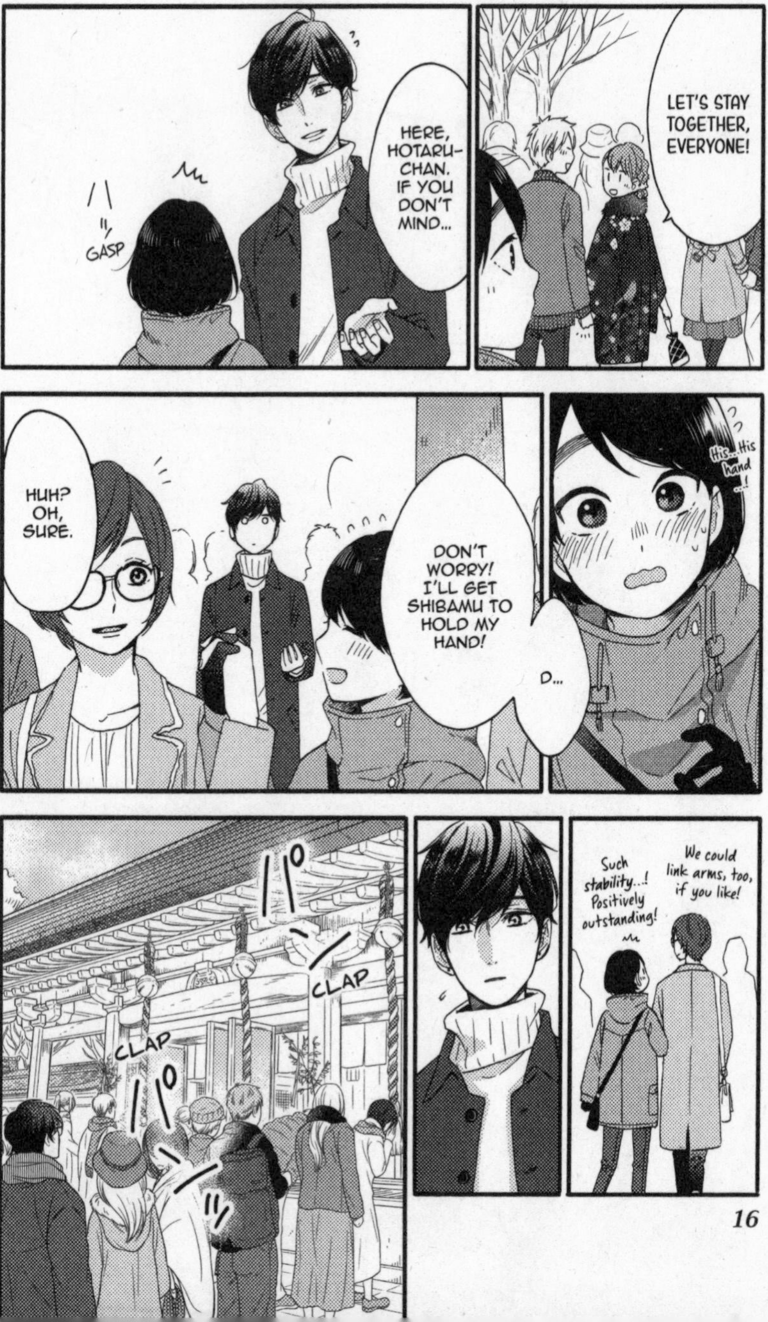
LET'S STAY TOGETHER, EVERYONE!
HERE, HOTARU-CHAN. IF YOU DON'T MIND...
GASP
His... His hand...!
D...
DON'T WORRY! I'LL GET SHIBAMU TO HOLD MY HAND!
HUH? OH, SURE.
We could link arms, too, if you like!
Such stability...! Positively outstanding!
CLAP
CLAP

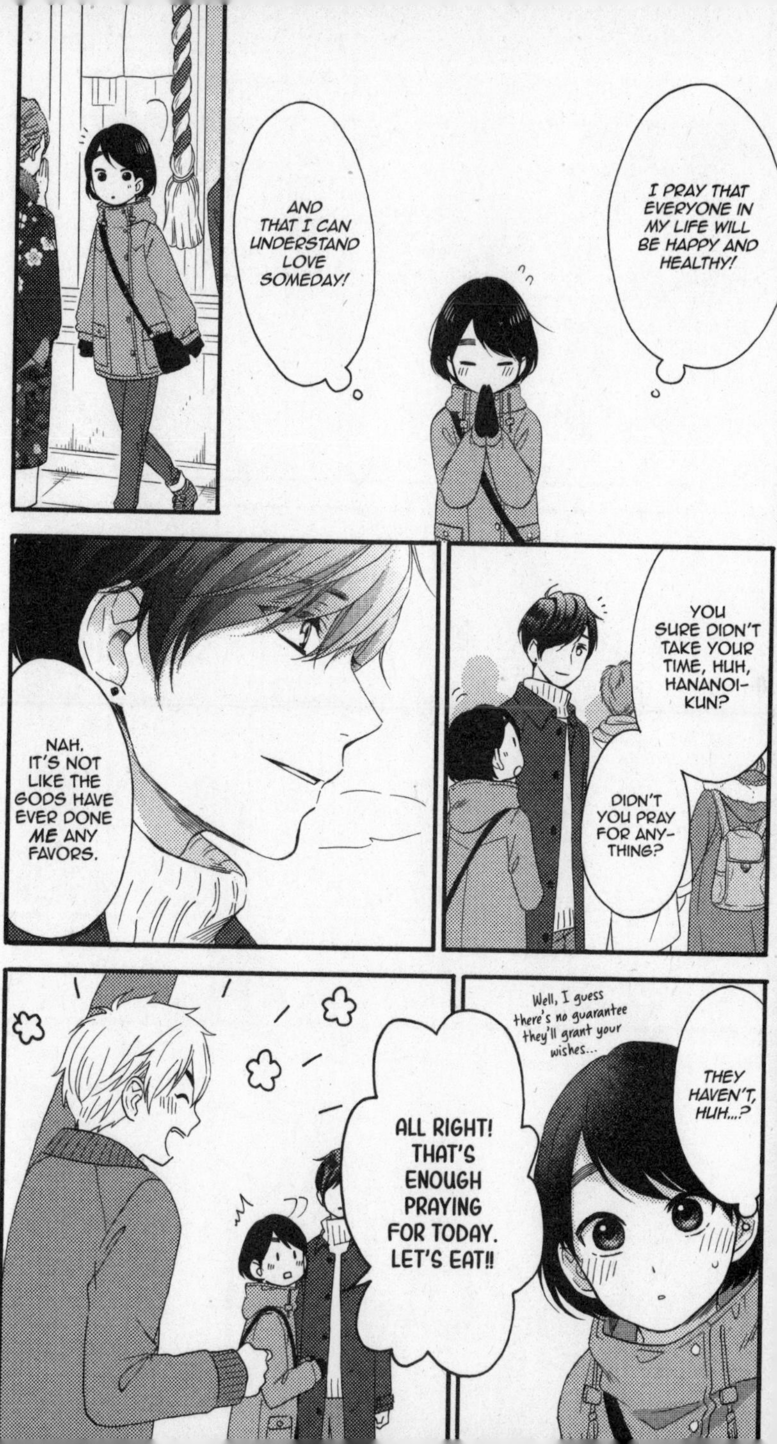
I PRAY THAT EVERYONE IN MY LIFE WILL BE HAPPY AND HEALTHY!
AND THAT I CAN UNDERSTAND LOVE SOMEDAY!
YOU SURE DIDN'T TAKE YOUR TIME, HUH, HANANOI-KUN?
DIDN'T YOU PRAY FOR ANYTHING?
NAH. IT'S NOT LIKE THE GODS HAVE EVER DONE *ME* ANY FAVORS.
Well, I guess there's no guarantee they'll grant your wishes...
THEY HAVEN'T, HUH...?
ALL RIGHT! THAT'S ENOUGH PRAYING FOR TODAY. LET'S EAT!!

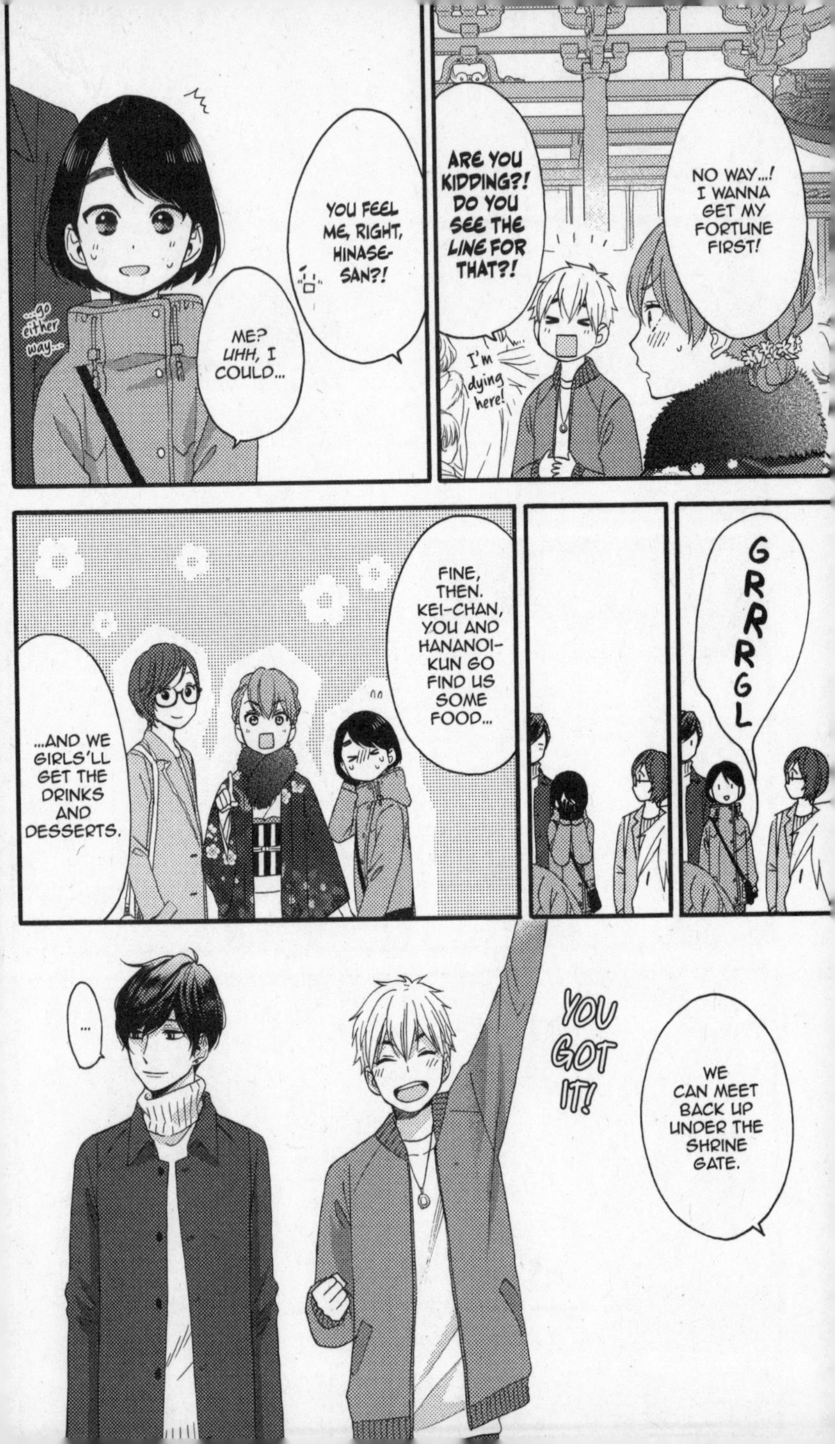
NO WAY...! I WANNA GET MY FORTUNE FIRST!
ARE YOU KIDDING?! DO YOU SEE THE LINE FOR THAT?!
I'm dying here!
YOU FEEL ME, RIGHT, HINASE-SAN?!
ME? UHH, I COULD...
...go either way...
GRRRGL
FINE, THEN. KEI-CHAN, YOU AND HANANOI-KUN GO FIND US SOME FOOD...
...AND WE GIRLS'LL GET THE DRINKS AND DESSERTS.
WE CAN MEET BACK UP UNDER THE SHRINE GATE.
YOU GOT IT!
...

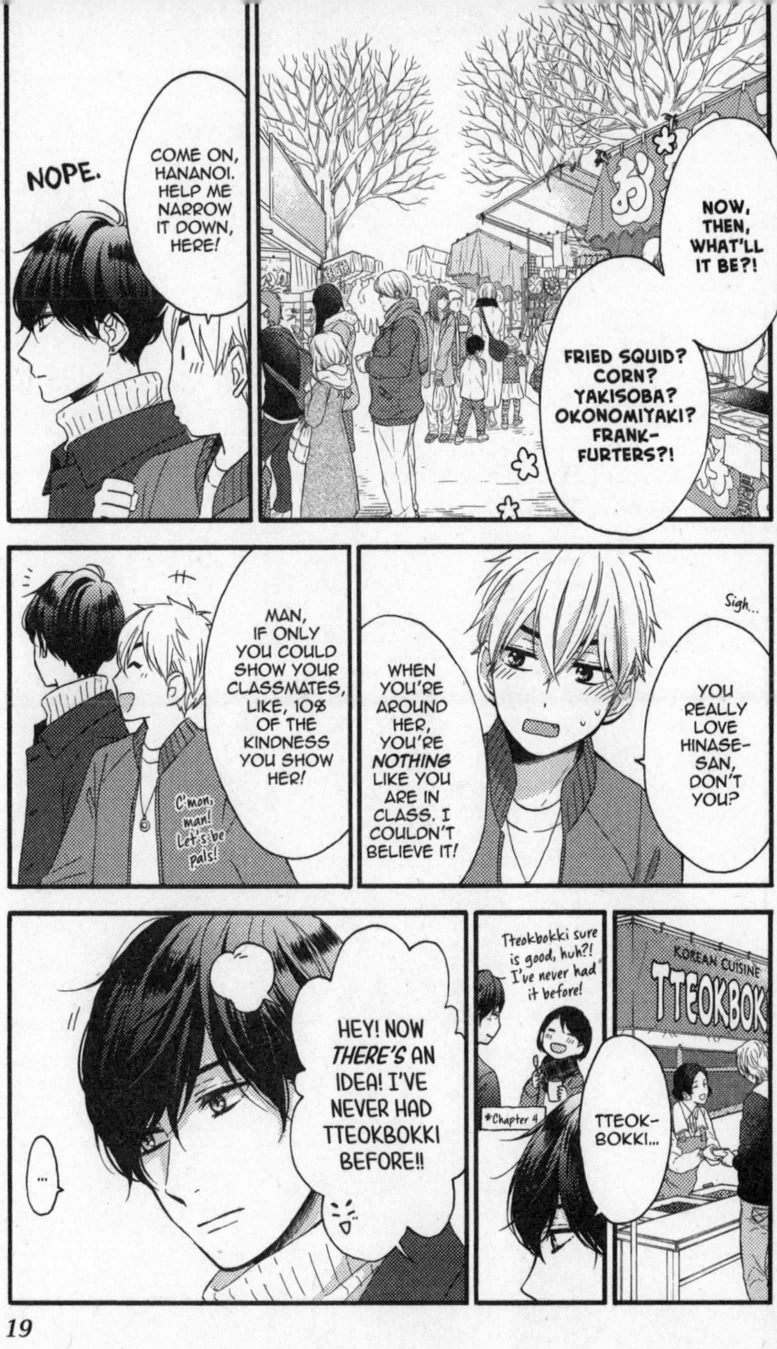
NOW, THEN, WHAT'LL IT BE?!
FRIED SQUID? CORN? YAKISOBA? OKONOMIYAKI? FRANK-FURTERS?!
COME ON, HANANOI. HELP ME NARROW IT DOWN, HERE!
NOPE.
Sigh...
YOU REALLY LOVE HINASE-SAN, DON'T YOU?
WHEN YOU'RE AROUND HER, YOU'RE *NOTHING* LIKE YOU ARE IN CLASS. I COULDN'T BELIEVE IT!
MAN, IF ONLY YOU COULD SHOW YOUR CLASSMATES, LIKE, 10% OF THE KINDNESS YOU SHOW HER!
C'mon, man! Let's be pals!
KOREAN CUISINE
TTEOKBOK
Tteokbokki sure is good, huh?! I've never had it before!
*Chapter 4
TTEOK-BOKKI...
HEY! NOW *THERE'S* AN IDEA! I'VE NEVER HAD TTEOKBOKKI BEFORE!!
...

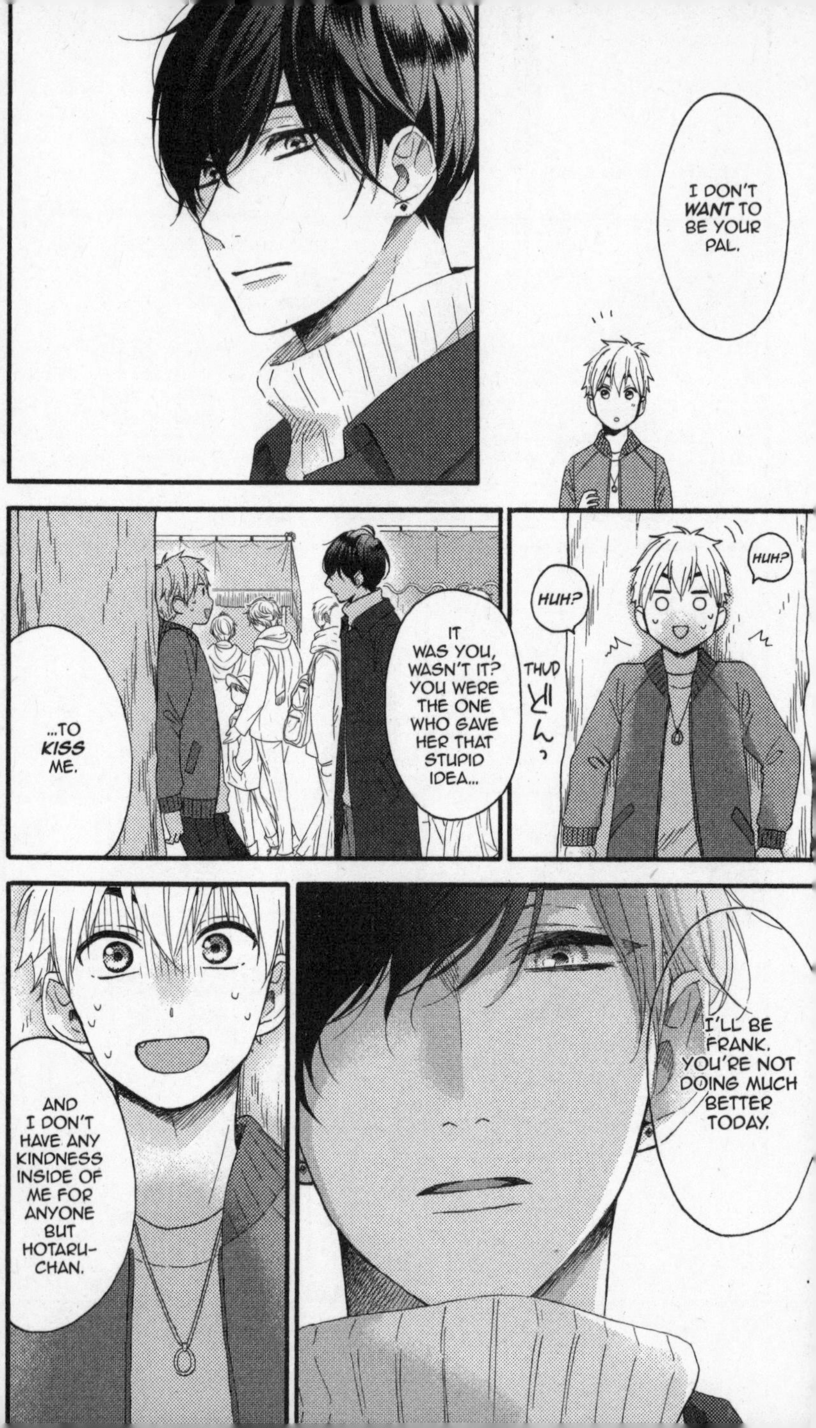

I DON'T *WANT* TO BE YOUR PAL.
HUH?
HUH?
THUD どん
IT WAS YOU, WASN'T IT? YOU WERE THE ONE WHO GAVE HER THAT STUPID IDEA...
...TO *KISS* ME.
I'LL BE FRANK. YOU'RE NOT DOING MUCH BETTER TODAY.
AND I DON'T HAVE ANY KINDNESS INSIDE OF ME FOR ANYONE BUT HOTARU-CHAN.

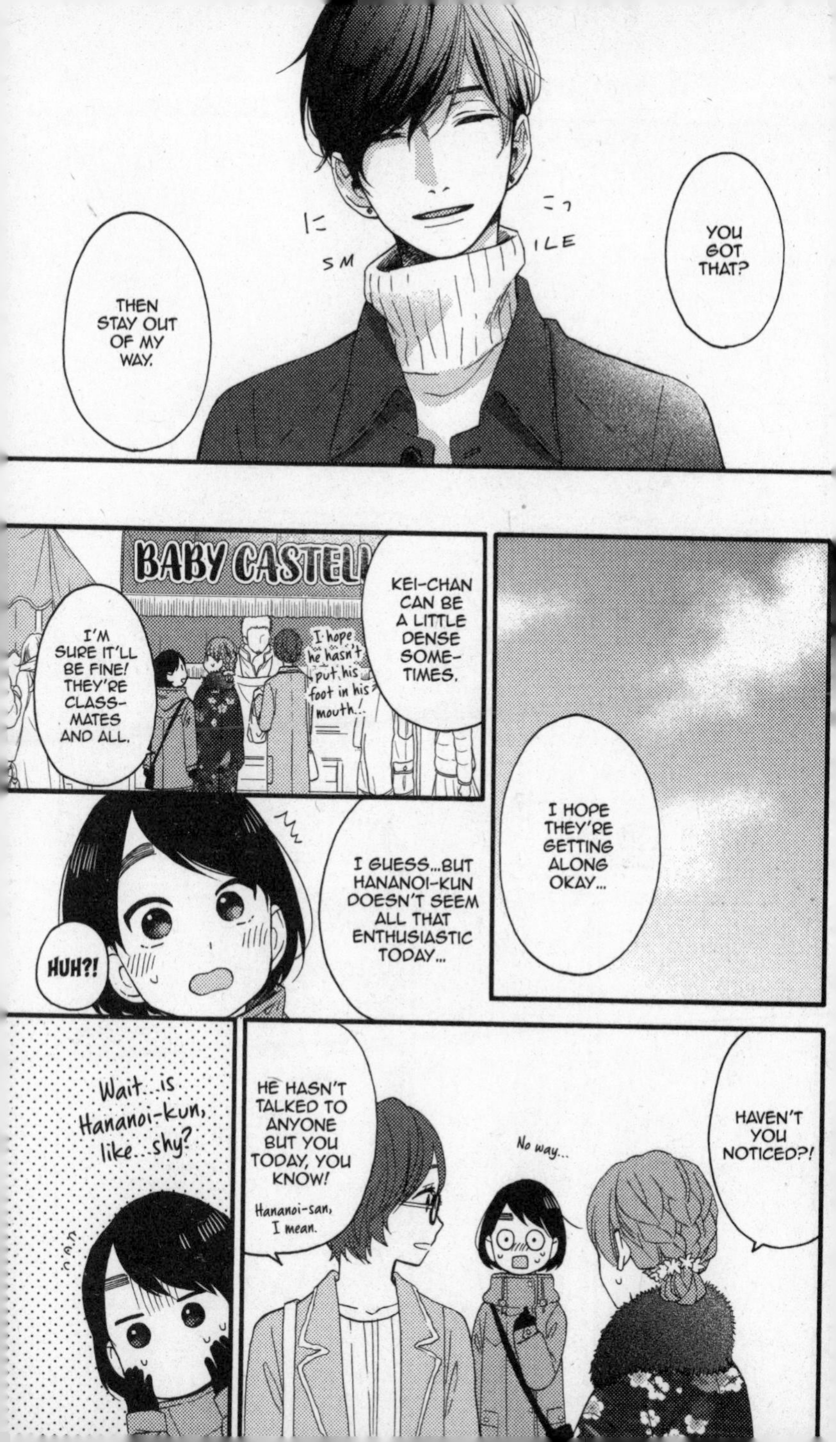
YOU GOT THAT?
SM ILE
THEN STAY OUT OF MY WAY.
I HOPE THEY'RE GETTING ALONG OKAY...
KEI-CHAN CAN BE A LITTLE DENSE SOMETIMES.
I hope he hasn't put his foot in his mouth!
I'M SURE IT'LL BE FINE! THEY'RE CLASSMATES AND ALL.
I GUESS...BUT HANANOI-KUN DOESN'T SEEM ALL THAT ENTHUSIASTIC TODAY...
HUH?!
HAVEN'T YOU NOTICED?!
No way...
HE HASN'T TALKED TO ANYONE BUT YOU TODAY, YOU KNOW!
Hananoi-san, I mean.
Wait...is Hananoi-kun, like...shy?

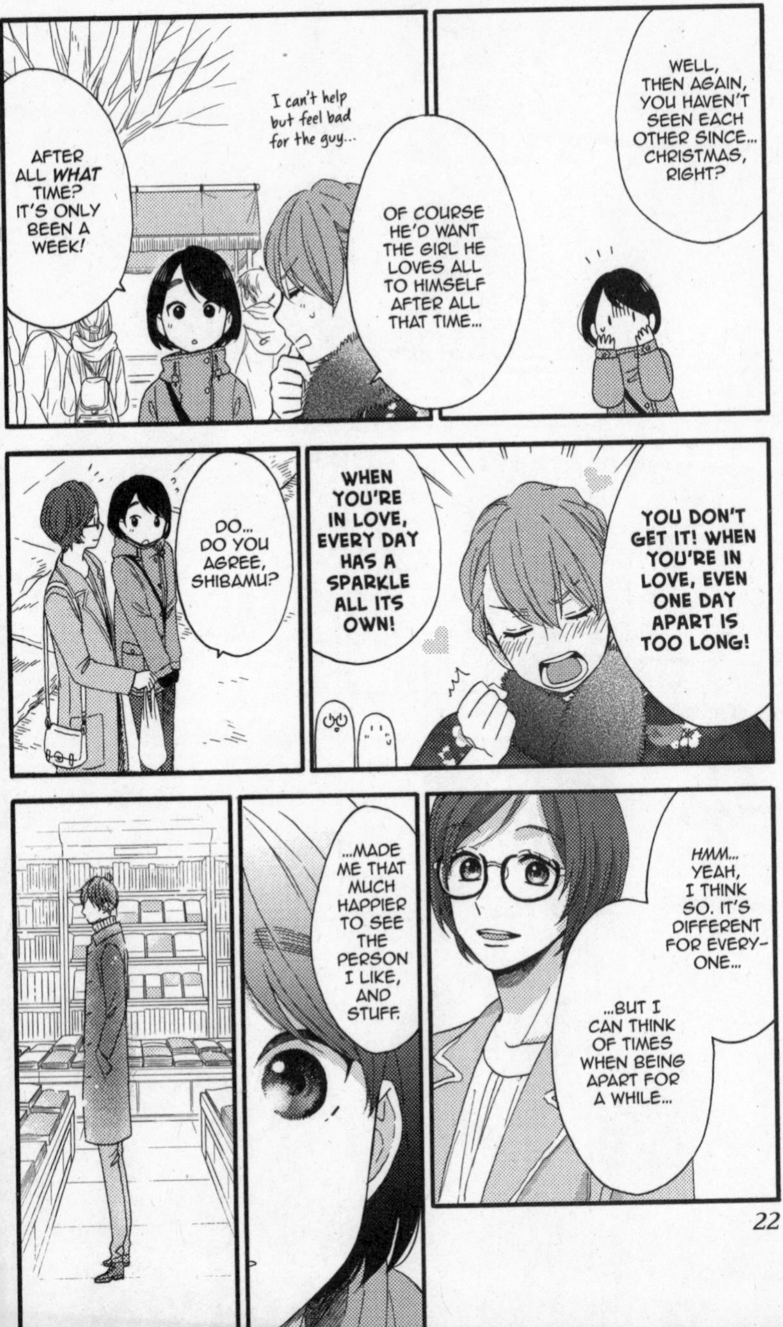
WELL, THEN AGAIN, YOU HAVEN'T SEEN EACH OTHER SINCE... CHRISTMAS, RIGHT?
OF COURSE HE'D WANT THE GIRL HE LOVES ALL TO HIMSELF AFTER ALL THAT TIME...
I can't help but feel bad for the guy...
AFTER ALL *WHAT* TIME? IT'S ONLY BEEN A WEEK!
YOU DON'T GET IT! WHEN YOU'RE IN LOVE, EVEN ONE DAY APART IS TOO LONG!
WHEN YOU'RE IN LOVE, EVERY DAY HAS A SPARKLE ALL ITS OWN!
DO... DO YOU AGREE, SHIBAMU?
HMM... YEAH, I THINK SO. IT'S DIFFERENT FOR EVERY-ONE...
...BUT I CAN THINK OF TIMES WHEN BEING APART FOR A WHILE...
...MADE ME THAT MUCH HAPPIER TO SEE THE PERSON I LIKE, AND STUFF.

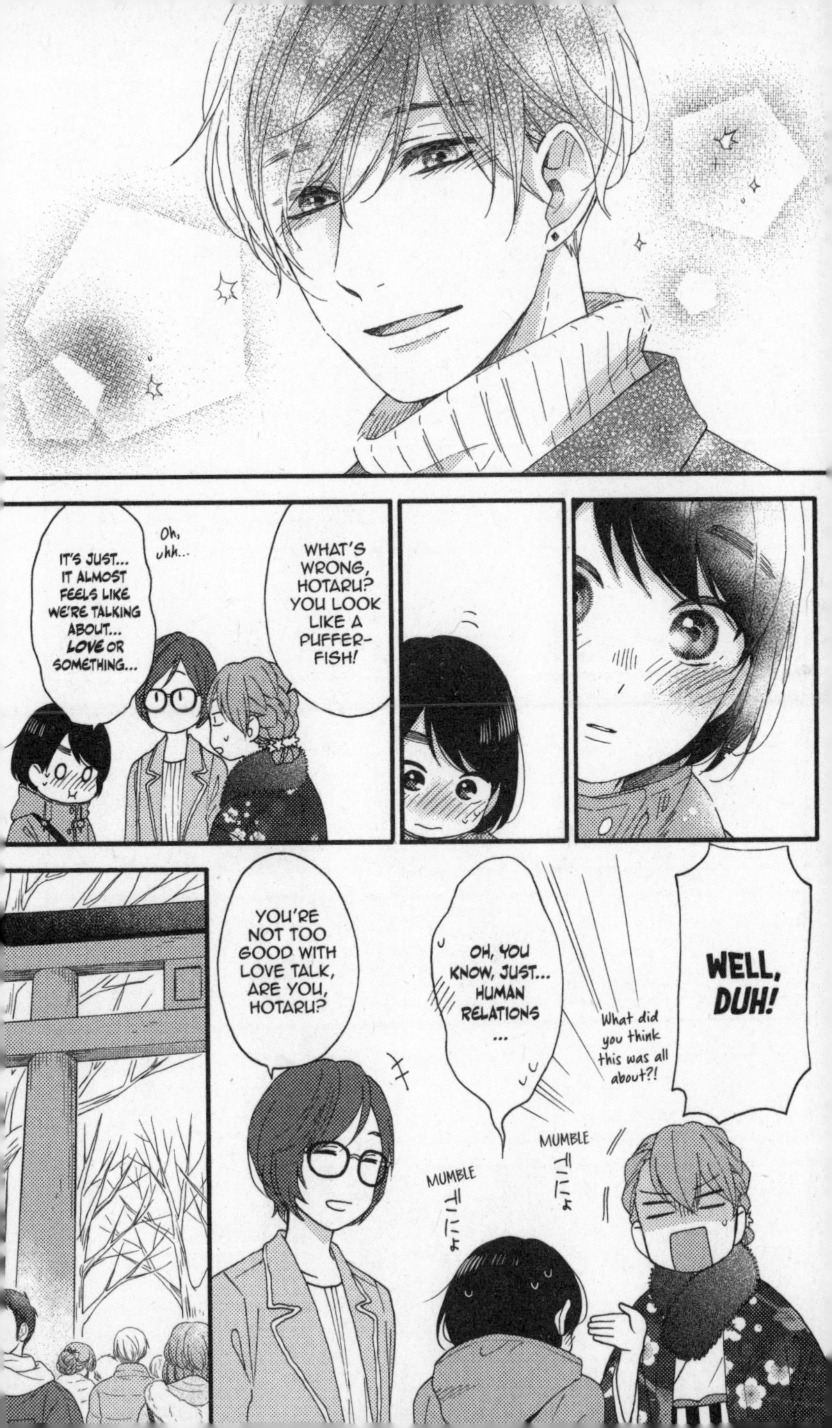

WHAT'S WRONG, HOTARU? YOU LOOK LIKE A PUFFER-FISH!
Oh, uhh...
IT'S JUST... IT ALMOST FEELS LIKE WE'RE TALKING ABOUT... *LOVE* OR SOMETHING...
WELL, DUH!
What did you think this was all about?!
OH, YOU KNOW, JUST... HUMAN RELATIONS ...
YOU'RE NOT TOO GOOD WITH LOVE TALK, ARE YOU, HOTARU?
MUMBLE
MUMBLE

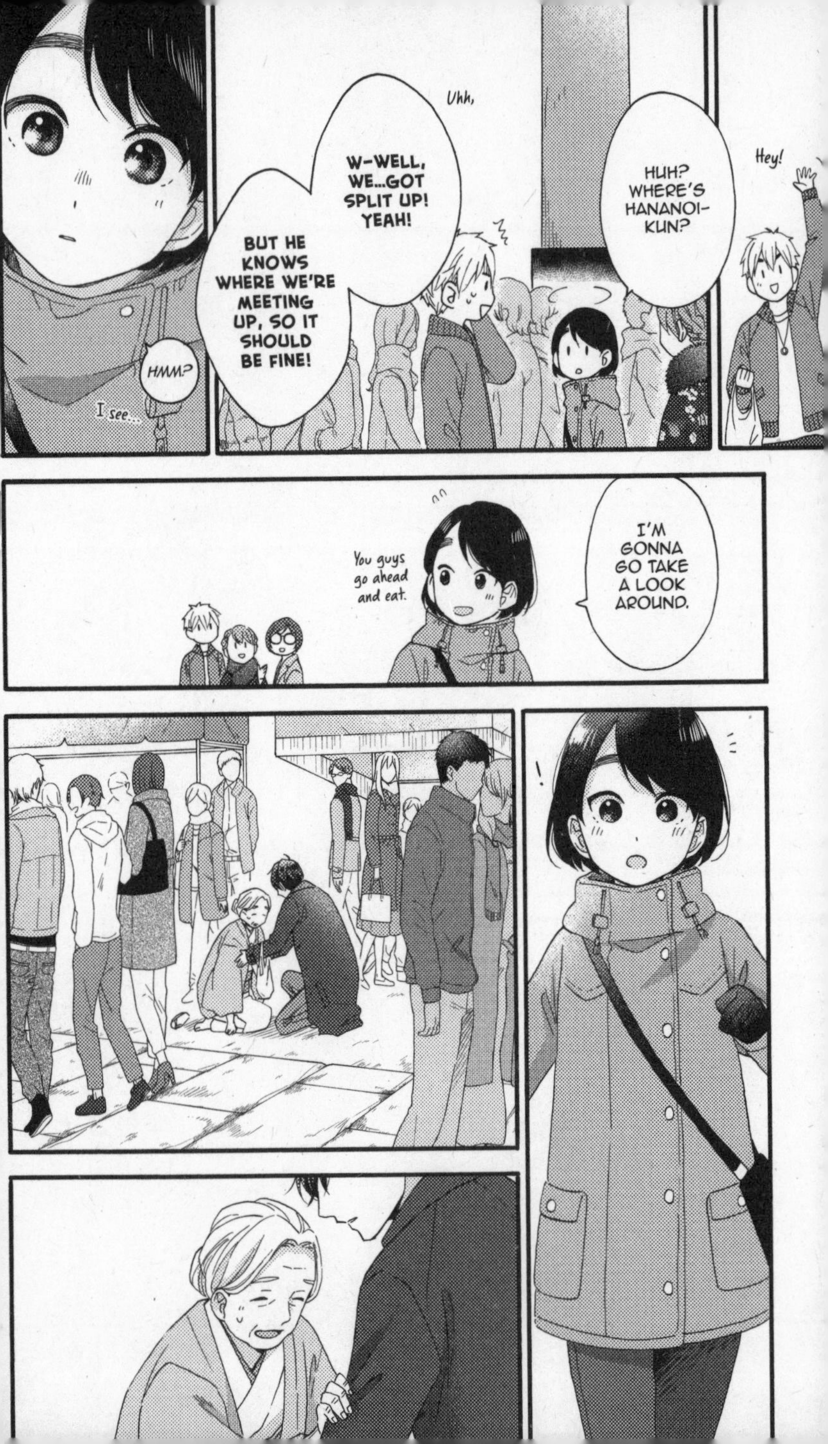
Hey!
HUH? WHERE'S HANANOI-KUN?
Uhh,
W-WELL, WE...GOT SPLIT UP! YEAH!
BUT HE KNOWS WHERE WE'RE MEETING UP, SO IT SHOULD BE FINE!
HMM?
I see...
I'M GONNA GO TAKE A LOOK AROUND.
You guys go ahead and eat.

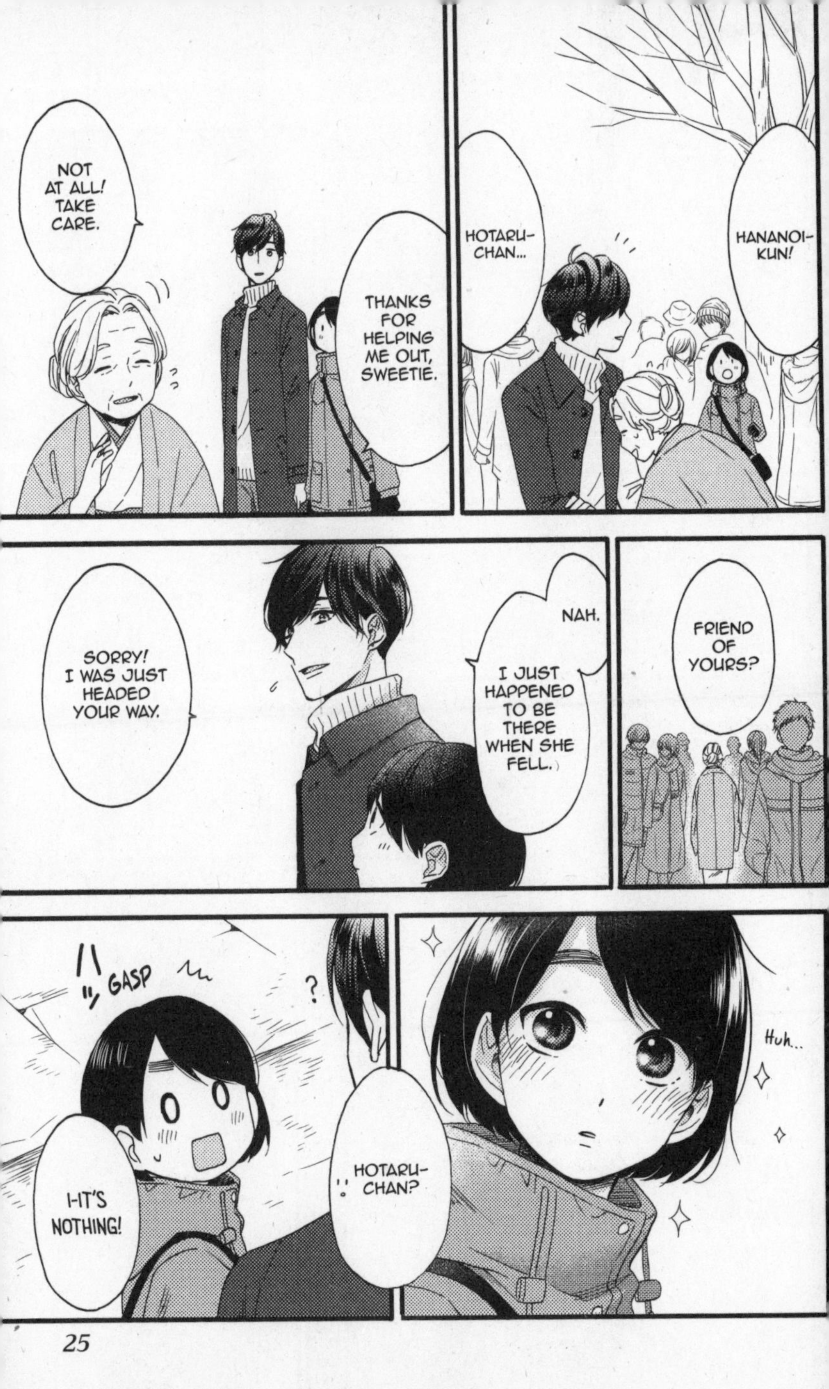
HANANOI-KUN!
HOTARU-CHAN...
THANKS FOR HELPING ME OUT, SWEETIE.
NOT AT ALL! TAKE CARE.
FRIEND OF YOURS?
NAH.
I JUST HAPPENED TO BE THERE WHEN SHE FELL.
SORRY! I WAS JUST HEADED YOUR WAY.
Huh...
HOTARU-CHAN?
GASP
I-IT'S NOTHING!

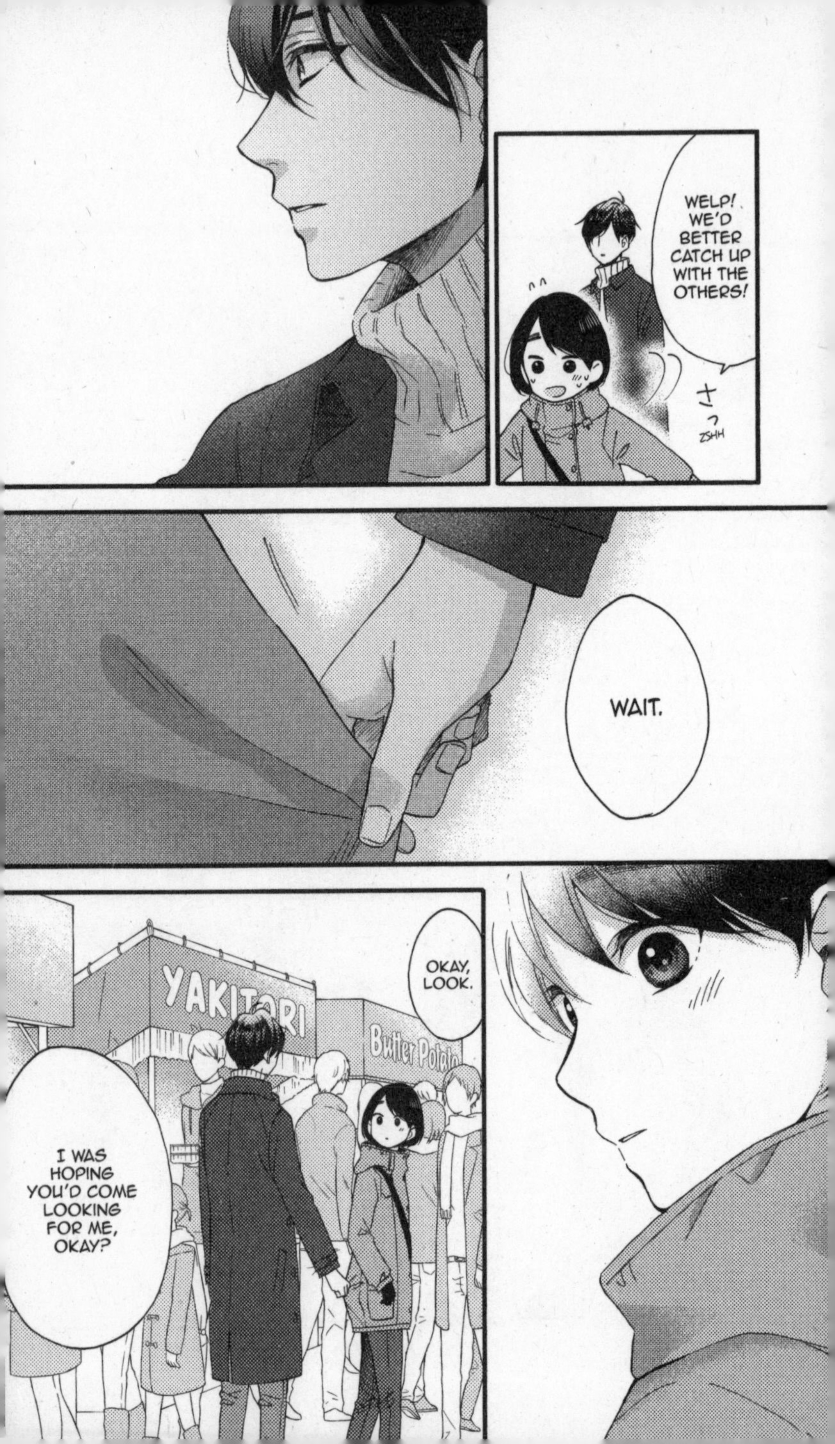
WELP! WE'D BETTER CATCH UP WITH THE OTHERS!
さっ
ZSHH
WAIT.
OKAY, LOOK.
I WAS HOPING YOU'D COME LOOKING FOR ME, OKAY?
YAKITORI
Butter Potato

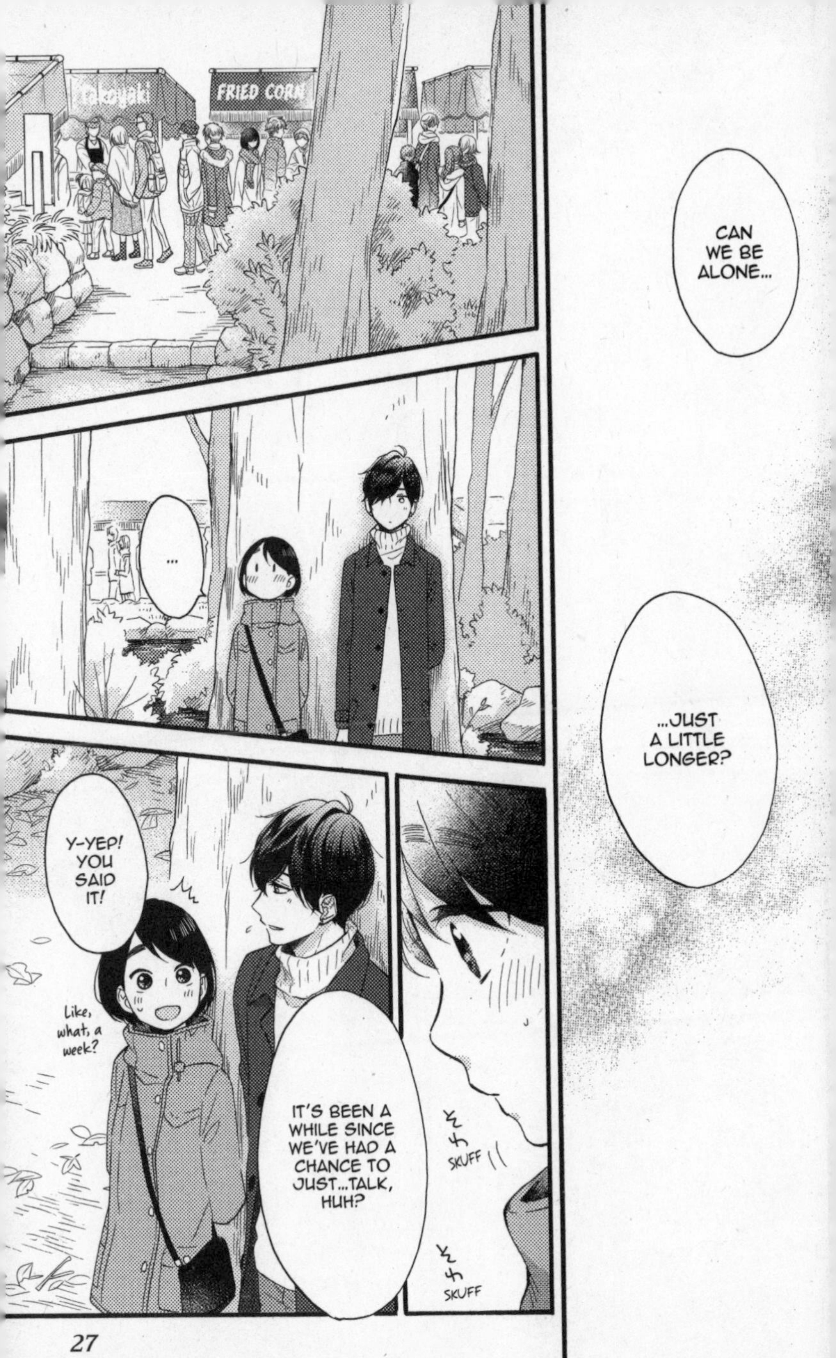
CAN WE BE ALONE...
...JUST A LITTLE LONGER?
Takoyaki
FRIED CORN
...
そわ
SKUFF
そわ
SKUFF
IT'S BEEN A WHILE SINCE WE'VE HAD A CHANCE TO JUST...TALK, HUH?
Y-YEP! YOU SAID IT!
Like, what, a week?

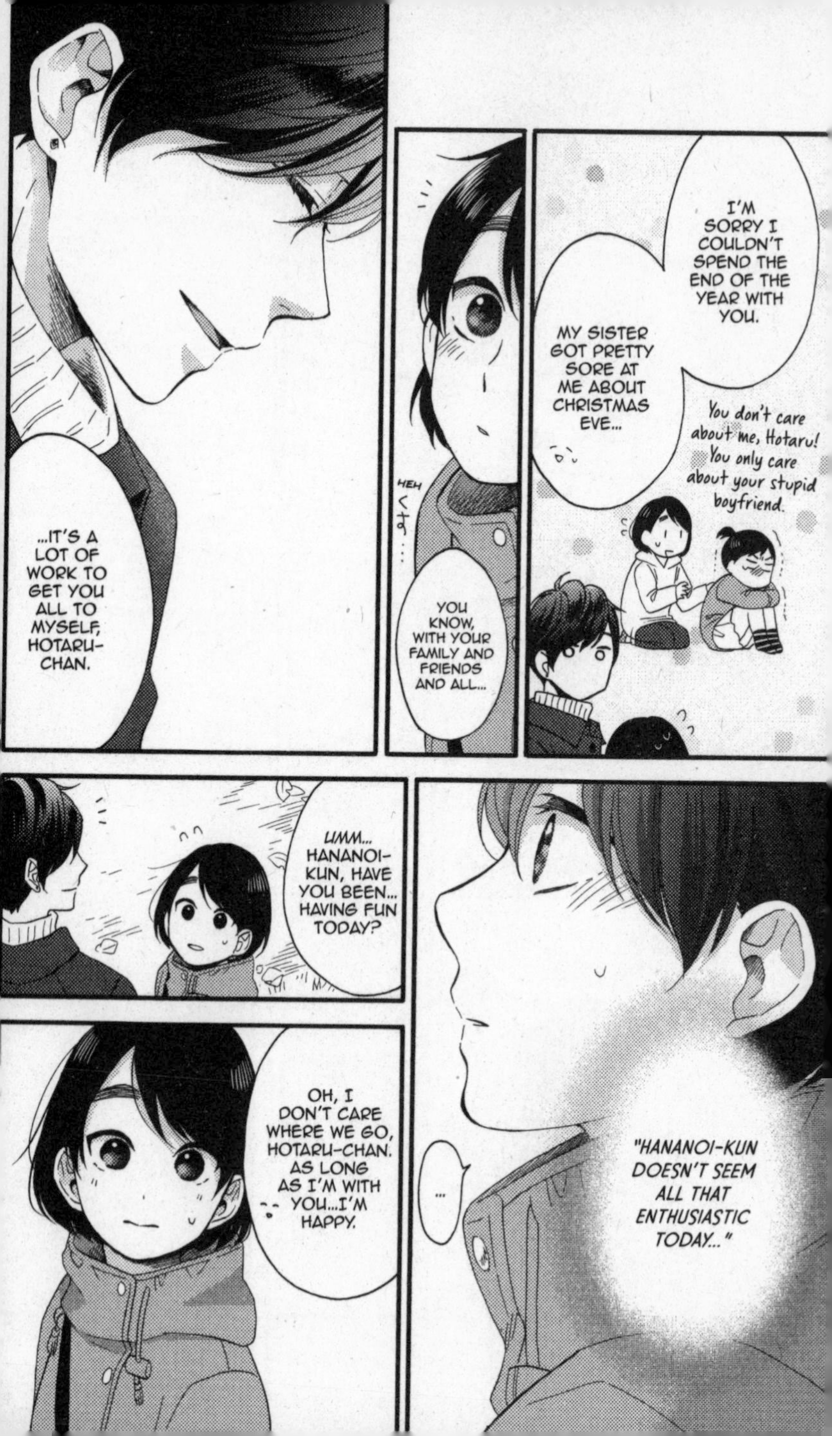
I'M SORRY I COULDN'T SPEND THE END OF THE YEAR WITH YOU.
MY SISTER GOT PRETTY SORE AT ME ABOUT CHRISTMAS EVE...
You don't care about me, Hotaru! You only care about your stupid boyfriend.
HEH
くす…
YOU KNOW, WITH YOUR FAMILY AND FRIENDS AND ALL...
...IT'S A LOT OF WORK TO GET YOU ALL TO MYSELF, HOTARU-CHAN.
...
"HANANOI-KUN DOESN'T SEEM ALL THAT ENTHUSIASTIC TODAY..."
UMM... HANANOI-KUN, HAVE YOU BEEN... HAVING FUN TODAY?
OH, I DON'T CARE WHERE WE GO, HOTARU-CHAN. AS LONG AS I'M WITH YOU...I'M HAPPY.

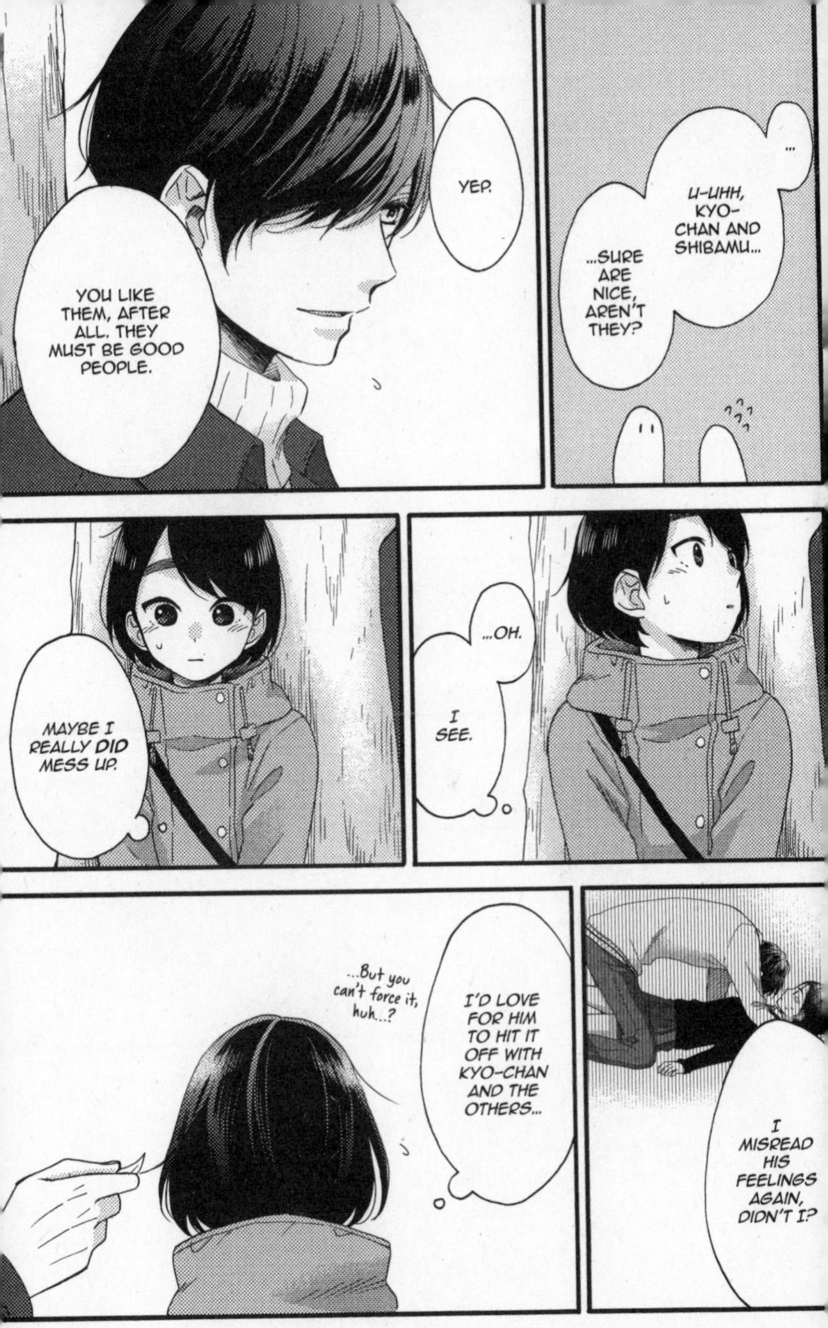
...
U-UHH, KYO-CHAN AND SHIBAMU...
...SURE ARE NICE, AREN'T THEY?
YEP.
YOU LIKE THEM, AFTER ALL. THEY MUST BE GOOD PEOPLE.
...OH.
I SEE.
MAYBE I REALLY DID MESS UP.
I MISREAD HIS FEELINGS AGAIN, DIDN'T I?
I'D LOVE FOR HIM TO HIT IT OFF WITH KYO-CHAN AND THE OTHERS...
...But you can't force it, huh...?

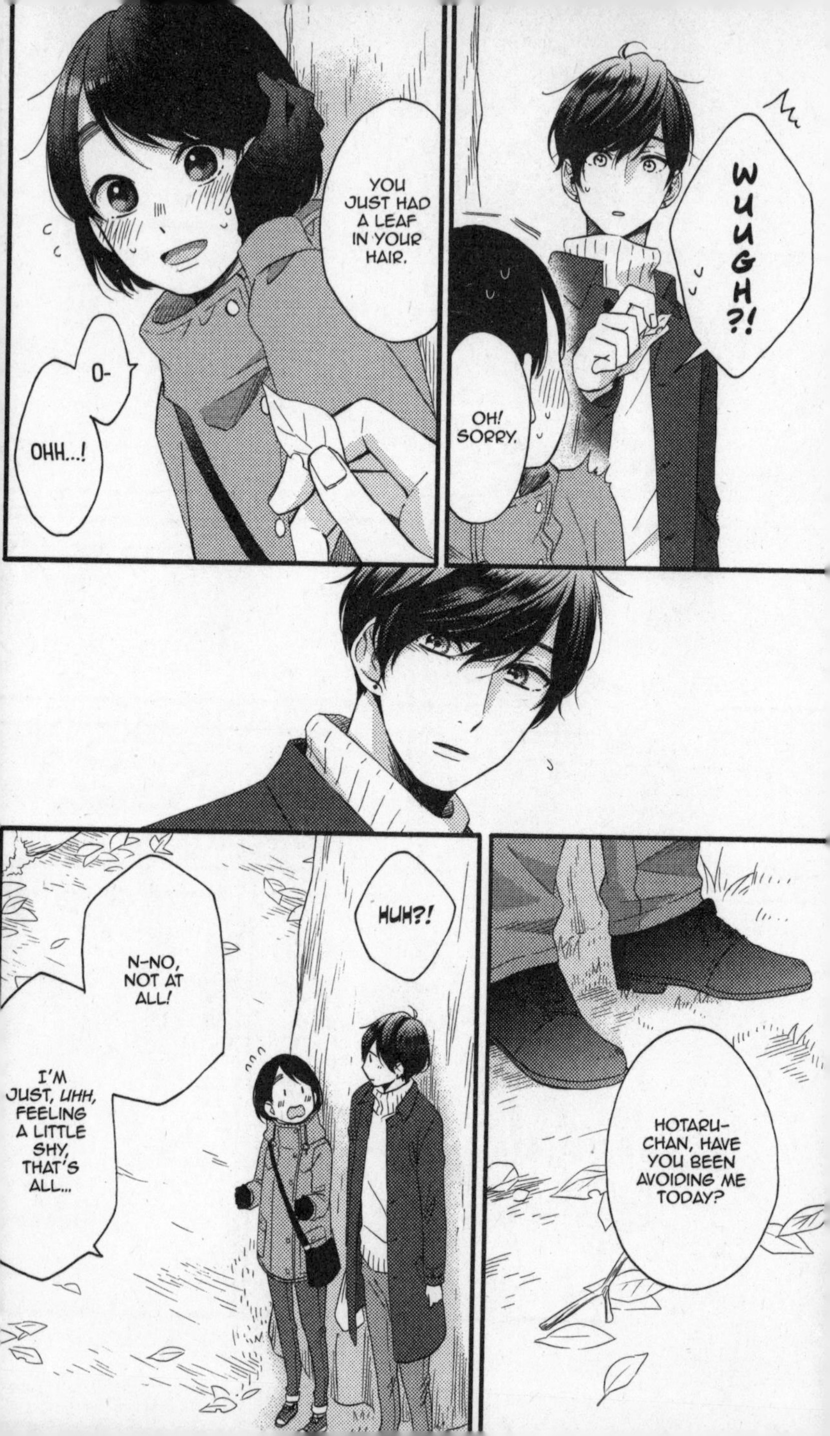
WUUGH?!
OH! SORRY.
YOU JUST HAD A LEAF IN YOUR HAIR.
O- OHH...!
HOTARU-CHAN, HAVE YOU BEEN AVOIDING ME TODAY?
HUH?!
N-NO, NOT AT ALL!
I'M JUST, *UHH*, FEELING A LITTLE SHY, THAT'S ALL...

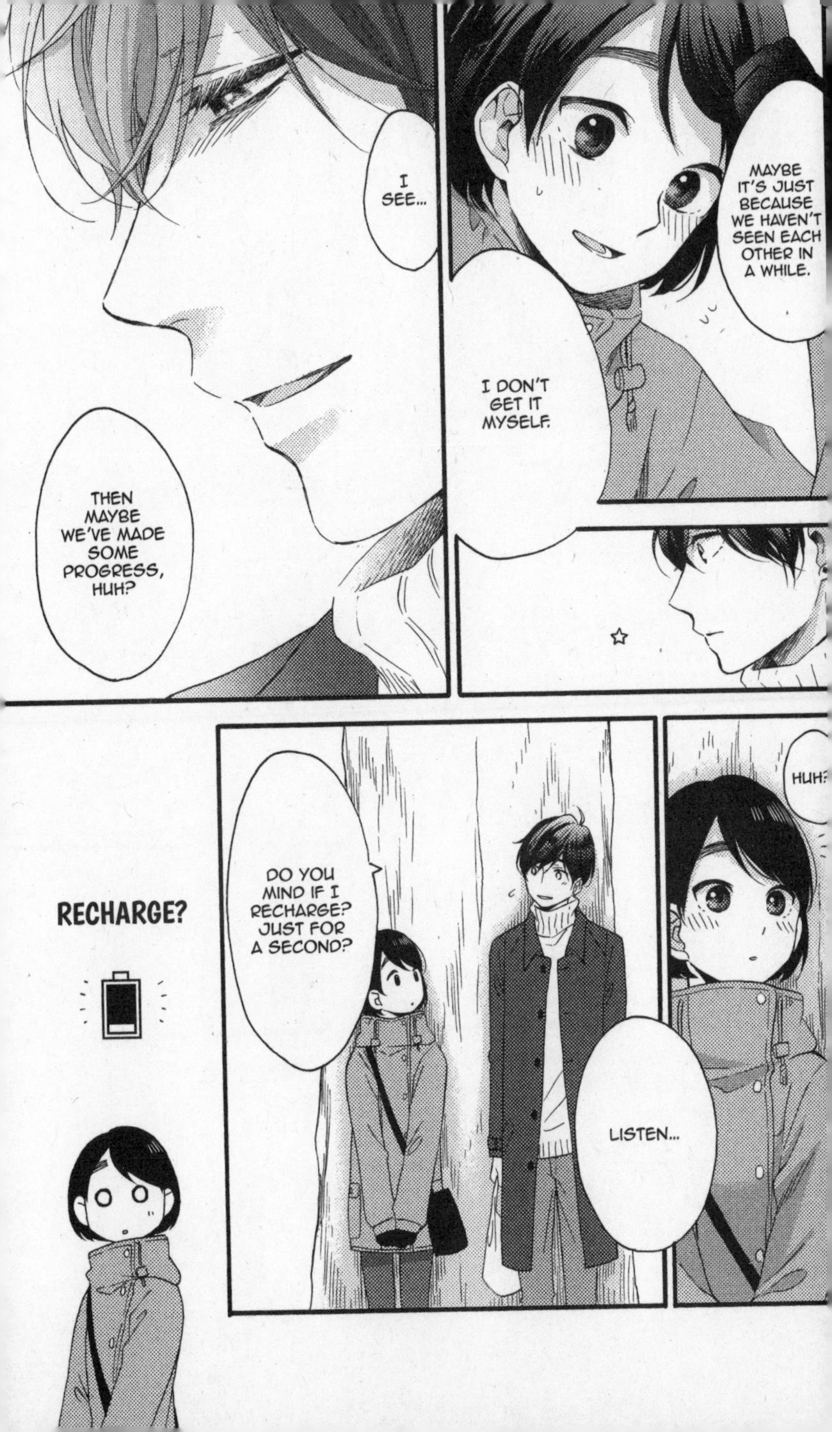
MAYBE IT'S JUST BECAUSE WE HAVEN'T SEEN EACH OTHER IN A WHILE.
I DON'T GET IT MYSELF.
I SEE...
THEN MAYBE WE'VE MADE SOME PROGRESS, HUH?
HUH?
LISTEN...
DO YOU MIND IF I RECHARGE? JUST FOR A SECOND?
RECHARGE?

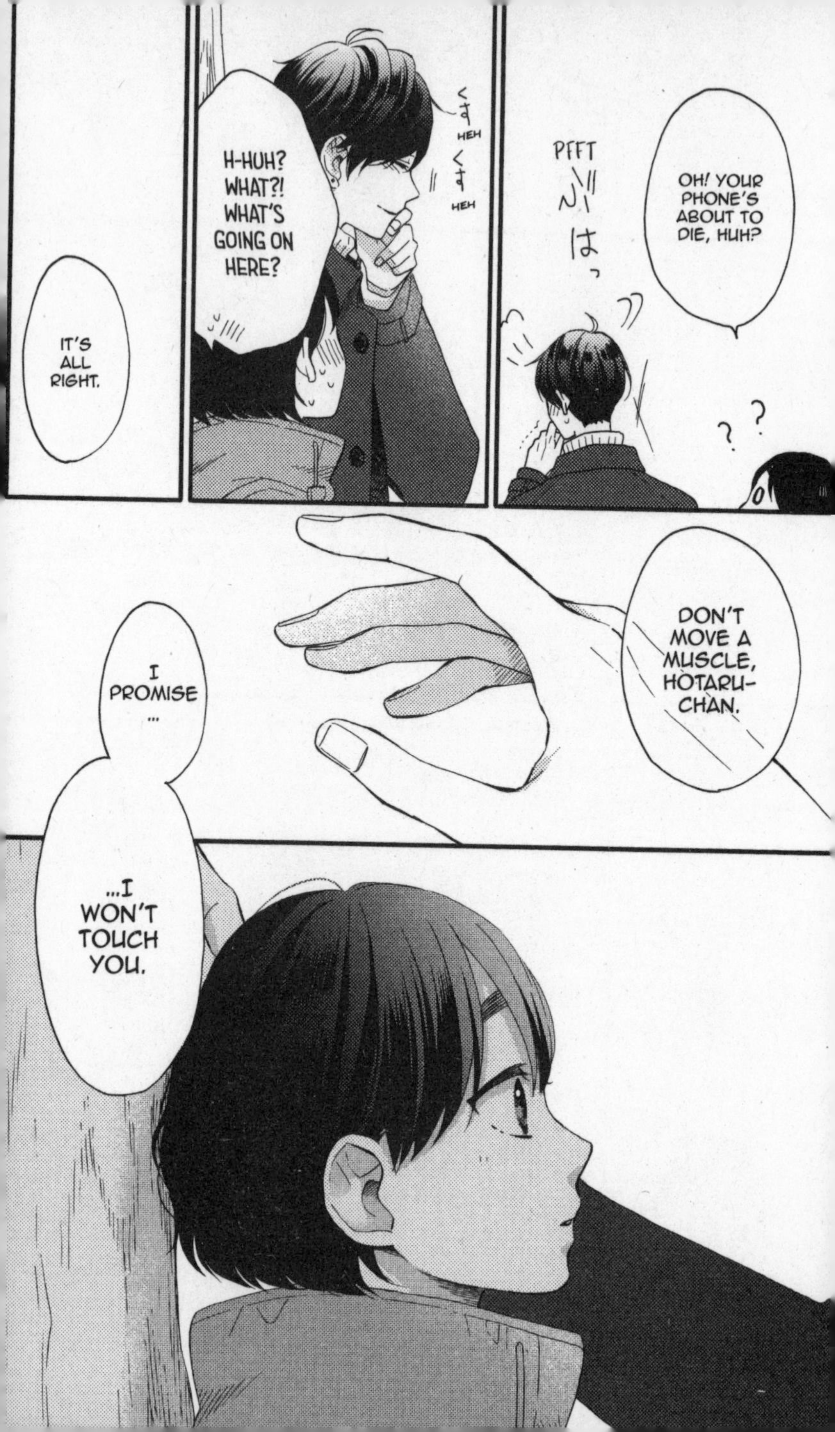
OH! YOUR PHONE'S ABOUT TO DIE, HUH?
? ?
PFFT
ぷはっ
くす HEH くす HEH
H-HUH? WHAT?! WHAT'S GOING ON HERE?
IT'S ALL RIGHT.
DON'T MOVE A MUSCLE, HOTARU-CHAN.
I PROMISE ...
...I WON'T TOUCH YOU.

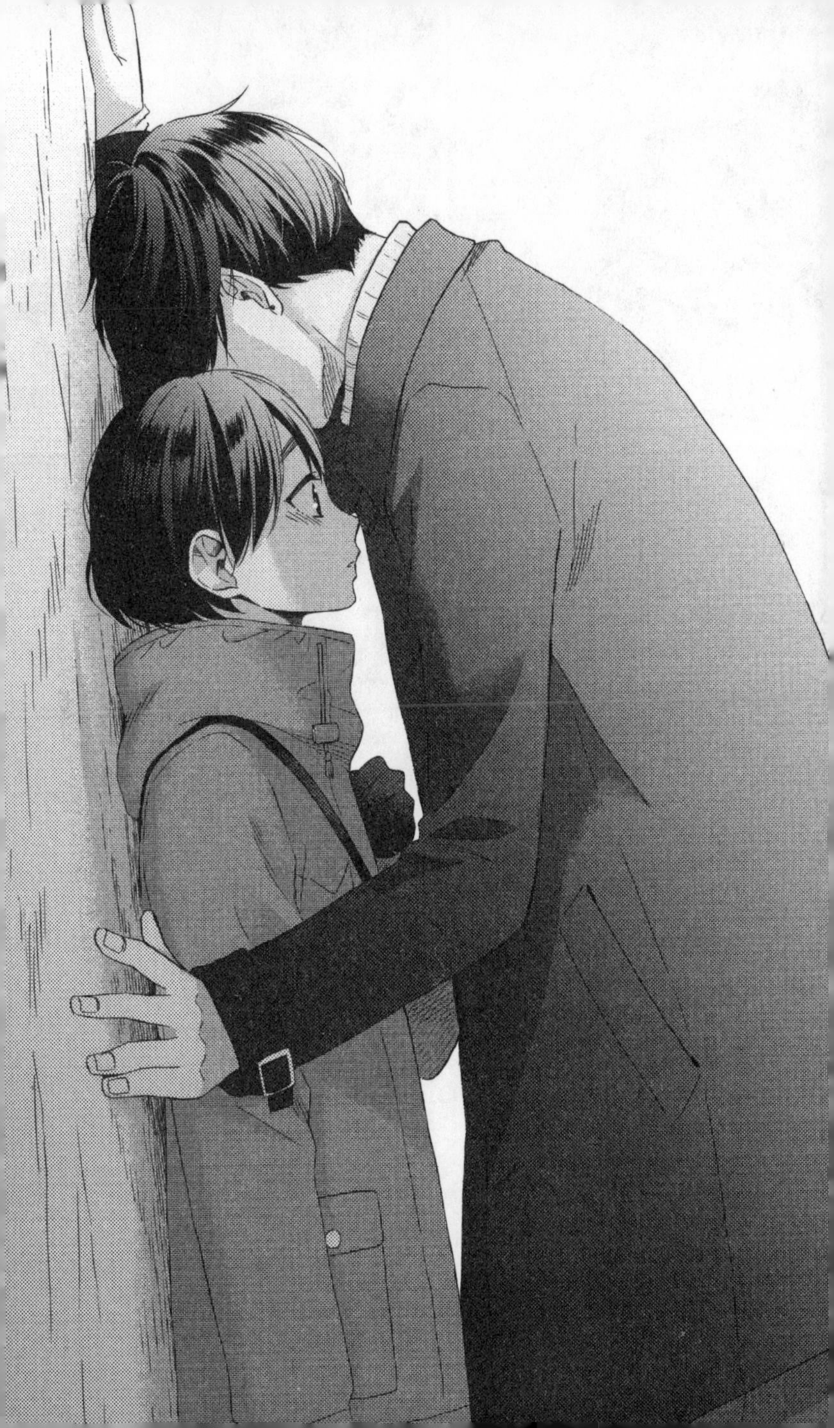

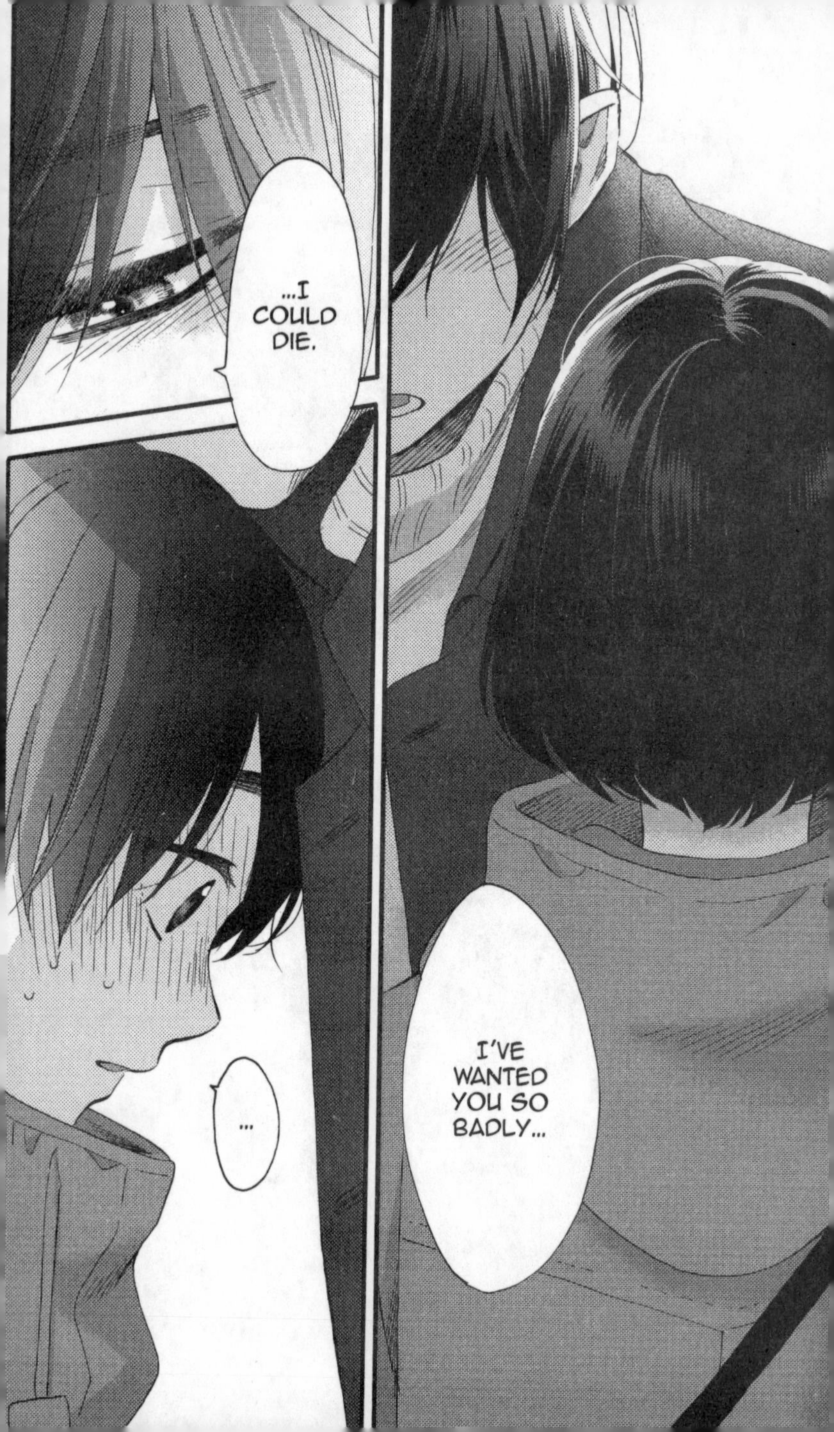
I'VE WANTED YOU SO BADLY...
...I COULD DIE.
...

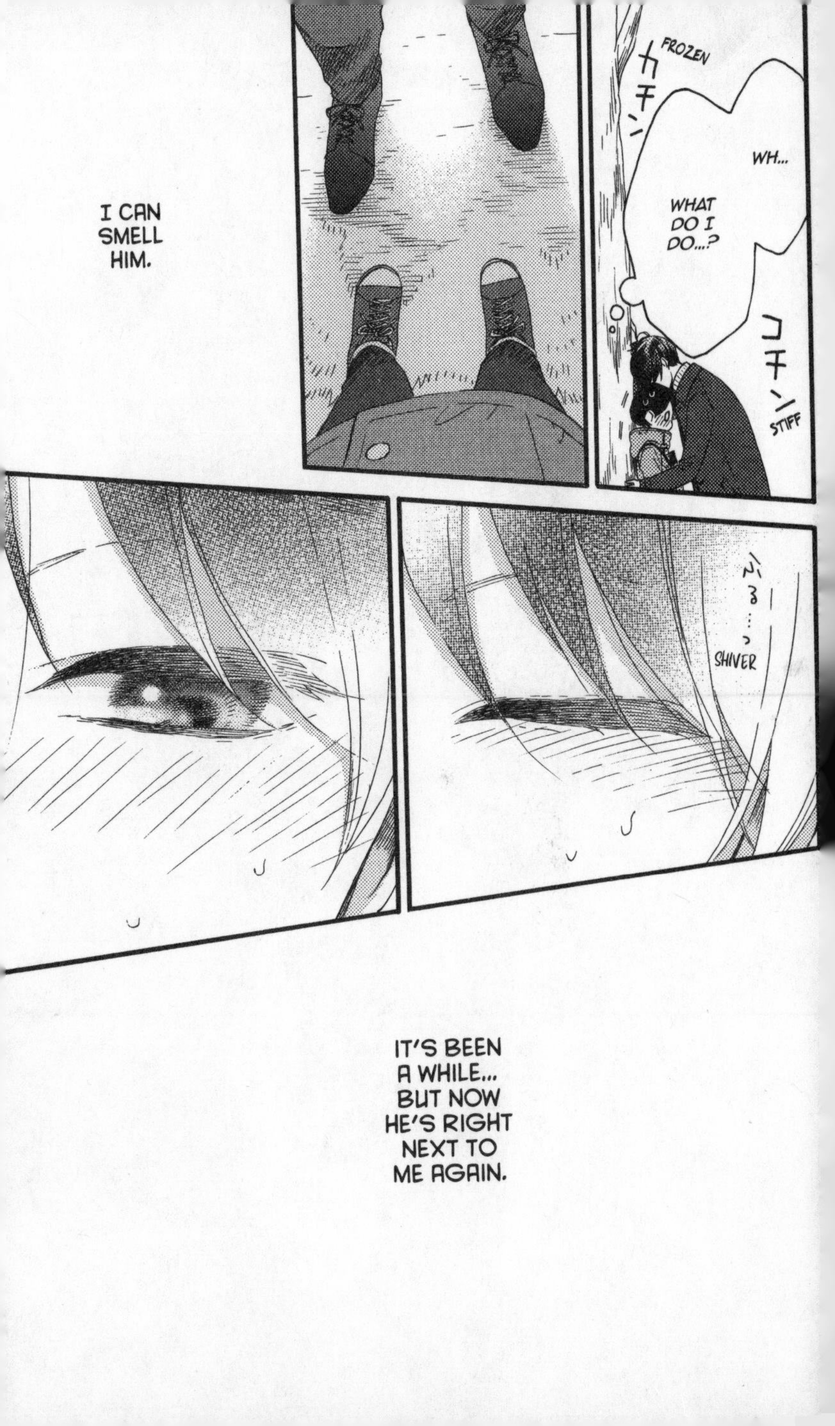
カチン
FROZEN
WH...
WHAT DO I DO...?
コチン
STIFF
I CAN SMELL HIM.
ふる…っ
SHIVER
IT'S BEEN A WHILE... BUT NOW HE'S RIGHT NEXT TO ME AGAIN.

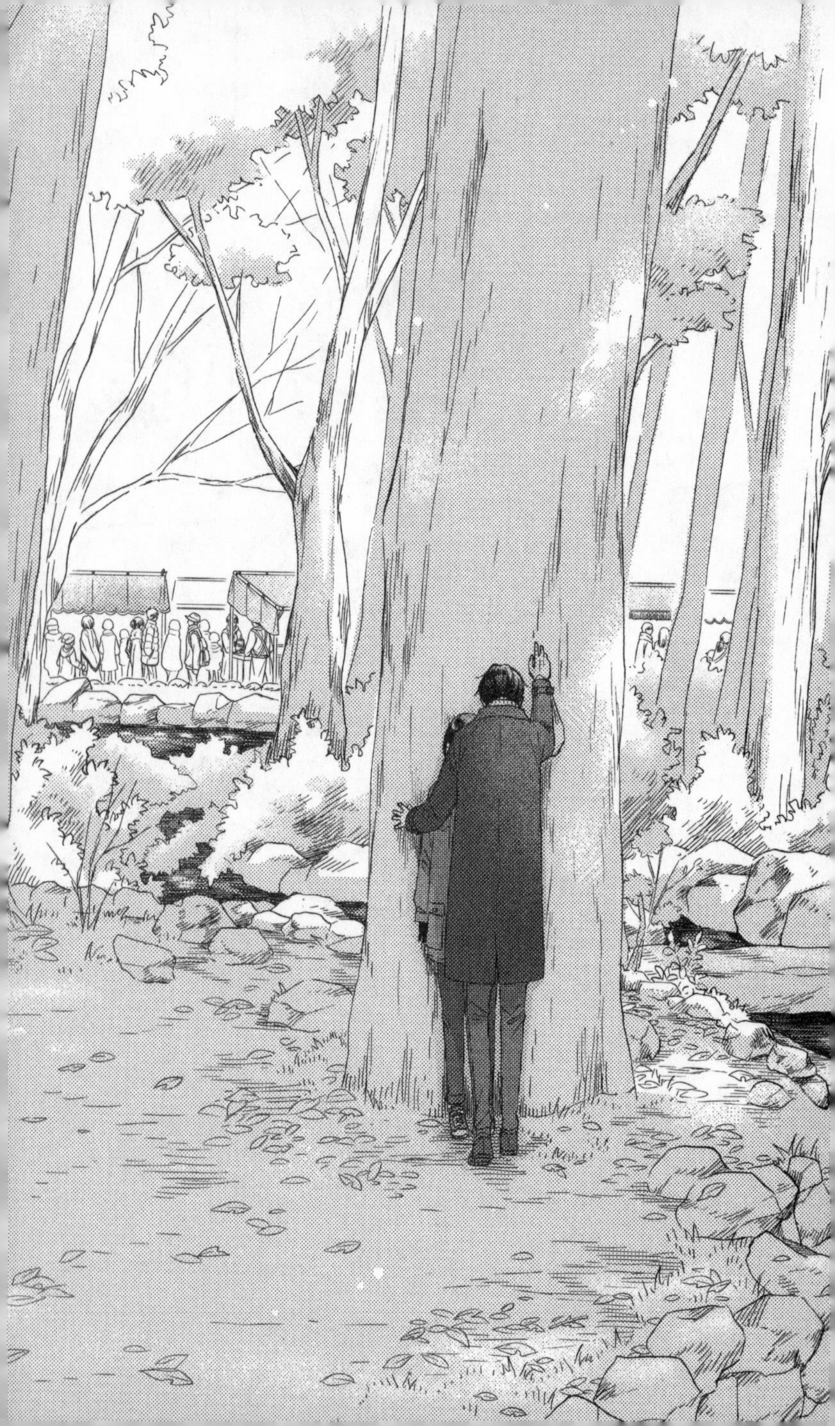

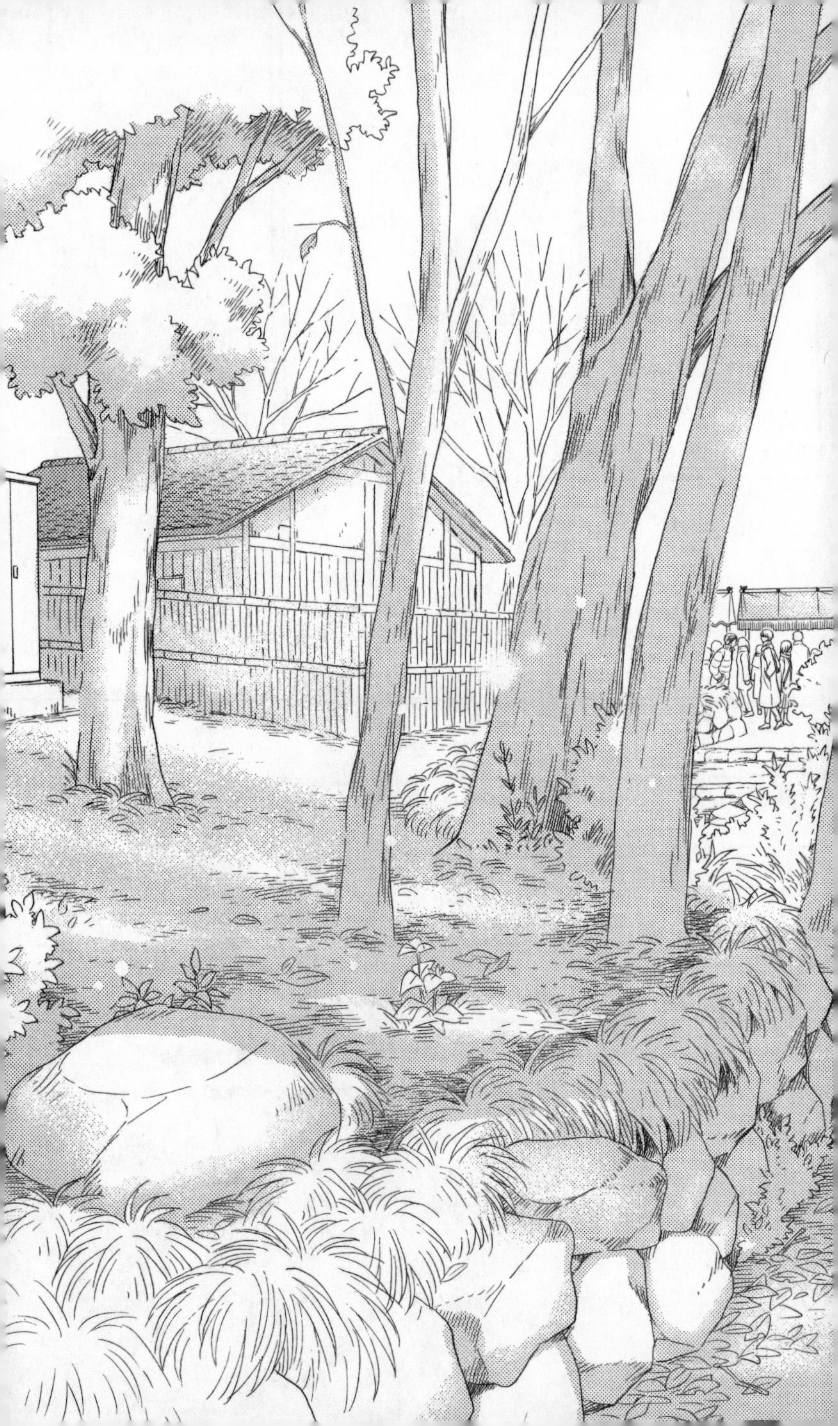

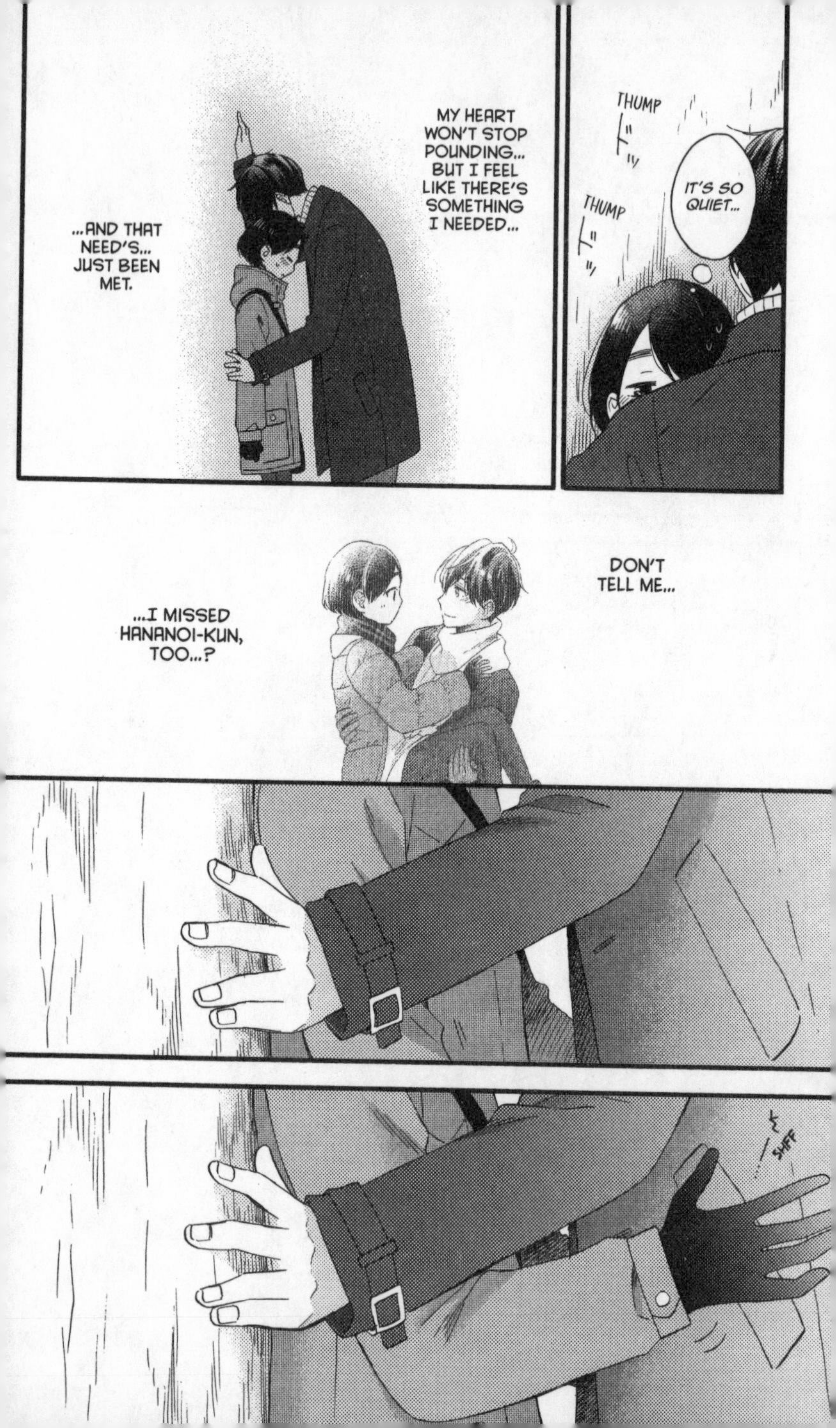
THUMP
IT'S SO QUIET...
THUMP
MY HEART WON'T STOP POUNDING... BUT I FEEL LIKE THERE'S SOMETHING I NEEDED...
...AND THAT NEED'S... JUST BEEN MET.
DON'T TELL ME...
...I MISSED HANANOI-KUN, TOO...?
SHFF

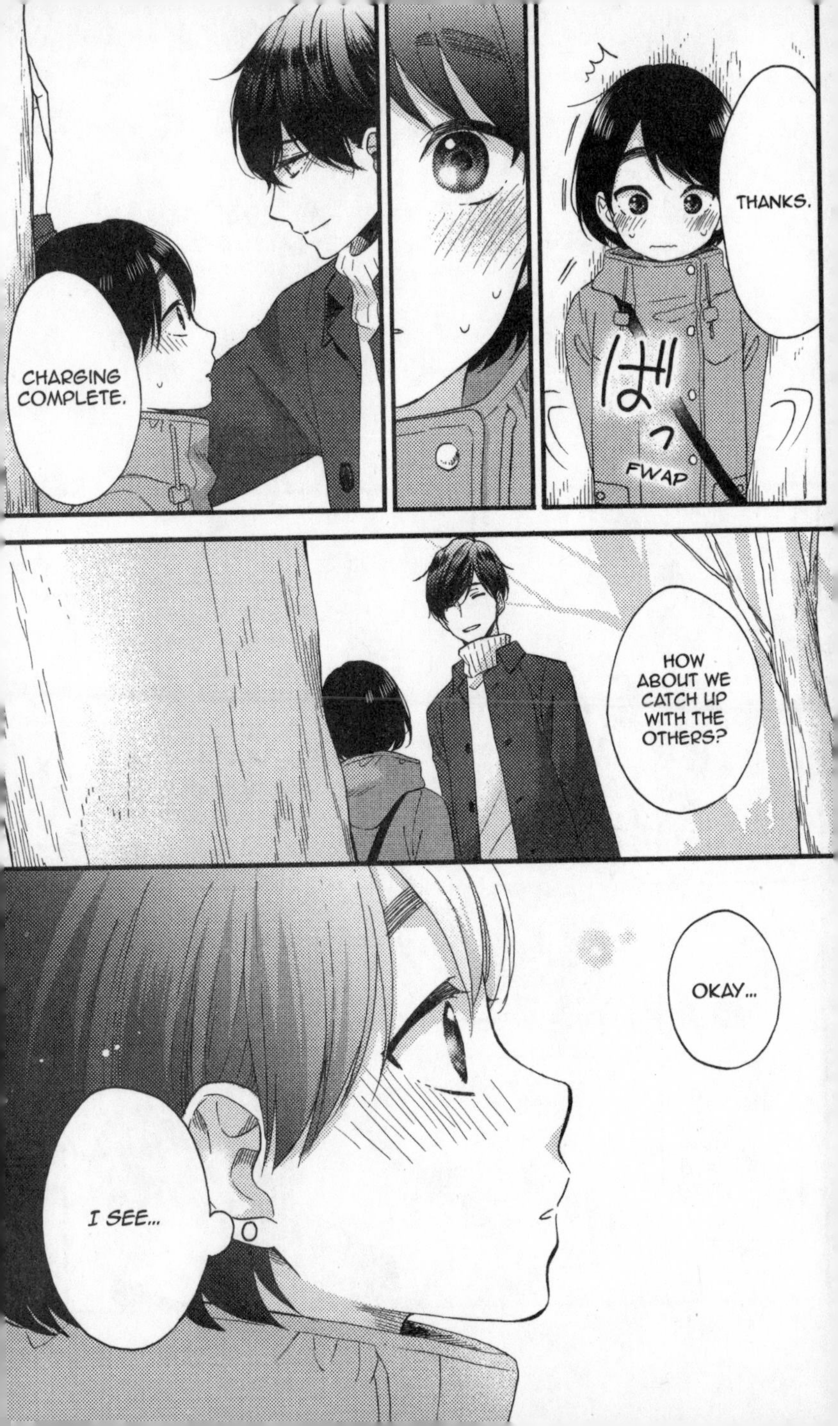
THANKS.
ぱっ
FWAP
CHARGING COMPLETE.
HOW ABOUT WE CATCH UP WITH THE OTHERS?
OKAY...
I SEE...

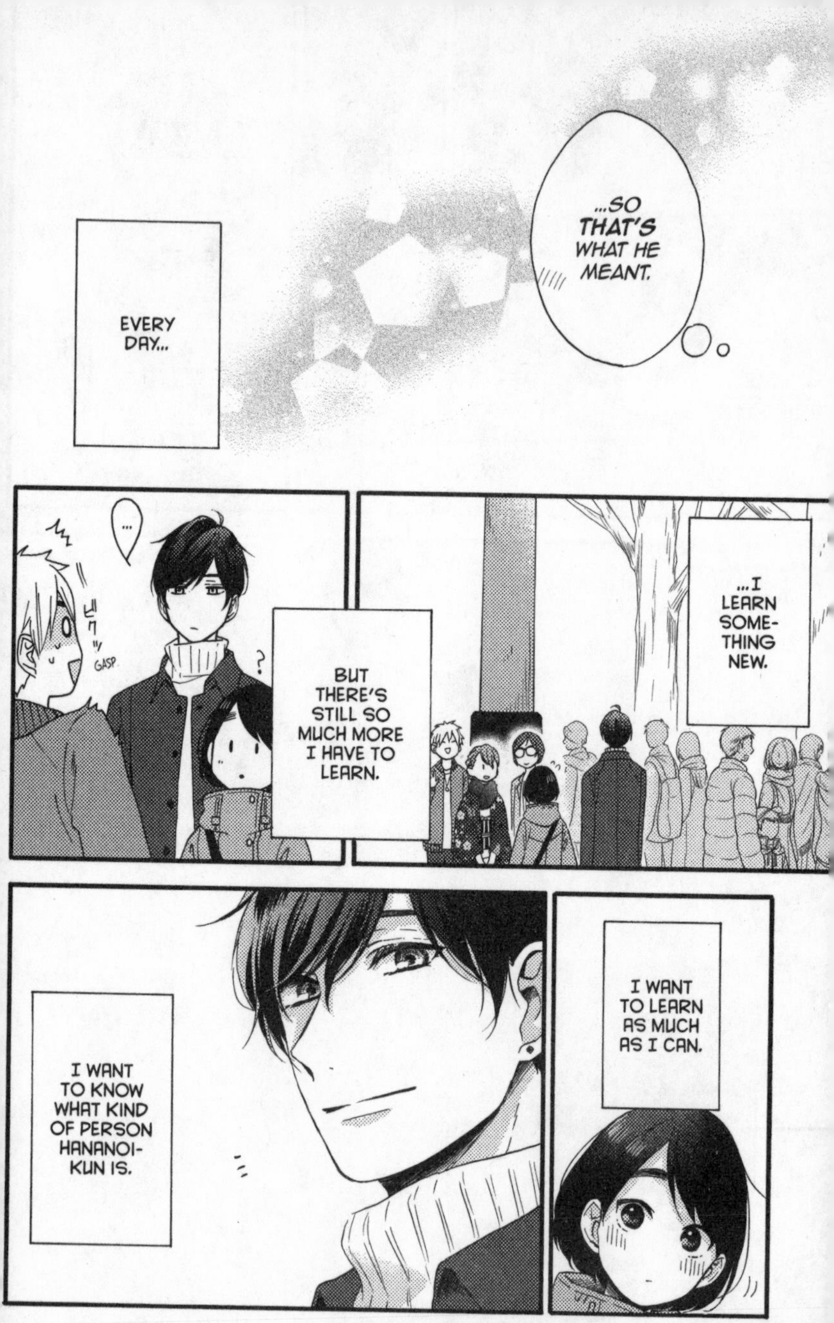
...SO THAT'S WHAT HE MEANT.
EVERY DAY...
...I LEARN SOMETHING NEW.
BUT THERE'S STILL SO MUCH MORE I HAVE TO LEARN.
...
?
ビクッ
GASP
I WANT TO LEARN AS MUCH AS I CAN.
I WANT TO KNOW WHAT KIND OF PERSON HANANOI-KUN IS.

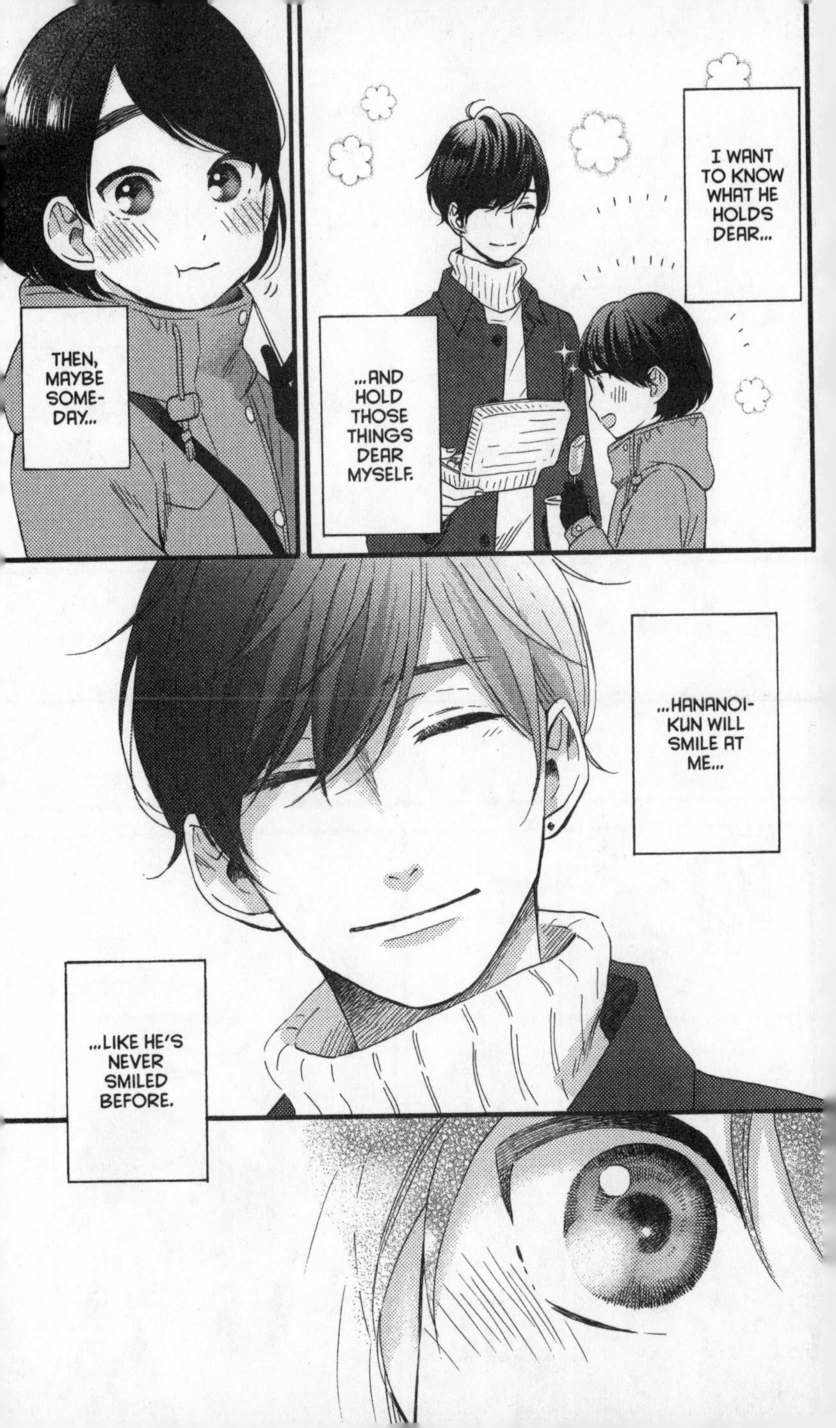
I WANT TO KNOW WHAT HE HOLDS DEAR...
...AND HOLD THOSE THINGS DEAR MYSELF.
THEN, MAYBE SOME-DAY...
...HANANOI-KUN WILL SMILE AT ME...
...LIKE HE'S NEVER SMILED BEFORE.

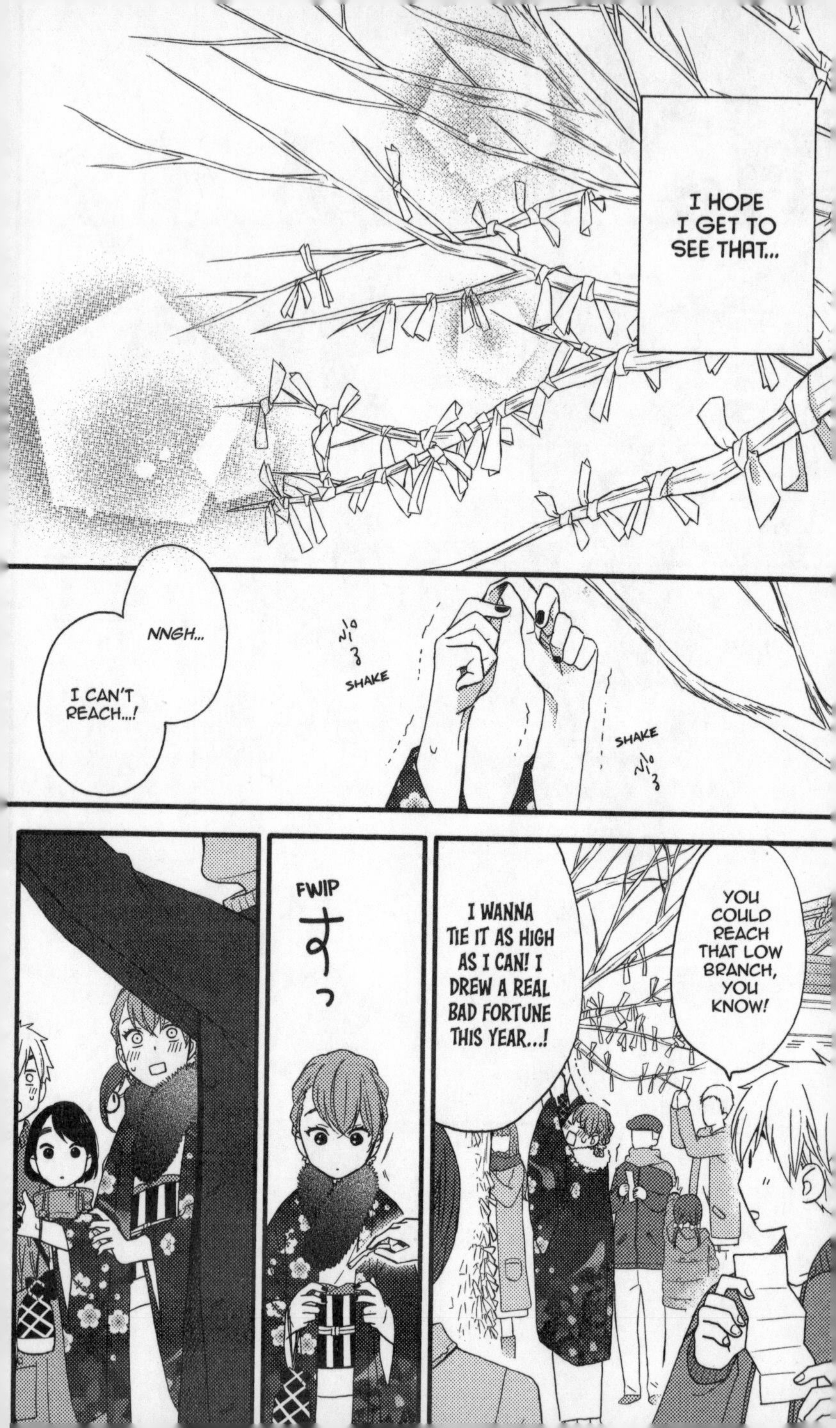
I HOPE I GET TO SEE THAT...
SHAKE
SHAKE
NNGH...
I CAN'T REACH...!
YOU COULD REACH THAT LOW BRANCH, YOU KNOW!
I WANNA TIE IT AS HIGH AS I CAN! I DREW A REAL BAD FORTUNE THIS YEAR...!
FWIP
すっ

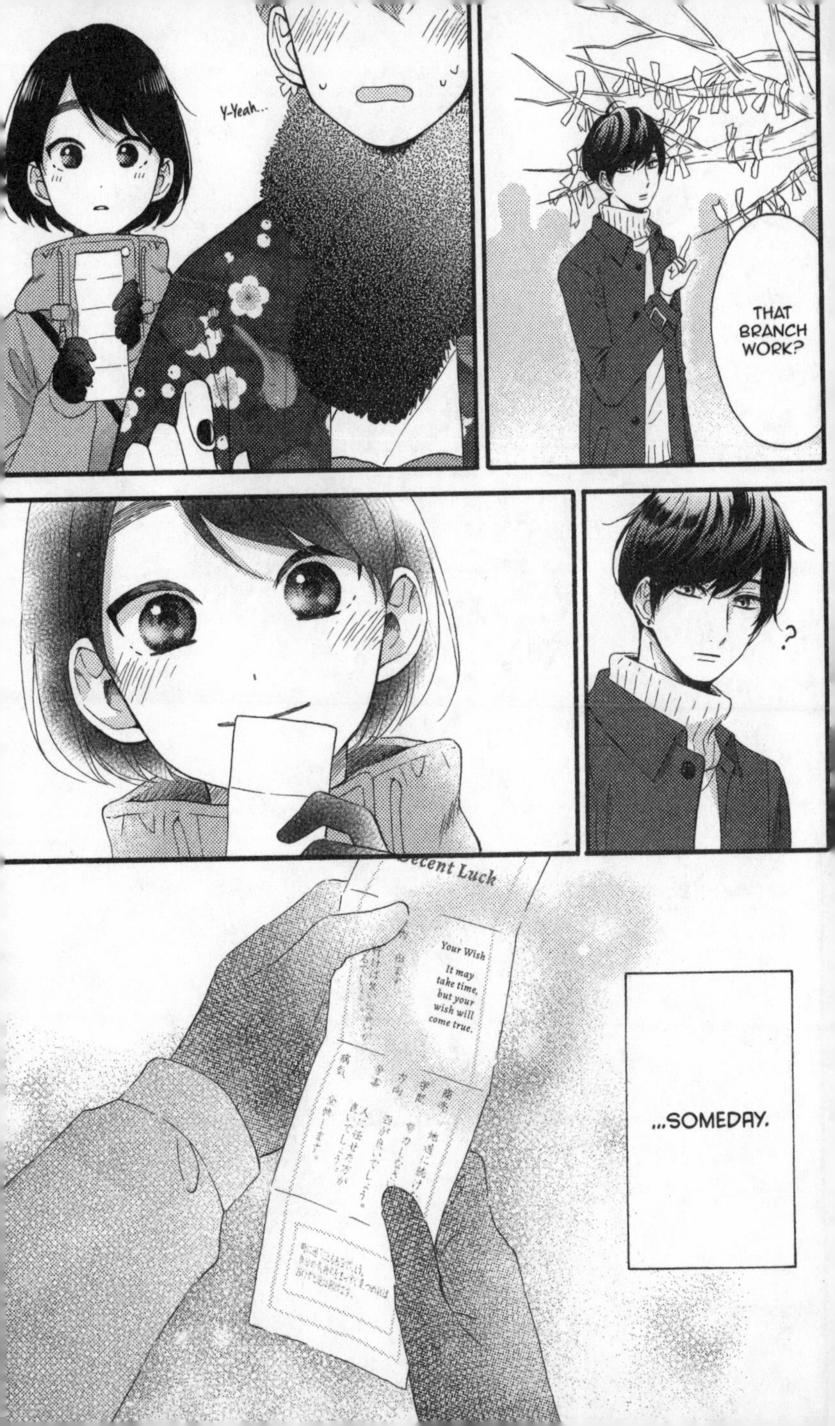
THAT BRANCH WORK?
Y-Yeah...
?
ecent Luck
Your Wish
It may take time, but your wish will come true.
...SOMEDAY.

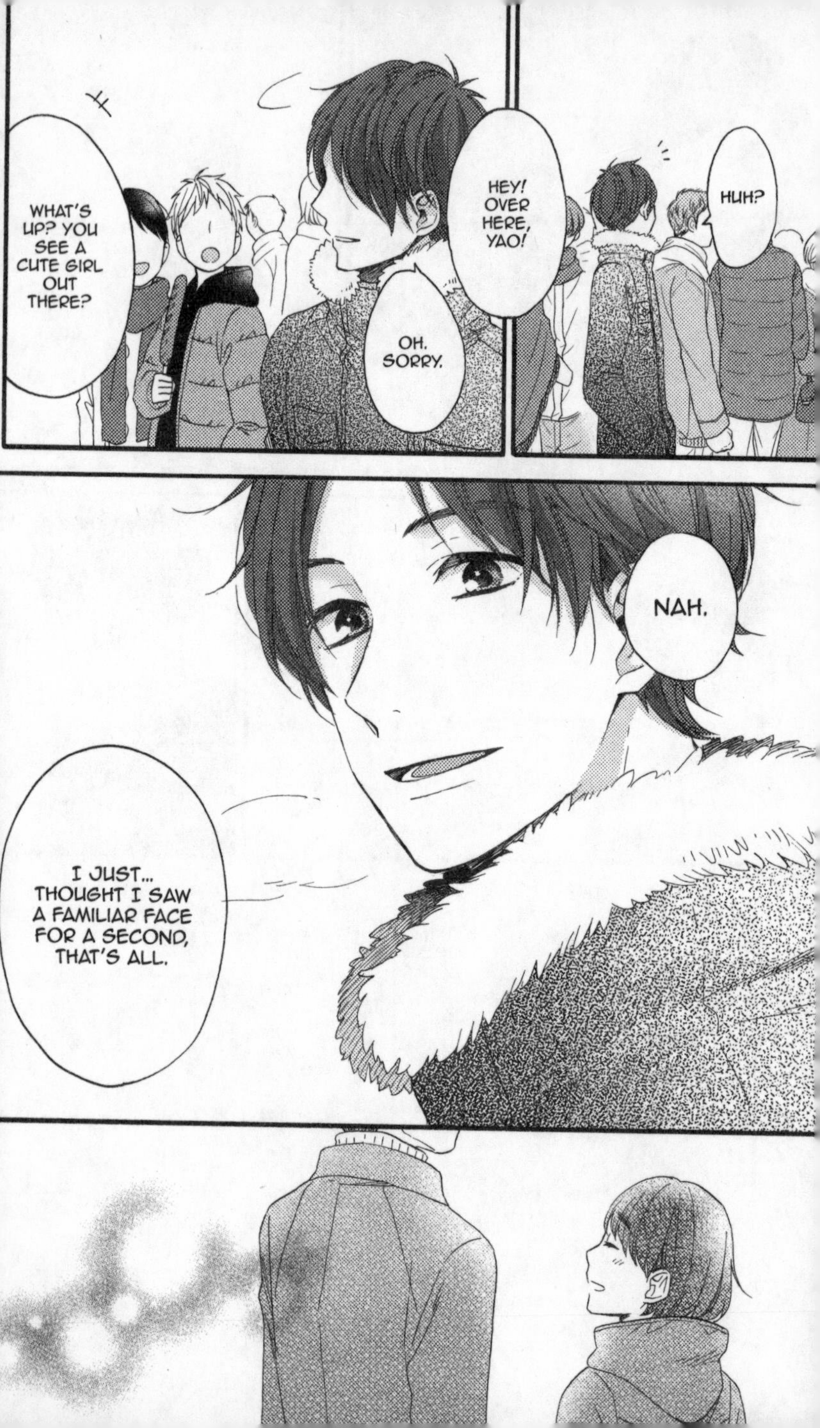
HUH?
HEY! OVER HERE, YAO!
OH. SORRY.
WHAT'S UP? YOU SEE A CUTE GIRL OUT THERE?
NAH.
I JUST... THOUGHT I SAW A FAMILIAR FACE FOR A SECOND, THAT'S ALL.

Never-Before-Seen A Condition Called Love

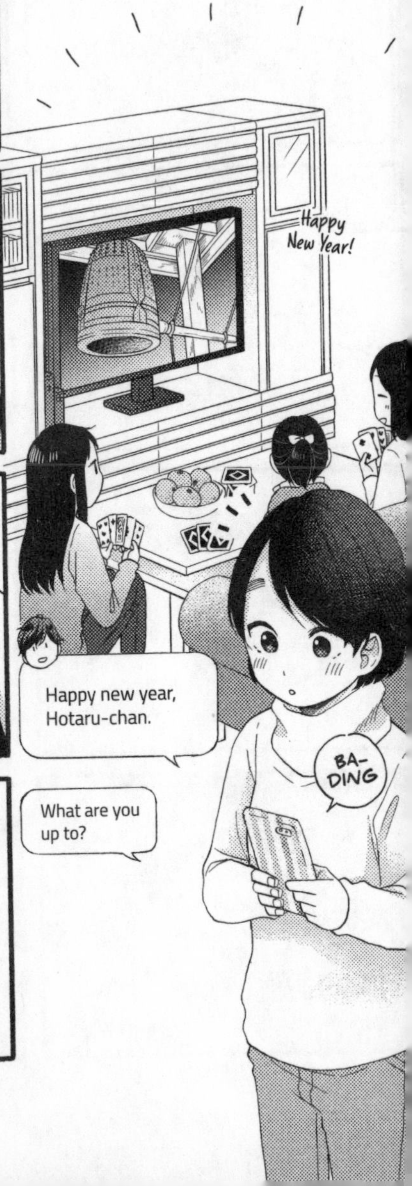
Happy New Year!
Happy new year, Hotaru-chan.
What are you up to?
BA-DING

Ringing in the New Year with Hananoi-kun (1)

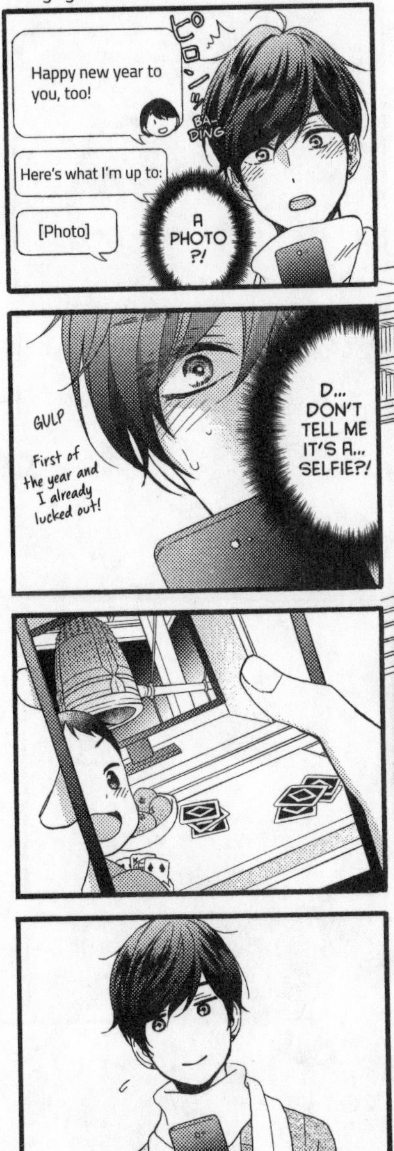
BA-DING
Happy new year to you, too!
Here's what I'm up to:
A PHOTO?!
[Photo]
D... DON'T TELL ME IT'S A... SELFIE?!
GULP
First of the year and I already lucked out!

Ringing in the New Year with Hananoi-kun (2)

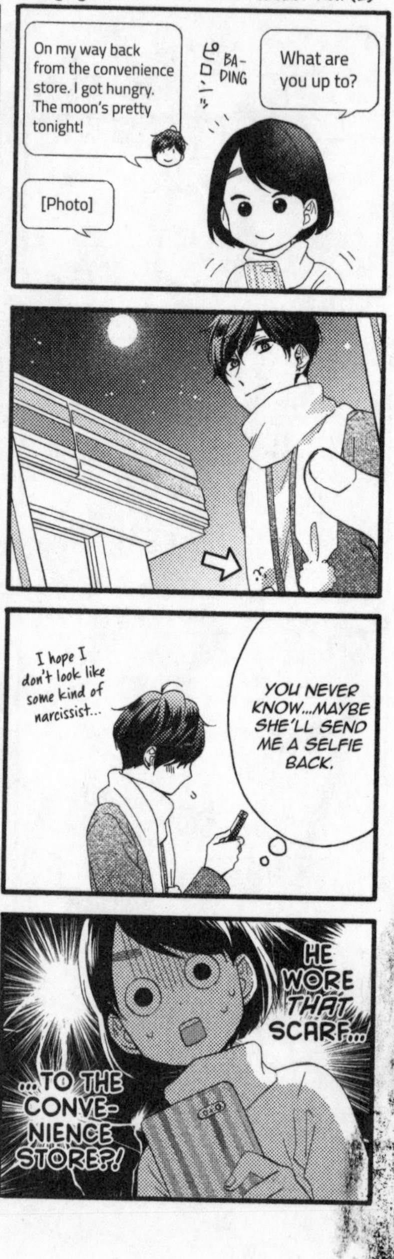
What are you up to?
BA-DING
On my way back from the convenience store. I got hungry. The moon's pretty tonight!
[Photo]
YOU NEVER KNOW...MAYBE SHE'LL SEND ME A SELFIE BACK.
I hope I don't look like some kind of narcissist...
HE WORE THAT SCARF...
...TO THE CONVENIENCE STORE?!

Ringing in the New Year with Hananoi-kun (3)

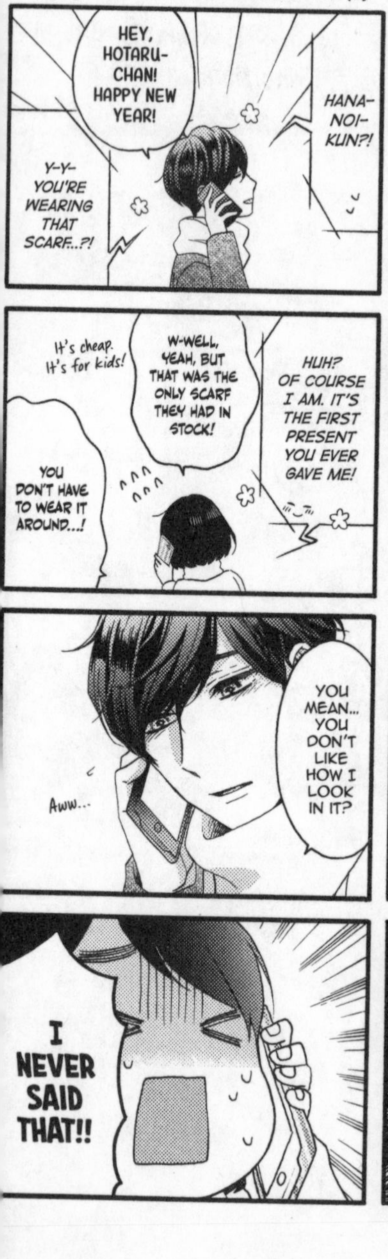
HEY, HOTARU-CHAN! HAPPY NEW YEAR!
HANA-NOI-KUN?!
Y-Y-YOU'RE WEARING THAT SCARF...?!
HUH? OF COURSE I AM. IT'S THE FIRST PRESENT YOU EVER GAVE ME!
W-WELL, YEAH, BUT THAT WAS THE ONLY SCARF THEY HAD IN STOCK!
It's cheap. It's for kids!
YOU DON'T HAVE TO WEAR IT AROUND...!
YOU MEAN... YOU DON'T LIKE HOW I LOOK IN IT?
Aww...
I NEVER SAID THAT!!

CHAPTER 6

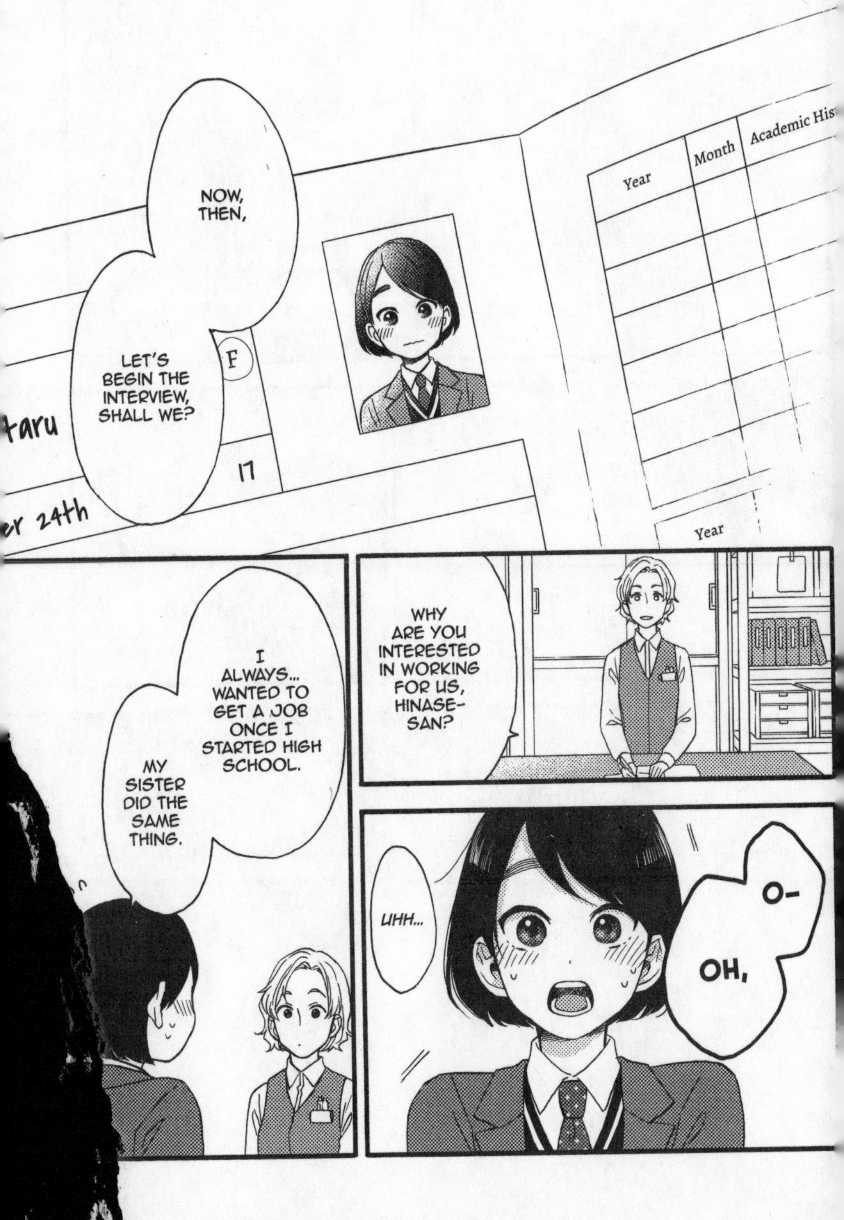

Academic Hist
Month
Year
F
taru
17
er 24th
Year
NOW, THEN,
LET'S BEGIN THE INTERVIEW, SHALL WE?
WHY ARE YOU INTERESTED IN WORKING FOR US, HINASE-SAN?
O- OH,
UHH...
I ALWAYS... WANTED TO GET A JOB ONCE I STARTED HIGH SCHOOL.
MY SISTER DID THE SAME THING.

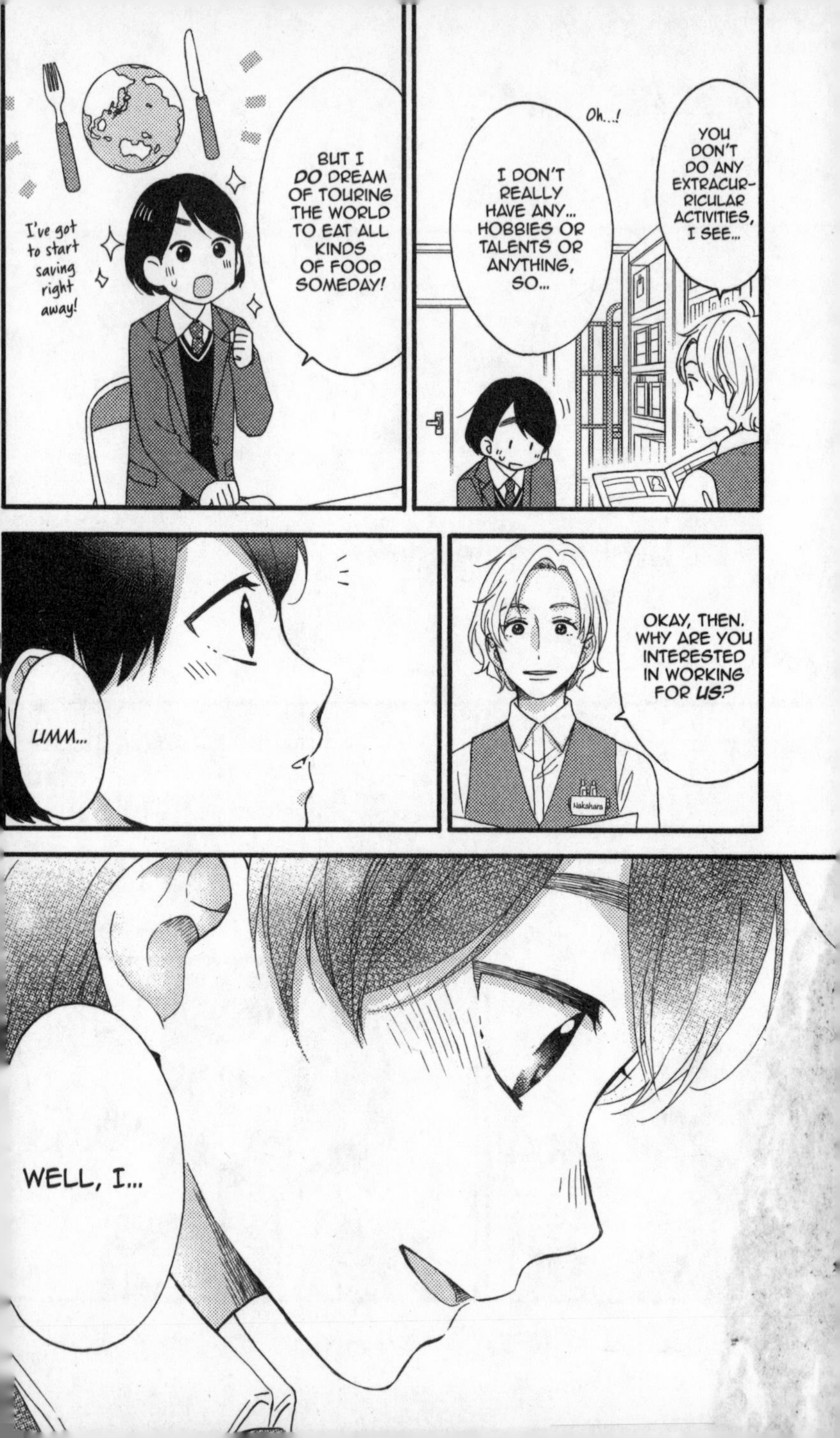
YOU DON'T DO ANY EXTRACURRICULAR ACTIVITIES, I SEE...
Oh...!
I DON'T REALLY HAVE ANY... HOBBIES OR TALENTS OR ANYTHING, SO...
BUT I DO DREAM OF TOURING THE WORLD TO EAT ALL KINDS OF FOOD SOMEDAY!
I've got to start saving right away!
OKAY, THEN. WHY ARE YOU INTERESTED IN WORKING FOR US?
Nakahara
UMM...
WELL, I...

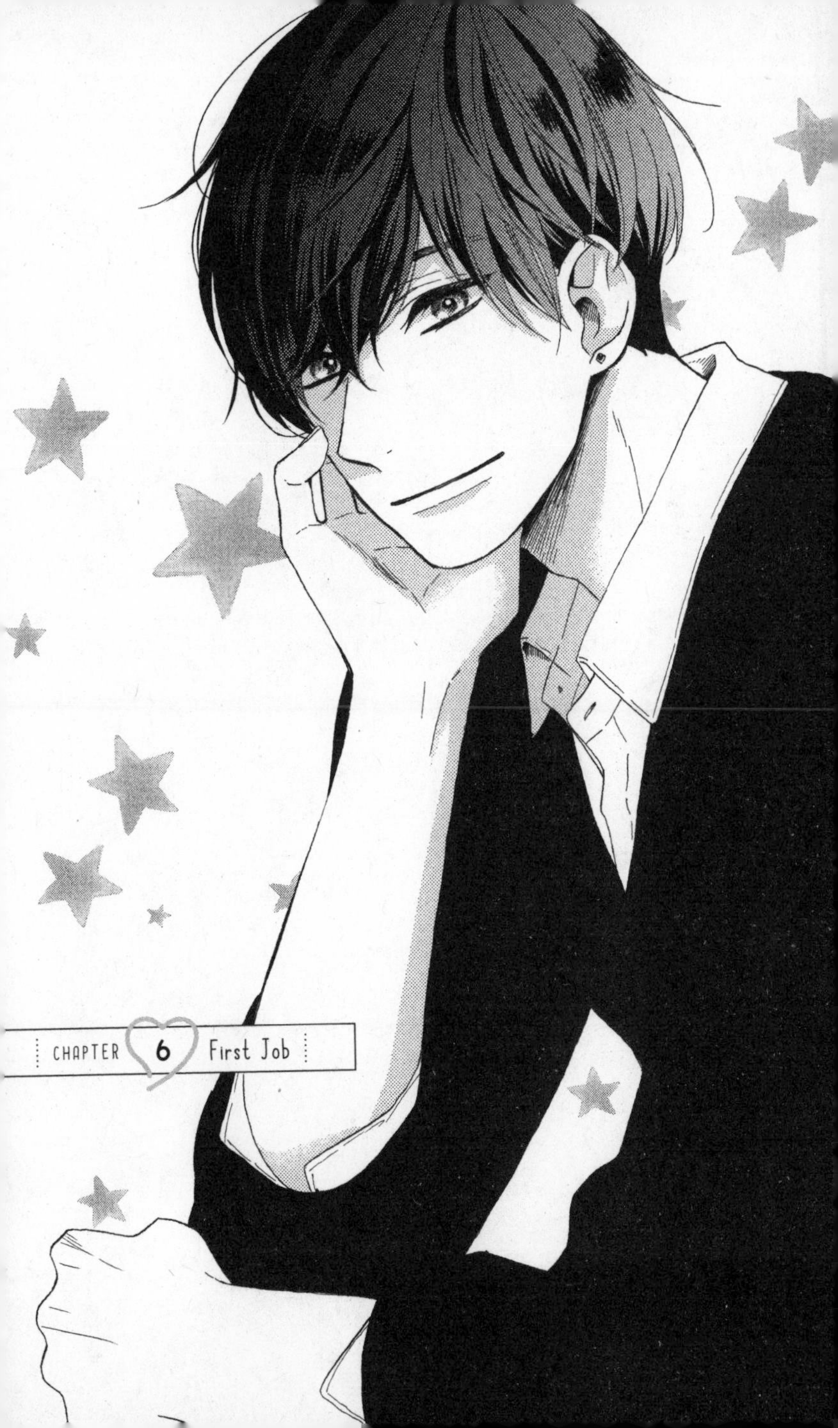
CHAPTER 6 First Job

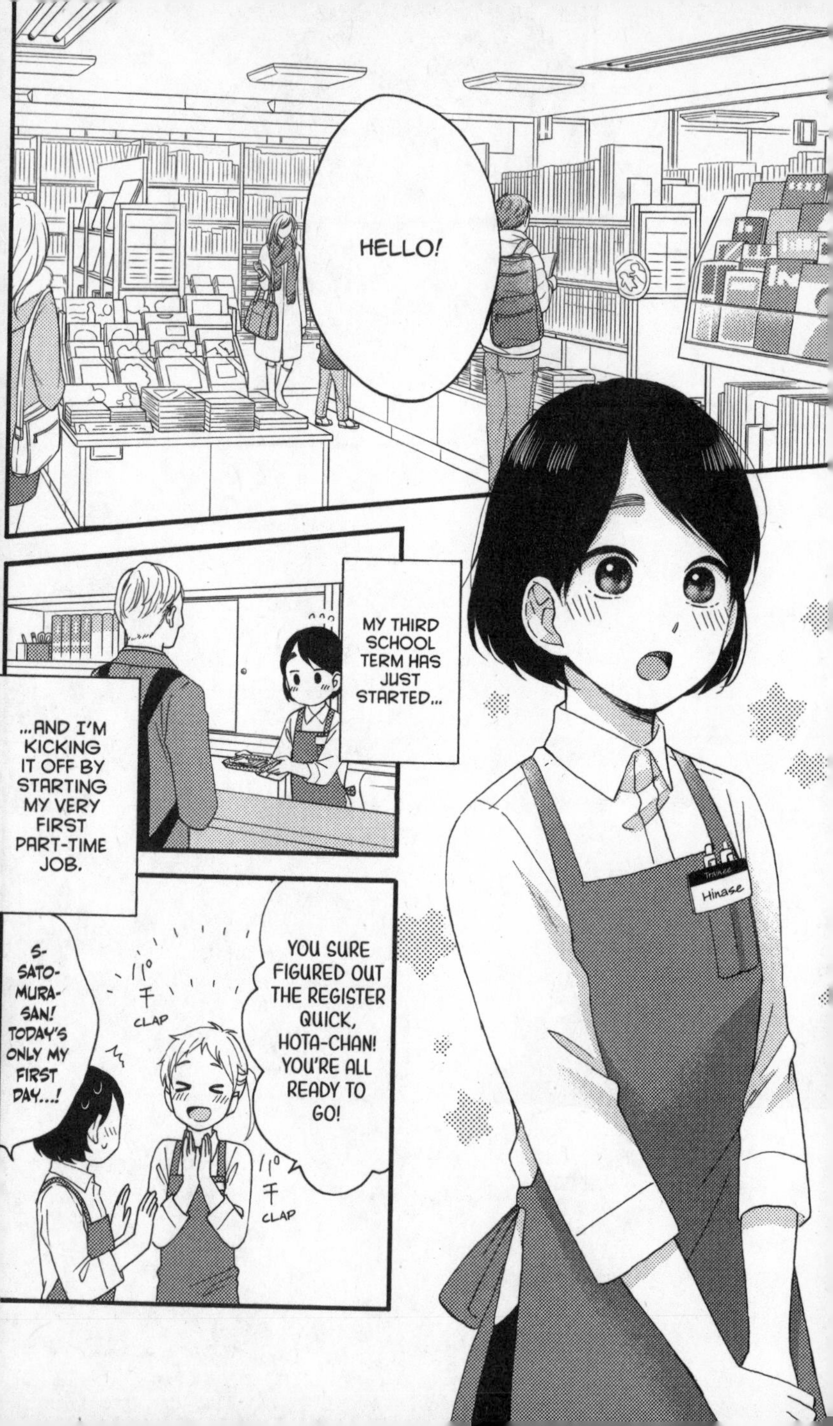
HELLO!
Trainee
Hinase
MY THIRD SCHOOL TERM HAS JUST STARTED...
...AND I'M KICKING IT OFF BY STARTING MY VERY FIRST PART-TIME JOB.
YOU SURE FIGURED OUT THE REGISTER QUICK, HOTA-CHAN! YOU'RE ALL READY TO GO!
パチ
CLAP
パチ
CLAP
S-SATO-MURA-SAN! TODAY'S ONLY MY FIRST DAY...!

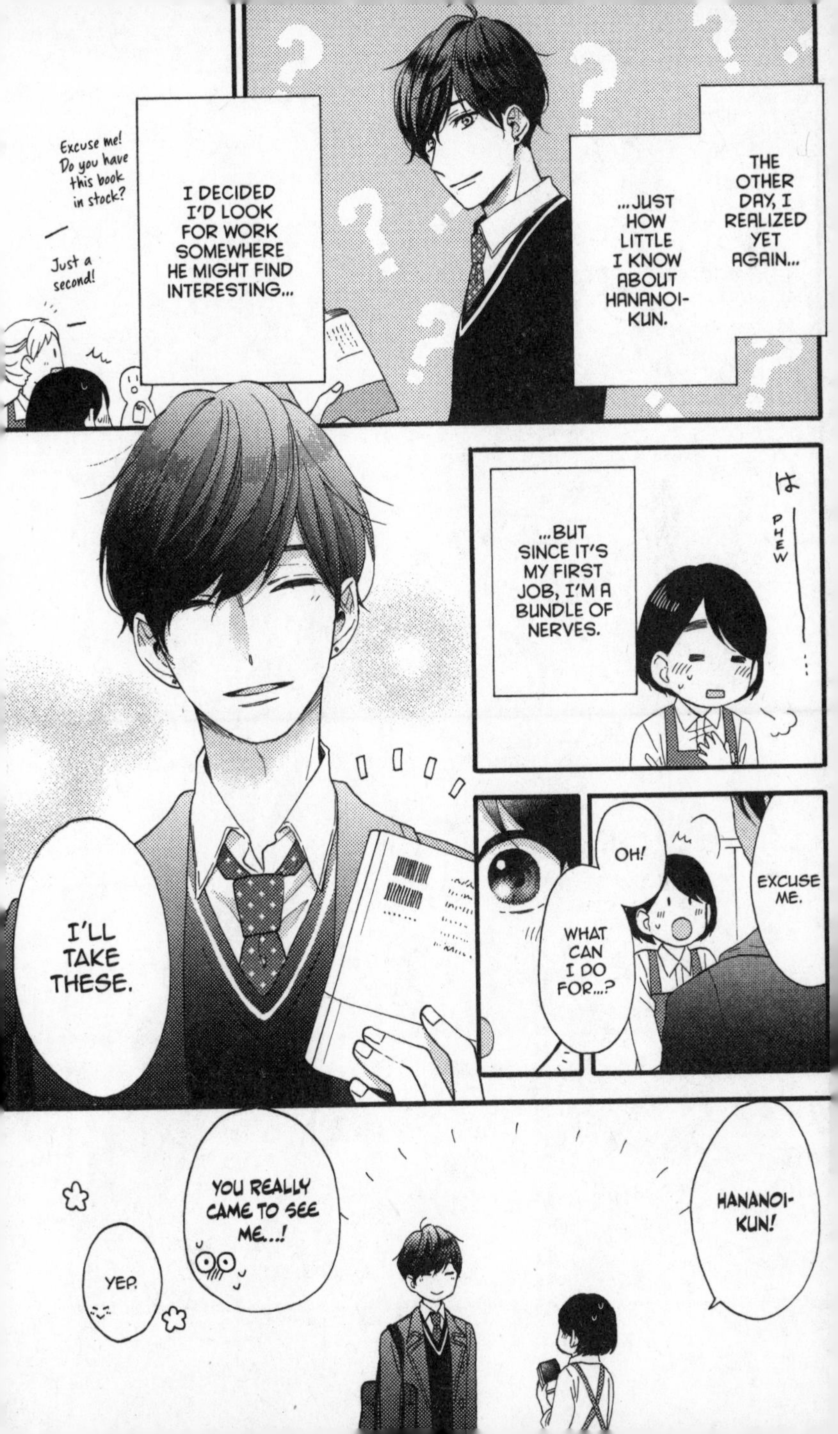
THE OTHER DAY, I REALIZED YET AGAIN...
...JUST HOW LITTLE I KNOW ABOUT HANANOI-KUN.
I DECIDED I'D LOOK FOR WORK SOMEWHERE HE MIGHT FIND INTERESTING...
Excuse me! Do you have this book in stock?
Just a second!
は
PHEW
...BUT SINCE IT'S MY FIRST JOB, I'M A BUNDLE OF NERVES.
EXCUSE ME.
OH!
WHAT CAN I DO FOR...?
I'LL TAKE THESE.
HANANOI-KUN!
YOU REALLY CAME TO SEE ME...!
YEP.

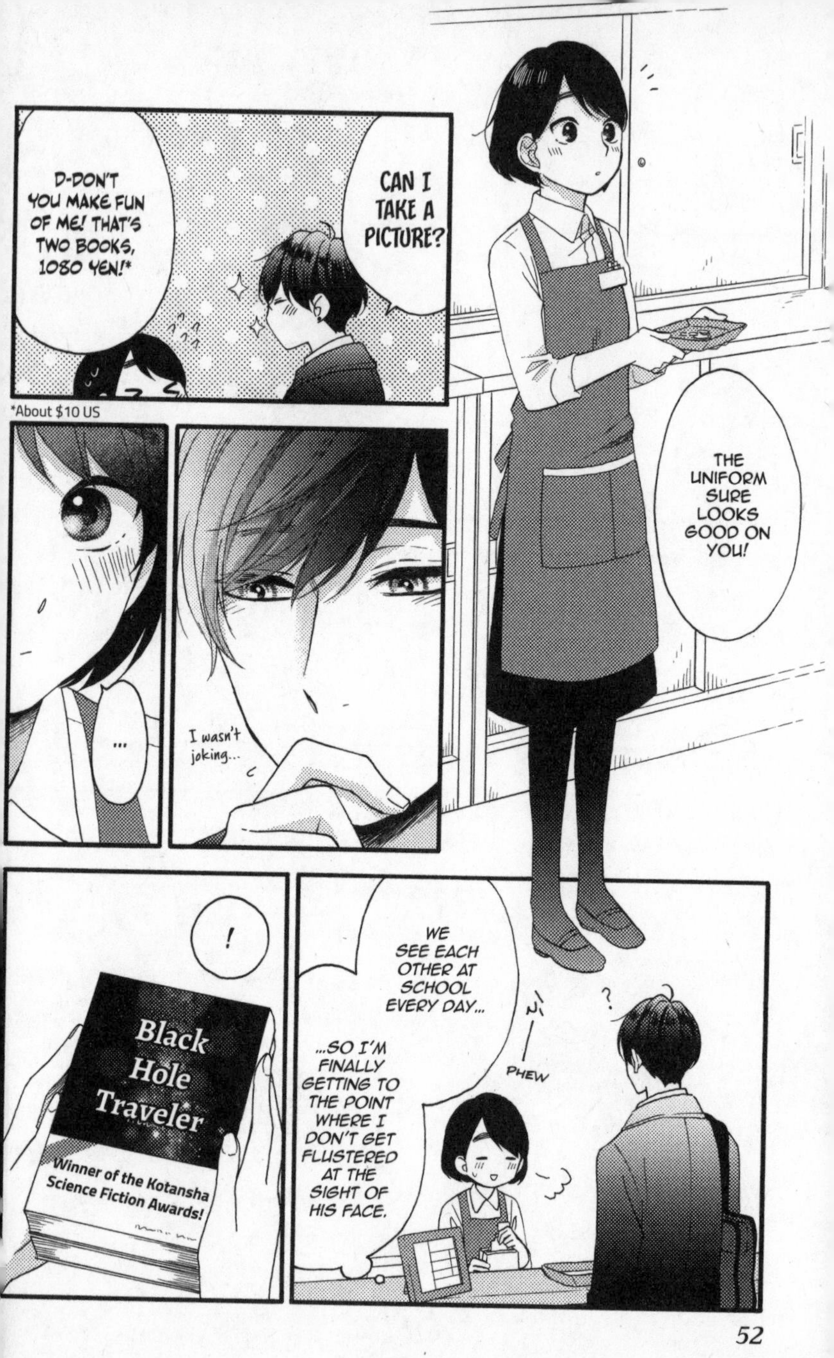

THE UNIFORM SURE LOOKS GOOD ON YOU!
CAN I TAKE A PICTURE?
D-DON'T YOU MAKE FUN OF ME! THAT'S TWO BOOKS, 1080 YEN!*
I wasn't joking...
...
WE SEE EACH OTHER AT SCHOOL EVERY DAY...
...SO I'M FINALLY GETTING TO THE POINT WHERE I DON'T GET FLUSTERED AT THE SIGHT OF HIS FACE.
?
N!
PHEW
!
Black Hole Traveler
Winner of the Kotansha Science Fiction Awards!

*About $10 US

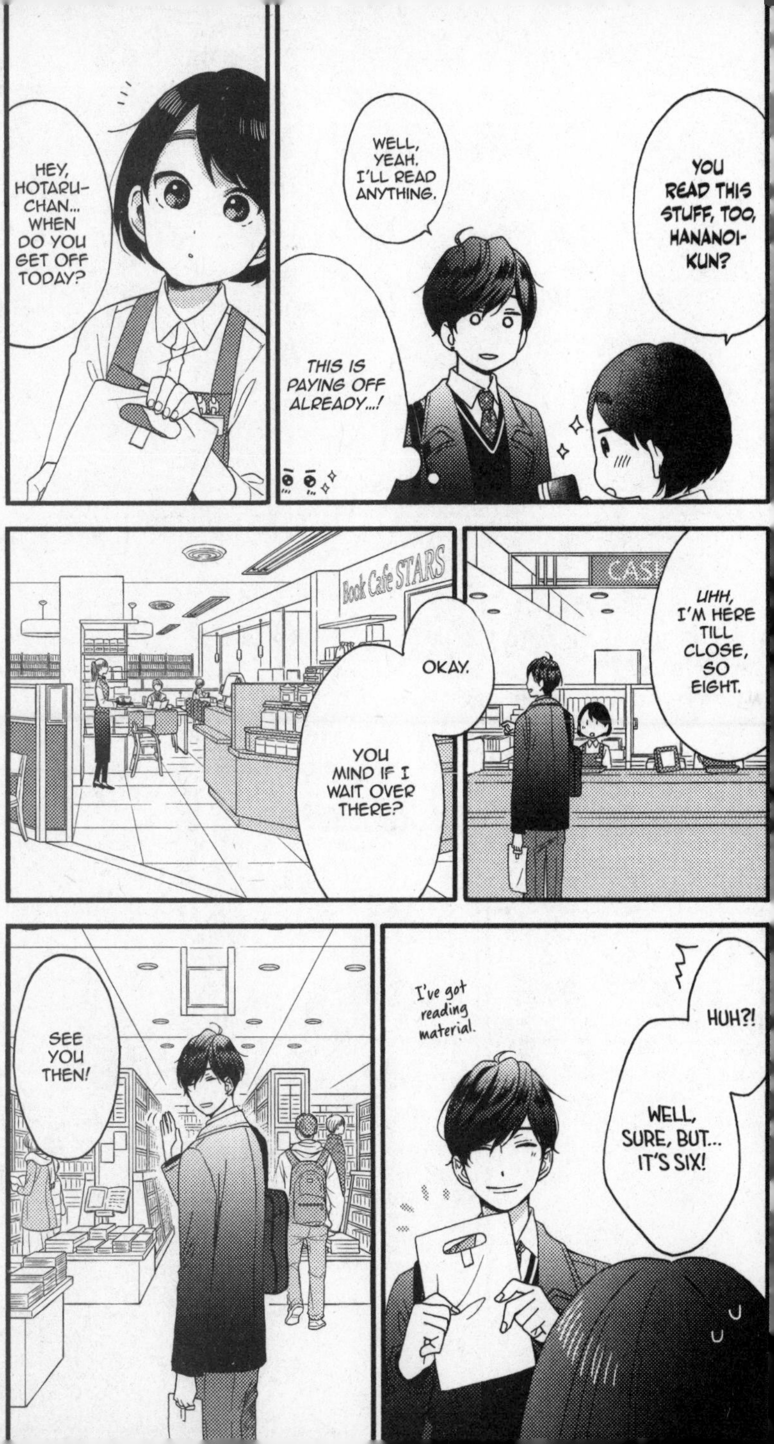
YOU READ THIS STUFF, TOO, HANANOI-KUN?
WELL, YEAH. I'LL READ ANYTHING.
THIS IS PAYING OFF ALREADY...!
HEY, HOTARU-CHAN... WHEN DO YOU GET OFF TODAY?
UHH, I'M HERE TILL CLOSE, SO EIGHT.
Book Cafe STARS
OKAY.
YOU MIND IF I WAIT OVER THERE?
HUH?!
WELL, SURE, BUT... IT'S SIX!
I've got reading material.
SEE YOU THEN!

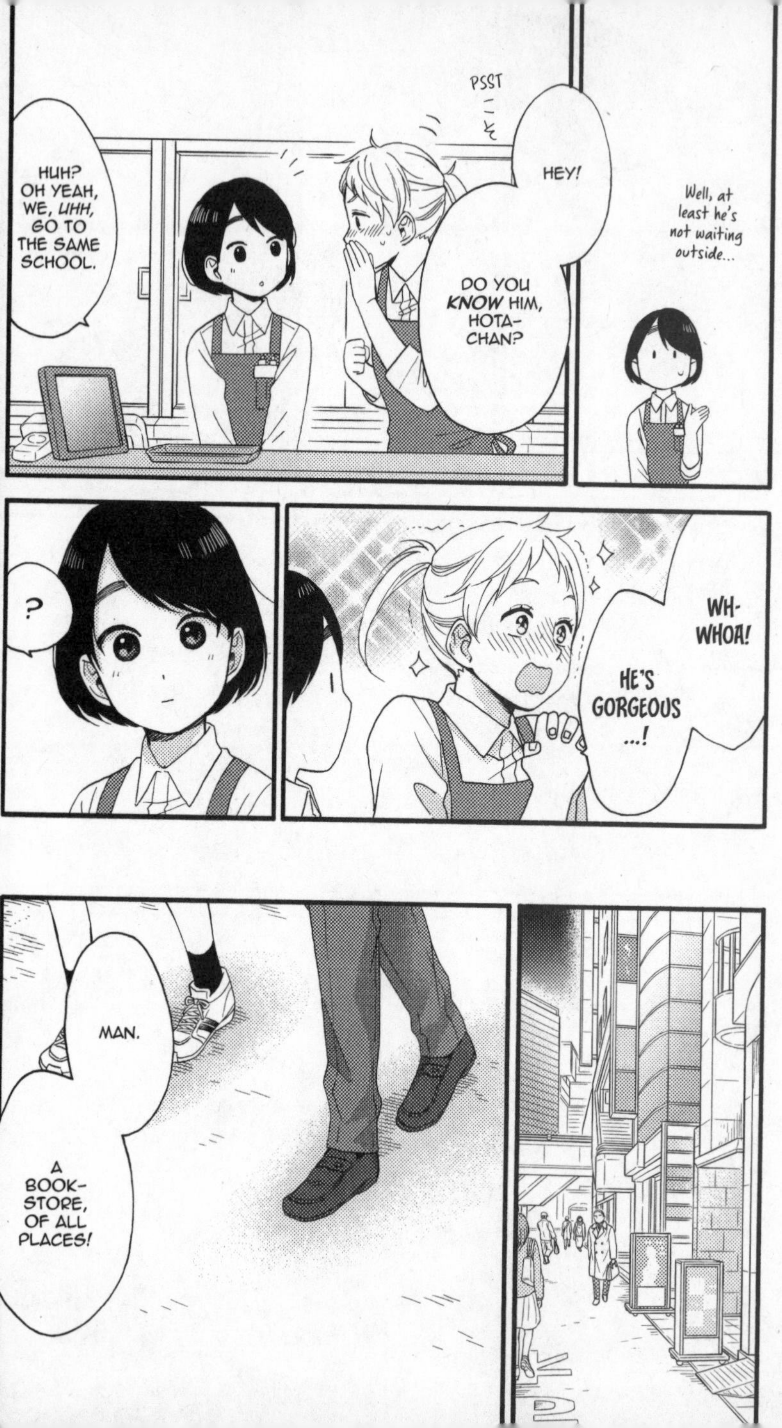
Well, at least he's not waiting outside...
PSST
HEY!
DO YOU KNOW HIM, HOTA-CHAN?
HUH? OH YEAH, WE, UHH, GO TO THE SAME SCHOOL.
WH-WHOA!
HE'S GORGEOUS ...!
?
MAN.
A BOOK-STORE, OF ALL PLACES!

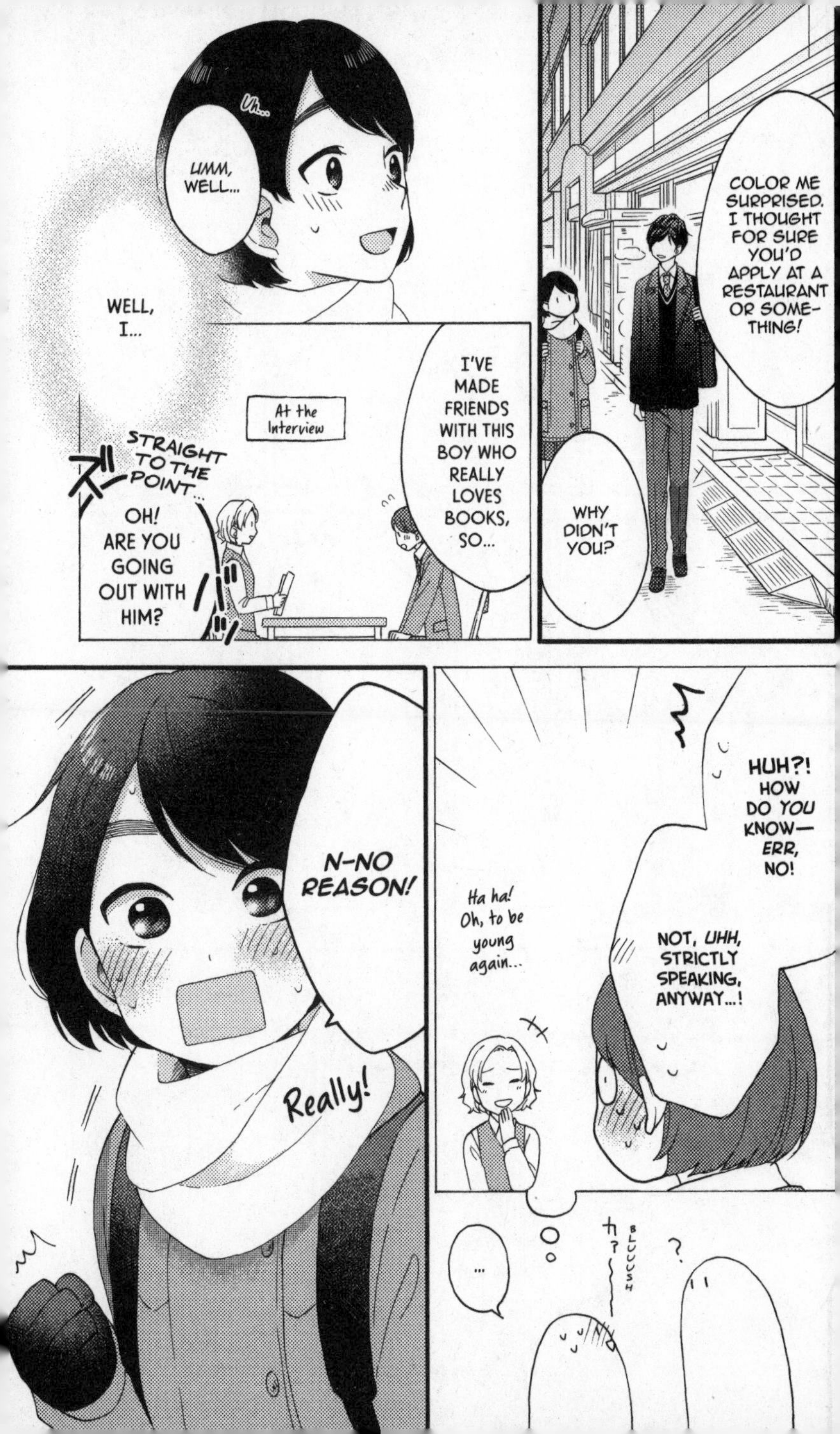
COLOR ME SURPRISED. I THOUGHT FOR SURE YOU'D APPLY AT A RESTAURANT OR SOME-THING!
WHY DIDN'T YOU?
Uh...
UMM, WELL...
WELL, I...
At the Interview
I'VE MADE FRIENDS WITH THIS BOY WHO REALLY LOVES BOOKS, SO...
STRAIGHT TO THE POINT...
OH! ARE YOU GOING OUT WITH HIM?
HUH?! HOW DO YOU KNOW— ERR, NO!
NOT, UHH, STRICTLY SPEAKING, ANYWAY...!
Ha ha! Oh, to be young again...
BLUUSH
...
N-NO REASON!
Really!

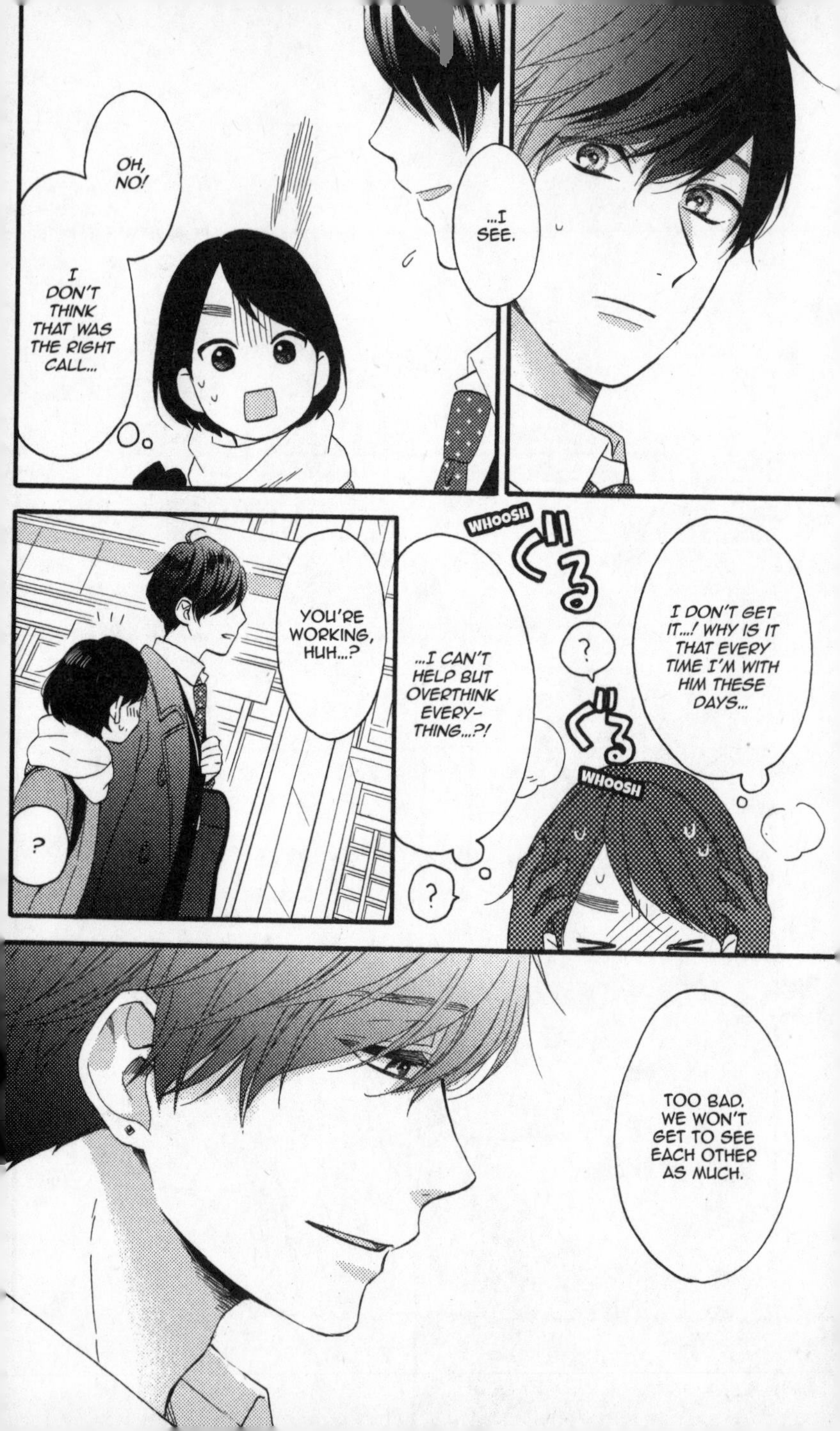
...I SEE.
OH, NO!
I DON'T THINK THAT WAS THE RIGHT CALL...
WHOOSH
ぐる
?
ぐる
WHOOSH
I DON'T GET IT...! WHY IS IT THAT EVERY TIME I'M WITH HIM THESE DAYS...
...I CAN'T HELP BUT OVERTHINK EVERY-THING...?!
?
YOU'RE WORKING, HUH...?
?
TOO BAD. WE WON'T GET TO SEE EACH OTHER AS MUCH.

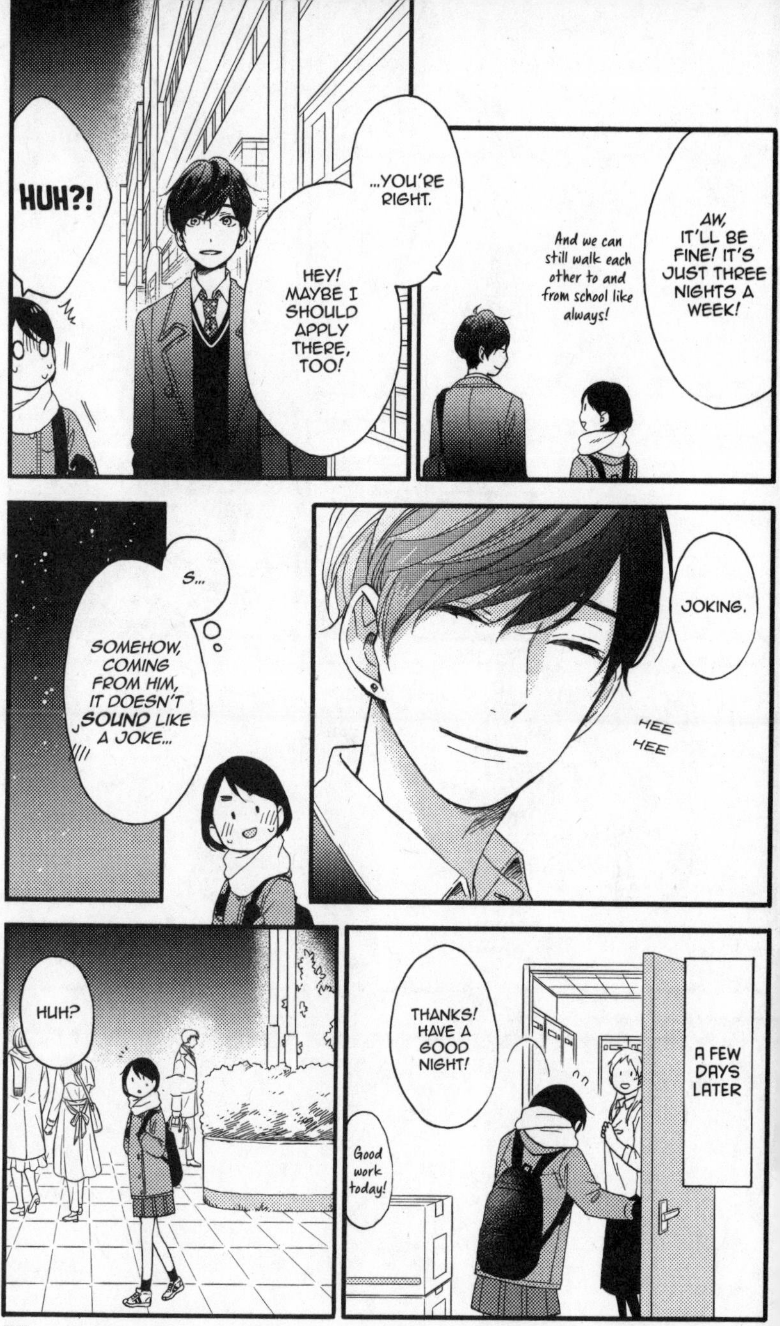
AW, IT'LL BE FINE! IT'S JUST THREE NIGHTS A WEEK!
And we can still walk each other to and from school like always!
...YOU'RE RIGHT.
HEY! MAYBE I SHOULD APPLY THERE, TOO!
HUH?!
JOKING.
HEE HEE
S...
SOMEHOW, COMING FROM HIM, IT DOESN'T **SOUND** LIKE A JOKE...
A FEW DAYS LATER
THANKS! HAVE A GOOD NIGHT!
Good work today!
HUH?

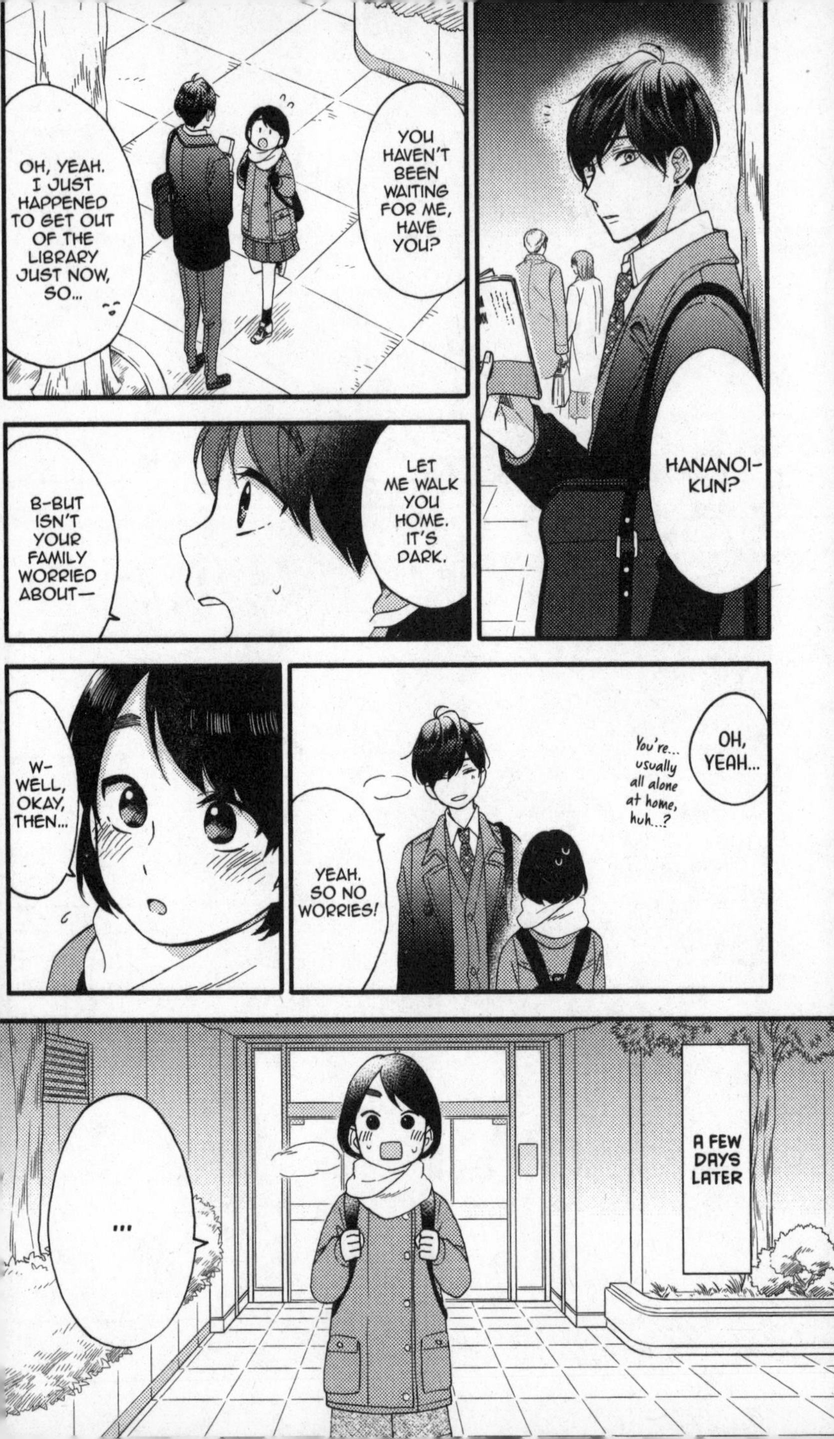
HANANOI-KUN?
YOU HAVEN'T BEEN WAITING FOR ME, HAVE YOU?
OH, YEAH. I JUST HAPPENED TO GET OUT OF THE LIBRARY JUST NOW, SO...
LET ME WALK YOU HOME. IT'S DARK.
B-BUT ISN'T YOUR FAMILY WORRIED ABOUT—
OH, YEAH...
You're... usually all alone at home, huh...?
YEAH. SO NO WORRIES!
W-WELL, OKAY, THEN...
A FEW DAYS LATER
...

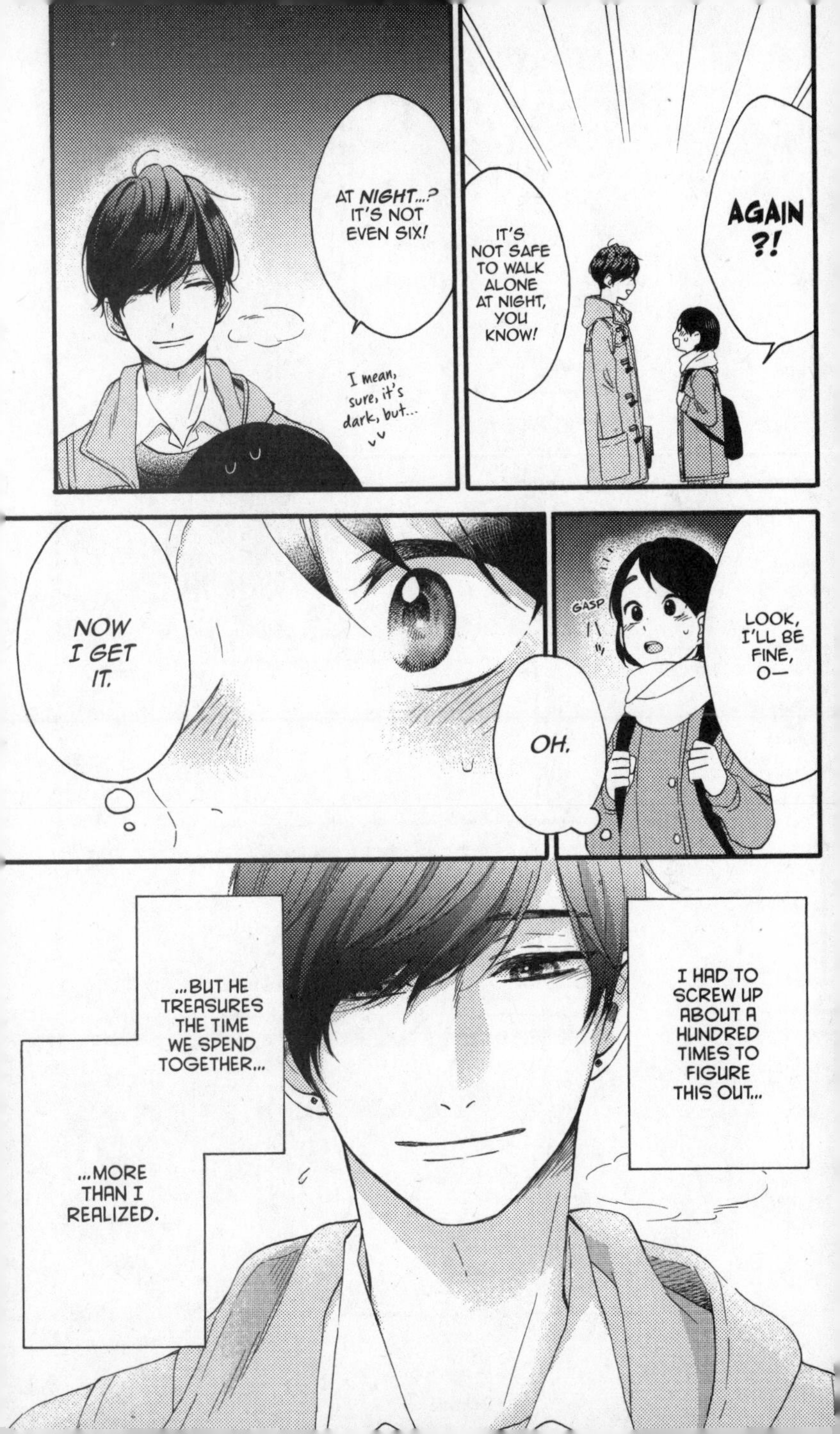
AGAIN ?!
IT'S NOT SAFE TO WALK ALONE AT NIGHT, YOU KNOW!
AT NIGHT...? IT'S NOT EVEN SIX!
I mean, sure, it's dark, but...
LOOK, I'LL BE FINE, O—
GASP
OH.
NOW I GET IT.
I HAD TO SCREW UP ABOUT A HUNDRED TIMES TO FIGURE THIS OUT...
...BUT HE TREASURES THE TIME WE SPEND TOGETHER...
...MORE THAN I REALIZED.

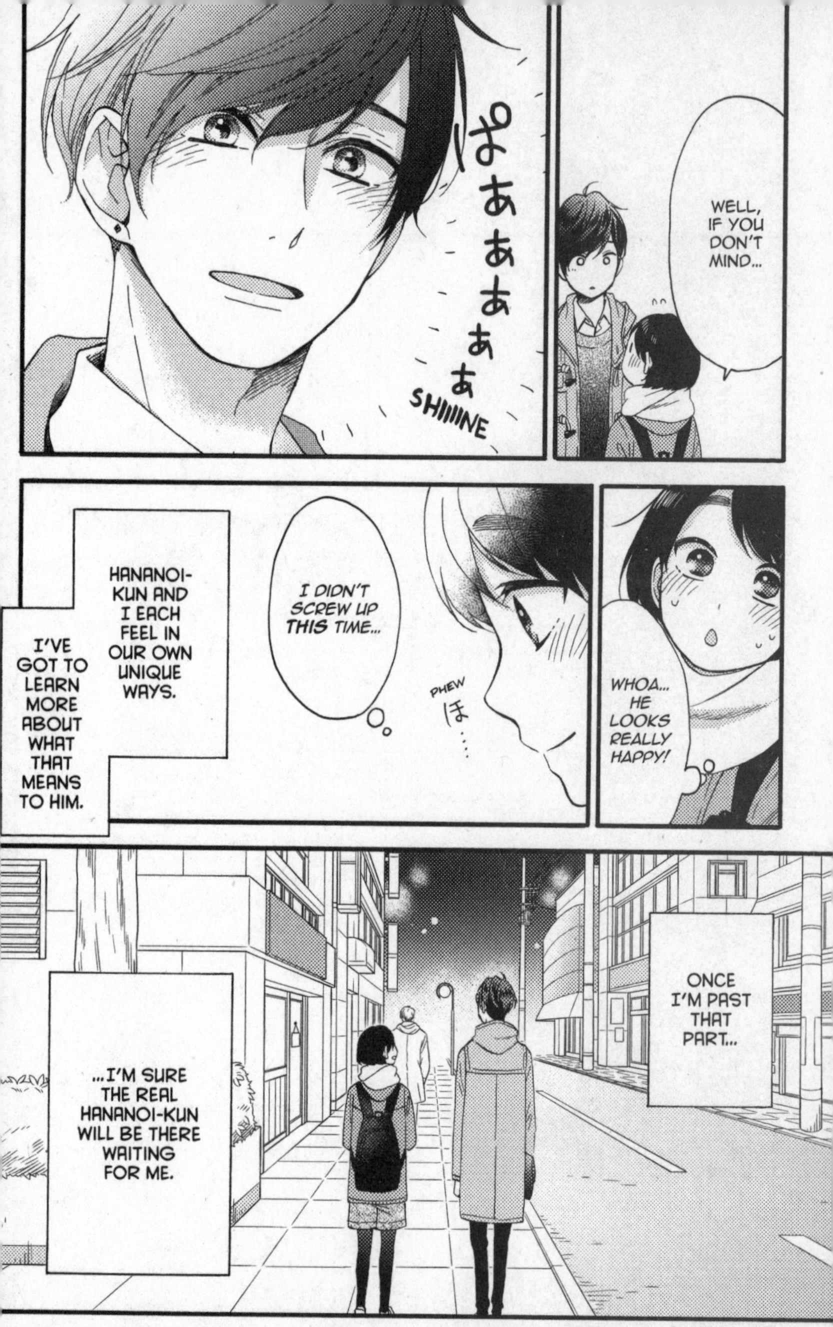
WELL, IF YOU DON'T MIND...
ぱあああ
SHIIIINE
WHOA... HE LOOKS REALLY HAPPY!
I DIDN'T SCREW UP THIS TIME...
PHEW
ほ...
HANANOI-KUN AND I EACH FEEL IN OUR OWN UNIQUE WAYS.
I'VE GOT TO LEARN MORE ABOUT WHAT THAT MEANS TO HIM.
ONCE I'M PAST THAT PART...
...I'M SURE THE REAL HANANOI-KUN WILL BE THERE WAITING FOR ME.

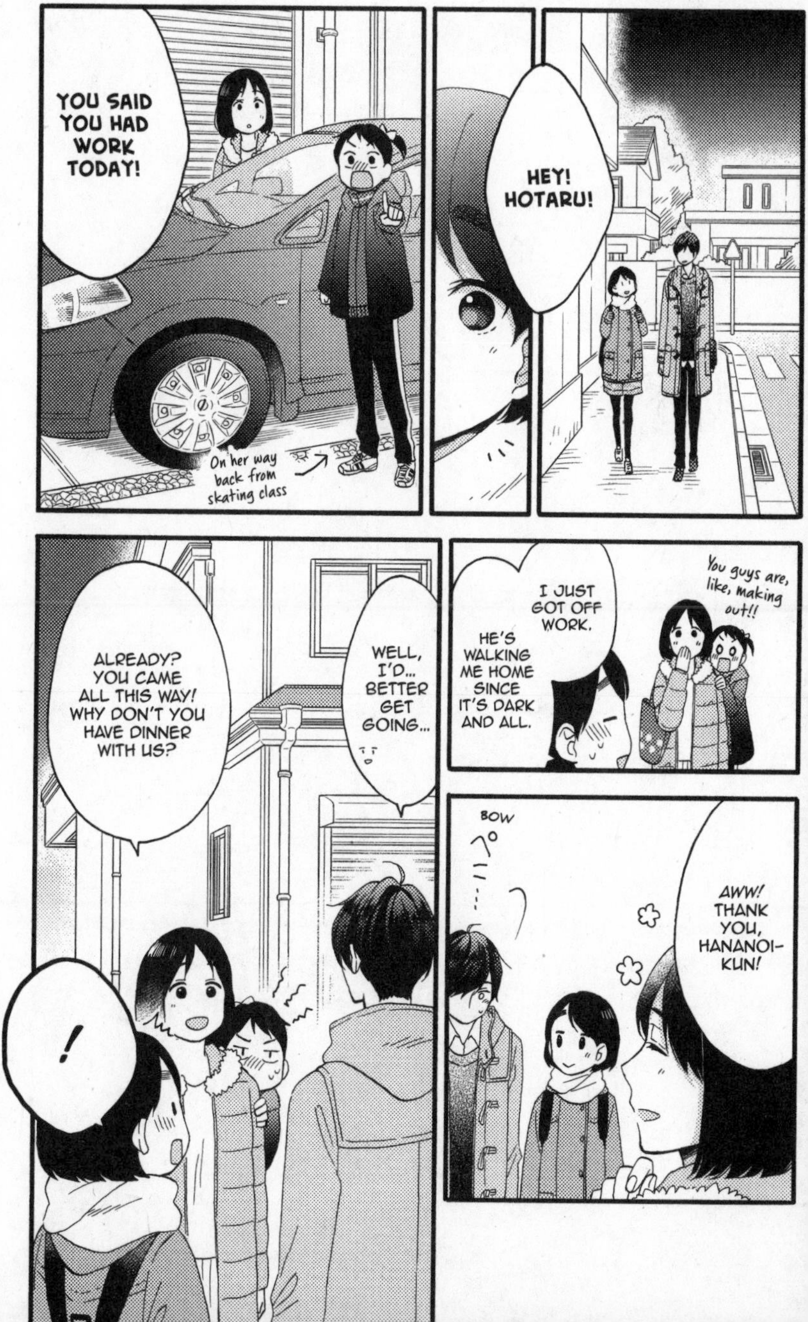
HEY! HOTARU!
YOU SAID YOU HAD WORK TODAY!
On her way back from skating class
You guys are, like, making out!!
I JUST GOT OFF WORK.
HE'S WALKING ME HOME SINCE IT'S DARK AND ALL.
AWW! THANK YOU, HANANOI-KUN!
BOW
WELL, I'D... BETTER GET GOING...
ALREADY? YOU CAME ALL THIS WAY! WHY DON'T YOU HAVE DINNER WITH US?
!

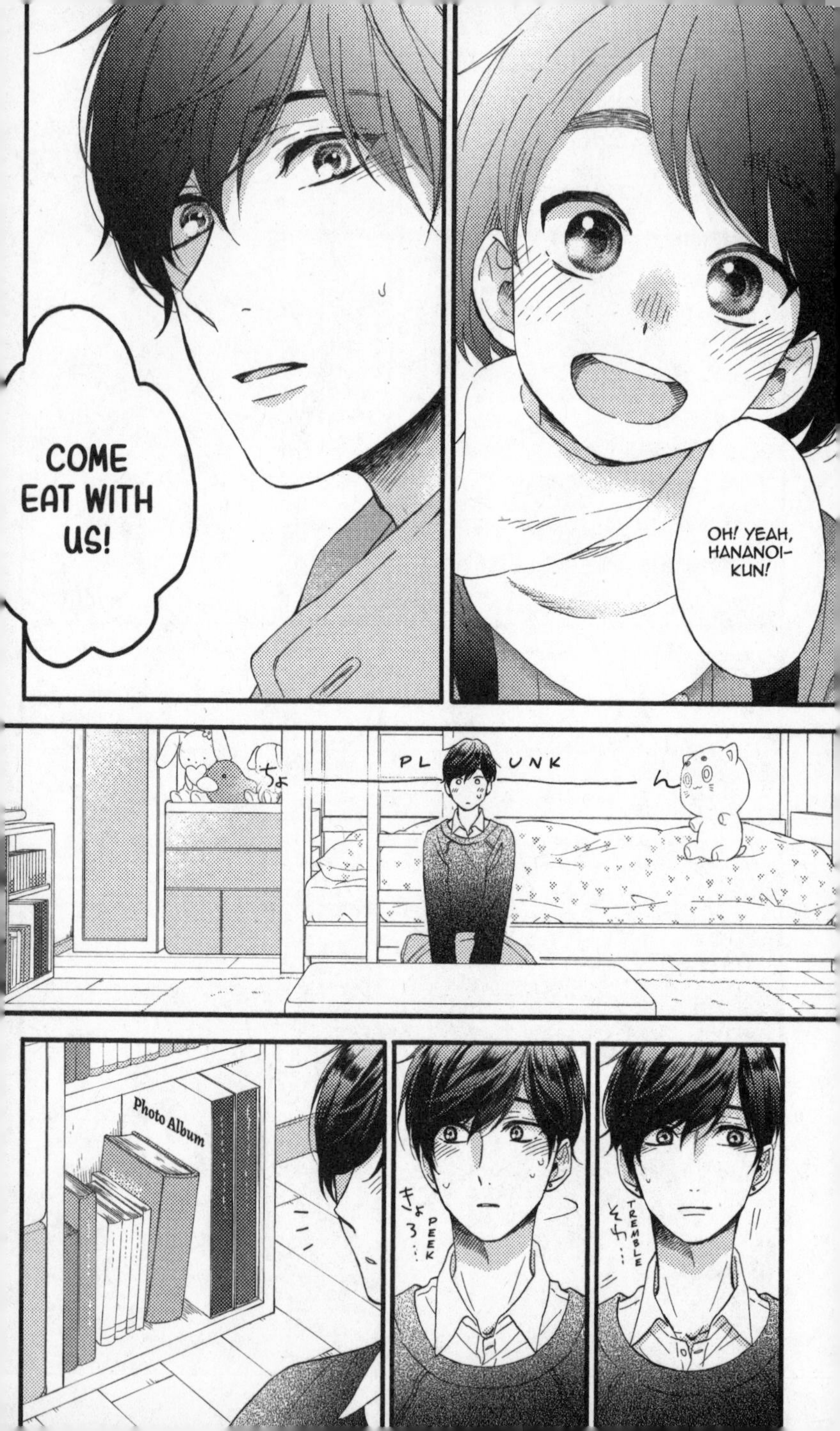
OH! YEAH, HANANOI-KUN!
COME EAT WITH US!
PL UNK
ちょ
ん
TREMBLE
きょろ…
PEEK

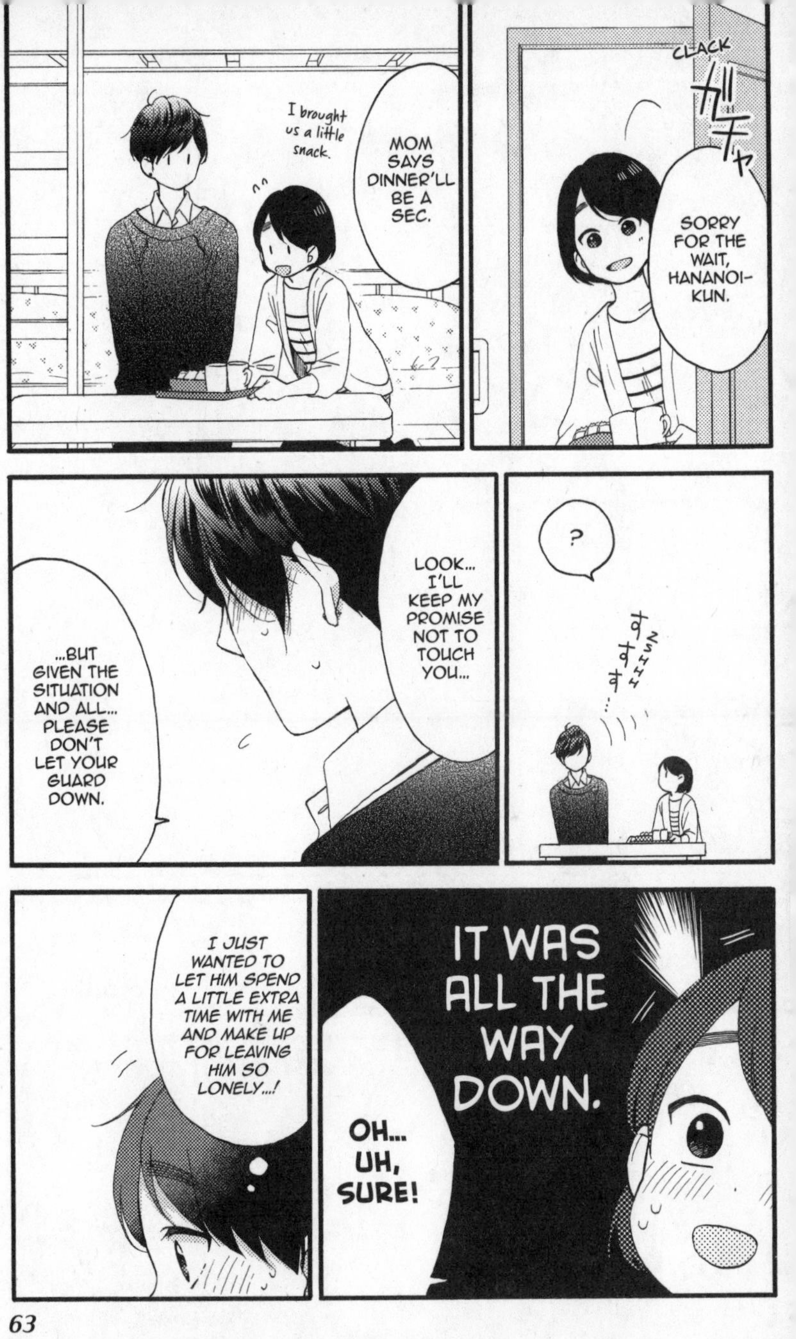
CLACK
ガチャ
SORRY FOR THE WAIT, HANANOI-KUN.
MOM SAYS DINNER'LL BE A SEC.
I brought us a little snack.
?
すすす…
SHHH
LOOK... I'LL KEEP MY PROMISE NOT TO TOUCH YOU...
...BUT GIVEN THE SITUATION AND ALL... PLEASE DON'T LET YOUR GUARD DOWN.
IT WAS ALL THE WAY DOWN.
OH... UH, SURE!
I JUST WANTED TO LET HIM SPEND A LITTLE EXTRA TIME WITH ME AND MAKE UP FOR LEAVING HIM SO LONELY...!

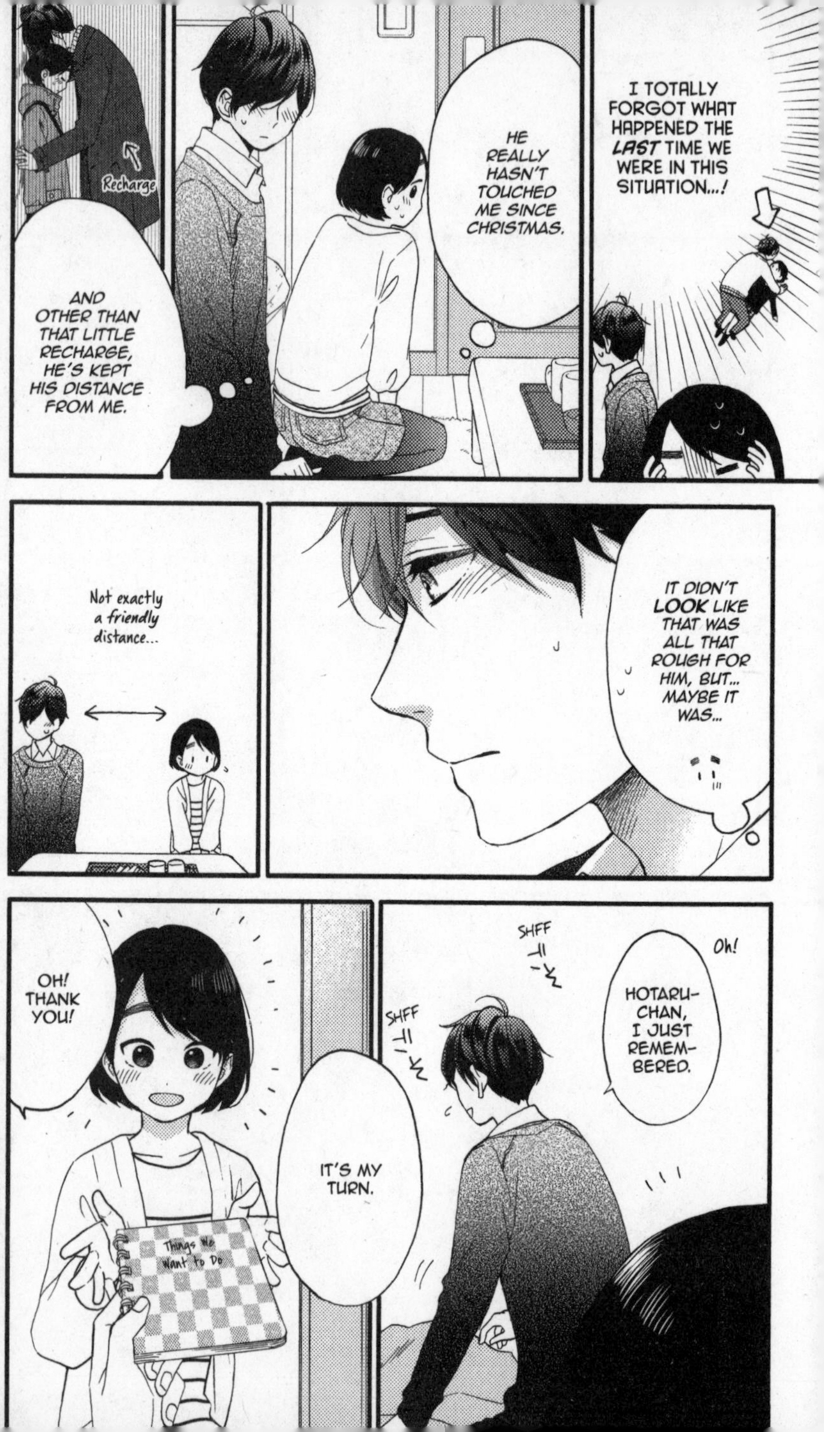
I TOTALLY FORGOT WHAT HAPPENED THE LAST TIME WE WERE IN THIS SITUATION...!
HE REALLY HASN'T TOUCHED ME SINCE CHRISTMAS.
Recharge
AND OTHER THAN THAT LITTLE RECHARGE, HE'S KEPT HIS DISTANCE FROM ME.
IT DIDN'T LOOK LIKE THAT WAS ALL THAT ROUGH FOR HIM, BUT... MAYBE IT WAS...
Not exactly a friendly distance...
Oh!
HOTARU-CHAN, I JUST REMEMBERED.
SHFF
SHFF
IT'S MY TURN.
OH! THANK YOU!
Things We Want to Do

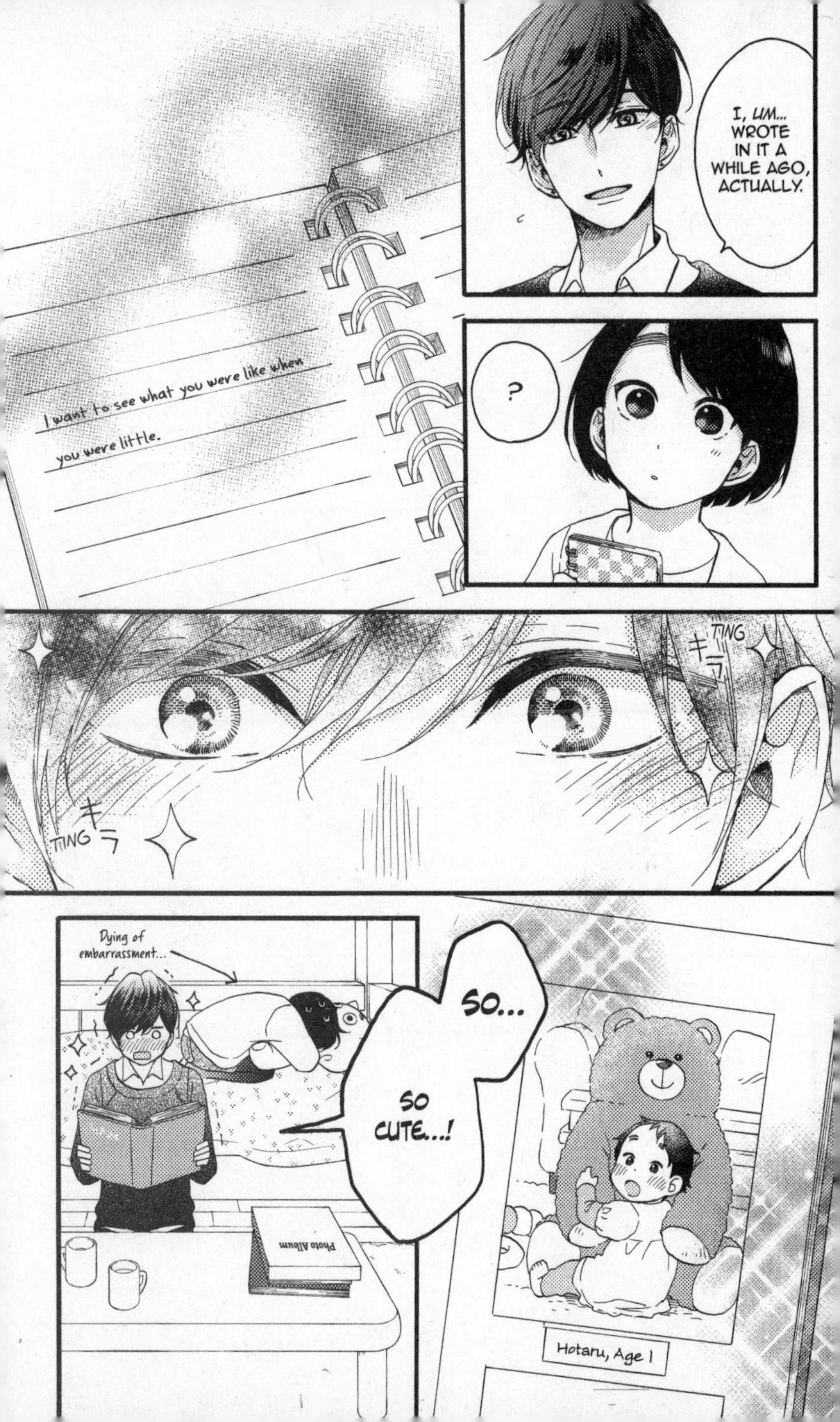
I, UM... WROTE IN IT A WHILE AGO, ACTUALLY.
?
I want to see what you were like when you were little.
TING キラ
TING キラ
SO...
SO CUTE...!
Hotaru, Age 1
Dying of embarrassment...
Photo Album

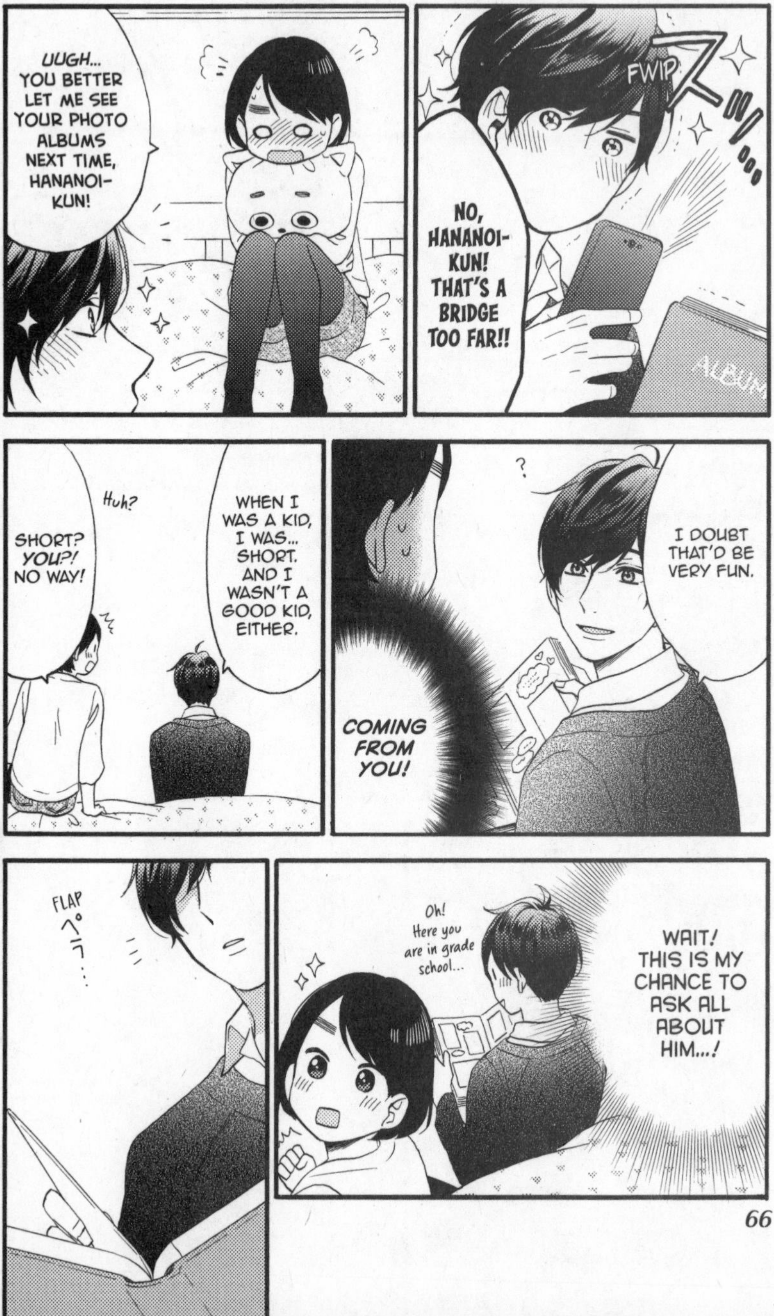
FWIP
NO, HANANOI-KUN! THAT'S A BRIDGE TOO FAR!!
ALBUM
UUGH... YOU BETTER LET ME SEE YOUR PHOTO ALBUMS NEXT TIME, HANANOI-KUN!
I DOUBT THAT'D BE VERY FUN.
?
COMING FROM YOU!
WHEN I WAS A KID, I WAS... SHORT. AND I WASN'T A GOOD KID, EITHER.
Huh?
SHORT? YOU?! NO WAY!
WAIT! THIS IS MY CHANCE TO ASK ALL ABOUT HIM...!
Oh! Here you are in grade school...
FLAP

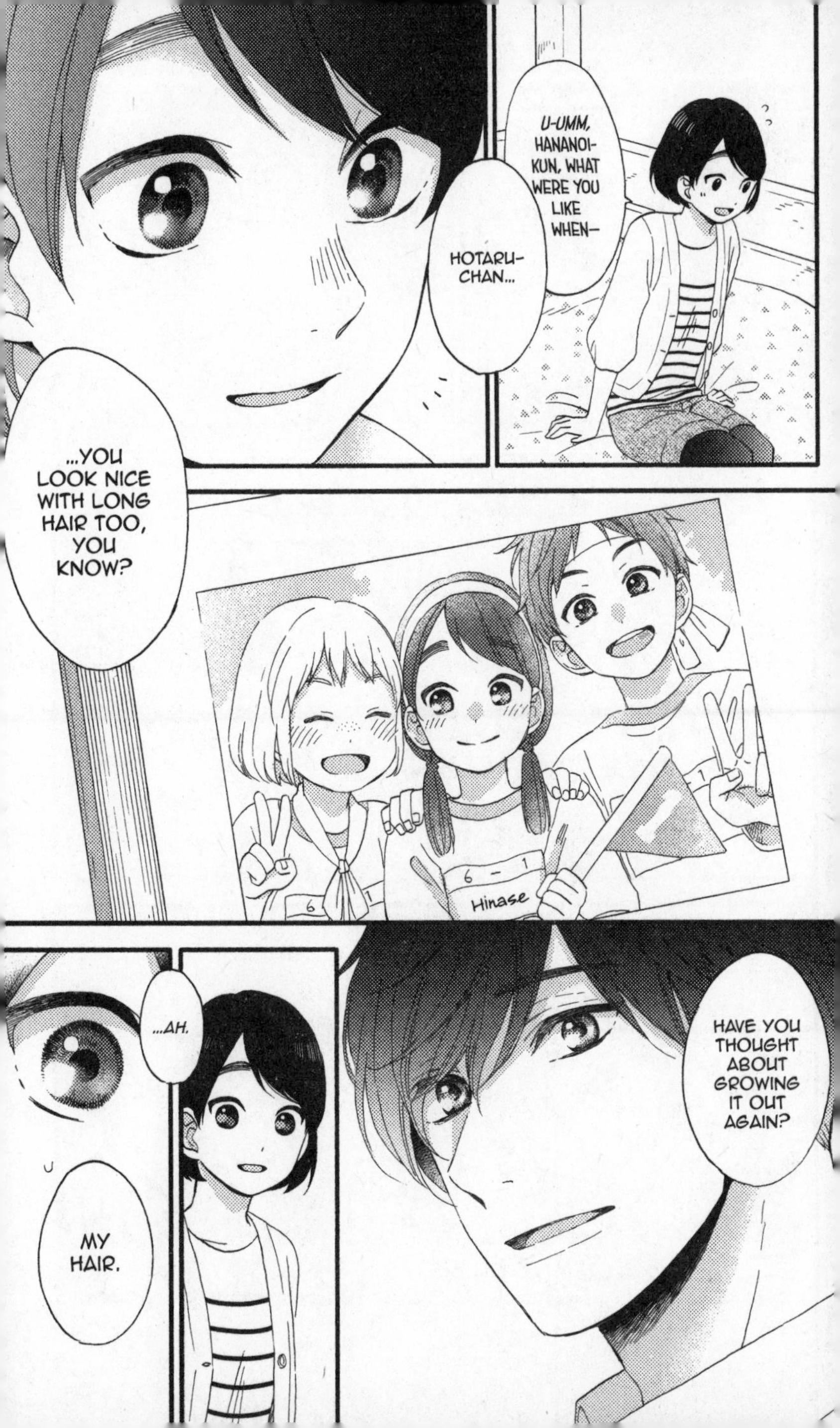
U-UMM, HANANOI-KUN, WHAT WERE YOU LIKE WHEN—
HOTARU-CHAN...
...YOU LOOK NICE WITH LONG HAIR TOO, YOU KNOW?
6 - 1
Hinase
HAVE YOU THOUGHT ABOUT GROWING IT OUT AGAIN?
...AH.
MY HAIR.

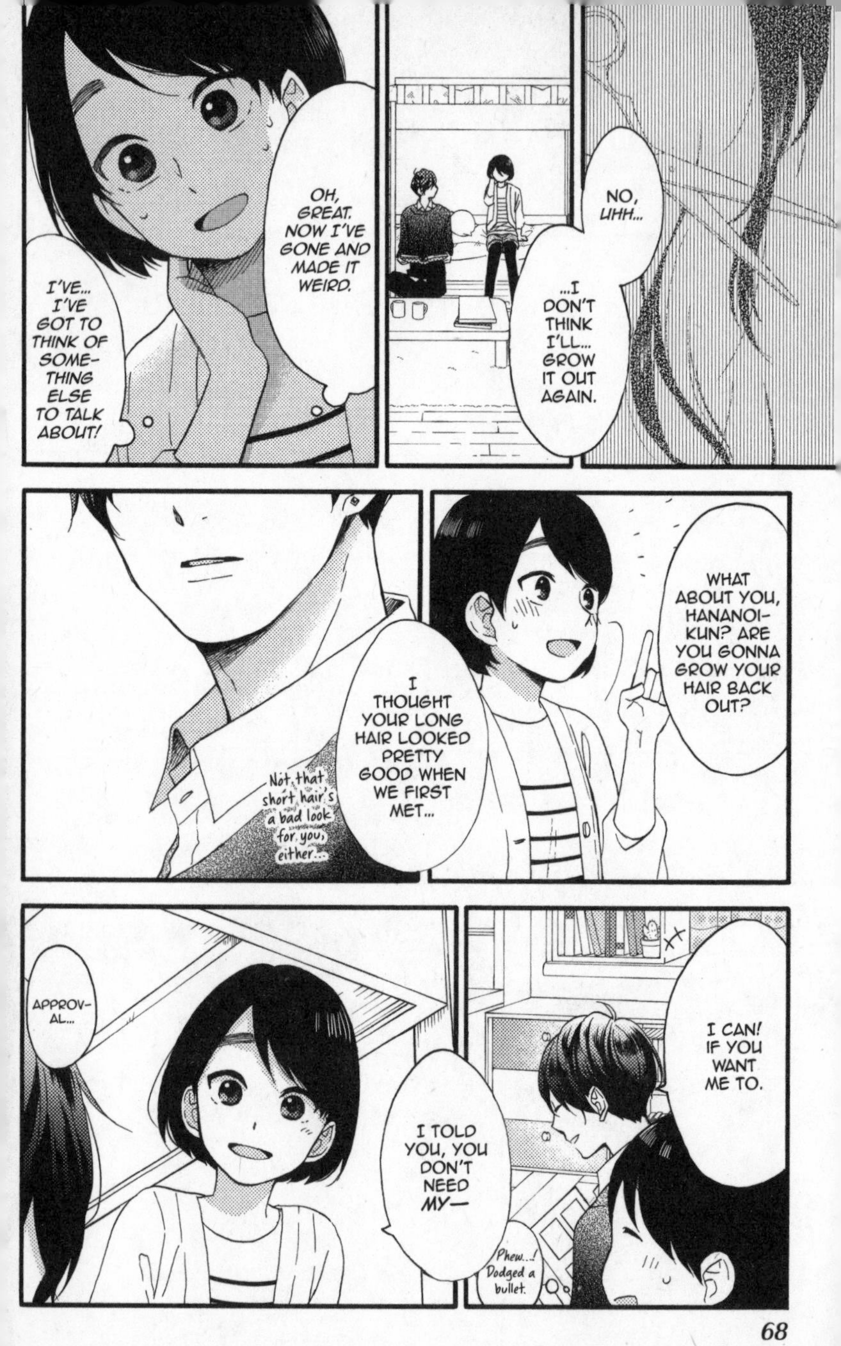
NO, UHH...
...I DON'T THINK I'LL... GROW IT OUT AGAIN.
OH, GREAT. NOW I'VE GONE AND MADE IT WEIRD.
I'VE... I'VE GOT TO THINK OF SOME-THING ELSE TO TALK ABOUT!
WHAT ABOUT YOU, HANANOI-KUN? ARE YOU GONNA GROW YOUR HAIR BACK OUT?
I THOUGHT YOUR LONG HAIR LOOKED PRETTY GOOD WHEN WE FIRST MET...
Not that short hair's a bad look for you, either...
I CAN! IF YOU WANT ME TO.
Phew...! Dodged a bullet.
I TOLD YOU, YOU DON'T NEED MY—
APPROV-AL...

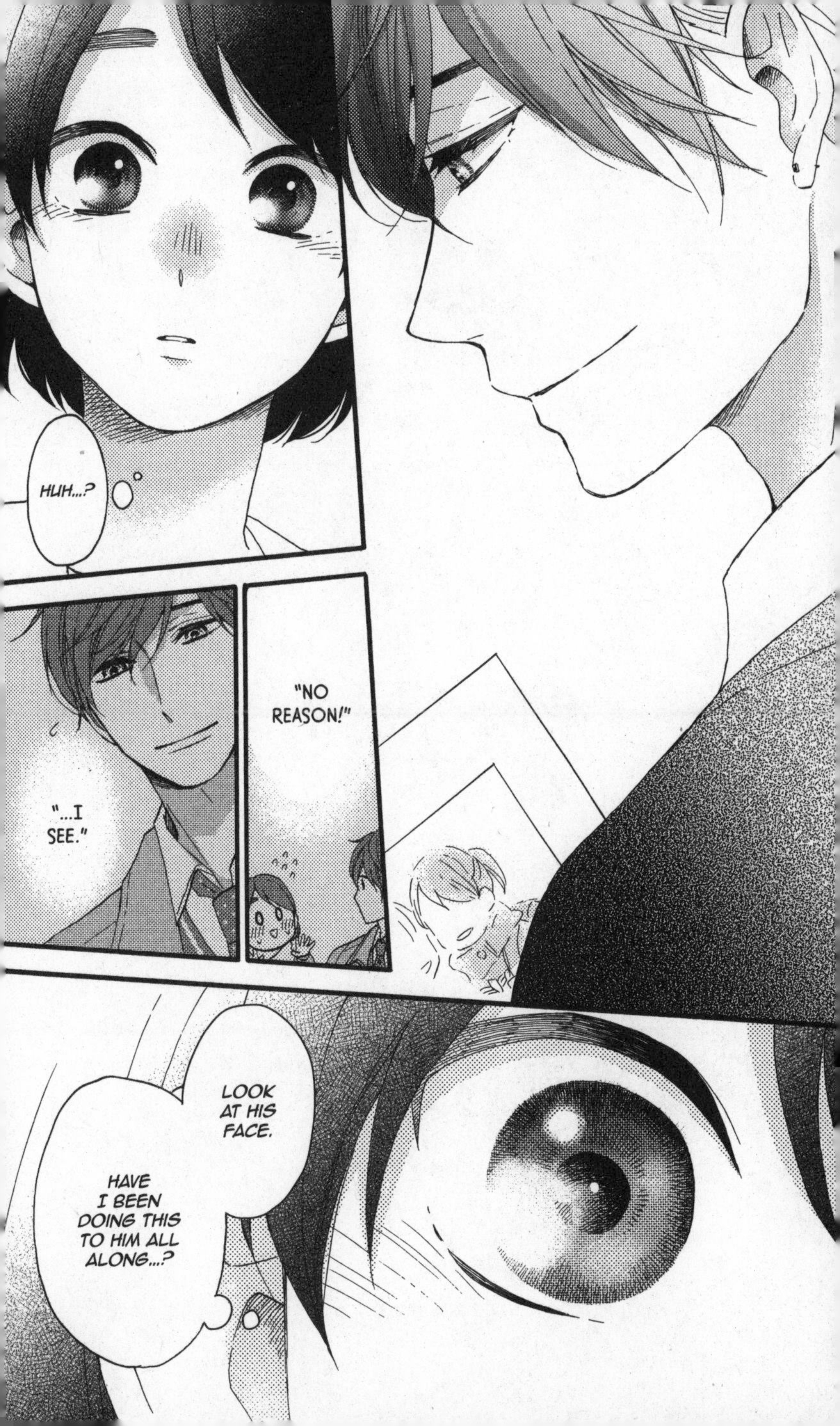
HUH...?
"NO REASON!"
"...I SEE."
LOOK AT HIS FACE.
HAVE I BEEN DOING THIS TO HIM ALL ALONG...?

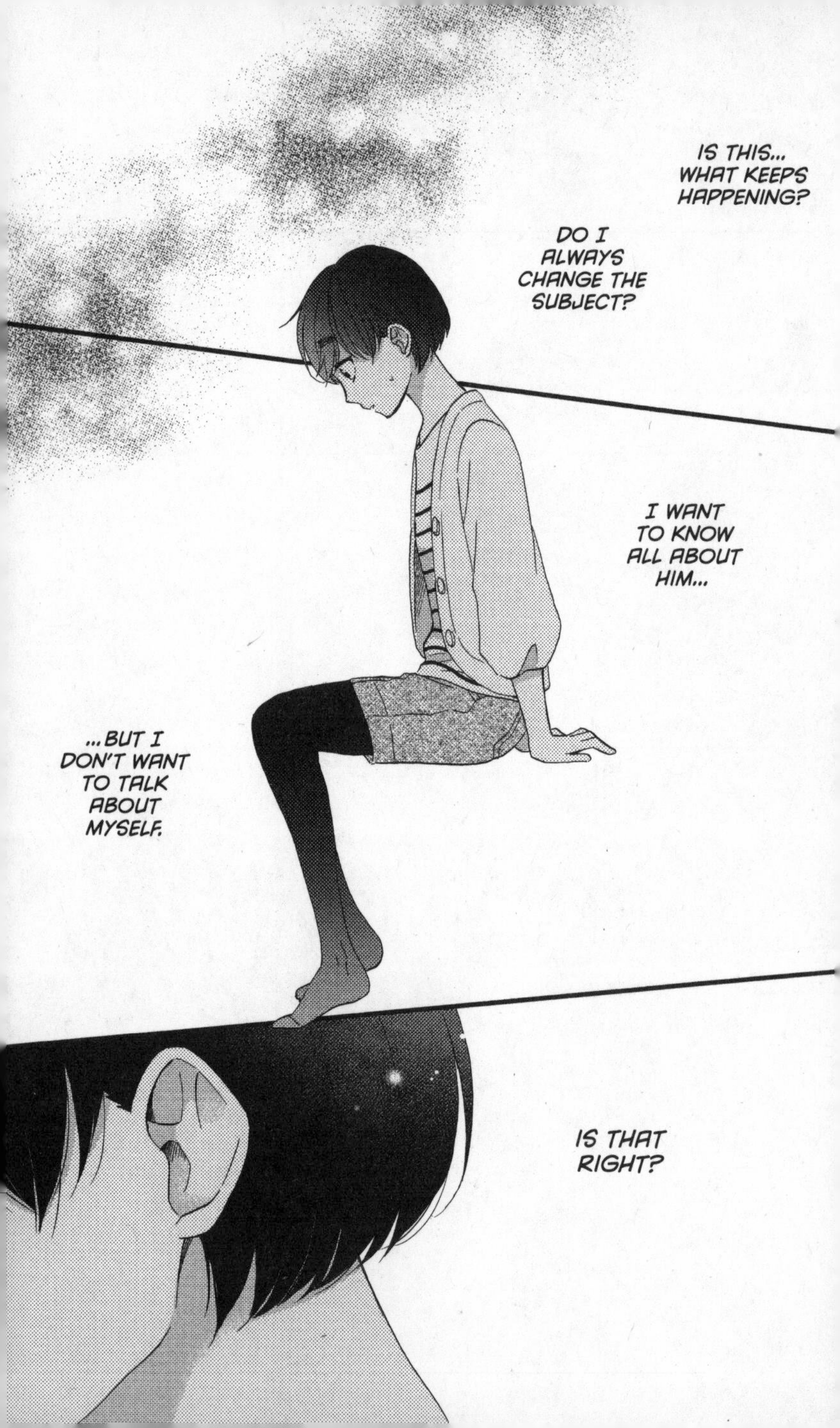
IS THIS... WHAT KEEPS HAPPENING?
DO I ALWAYS CHANGE THE SUBJECT?
I WANT TO KNOW ALL ABOUT HIM...
...BUT I DON'T WANT TO TALK ABOUT MYSELF.
IS THAT RIGHT?

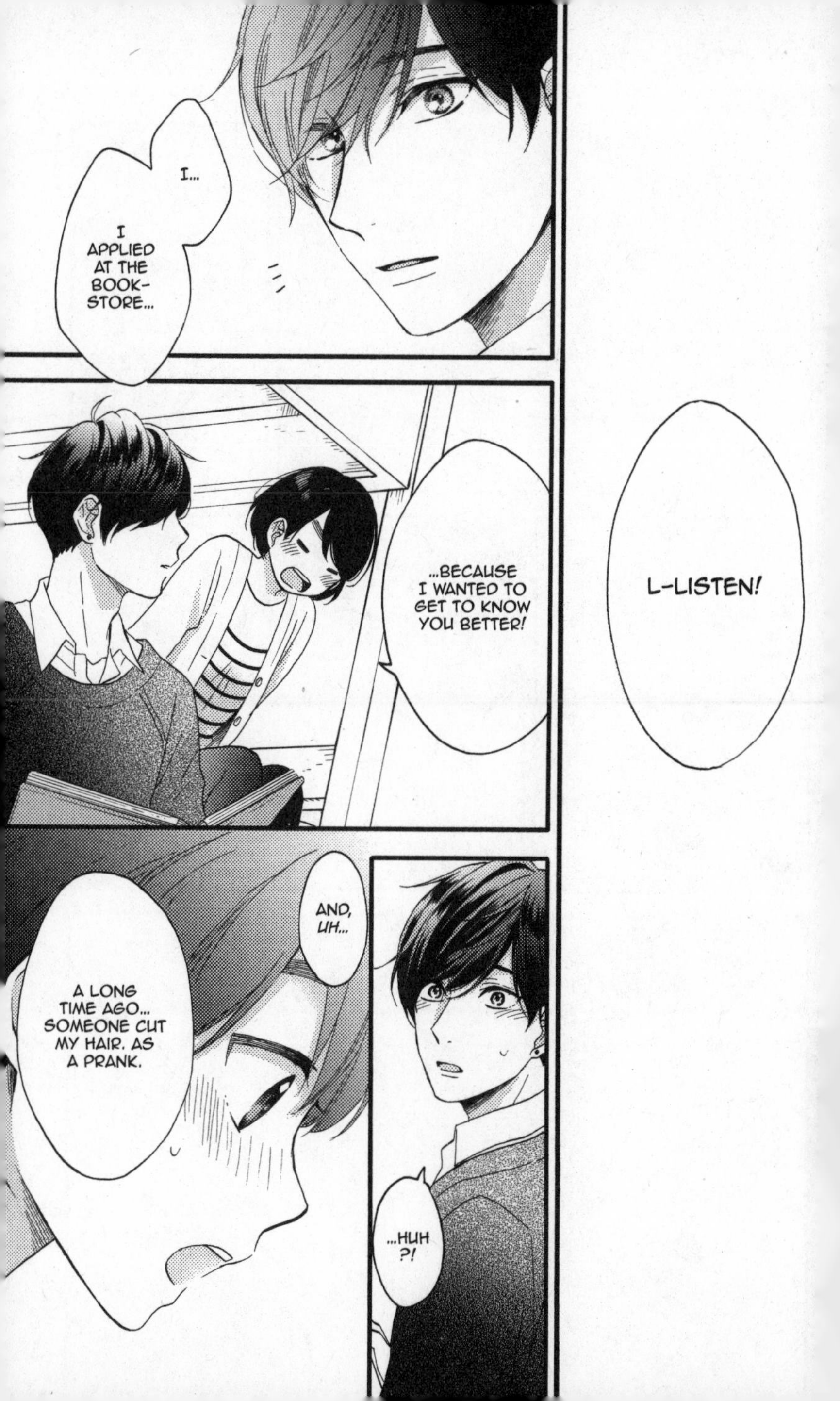
L-LISTEN!
I...
I APPLIED AT THE BOOK-STORE...
...BECAUSE I WANTED TO GET TO KNOW YOU BETTER!
AND, UH...
A LONG TIME AGO... SOMEONE CUT MY HAIR. AS A PRANK.
...HUH ?!

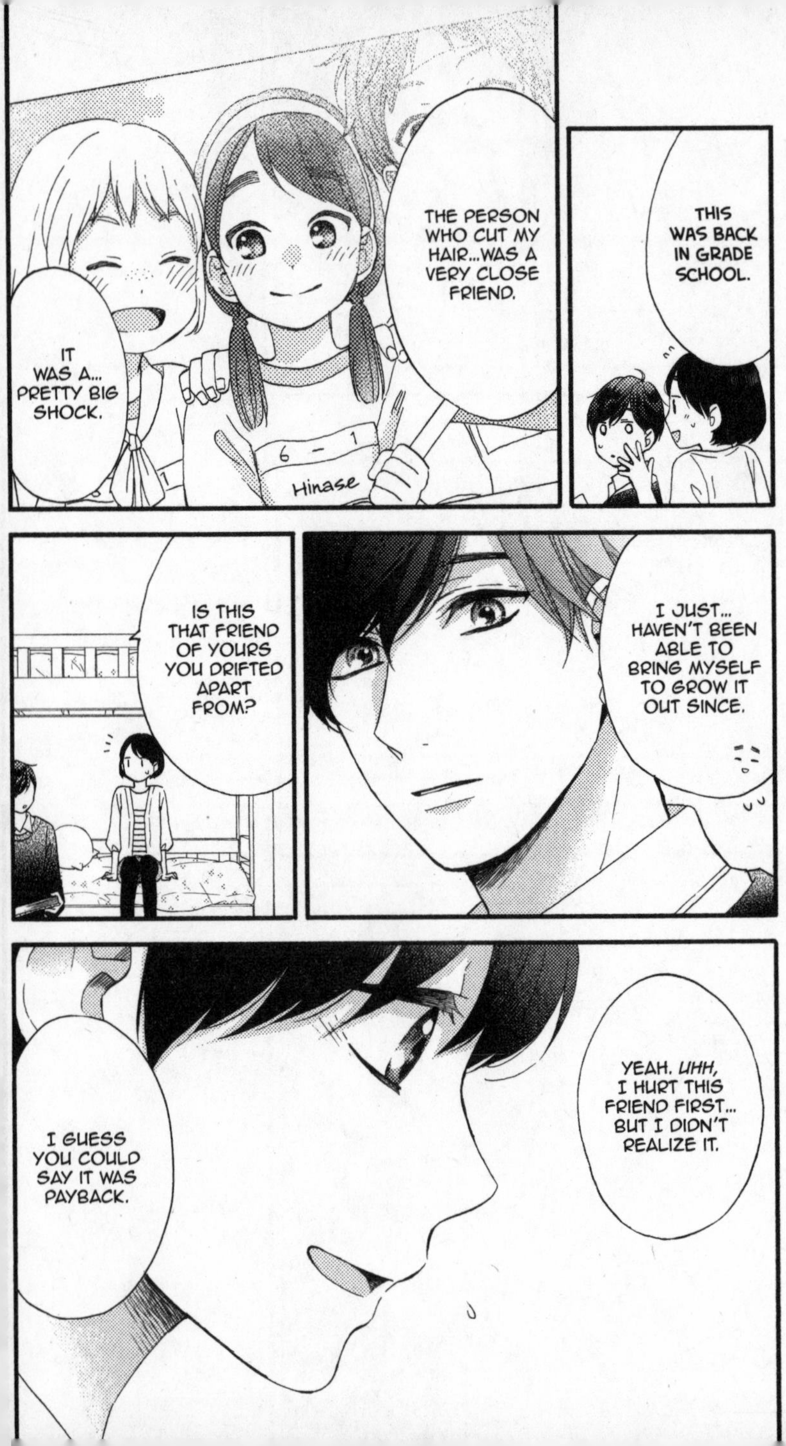
THIS WAS BACK IN GRADE SCHOOL.
THE PERSON WHO CUT MY HAIR...WAS A VERY CLOSE FRIEND.
6 - 1
Hinase
IT WAS A... PRETTY BIG SHOCK.
I JUST... HAVEN'T BEEN ABLE TO BRING MYSELF TO GROW IT OUT SINCE.
IS THIS THAT FRIEND OF YOURS YOU DRIFTED APART FROM?
YEAH. *UHH*, I HURT THIS FRIEND FIRST... BUT I DIDN'T REALIZE IT.
I GUESS YOU COULD SAY IT WAS PAYBACK.

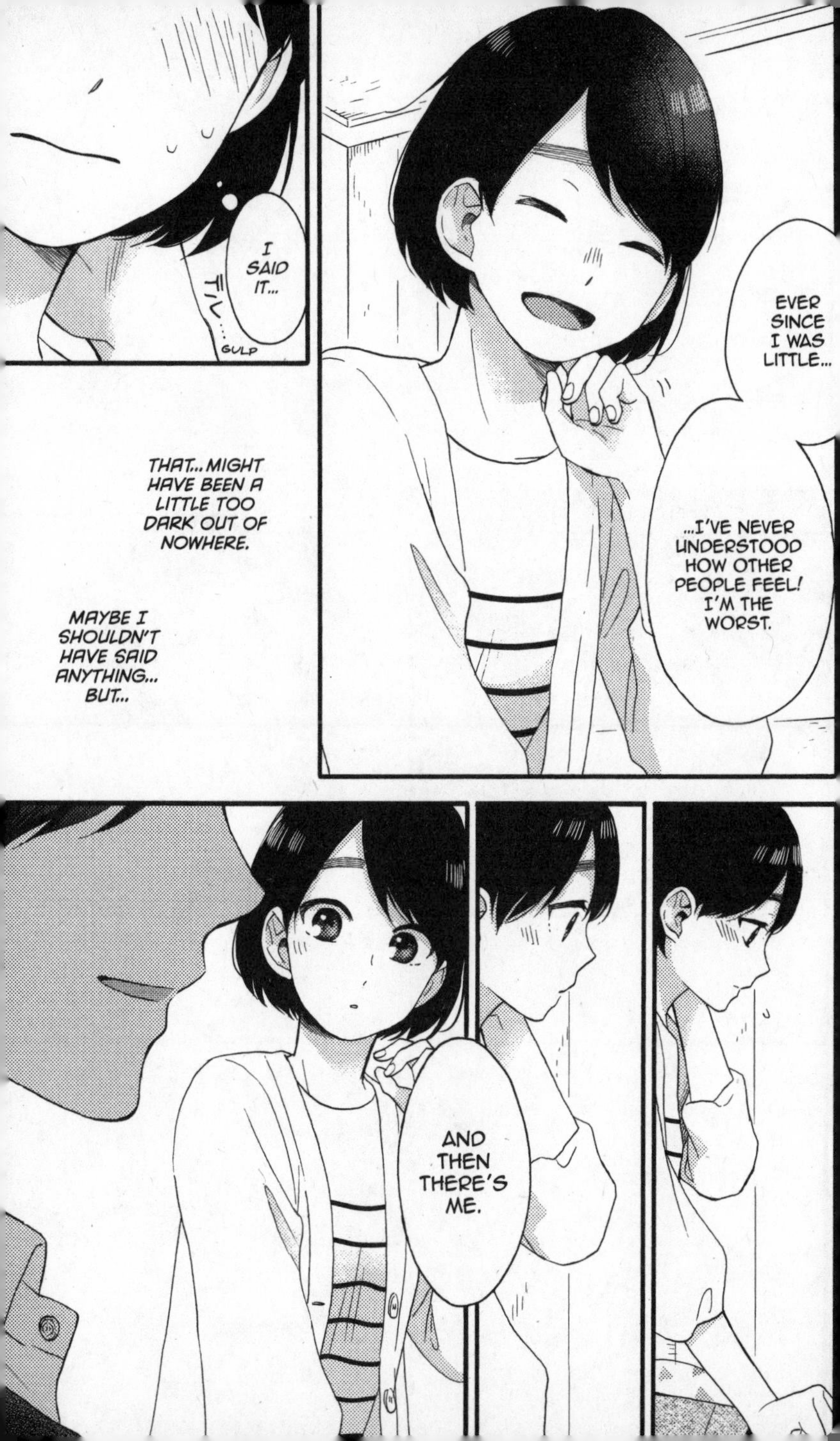
EVER SINCE I WAS LITTLE...
...I'VE NEVER UNDERSTOOD HOW OTHER PEOPLE FEEL! I'M THE WORST.
I SAID IT...
GULP
THAT... MIGHT HAVE BEEN A LITTLE TOO DARK OUT OF NOWHERE.
MAYBE I SHOULDN'T HAVE SAID ANYTHING... BUT...
AND THEN THERE'S ME.

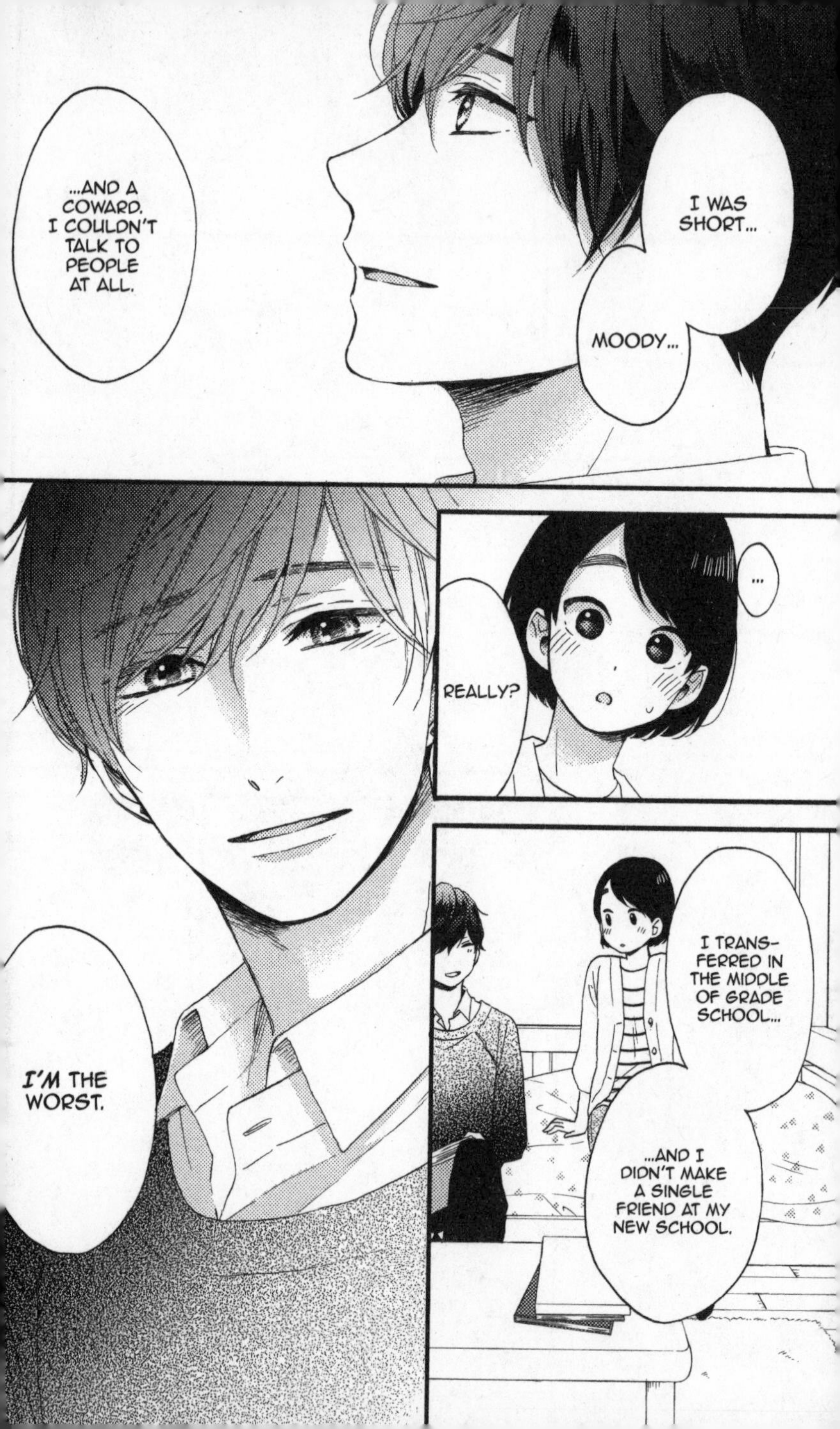
I WAS SHORT...
MOODY...
...AND A COWARD. I COULDN'T TALK TO PEOPLE AT ALL.
...
REALLY?
I TRANSFERRED IN THE MIDDLE OF GRADE SCHOOL...
...AND I DIDN'T MAKE A SINGLE FRIEND AT MY NEW SCHOOL.
I'M THE WORST.

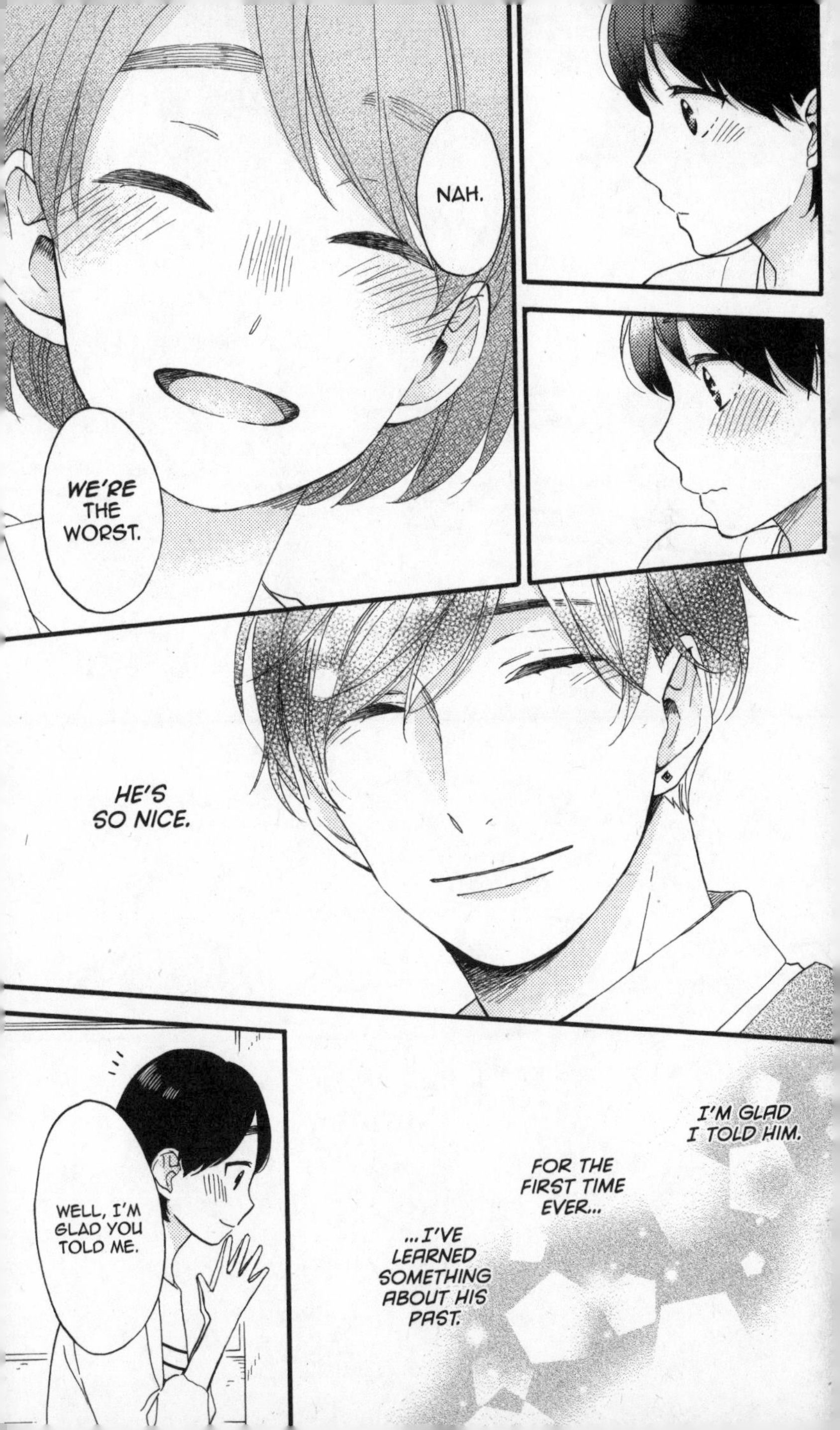
NAH.
WE'RE THE WORST.
HE'S SO NICE.
I'M GLAD I TOLD HIM.
FOR THE FIRST TIME EVER...
...I'VE LEARNED SOMETHING ABOUT HIS PAST.
WELL, I'M GLAD YOU TOLD ME.

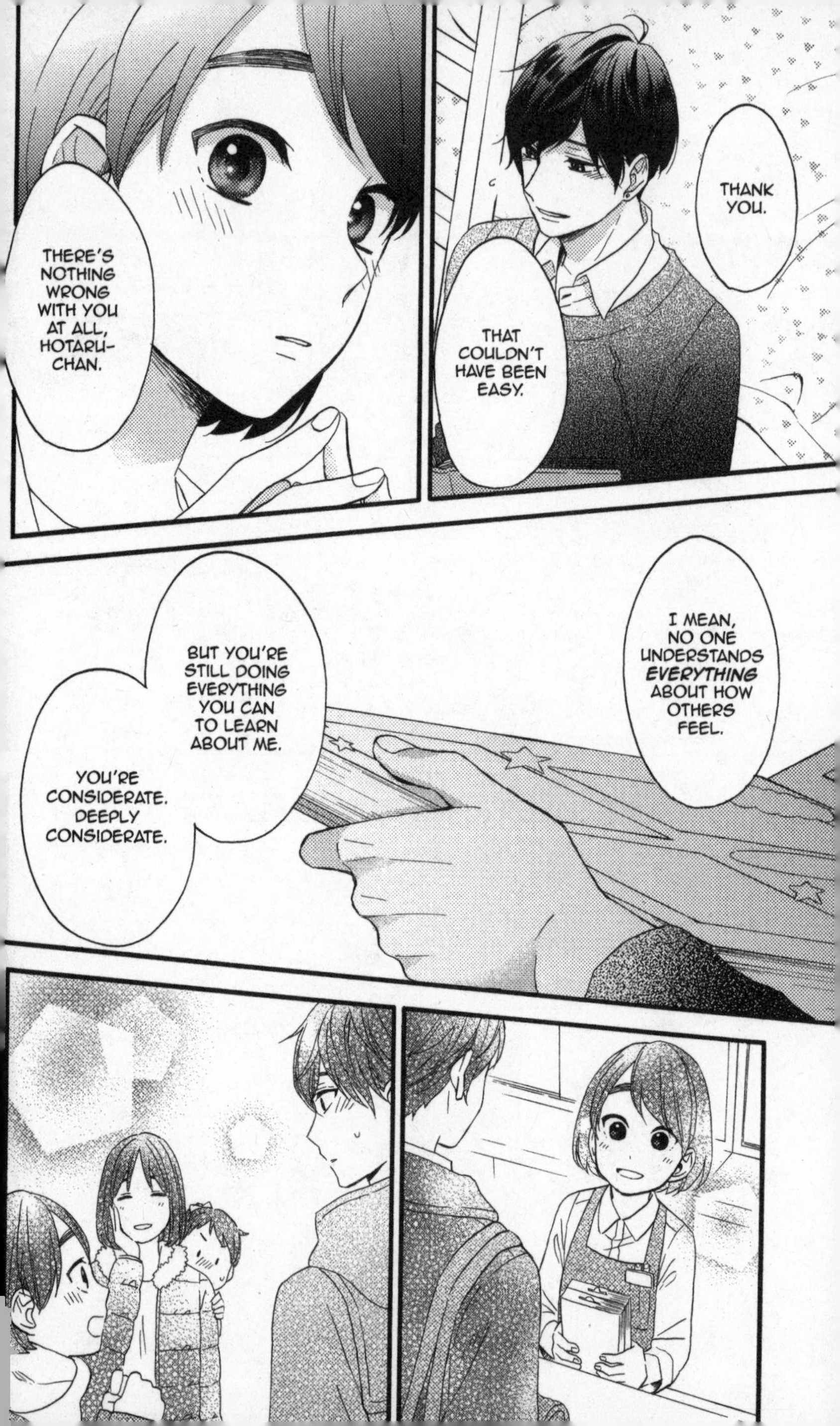
THANK YOU.
THAT COULDN'T HAVE BEEN EASY.
THERE'S NOTHING WRONG WITH YOU AT ALL, HOTARU-CHAN.
I MEAN, NO ONE UNDERSTANDS *EVERYTHING* ABOUT HOW OTHERS FEEL.
BUT YOU'RE STILL DOING EVERYTHING YOU CAN TO LEARN ABOUT ME.
YOU'RE CONSIDERATE. DEEPLY CONSIDERATE.

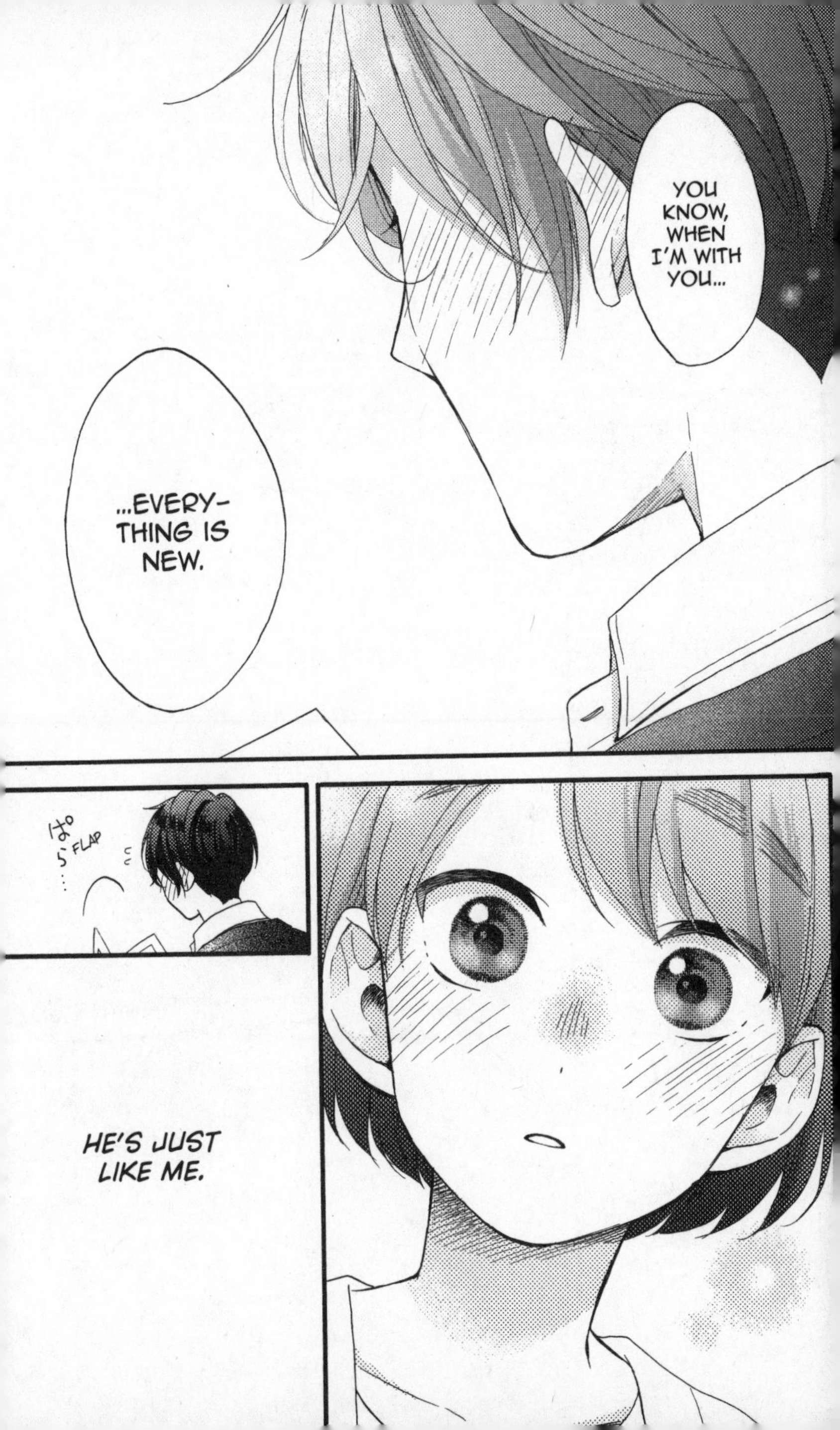
YOU KNOW, WHEN I'M WITH YOU...
...EVERY-THING IS NEW.
ぱら
FLAP
HE'S JUST LIKE ME.

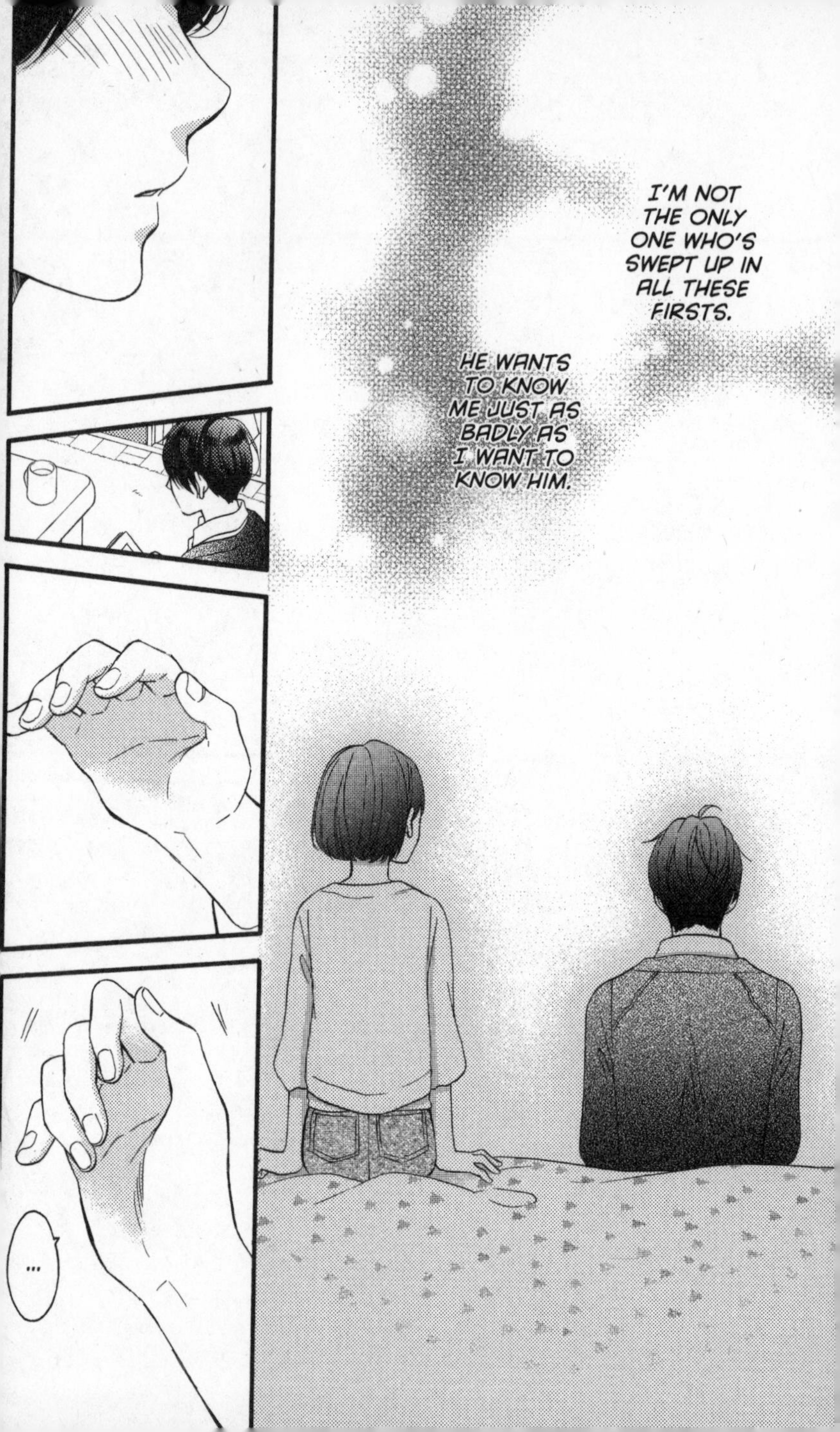
I'M NOT THE ONLY ONE WHO'S SWEPT UP IN ALL THESE FIRSTS.
HE WANTS TO KNOW ME JUST AS BADLY AS I WANT TO KNOW HIM.
...

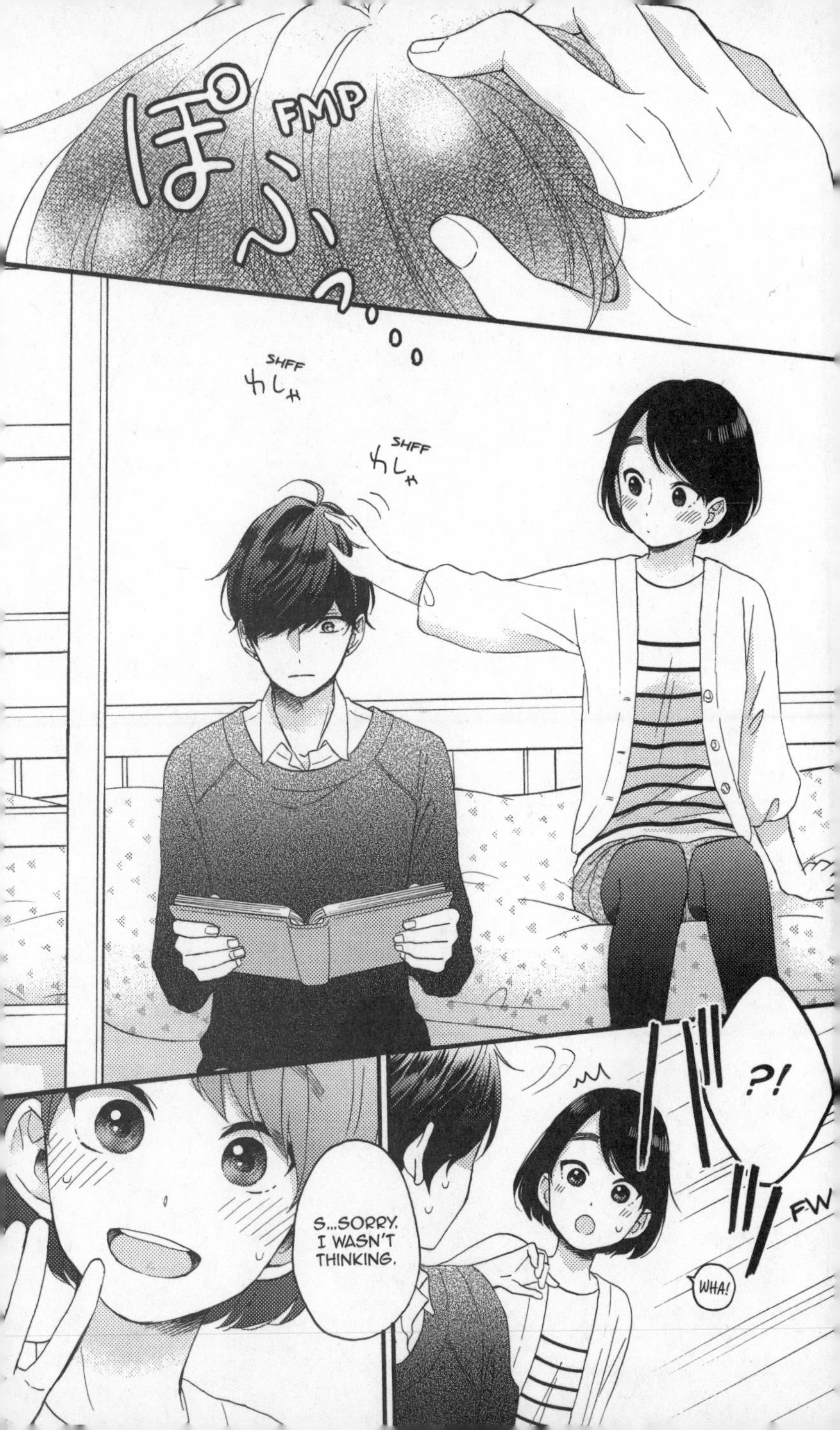
ぽふっ。。。
FMP
わしゃ
SHFF
わしゃ
SHFF
?!
FW
WHA!
S...SORRY. I WASN'T THINKING.

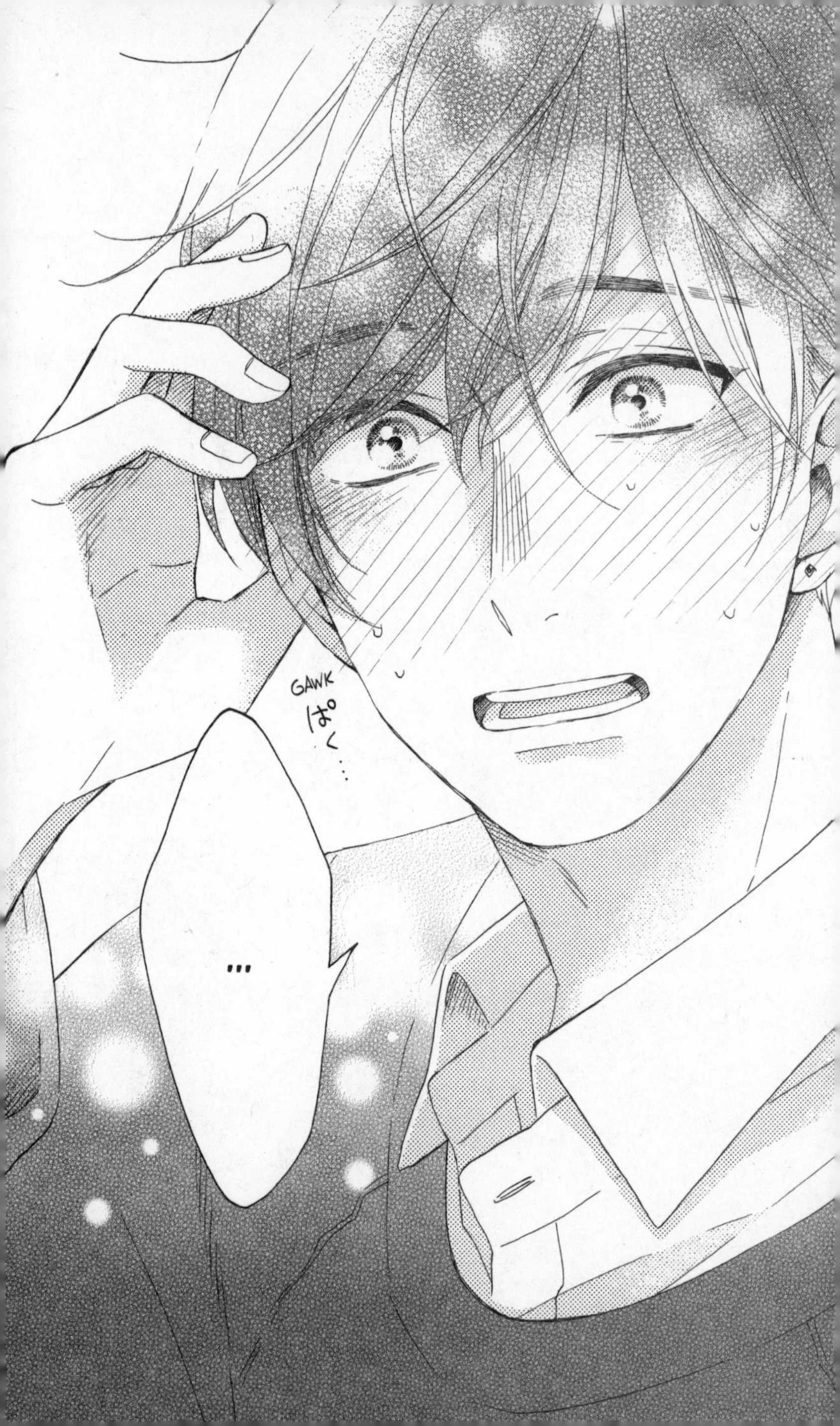
GAWK
ぱく…
...

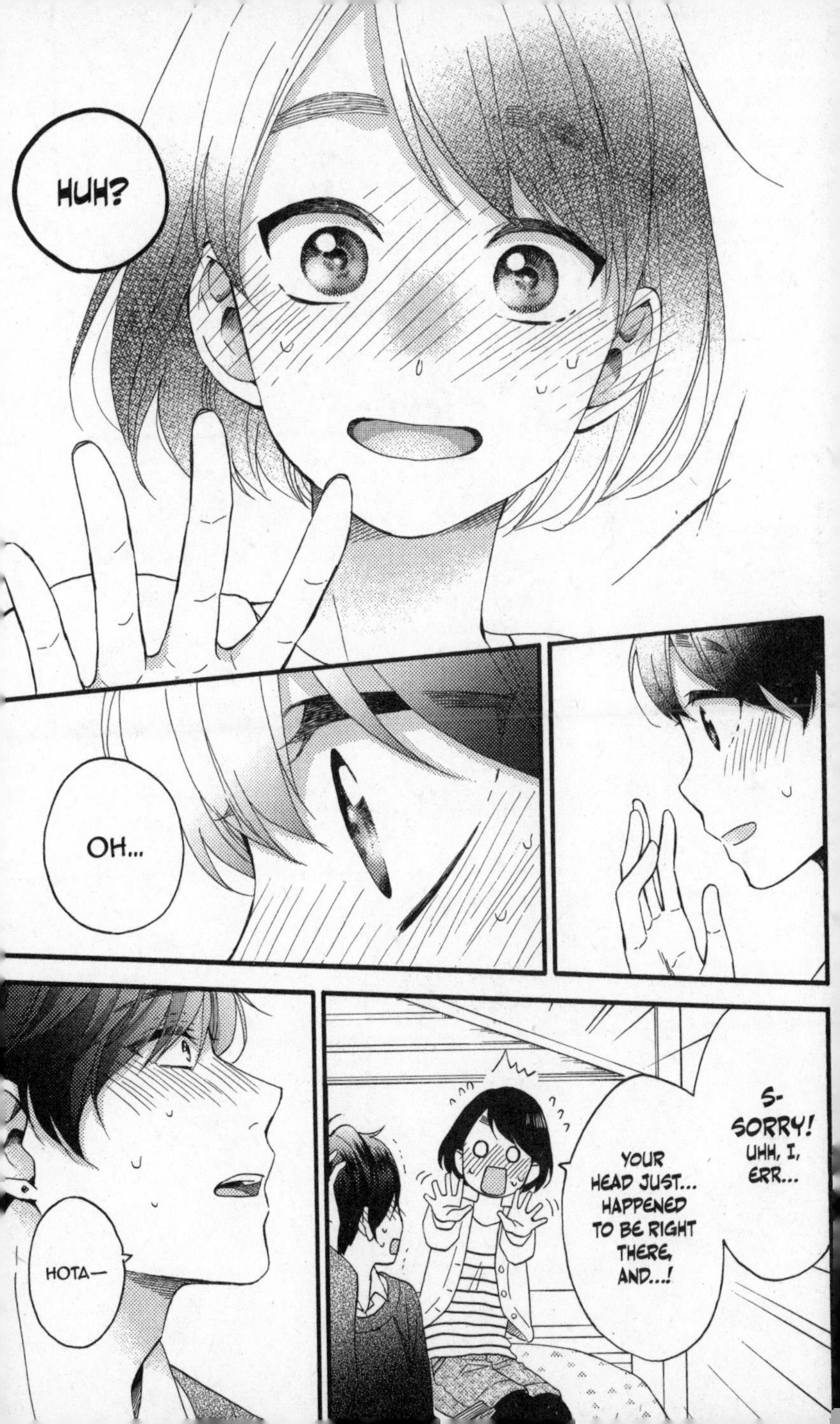
HUH?
OH...
S-SORRY! UHH, I, ERR...
YOUR HEAD JUST... HAPPENED TO BE RIGHT THERE, AND...!
HOTA—

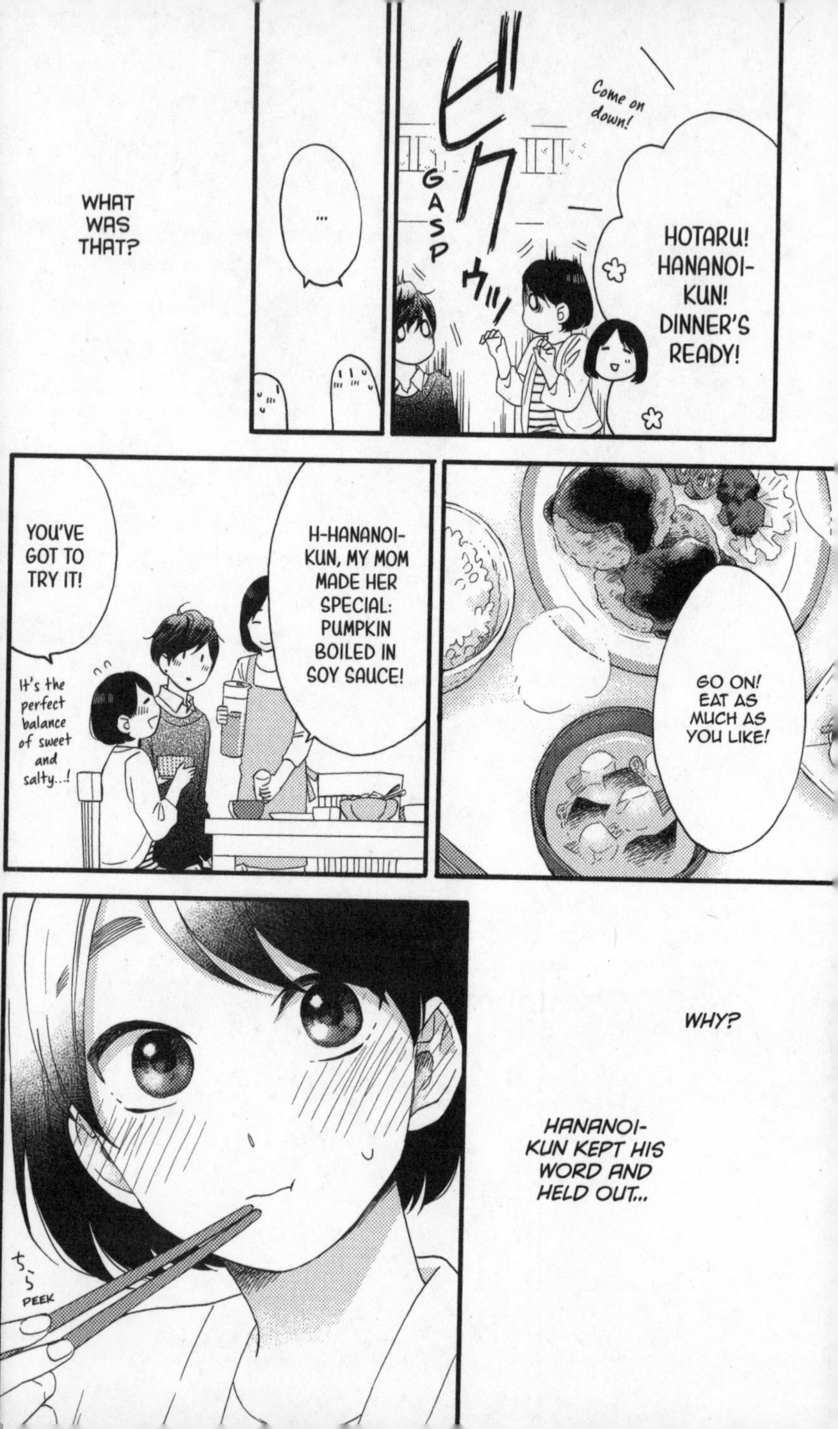
Come on down!
HOTARU! HANANOI-KUN! DINNER'S READY!
GASP
...
WHAT WAS THAT?
GO ON! EAT AS MUCH AS YOU LIKE!
H-HANANOI-KUN, MY MOM MADE HER SPECIAL: PUMPKIN BOILED IN SOY SAUCE!
YOU'VE GOT TO TRY IT!
It's the perfect balance of sweet and salty...!
WHY?
HANANOI-KUN KEPT HIS WORD AND HELD OUT...
PEEK

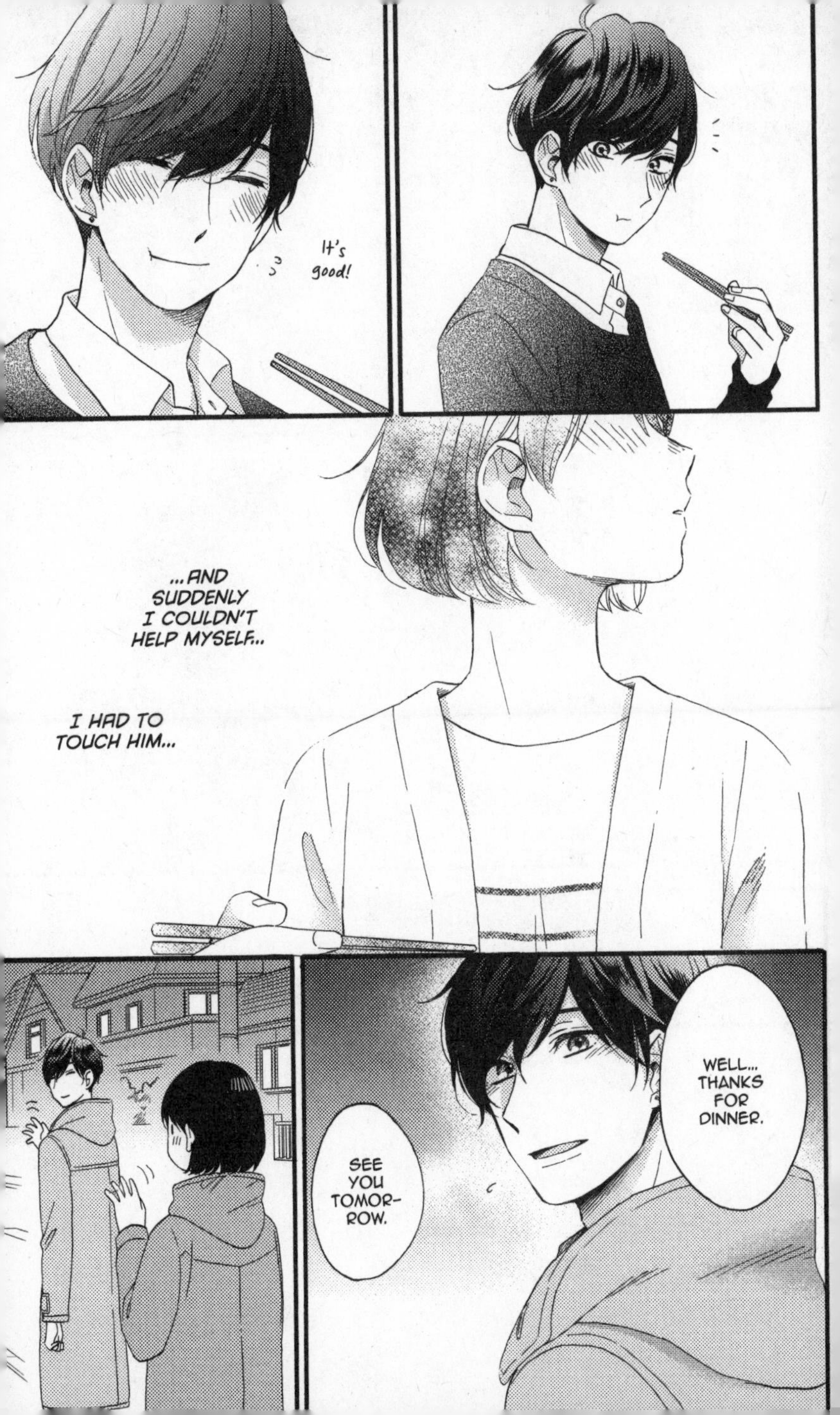
It's good!
...AND SUDDENLY I COULDN'T HELP MYSELF...
I HAD TO TOUCH HIM...
WELL... THANKS FOR DINNER.
SEE YOU TOMOR-ROW.

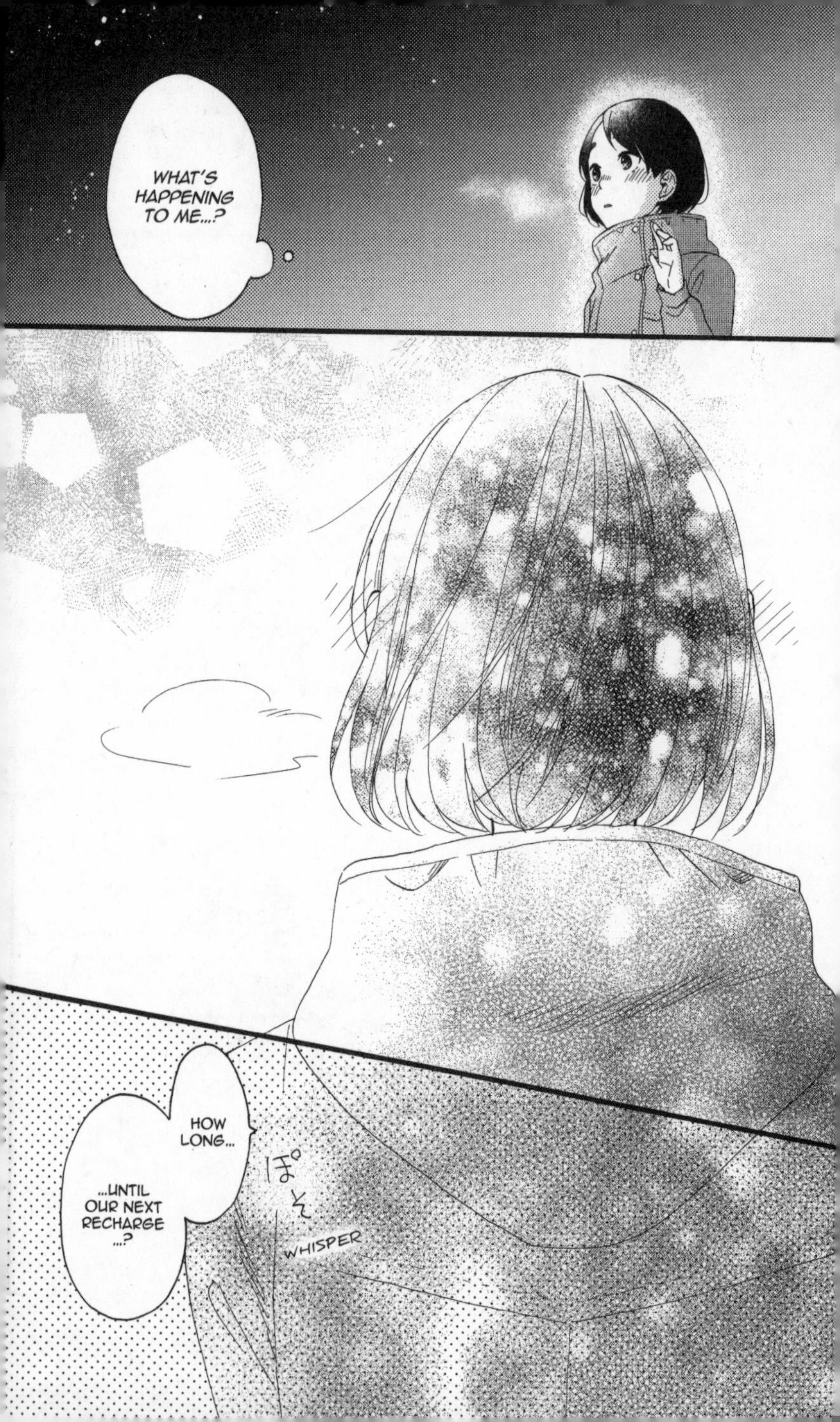
WHAT'S HAPPENING TO ME...?
HOW LONG...
...UNTIL OUR NEXT RECHARGE ...?
ぽそ
WHISPER

Deadly Eyes

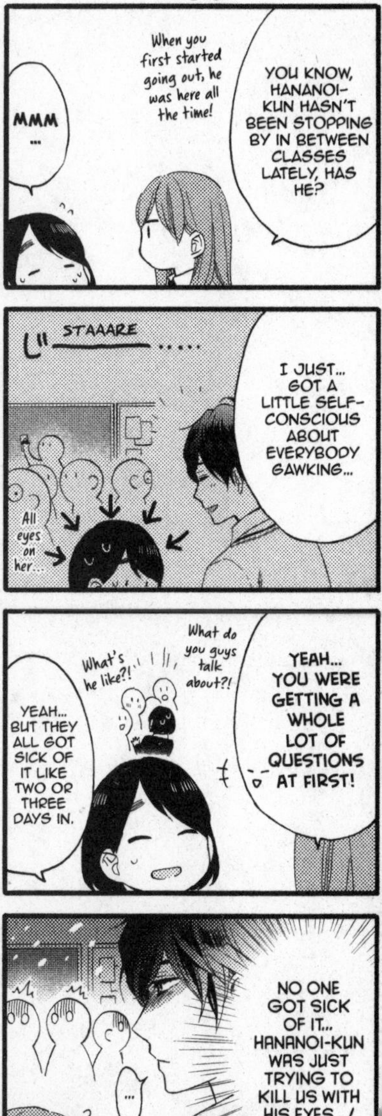
YOU KNOW, HANANOI-KUN HASN'T BEEN STOPPING BY IN BETWEEN CLASSES LATELY, HAS HE?
When you first started going out, he was here all the time!
MMM...
I JUST... GOT A LITTLE SELF-CONSCIOUS ABOUT EVERYBODY GAWKING...
じー STAAARE.....
All eyes on her...
YEAH... YOU WERE GETTING A WHOLE LOT OF QUESTIONS AT FIRST!
What do you guys talk about?!
What's he like?!
YEAH... BUT THEY ALL GOT SICK OF IT LIKE TWO OR THREE DAYS IN.
NO ONE GOT SICK OF IT... HANANOI-KUN WAS JUST TRYING TO KILL US WITH HIS EYES...!
...

What a Difference 11 Inches Makes (1)

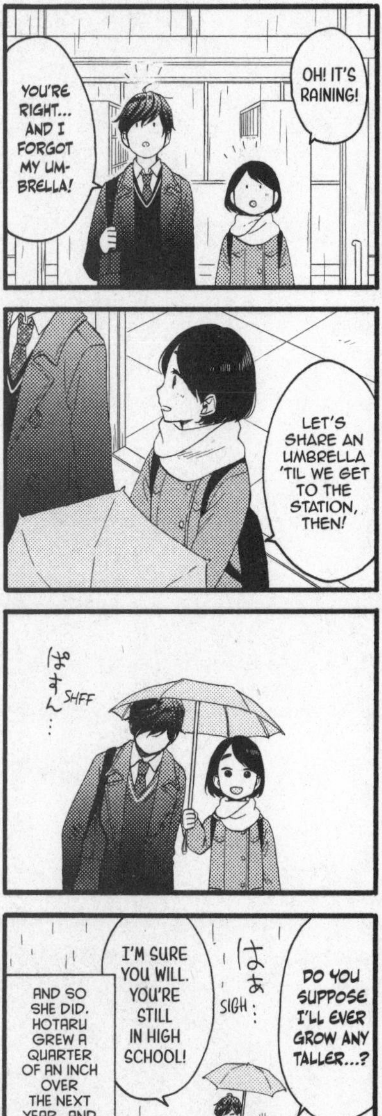
OH! IT'S RAINING!
YOU'RE RIGHT... AND I FORGOT MY UMBRELLA!
LET'S SHARE AN UMBRELLA 'TIL WE GET TO THE STATION, THEN!
ぽすん…
SHFF
DO YOU SUPPOSE I'LL EVER GROW ANY TALLER...?
はぁ…
SIGH
I'M SURE YOU WILL. YOU'RE STILL IN HIGH SCHOOL!
AND SO SHE DID. HOTARU GREW A QUARTER OF AN INCH OVER THE NEXT YEAR...AND HANANOI-KUN GREW OVER HALF AN INCH.

What a Difference 11 Inches Makes (2)

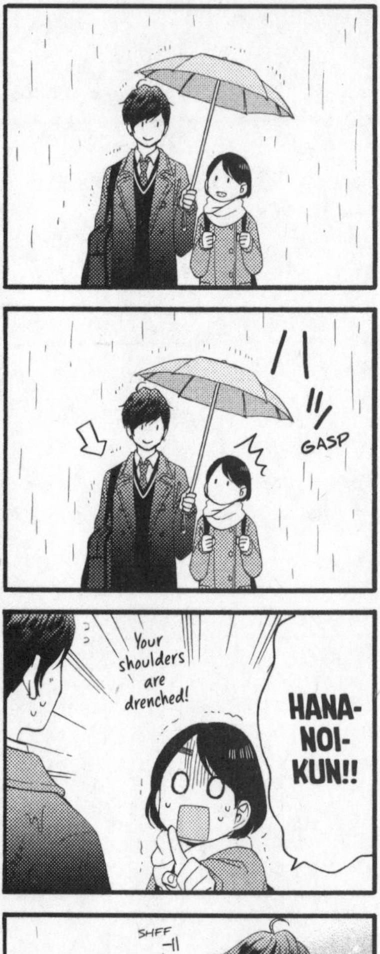
GASP
HANA-NOI-KUN!!
Your shoulders are drenched!
SHFF
SHFF
Jeez...
...
I'D BETTER START WORKING ON THAT GROWTH SPURT...!

What a Difference 11 Inches Makes (3)

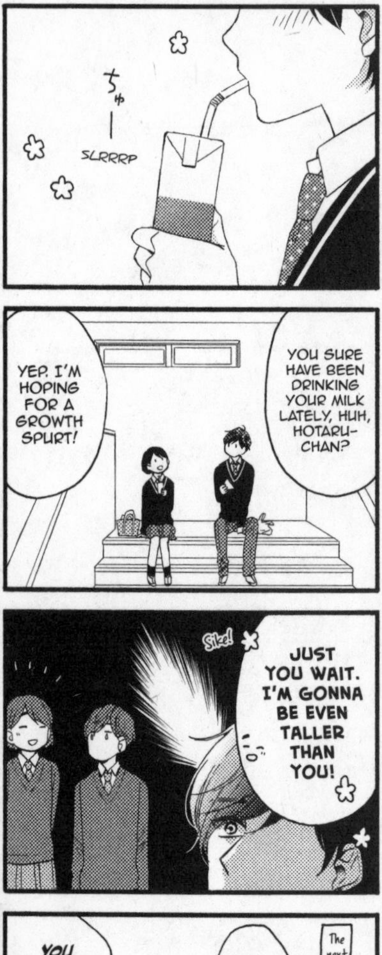
ちゅ
SLRRRP
YOU SURE HAVE BEEN DRINKING YOUR MILK LATELY, HUH, HOTARU-CHAN?
YEP. I'M HOPING FOR A GROWTH SPURT!
Sike!
JUST YOU WAIT. I'M GONNA BE EVEN TALLER THAN YOU!
The next day
HEY!
SLRRRP
ち
MILK
YOU CAN'T DRINK MILK TOO, HANANOI-KUN! THAT DEFEATS THE POINT!
MILK

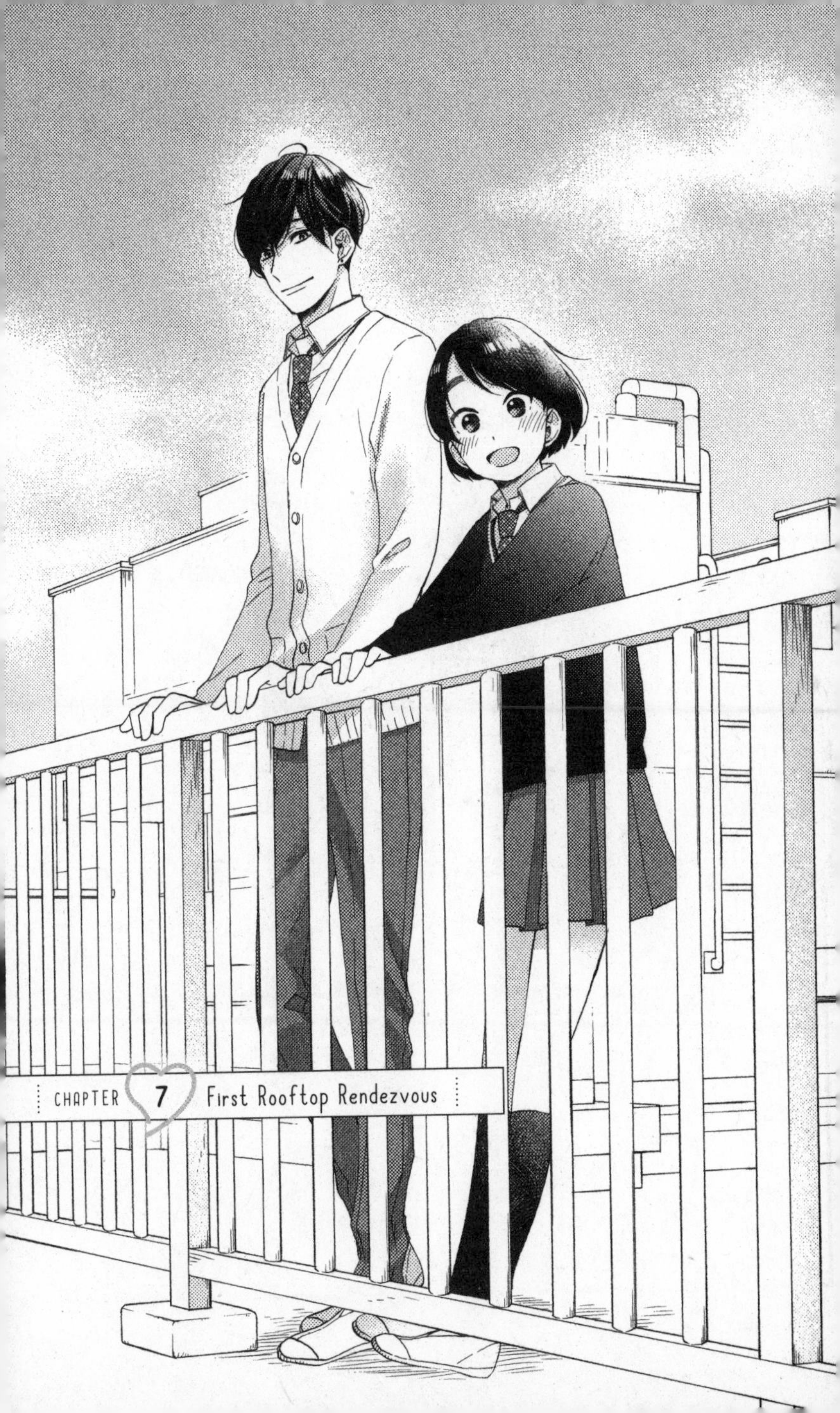
CHAPTER 7 First Rooftop Rendezvous

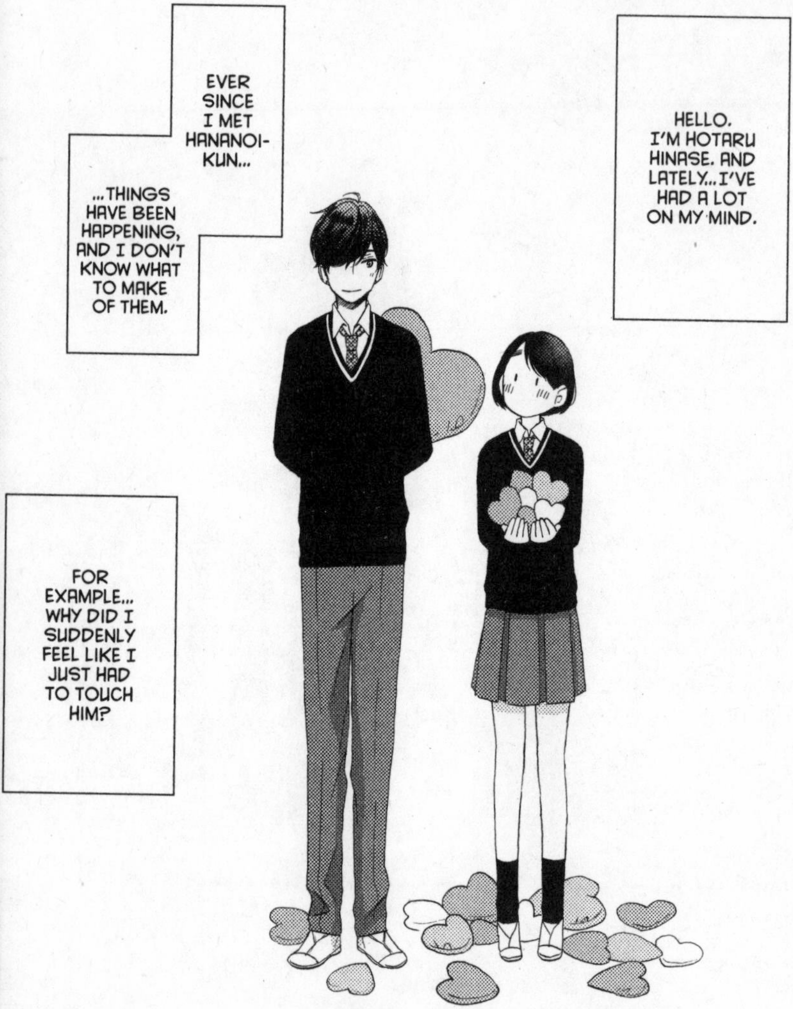
HELLO. I'M HOTARU HINASE. AND LATELY...I'VE HAD A LOT ON MY MIND.
EVER SINCE I MET HANANOI-KUN...
...THINGS HAVE BEEN HAPPENING, AND I DON'T KNOW WHAT TO MAKE OF THEM.
FOR EXAMPLE... WHY DID I SUDDENLY FEEL LIKE I JUST HAD TO TOUCH HIM?

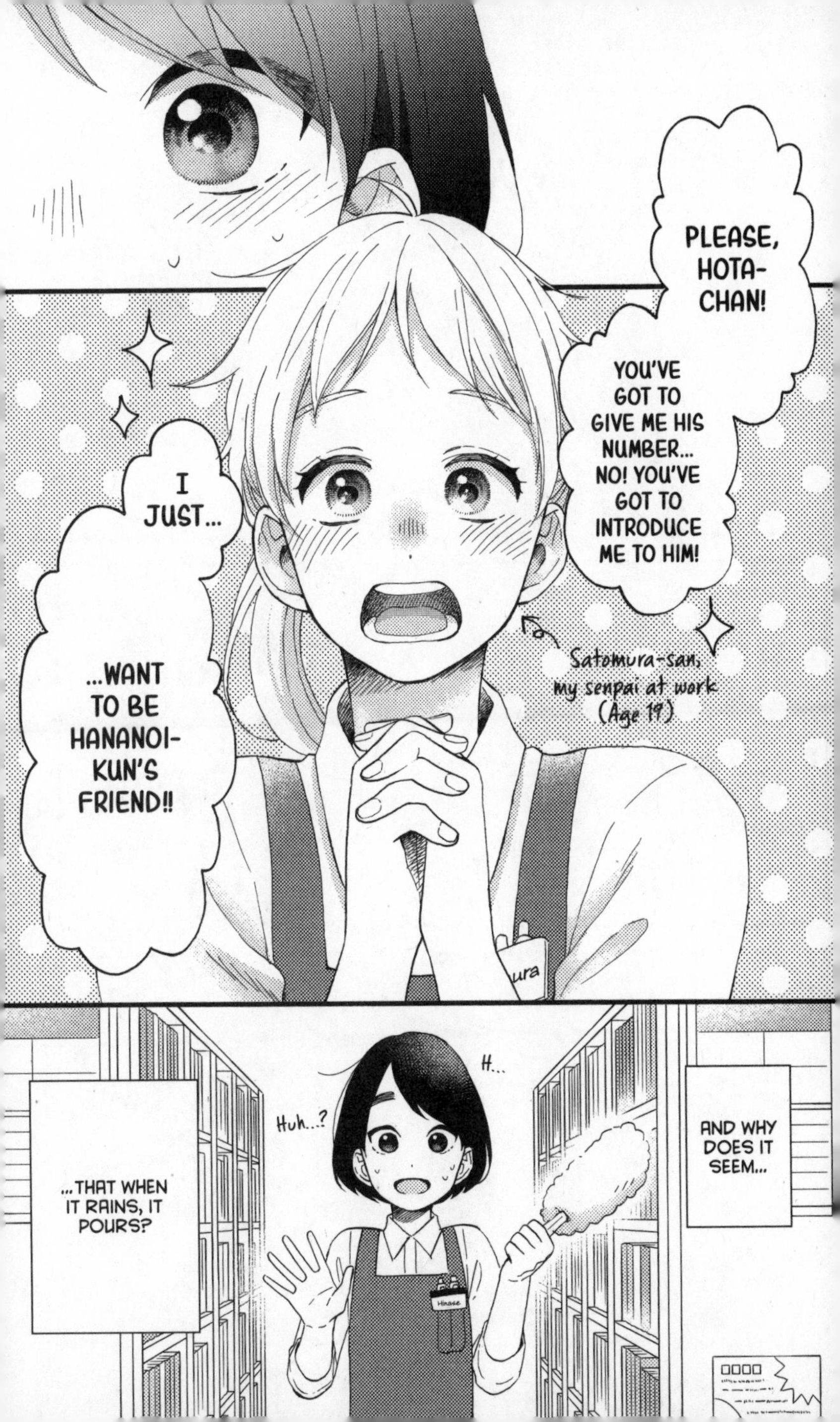
PLEASE, HOTA-CHAN!
YOU'VE GOT TO GIVE ME HIS NUMBER... NO! YOU'VE GOT TO INTRODUCE ME TO HIM!
Satomura-san, my senpai at work (Age 19)
I JUST...
...WANT TO BE HANANOI-KUN'S FRIEND!!
AND WHY DOES IT SEEM...
H...
Huh...?
...THAT WHEN IT RAINS, IT POURS?

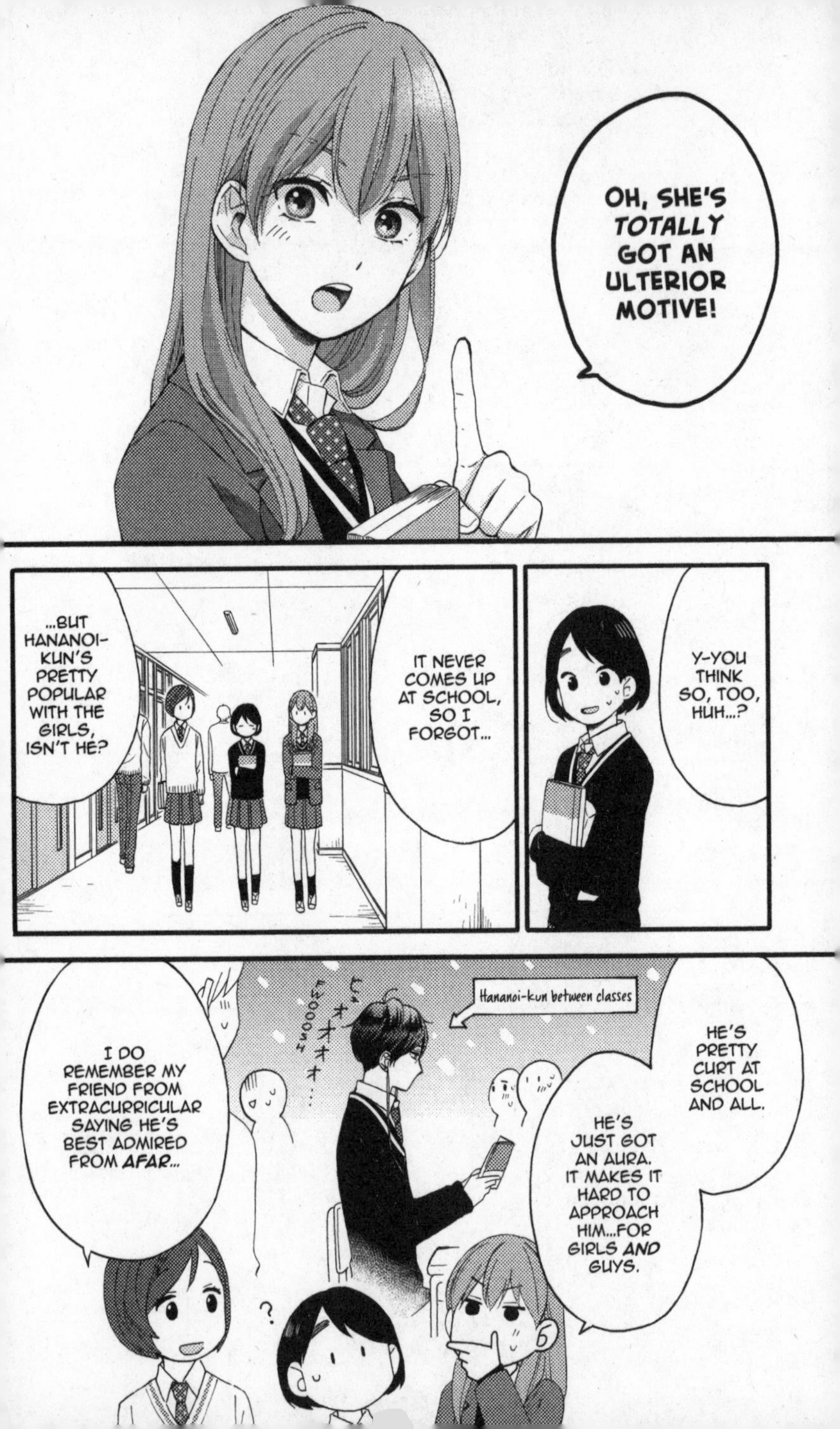
OH, SHE'S *TOTALLY* GOT AN ULTERIOR MOTIVE!
Y-YOU THINK SO, TOO, HUH...?
IT NEVER COMES UP AT SCHOOL, SO I FORGOT...
...BUT HANANOI-KUN'S PRETTY POPULAR WITH THE GIRLS, ISN'T HE?
HE'S PRETTY CURT AT SCHOOL AND ALL.
HE'S JUST GOT AN AURA. IT MAKES IT HARD TO APPROACH HIM...FOR GIRLS **AND** GUYS.
Hananoi-kun between classes
ジャオオオオ…
FWOOOSH
I DO REMEMBER MY FRIEND FROM EXTRACURRICULAR SAYING HE'S BEST ADMIRED FROM **AFAR**...

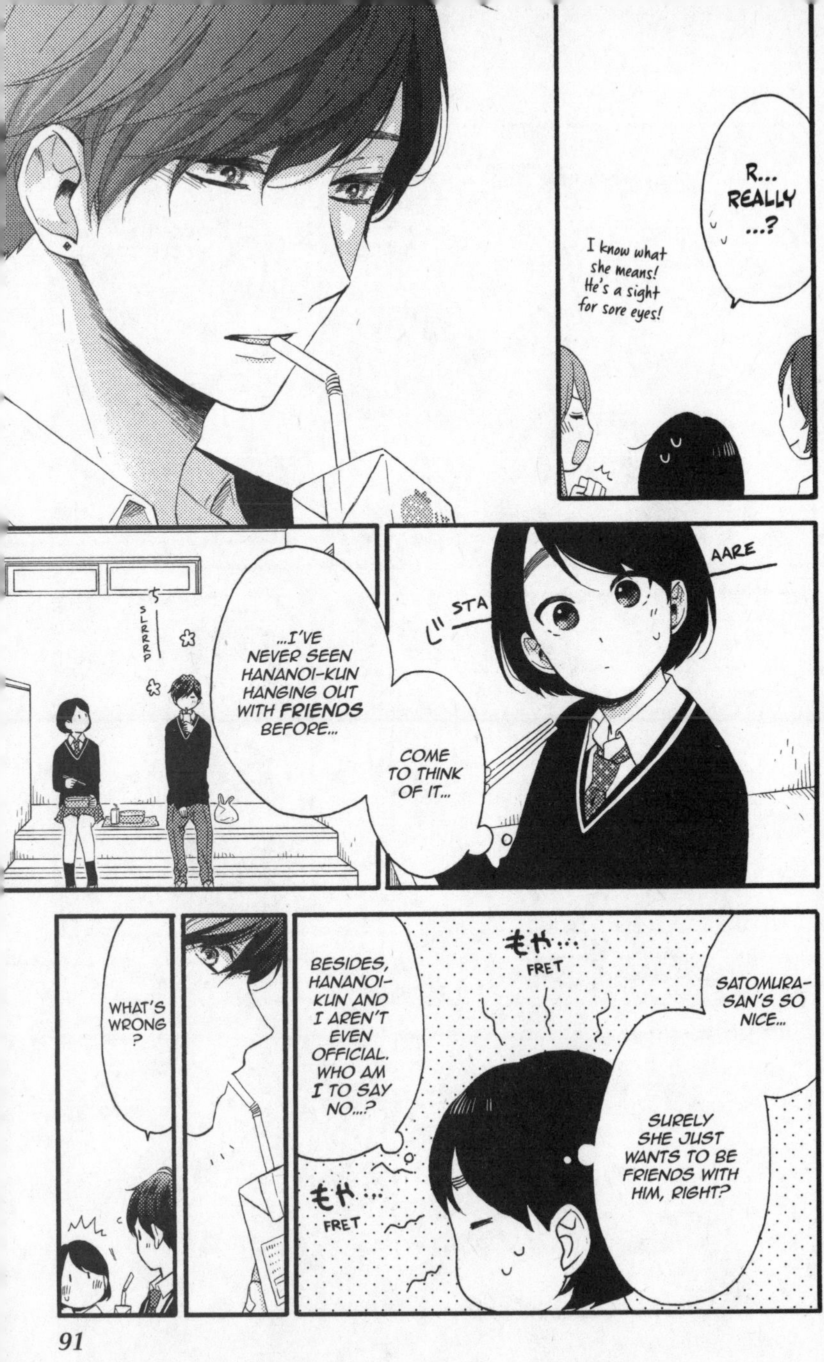
R... REALLY ...?
I know what she means! He's a sight for sore eyes!
AARE
じ STA
COME TO THINK OF IT...
...I'VE NEVER SEEN HANANOI-KUN HANGING OUT WITH FRIENDS BEFORE...
ち SLRRRP
SATOMURA-SAN'S SO NICE...
もや... FRET
SURELY SHE JUST WANTS TO BE FRIENDS WITH HIM, RIGHT?
BESIDES, HANANOI-KUN AND I AREN'T EVEN OFFICIAL. WHO AM I TO SAY NO...?
もや... FRET
WHAT'S WRONG ?

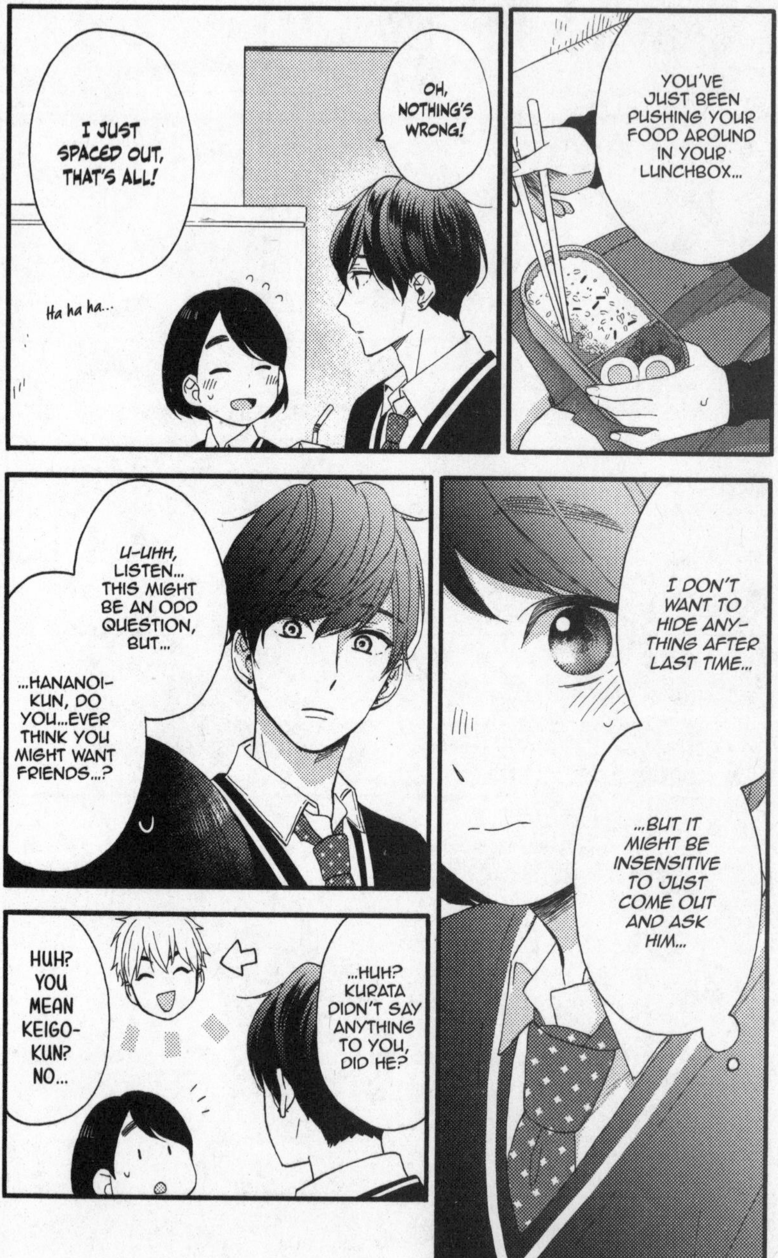
YOU'VE JUST BEEN PUSHING YOUR FOOD AROUND IN YOUR LUNCHBOX...
OH, NOTHING'S WRONG!
I JUST SPACED OUT, THAT'S ALL!
Ha ha ha...
I DON'T WANT TO HIDE ANY-THING AFTER LAST TIME...
...BUT IT MIGHT BE INSENSITIVE TO JUST COME OUT AND ASK HIM...
U-UHH, LISTEN... THIS MIGHT BE AN ODD QUESTION, BUT...
...HANANOI-KUN, DO YOU...EVER THINK YOU MIGHT WANT FRIENDS...?
...HUH? KURATA DIDN'T SAY ANYTHING TO YOU, DID HE?
HUH? YOU MEAN KEIGO-KUN? NO...

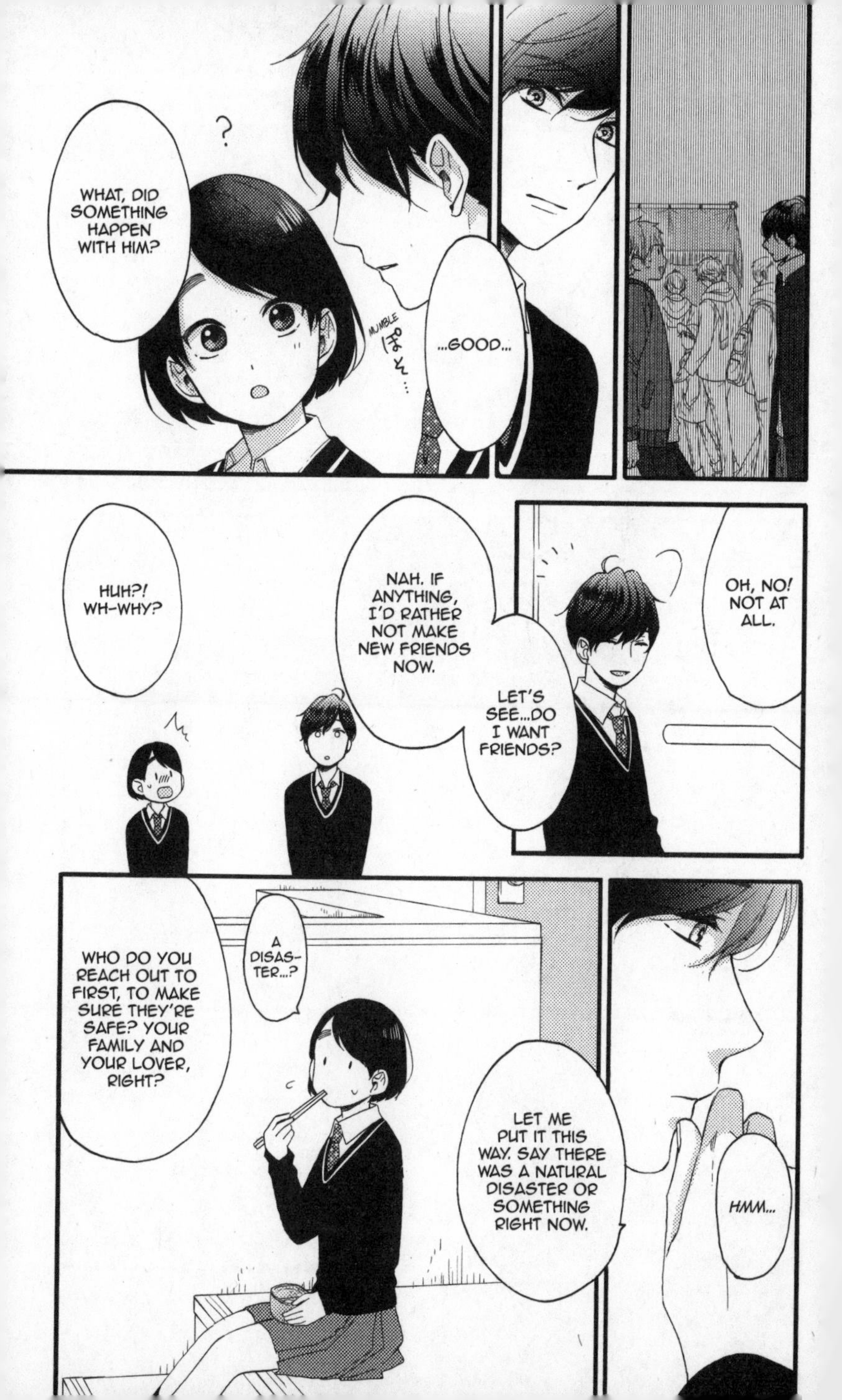
...GOOD...
MUMBLE
?
WHAT, DID SOMETHING HAPPEN WITH HIM?
OH, NO! NOT AT ALL.
LET'S SEE...DO I WANT FRIENDS?
NAH. IF ANYTHING, I'D RATHER NOT MAKE NEW FRIENDS NOW.
HUH?! WH-WHY?
HMM...
LET ME PUT IT THIS WAY. SAY THERE WAS A NATURAL DISASTER OR SOMETHING RIGHT NOW.
A DISAS-TER...?
WHO DO YOU REACH OUT TO FIRST, TO MAKE SURE THEY'RE SAFE? YOUR FAMILY AND YOUR LOVER, RIGHT?

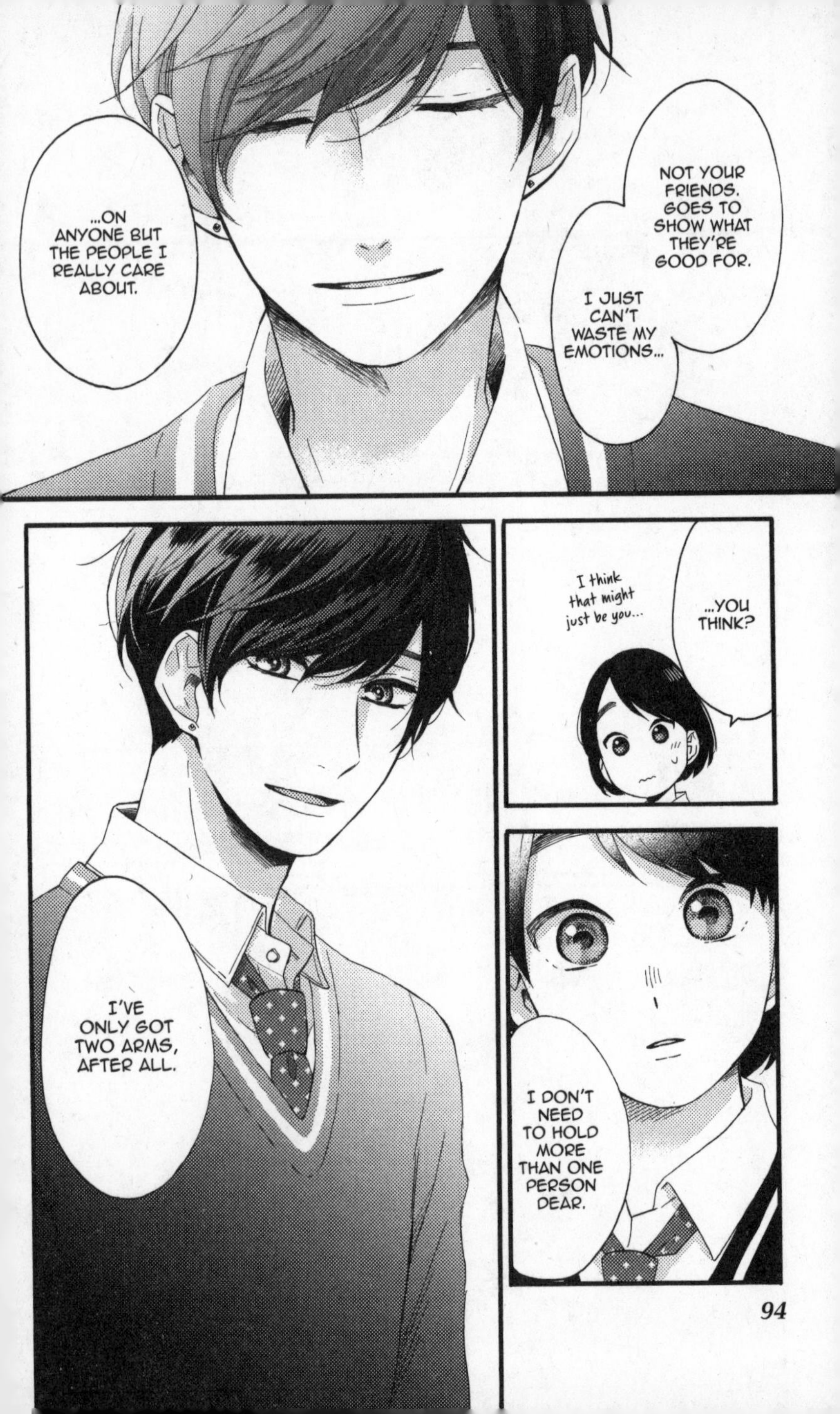
NOT YOUR FRIENDS. GOES TO SHOW WHAT THEY'RE GOOD FOR.
I JUST CAN'T WASTE MY EMOTIONS...
...ON ANYONE BUT THE PEOPLE I REALLY CARE ABOUT.
...YOU THINK?
I think that might just be you...
I DON'T NEED TO HOLD MORE THAN ONE PERSON DEAR.
I'VE ONLY GOT TWO ARMS, AFTER ALL.

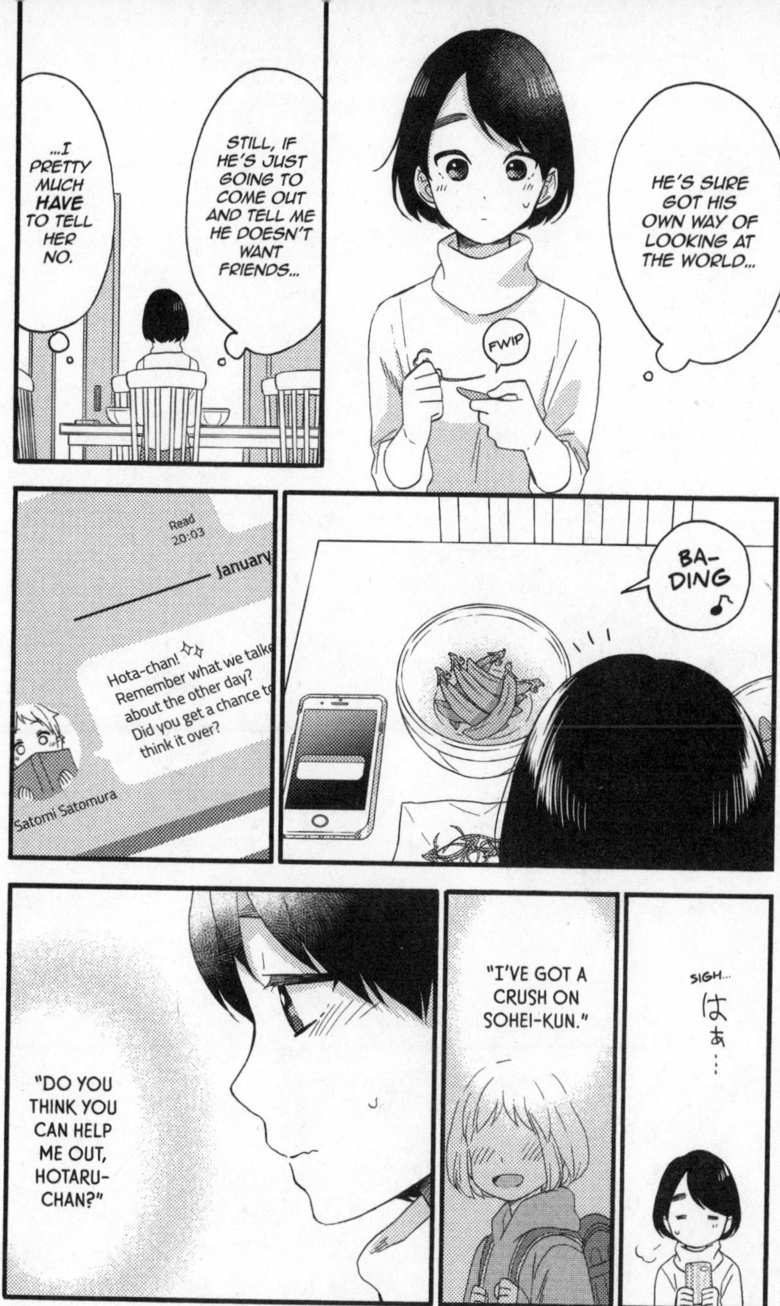
HE'S SURE GOT HIS OWN WAY OF LOOKING AT THE WORLD...
FWIP
STILL, IF HE'S JUST GOING TO COME OUT AND TELL ME HE DOESN'T WANT FRIENDS...
...I PRETTY MUCH **HAVE** TO TELL HER NO.
BA-DING ♪
Read 20:03
January
Hota-chan! ✧✧ Remember what we talke about the other day? Did you get a chance to think it over?
Satomi Satomura
SIGH...
はぁ…
"I'VE GOT A CRUSH ON SOHEI-KUN."
"DO YOU THINK YOU CAN HELP ME OUT, HOTARU-CHAN?"

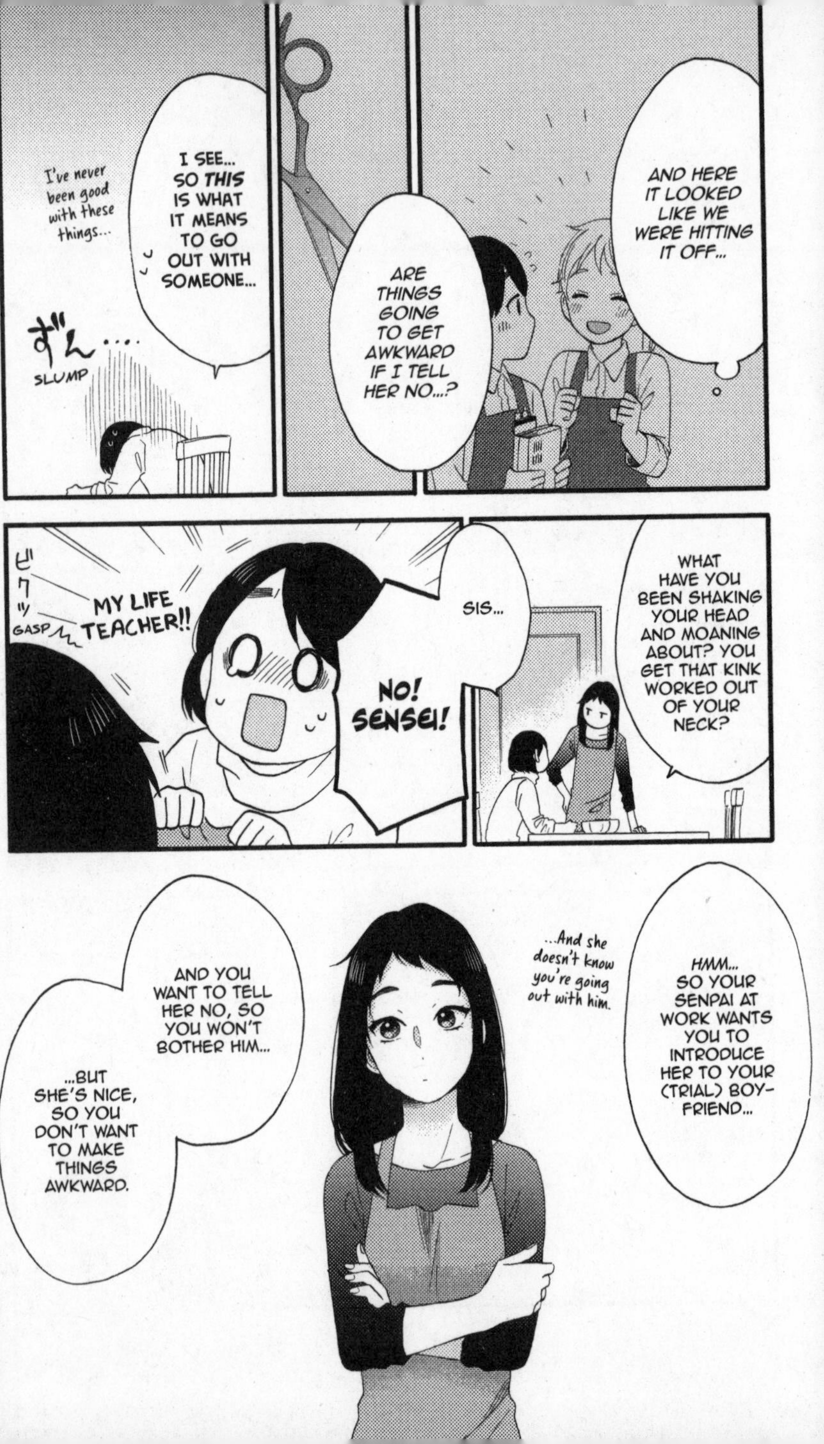
AND HERE IT LOOKED LIKE WE WERE HITTING IT OFF...
ARE THINGS GOING TO GET AWKWARD IF I TELL HER NO...?
I SEE... SO **THIS** IS WHAT IT MEANS TO GO OUT WITH SOMEONE...
I've never been good with these things...
ずん...
SLUMP
WHAT HAVE YOU BEEN SHAKING YOUR HEAD AND MOANING ABOUT? YOU GET THAT KINK WORKED OUT OF YOUR NECK?
SIS...
NO! SENSEI!
MY LIFE TEACHER!!
ビクッ
GASP
HMM... SO YOUR SENPAI AT WORK WANTS YOU TO INTRODUCE HER TO YOUR (TRIAL) BOY-FRIEND...
...And she doesn't know you're going out with him.
AND YOU WANT TO TELL HER NO, SO YOU WON'T BOTHER HIM...
...BUT SHE'S NICE, SO YOU DON'T WANT TO MAKE THINGS AWKWARD.

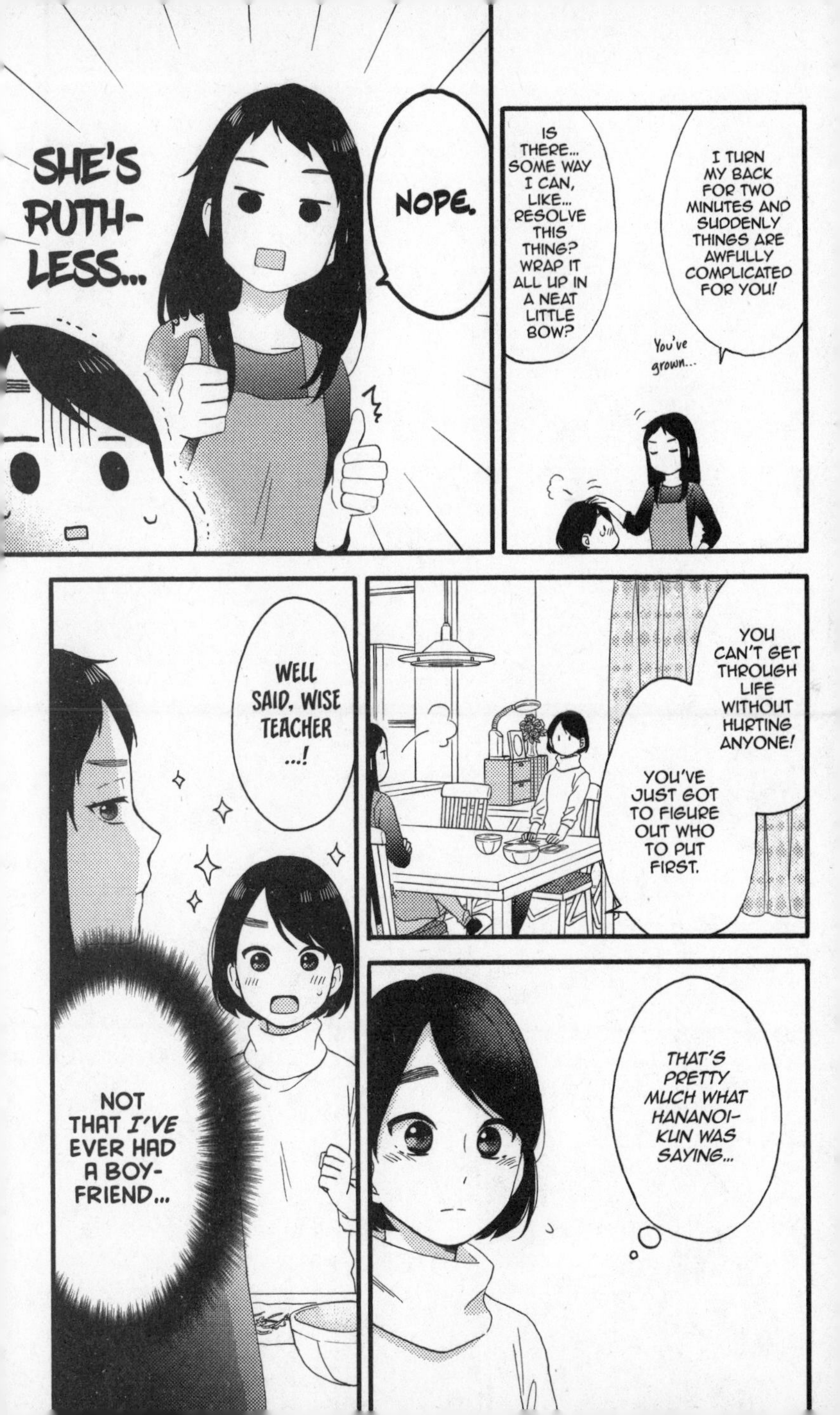
I TURN MY BACK FOR TWO MINUTES AND SUDDENLY THINGS ARE AWFULLY COMPLICATED FOR YOU!
IS THERE... SOME WAY I CAN, LIKE... RESOLVE THIS THING? WRAP IT ALL UP IN A NEAT LITTLE BOW?
You've grown...
NOPE.
SHE'S RUTH-LESS...
YOU CAN'T GET THROUGH LIFE WITHOUT HURTING ANYONE!
YOU'VE JUST GOT TO FIGURE OUT WHO TO PUT FIRST.
THAT'S PRETTY MUCH WHAT HANANOI-KUN WAS SAYING...
WELL SAID, WISE TEACHER ...!
NOT THAT *I'VE* EVER HAD A BOY-FRIEND...

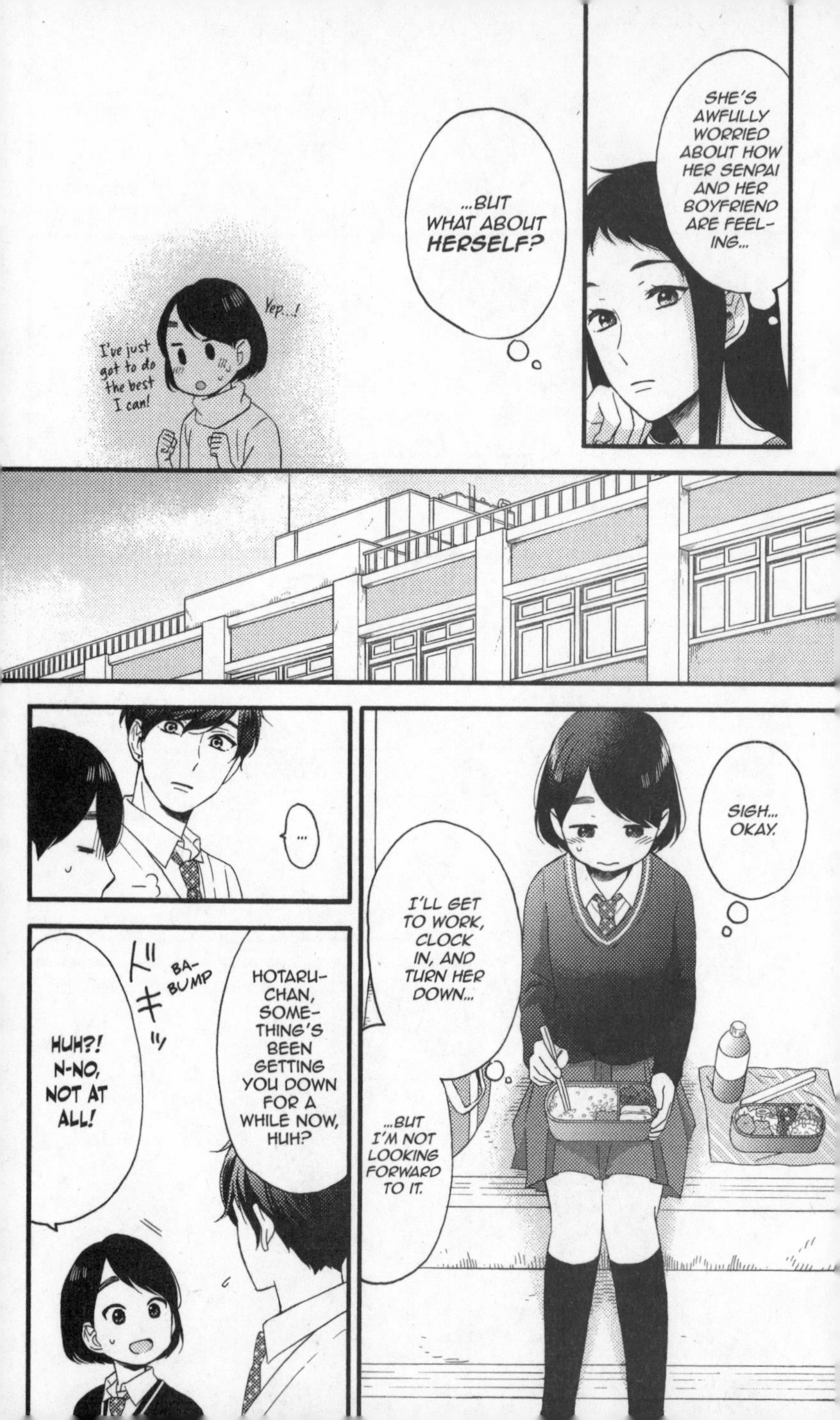
SHE'S AWFULLY WORRIED ABOUT HOW HER SENPAI AND HER BOYFRIEND ARE FEELING...
...BUT WHAT ABOUT HERSELF?
Yep...!
I've just got to do the best I can!
SIGH... OKAY.
I'LL GET TO WORK, CLOCK IN, AND TURN HER DOWN...
...BUT I'M NOT LOOKING FORWARD TO IT.
...
HOTARU-CHAN, SOMETHING'S BEEN GETTING YOU DOWN FOR A WHILE NOW, HUH?
ドキ
BA-BUMP
HUH?! N-NO, NOT AT ALL!

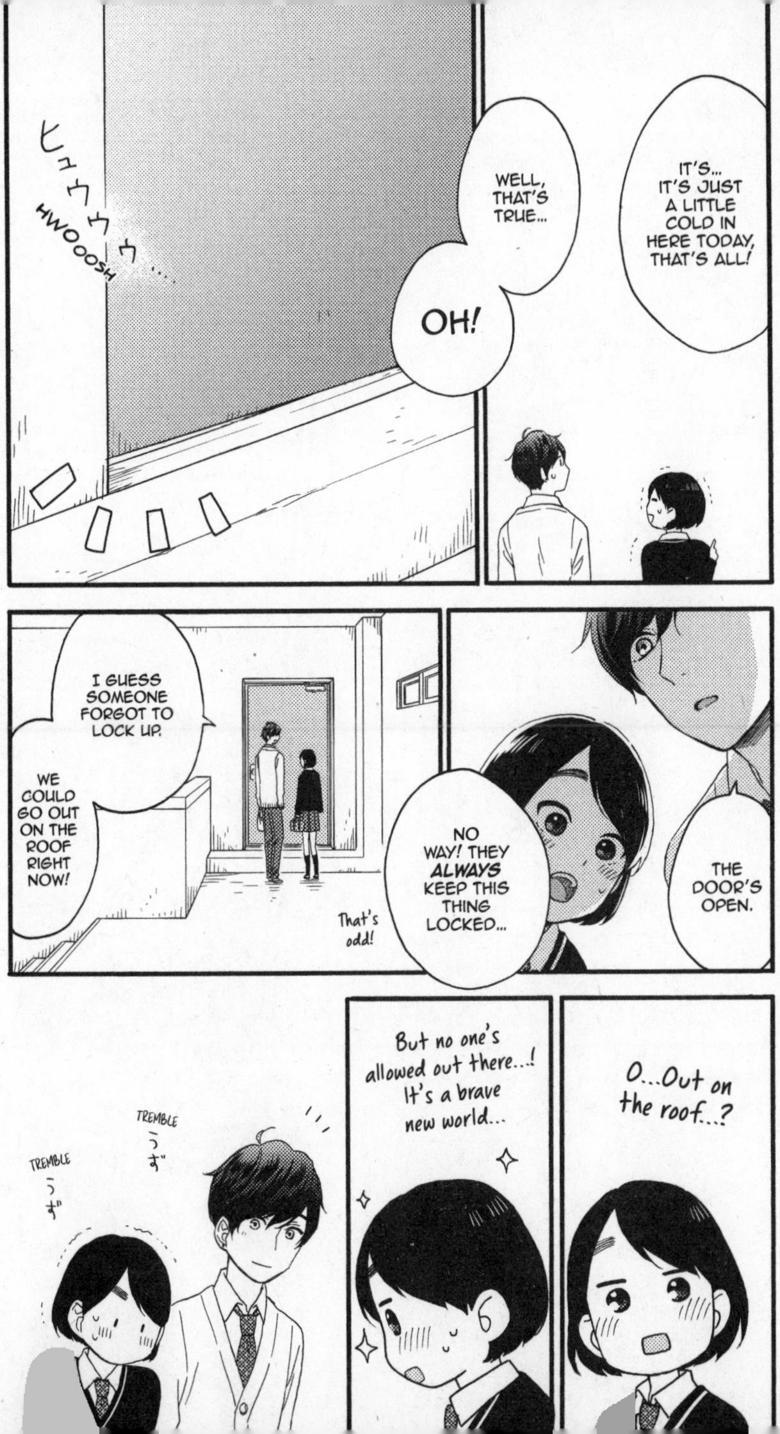
IT'S... IT'S JUST A LITTLE COLD IN HERE TODAY, THAT'S ALL!
WELL, THAT'S TRUE...
OH!
ヒュウウウ
HWOOOSH
THE DOOR'S OPEN.
NO WAY! THEY **ALWAYS** KEEP THIS THING LOCKED...
That's odd!
I GUESS SOMEONE FORGOT TO LOCK UP.
WE COULD GO OUT ON THE ROOF RIGHT NOW!
O...Out on the roof...?
But no one's allowed out there...! It's a brave new world...
TREMBLE
うず
TREMBLE
うず

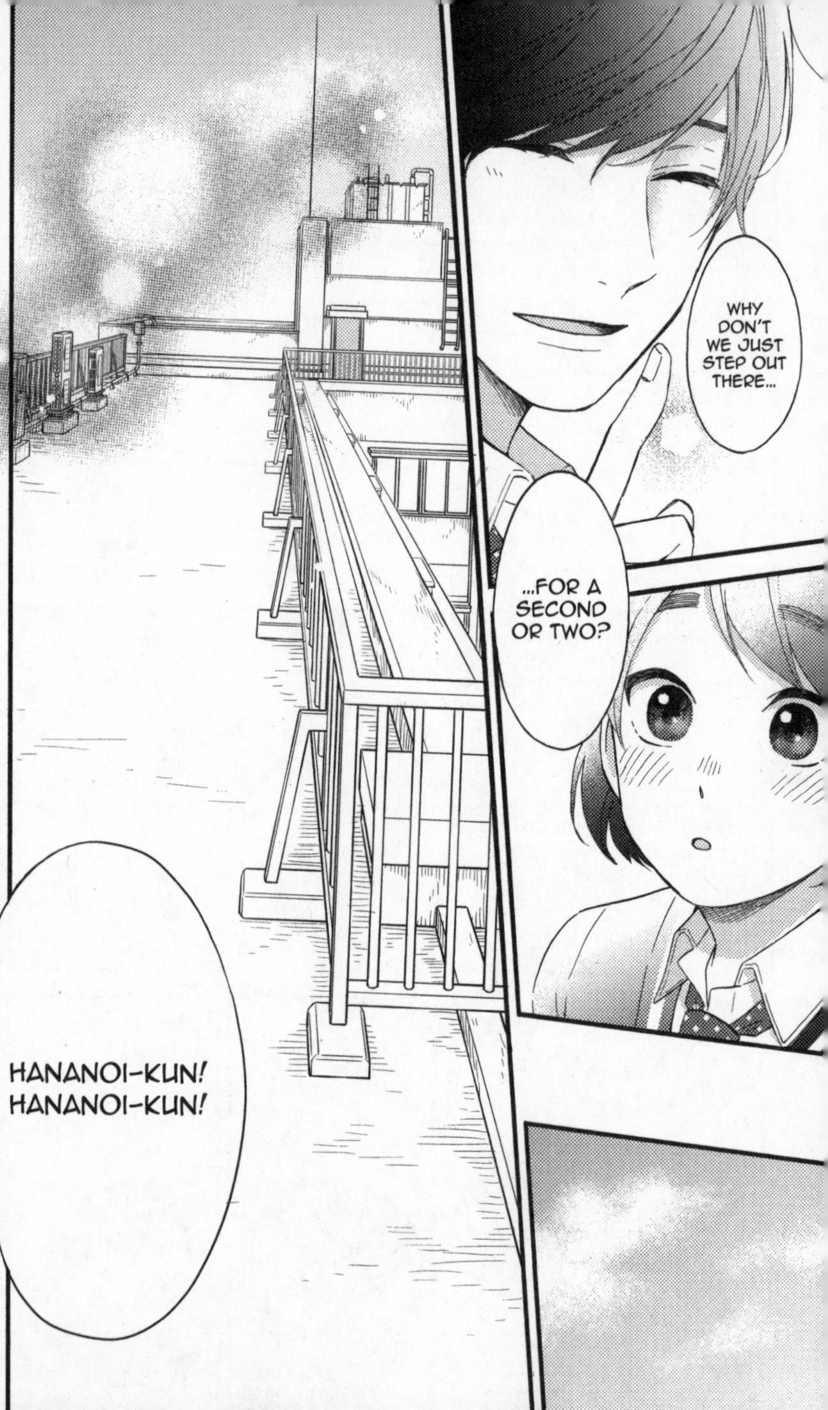
WHY DON'T WE JUST STEP OUT THERE...
...FOR A SECOND OR TWO?
HANANOI-KUN! HANANOI-KUN!

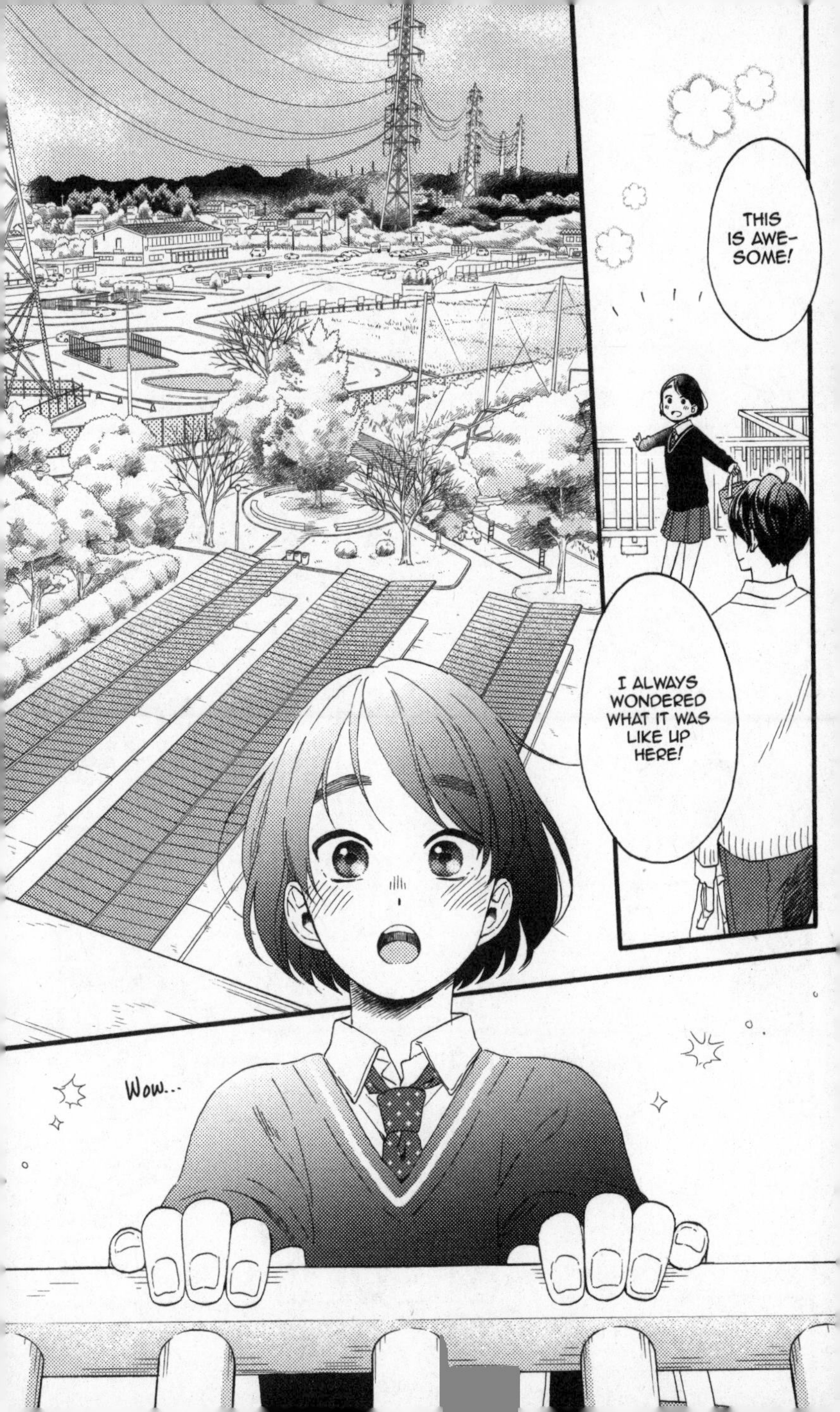
THIS IS AWE-SOME!
I ALWAYS WONDERED WHAT IT WAS LIKE UP HERE!
Wow...

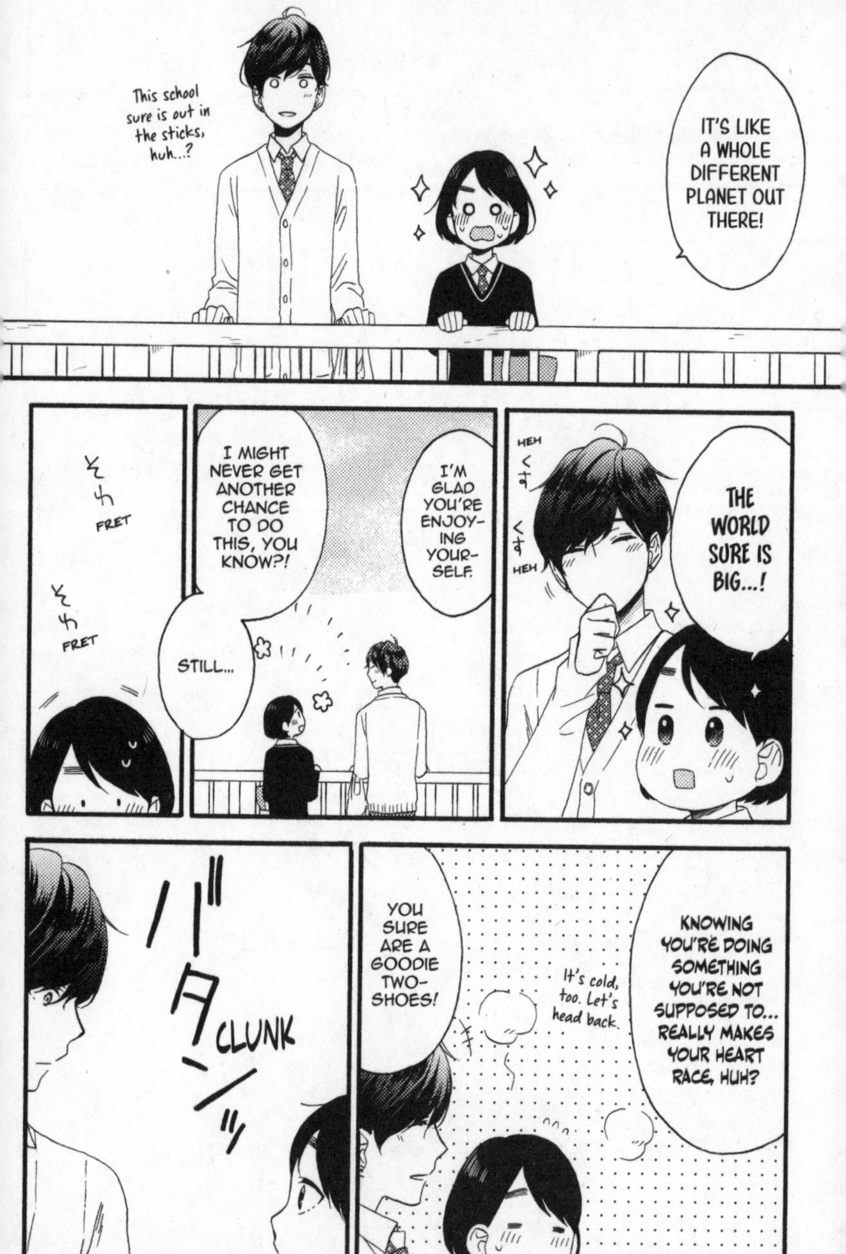
IT'S LIKE A WHOLE DIFFERENT PLANET OUT THERE!
This school sure is out in the sticks, huh...?
THE WORLD SURE IS BIG...!
くす HEH
くす HEH
I'M GLAD YOU'RE ENJOYING YOURSELF.
I MIGHT NEVER GET ANOTHER CHANCE TO DO THIS, YOU KNOW?!
STILL...
そわ FRET
そわ FRET
KNOWING YOU'RE DOING SOMETHING YOU'RE NOT SUPPOSED TO... REALLY MAKES YOUR HEART RACE, HUH?
It's cold, too. Let's head back.
YOU SURE ARE A GOODIE TWO-SHOES!
バタン
CLUNK

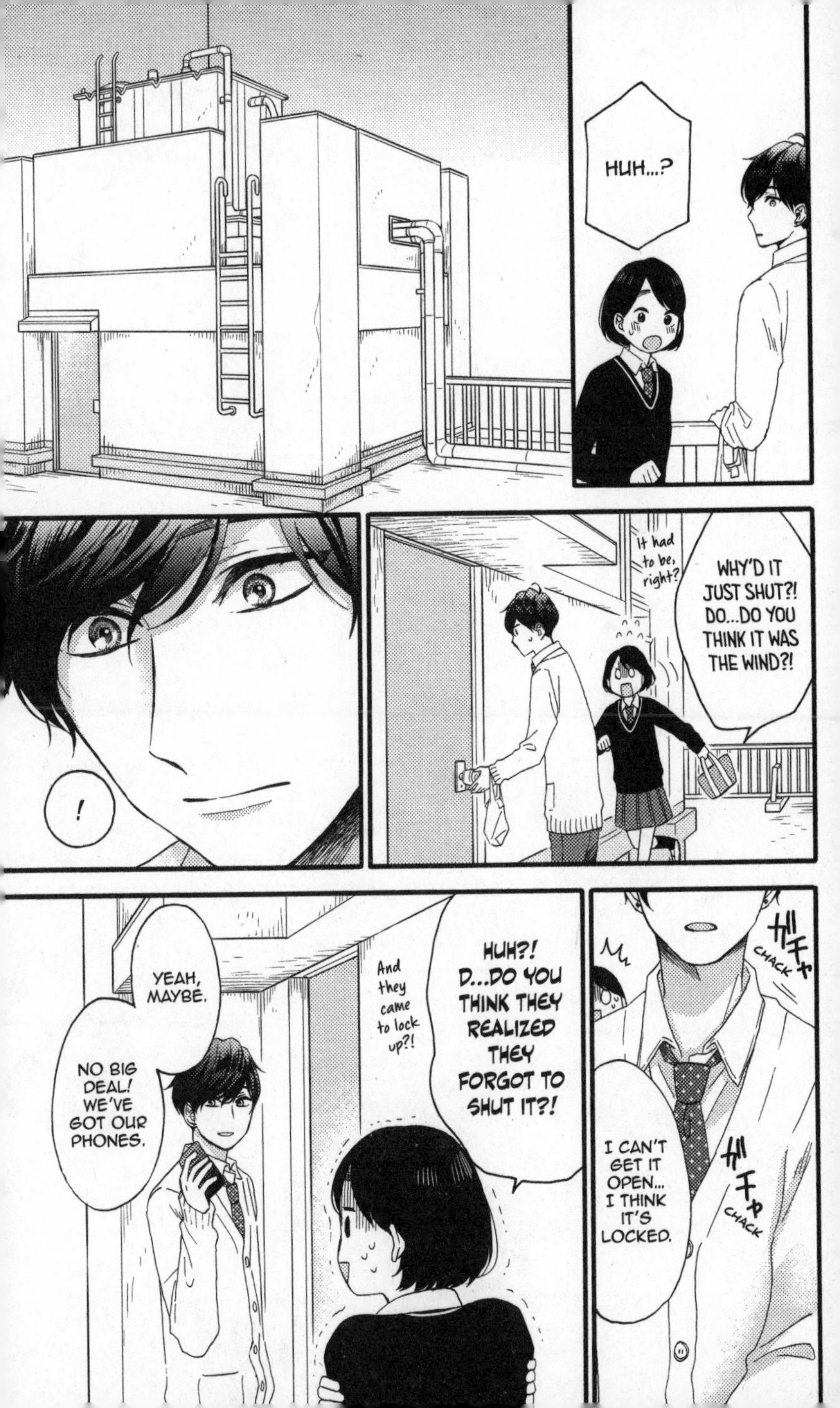
HUH...?
WHY'D IT JUST SHUT?! DO...DO YOU THINK IT WAS THE WIND?!
It had to be, right?
!
ガチャ
CHACK
I CAN'T GET IT OPEN... I THINK IT'S LOCKED.
ガチャ
CHACK
HUH?! D...DO YOU THINK THEY REALIZED THEY FORGOT TO SHUT IT?!
And they came to lock up?!
YEAH, MAYBE.
NO BIG DEAL! WE'VE GOT OUR PHONES.

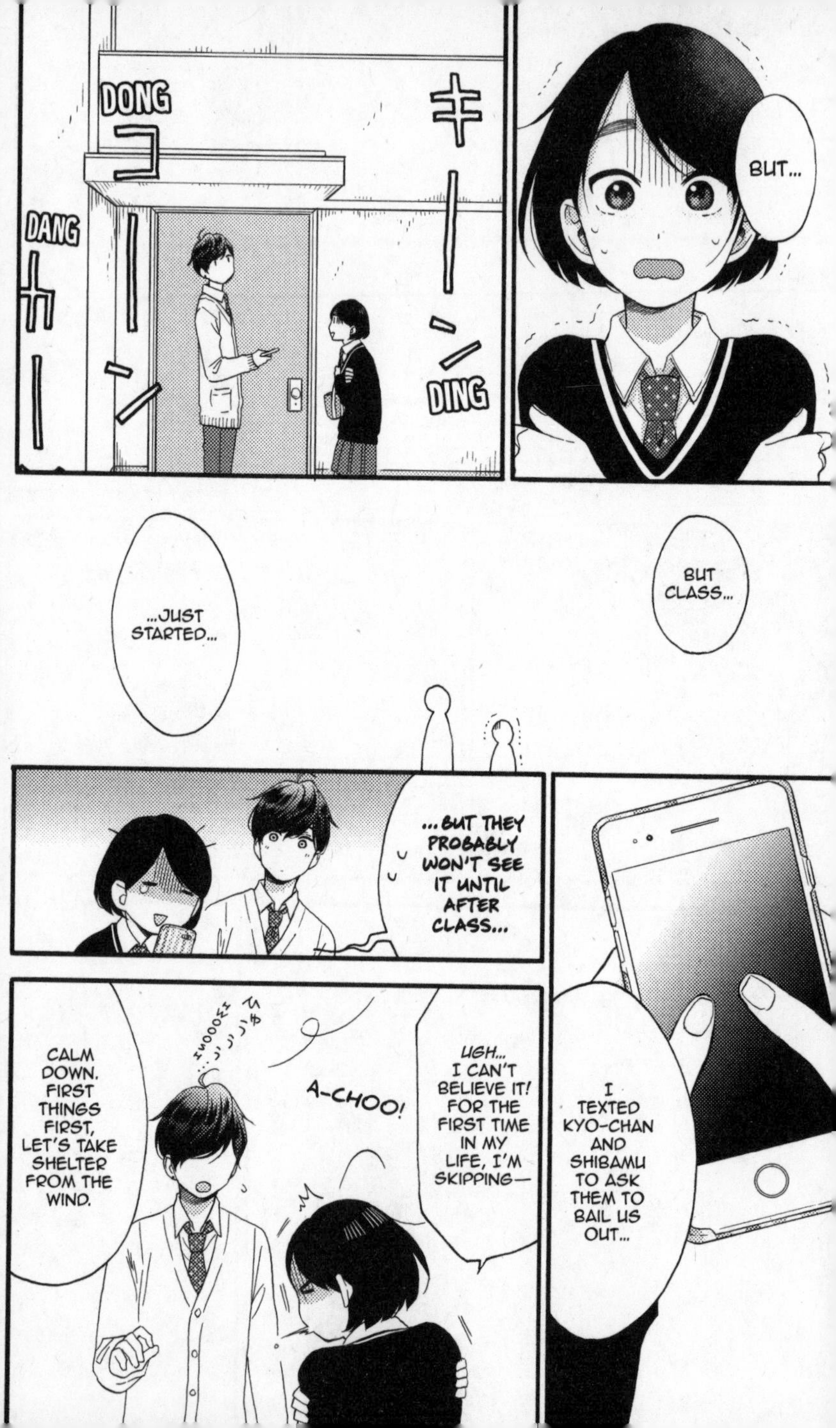

BUT...
DING
DONG
DANG
BUT CLASS...
...JUST STARTED...
I TEXTED KYO-CHAN AND SHIBAMU TO ASK THEM TO BAIL US OUT...
...BUT THEY PROBABLY WON'T SEE IT UNTIL AFTER CLASS...
UGH... I CAN'T BELIEVE IT! FOR THE FIRST TIME IN MY LIFE, I'M SKIPPING—
A-CHOO!
CALM DOWN. FIRST THINGS FIRST, LET'S TAKE SHELTER FROM THE WIND.

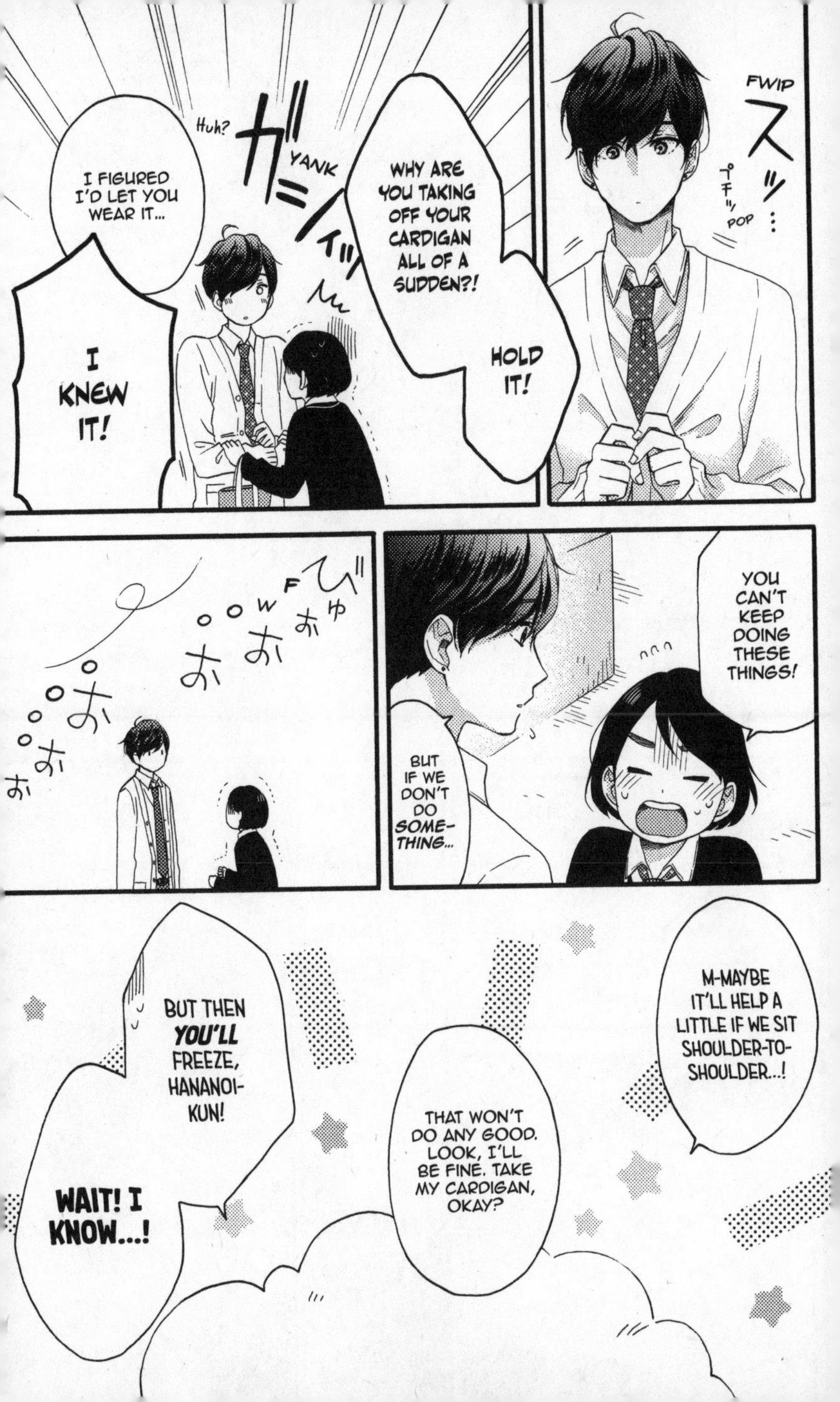
FWIP
POP
WHY ARE YOU TAKING OFF YOUR CARDIGAN ALL OF A SUDDEN?!
HOLD IT!
YANK
Huh?
I FIGURED I'D LET YOU WEAR IT...
I KNEW IT!
YOU CAN'T KEEP DOING THESE THINGS!
BUT IF WE DON'T DO SOMETHING...
FWOOO
M-MAYBE IT'LL HELP A LITTLE IF WE SIT SHOULDER-TO-SHOULDER...!
THAT WON'T DO ANY GOOD. LOOK, I'LL BE FINE. TAKE MY CARDIGAN, OKAY?
BUT THEN YOU'LL FREEZE, HANANOI-KUN!
WAIT! I KNOW...!

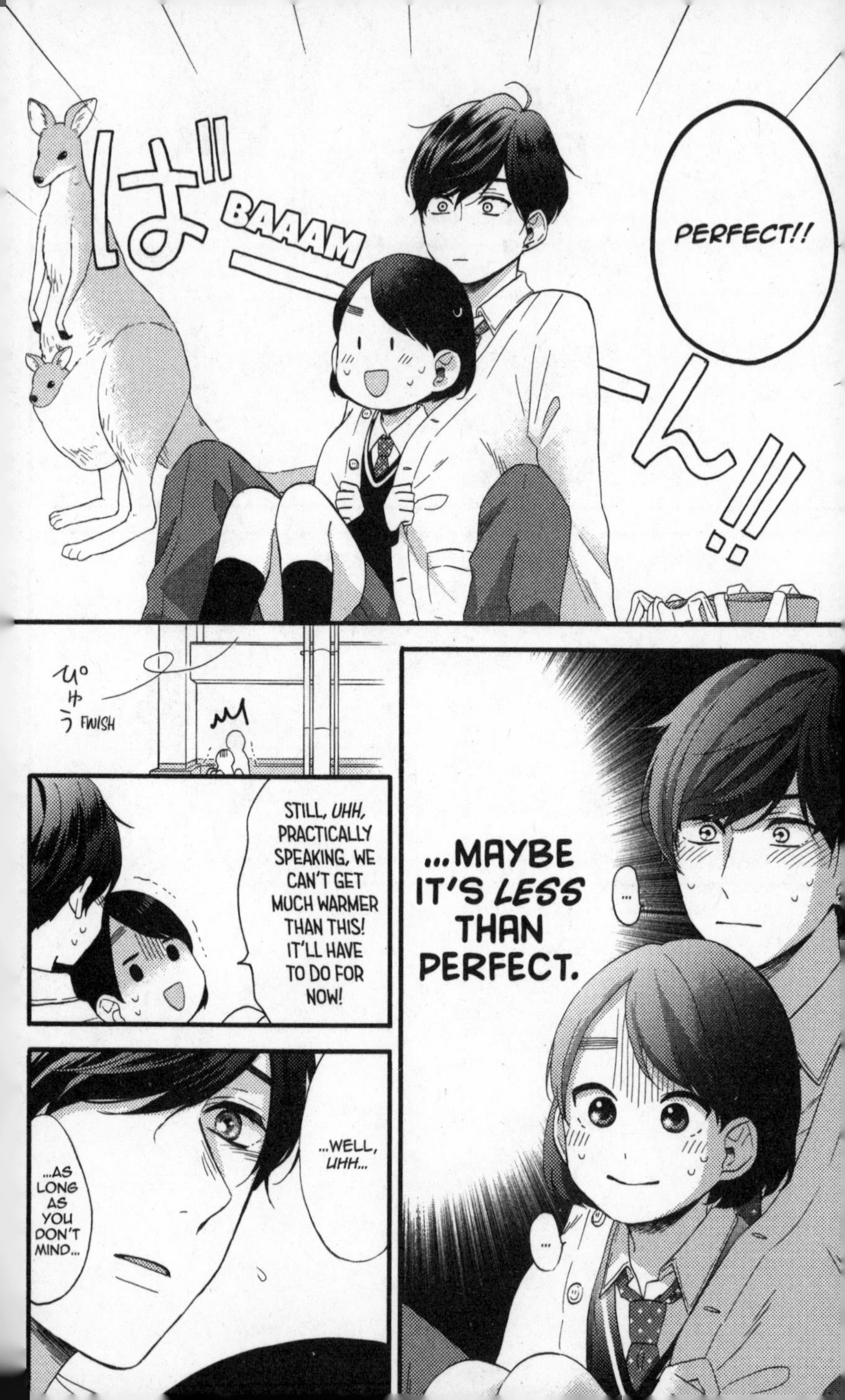

PERFECT!!
ば BAAAM
ん!!
...
...MAYBE IT'S LESS THAN PERFECT.
...
ぴゅう FWISH
STILL, UHH, PRACTICALLY SPEAKING, WE CAN'T GET MUCH WARMER THAN THIS! IT'LL HAVE TO DO FOR NOW!
...WELL, UHH...
...AS LONG AS YOU DON'T MIND...

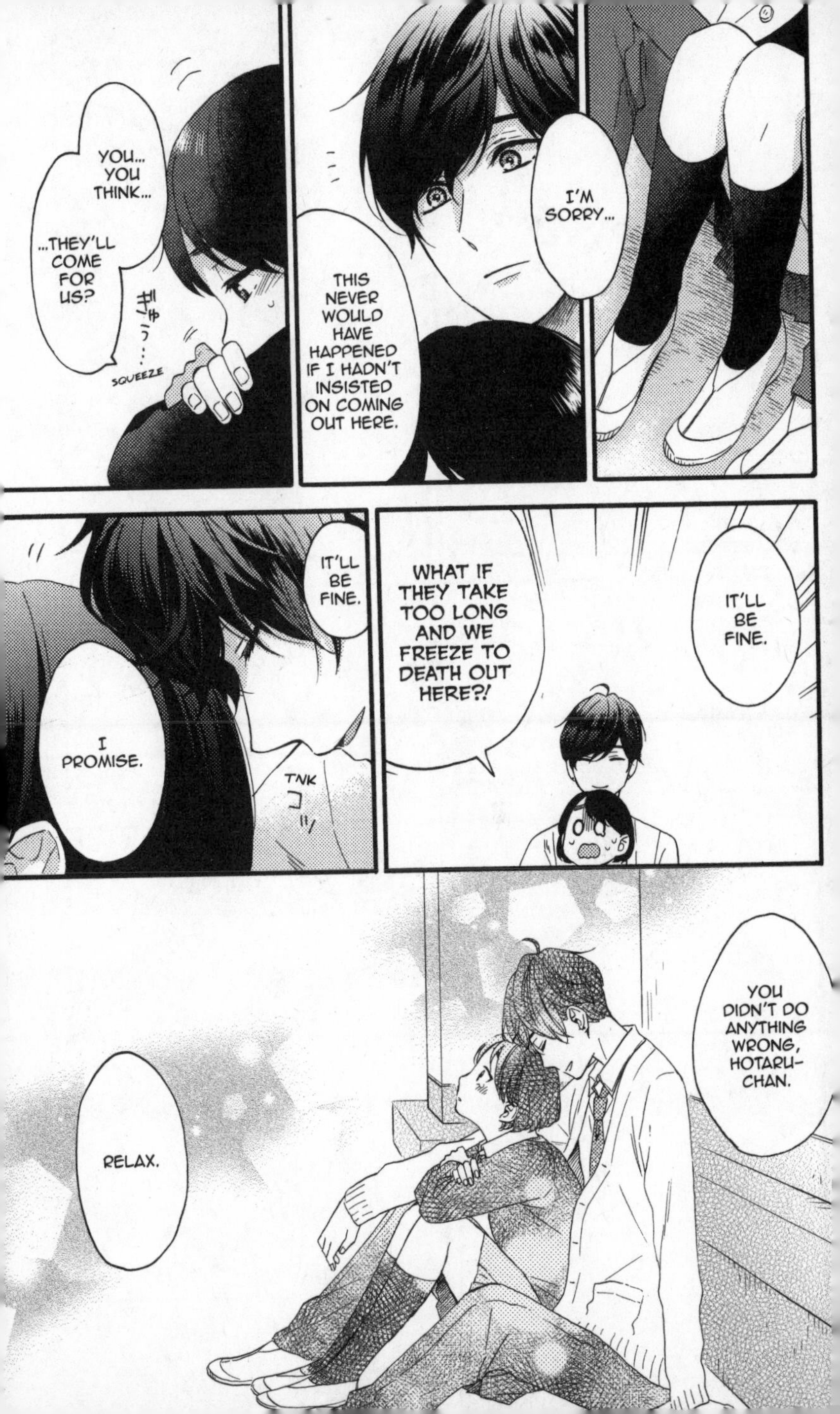
I'M SORRY...
THIS NEVER WOULD HAVE HAPPENED IF I HADN'T INSISTED ON COMING OUT HERE.
YOU... YOU THINK...
...THEY'LL COME FOR US?
SQUEEZE
IT'LL BE FINE.
WHAT IF THEY TAKE TOO LONG AND WE FREEZE TO DEATH OUT HERE?!
IT'LL BE FINE.
I PROMISE.
TNK
YOU DIDN'T DO ANYTHING WRONG, HOTARU-CHAN.
RELAX.

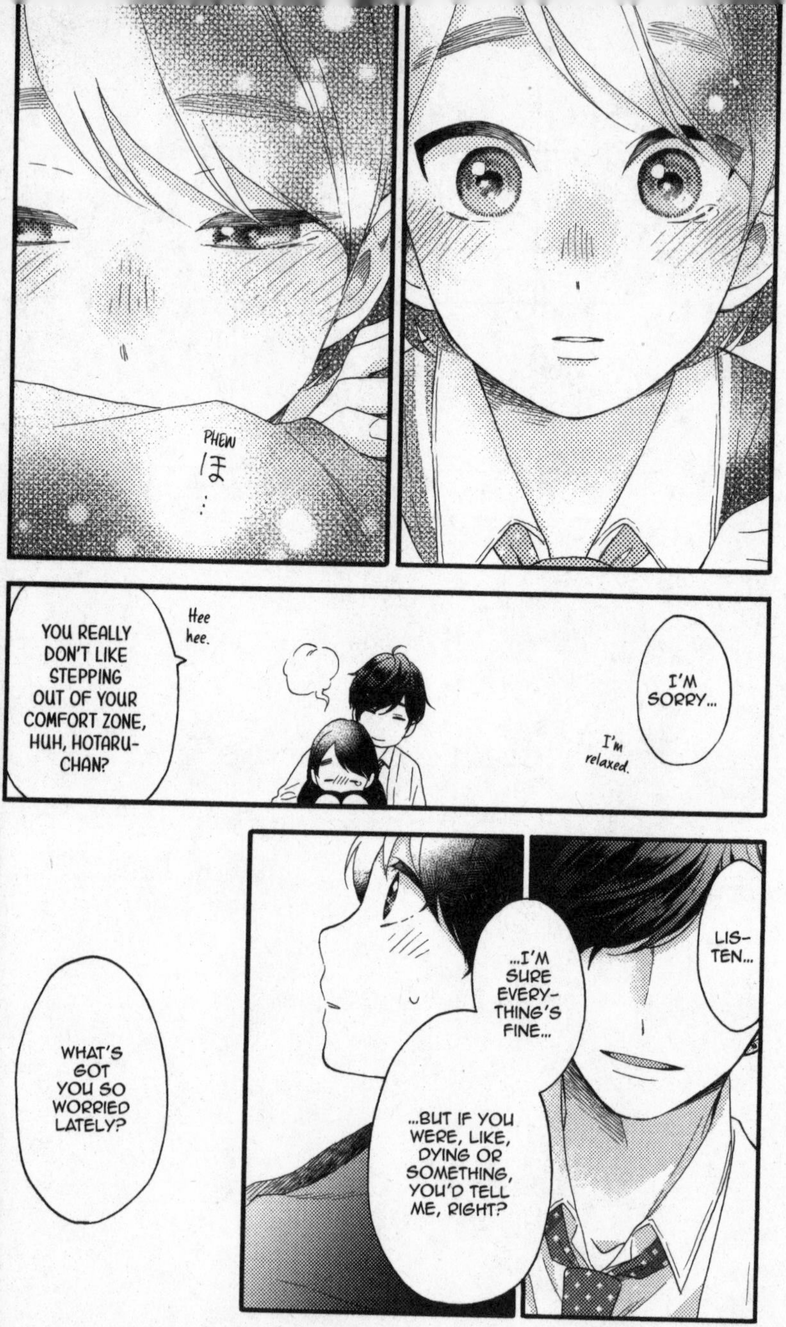
PHEW
ほ…
I'M SORRY...
I'm relaxed.
Hee hee.
YOU REALLY DON'T LIKE STEPPING OUT OF YOUR COMFORT ZONE, HUH, HOTARU-CHAN?
LIS-TEN...
...I'M SURE EVERY-THING'S FINE...
...BUT IF YOU WERE, LIKE, DYING OR SOMETHING, YOU'D TELL ME, RIGHT?
WHAT'S GOT YOU SO WORRIED LATELY?

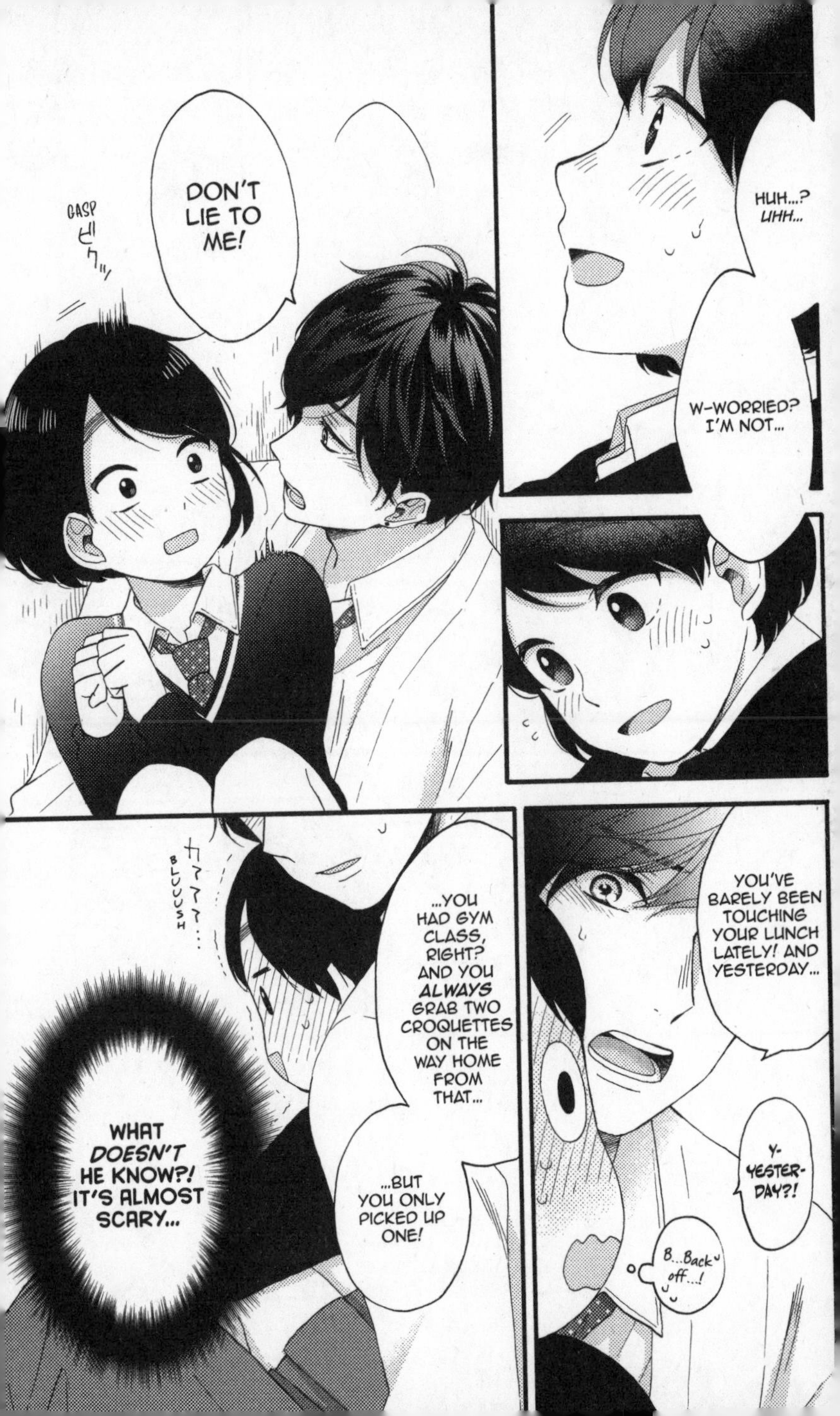
HUH...? UHH...
W-WORRIED? I'M NOT...
DON'T LIE TO ME!
GASP
ビクッ
YOU'VE BARELY BEEN TOUCHING YOUR LUNCH LATELY! AND YESTERDAY...
Y-YESTER-DAY?!
B...Back off...!
...YOU HAD GYM CLASS, RIGHT? AND YOU ALWAYS GRAB TWO CROQUETTES ON THE WAY HOME FROM THAT...
...BUT YOU ONLY PICKED UP ONE!
カァァァ...
BLUUUSH
WHAT DOESN'T HE KNOW?! IT'S ALMOST SCARY...

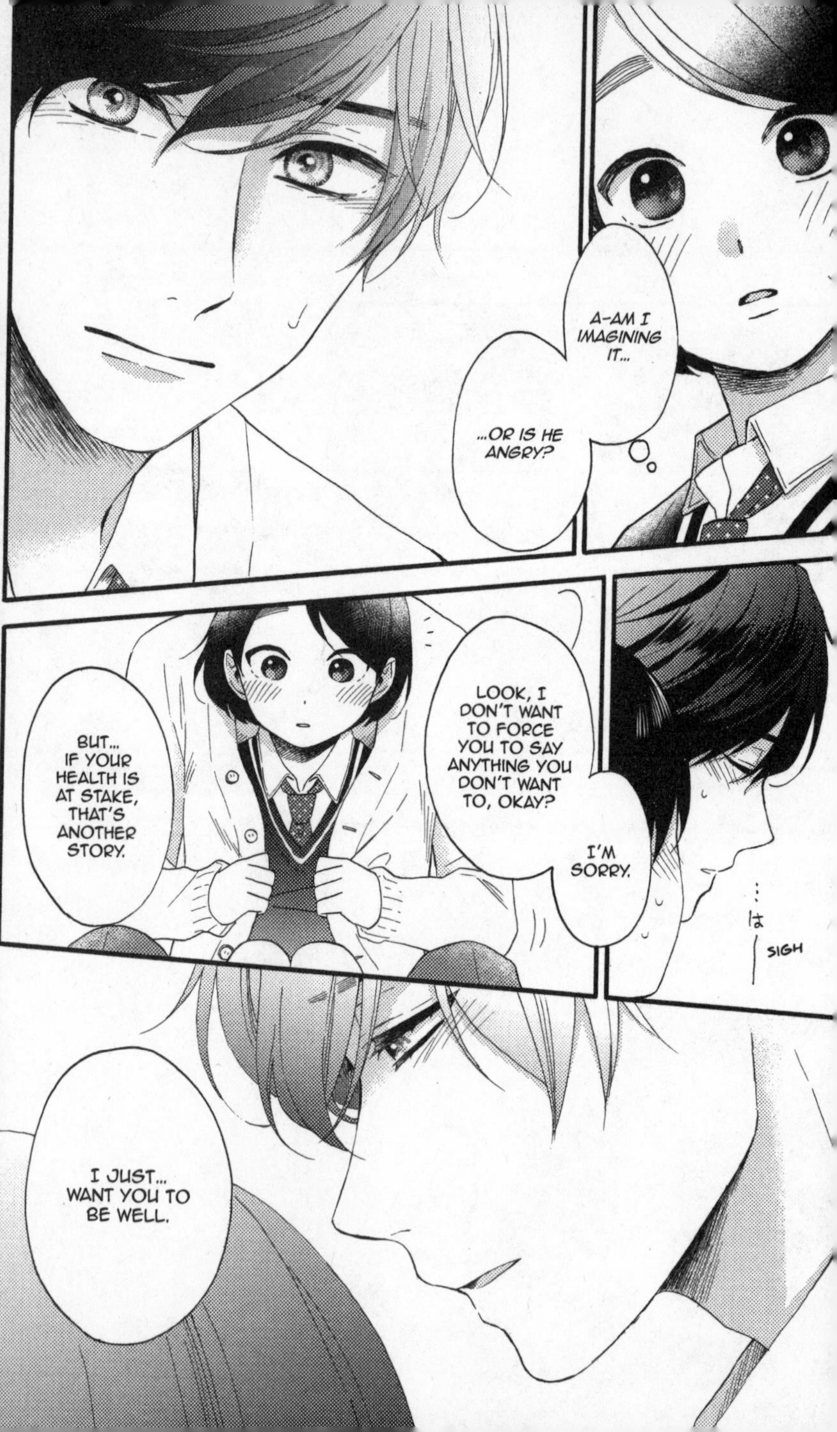
A-AM I IMAGINING IT...
...OR IS HE ANGRY?
…はー
SIGH
I'M SORRY.
LOOK, I DON'T WANT TO FORCE YOU TO SAY ANYTHING YOU DON'T WANT TO, OKAY?
BUT... IF YOUR HEALTH IS AT STAKE, THAT'S ANOTHER STORY.
I JUST... WANT YOU TO BE WELL.

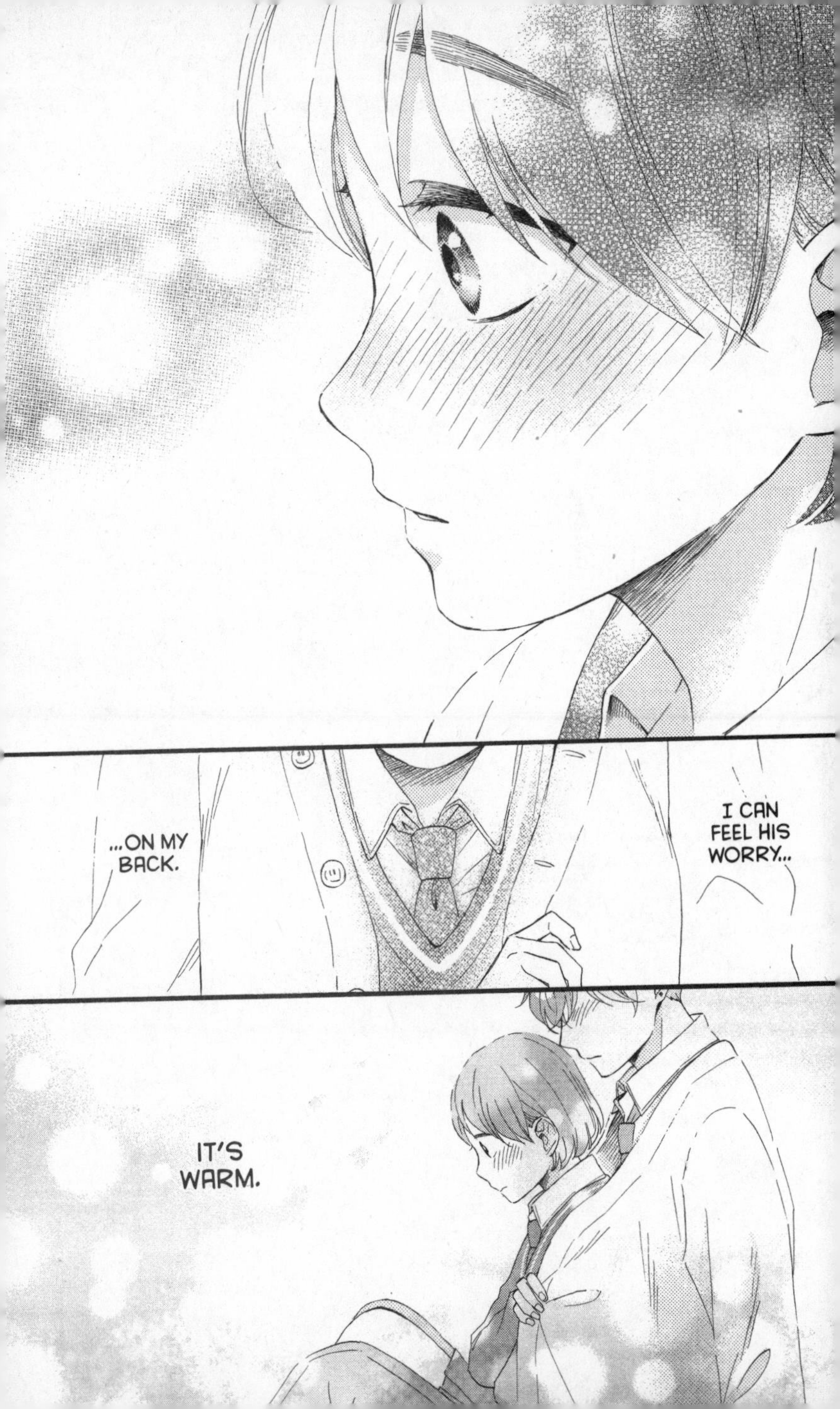
I CAN FEEL HIS WORRY...
...ON MY BACK.
IT'S WARM.

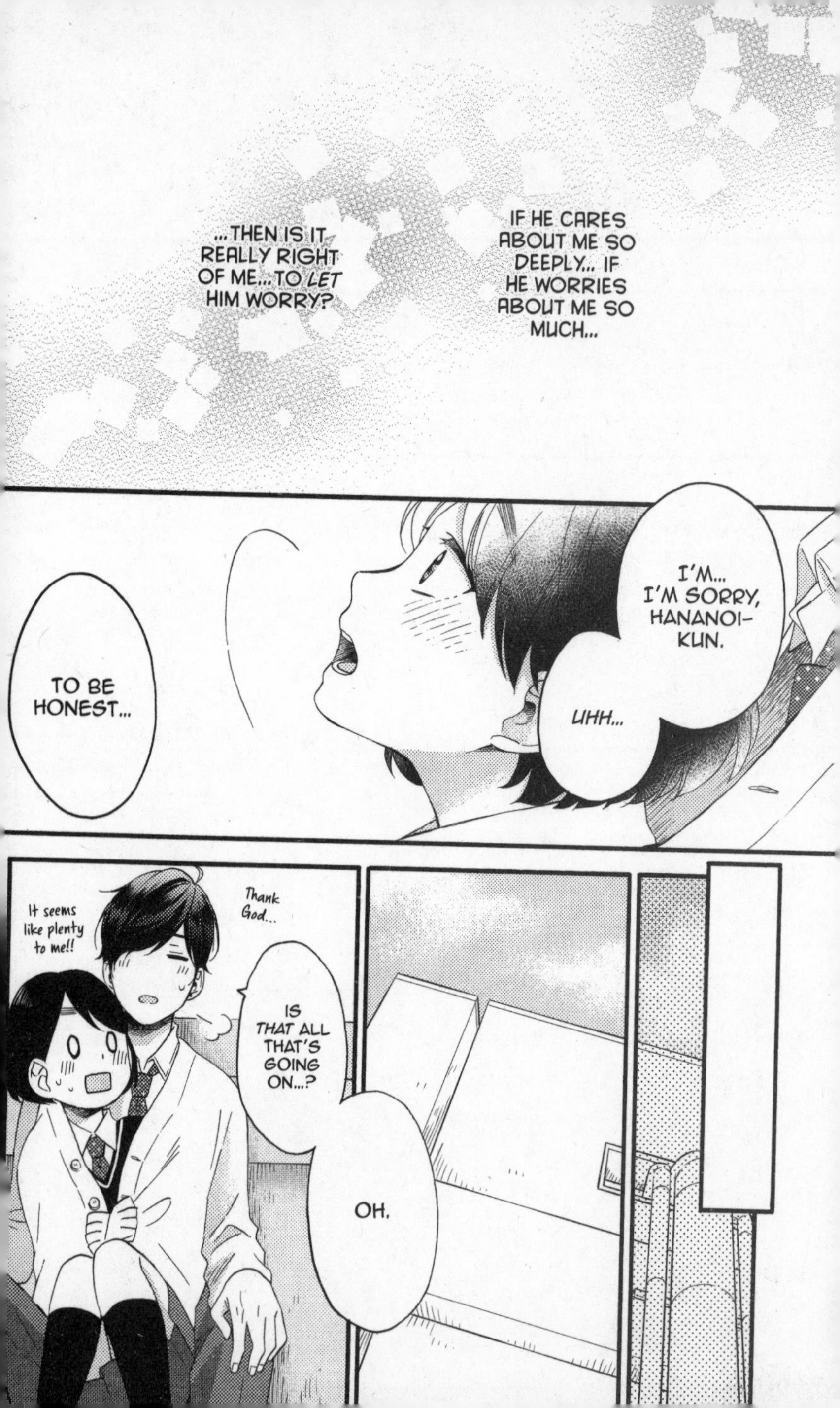
IF HE CARES ABOUT ME SO DEEPLY... IF HE WORRIES ABOUT ME SO MUCH...
...THEN IS IT REALLY RIGHT OF ME...TO *LET* HIM WORRY?
I'M... I'M SORRY, HANANOI-KUN.
UHH...
TO BE HONEST...
OH.
IS *THAT ALL* THAT'S GOING ON...?
Thank God...
It seems like plenty to me!!

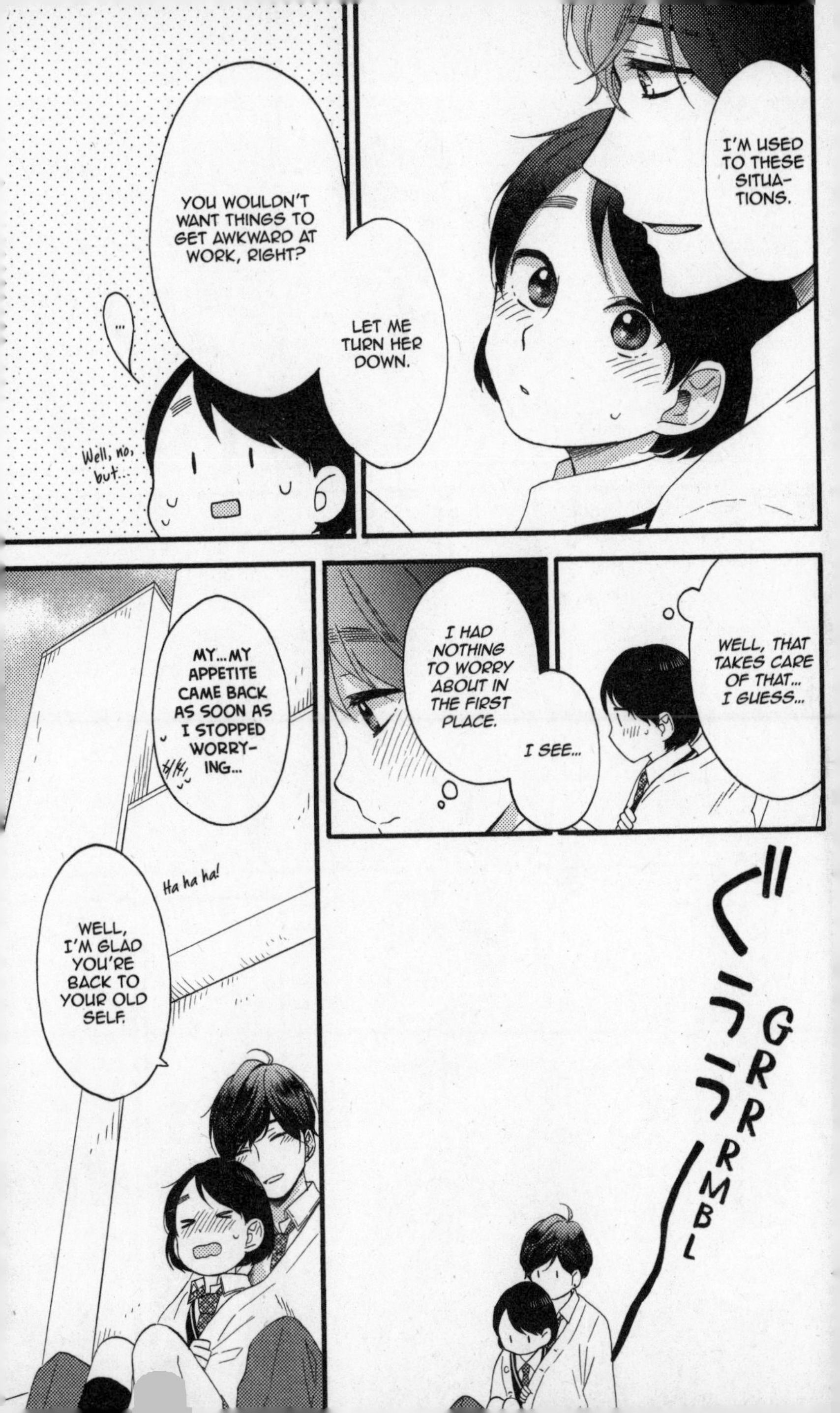
I'M USED TO THESE SITUATIONS.
LET ME TURN HER DOWN.
YOU WOULDN'T WANT THINGS TO GET AWKWARD AT WORK, RIGHT?
...
Well, no, but...
WELL, THAT TAKES CARE OF THAT... I GUESS...
I HAD NOTHING TO WORRY ABOUT IN THE FIRST PLACE.
I SEE...
GRRRMBL
MY...MY APPETITE CAME BACK AS SOON AS I STOPPED WORRYING...
Ha ha ha!
WELL, I'M GLAD YOU'RE BACK TO YOUR OLD SELF.

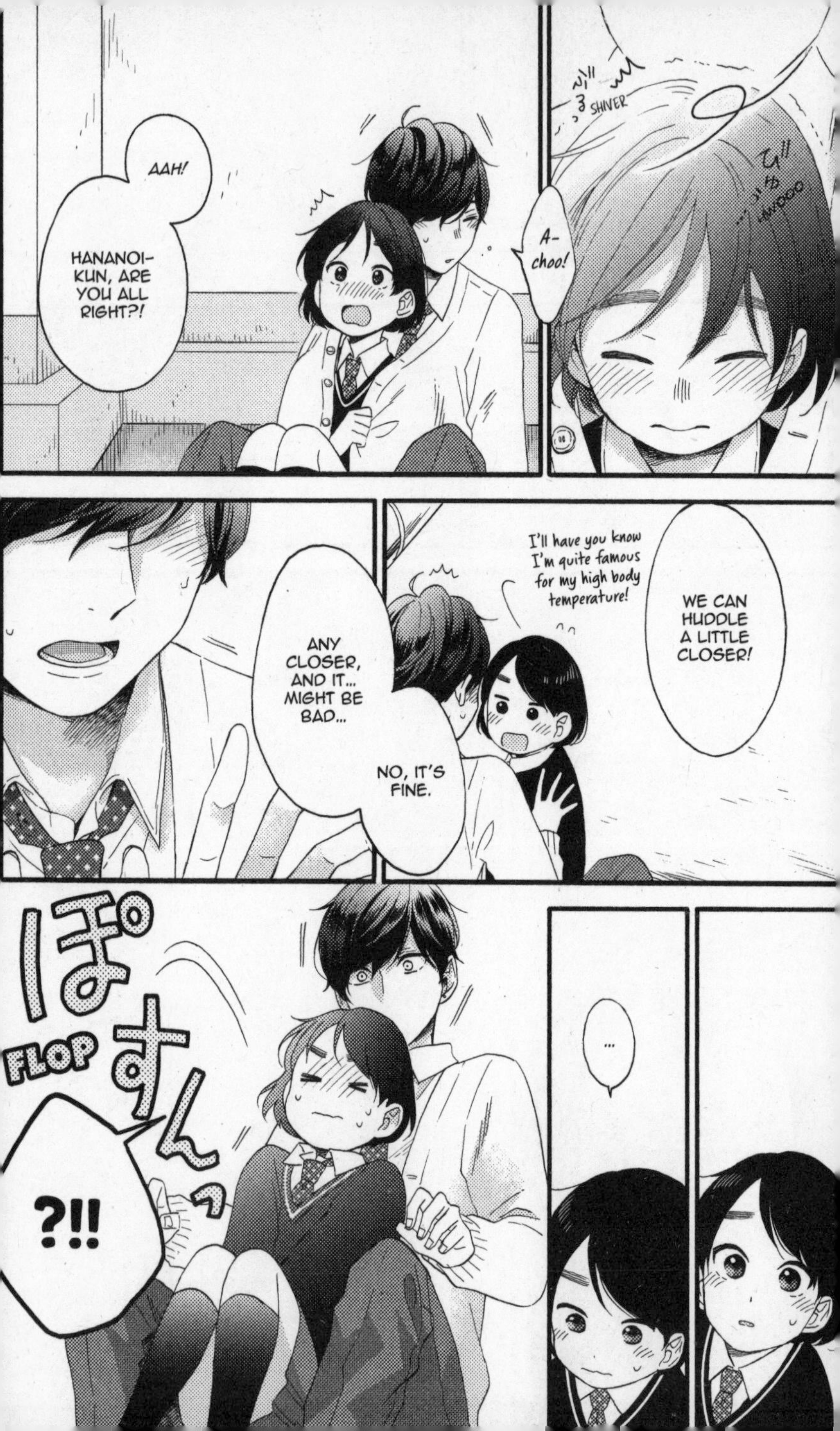
SHIVER
HWOOO
A-choo!
AAH!
HANANOI-KUN, ARE YOU ALL RIGHT?!
WE CAN HUDDLE A LITTLE CLOSER!
I'll have you know I'm quite famous for my high body temperature!
NO, IT'S FINE.
ANY CLOSER, AND IT... MIGHT BE BAD...
...
FLOP
?!!

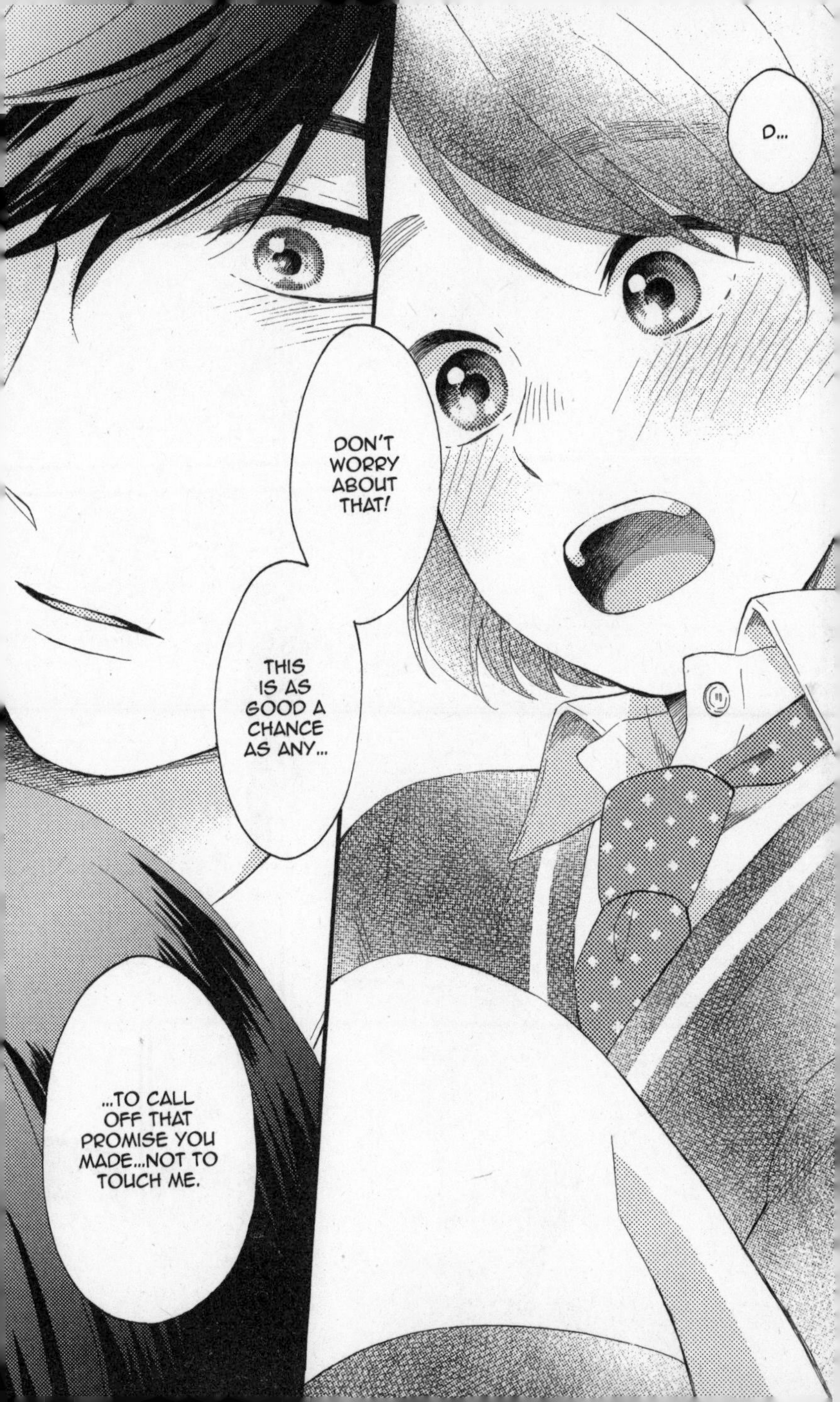
D...
DON'T WORRY ABOUT THAT!
THIS IS AS GOOD A CHANCE AS ANY...
...TO CALL OFF THAT PROMISE YOU MADE...NOT TO TOUCH ME.

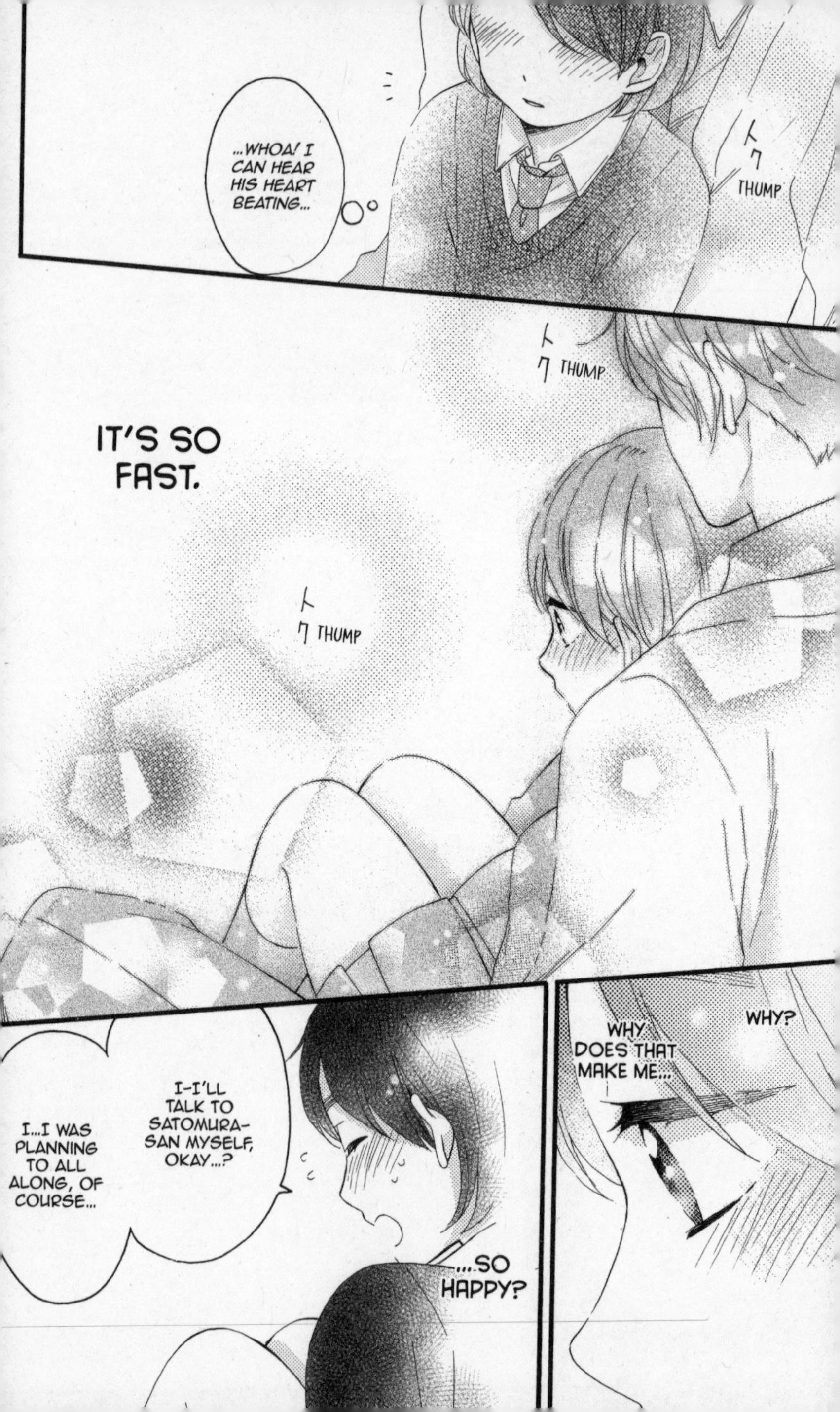

トク THUMP
...WHOA! I CAN HEAR HIS HEART BEATING...
トク THUMP
IT'S SO FAST.
トク THUMP
WHY?
WHY DOES THAT MAKE ME...
I-I'LL TALK TO SATOMURA-SAN MYSELF, OKAY...?
I...I WAS PLANNING TO ALL ALONG, OF COURSE...
...SO HAPPY?

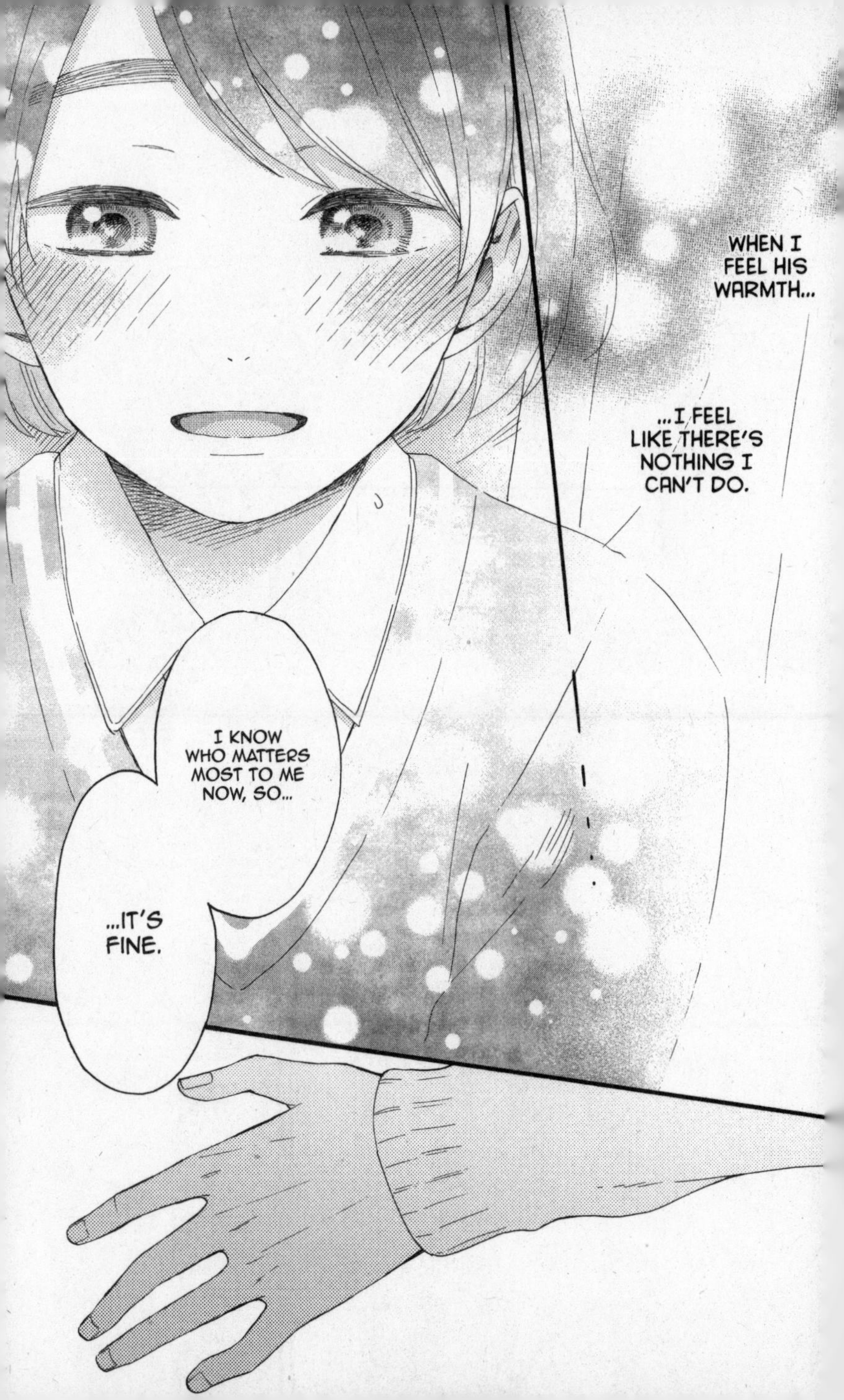
WHEN I FEEL HIS WARMTH...
...I FEEL LIKE THERE'S NOTHING I CAN'T DO.
I KNOW WHO MATTERS MOST TO ME NOW, SO...
...IT'S FINE.

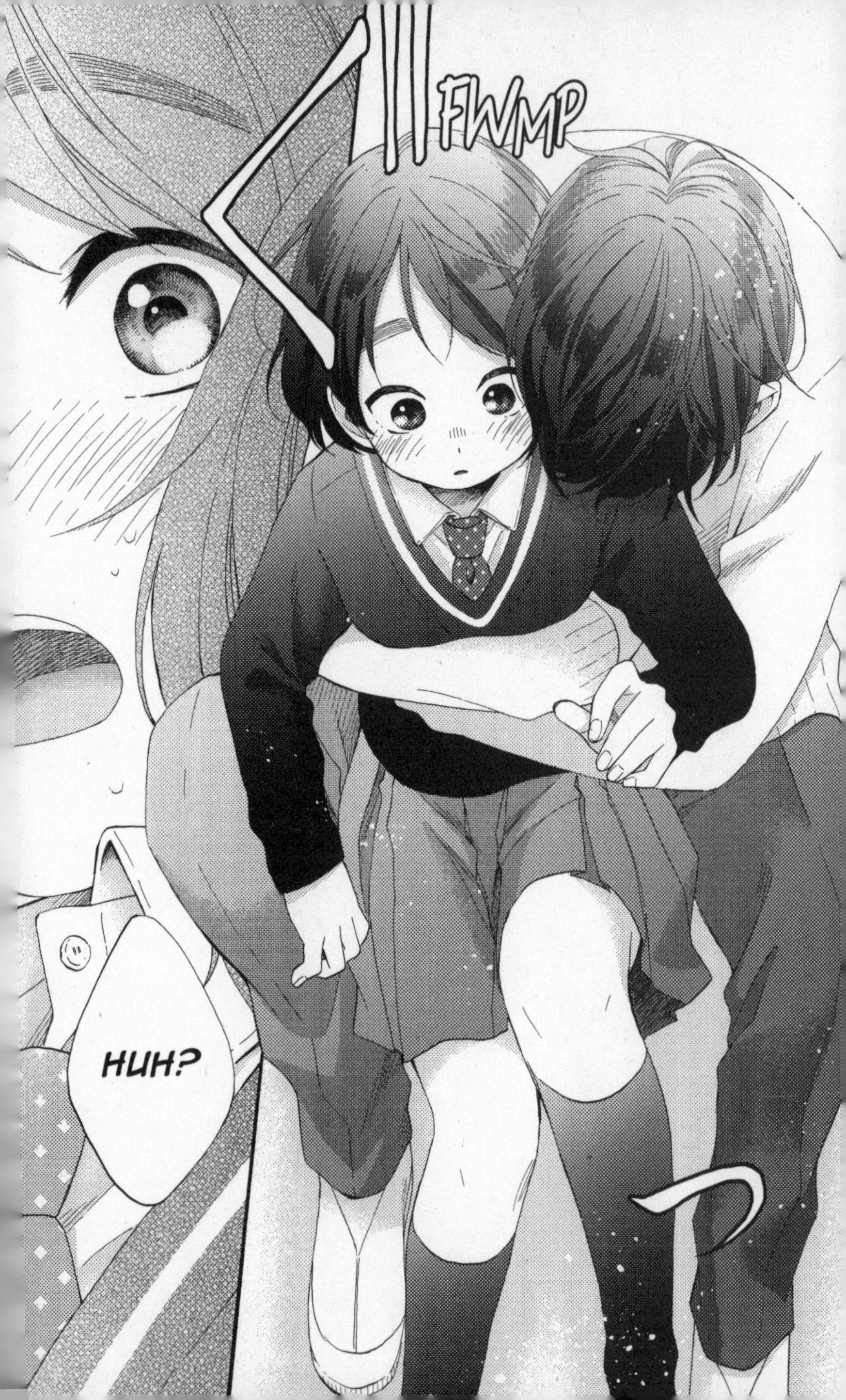
FWMP
HUH?

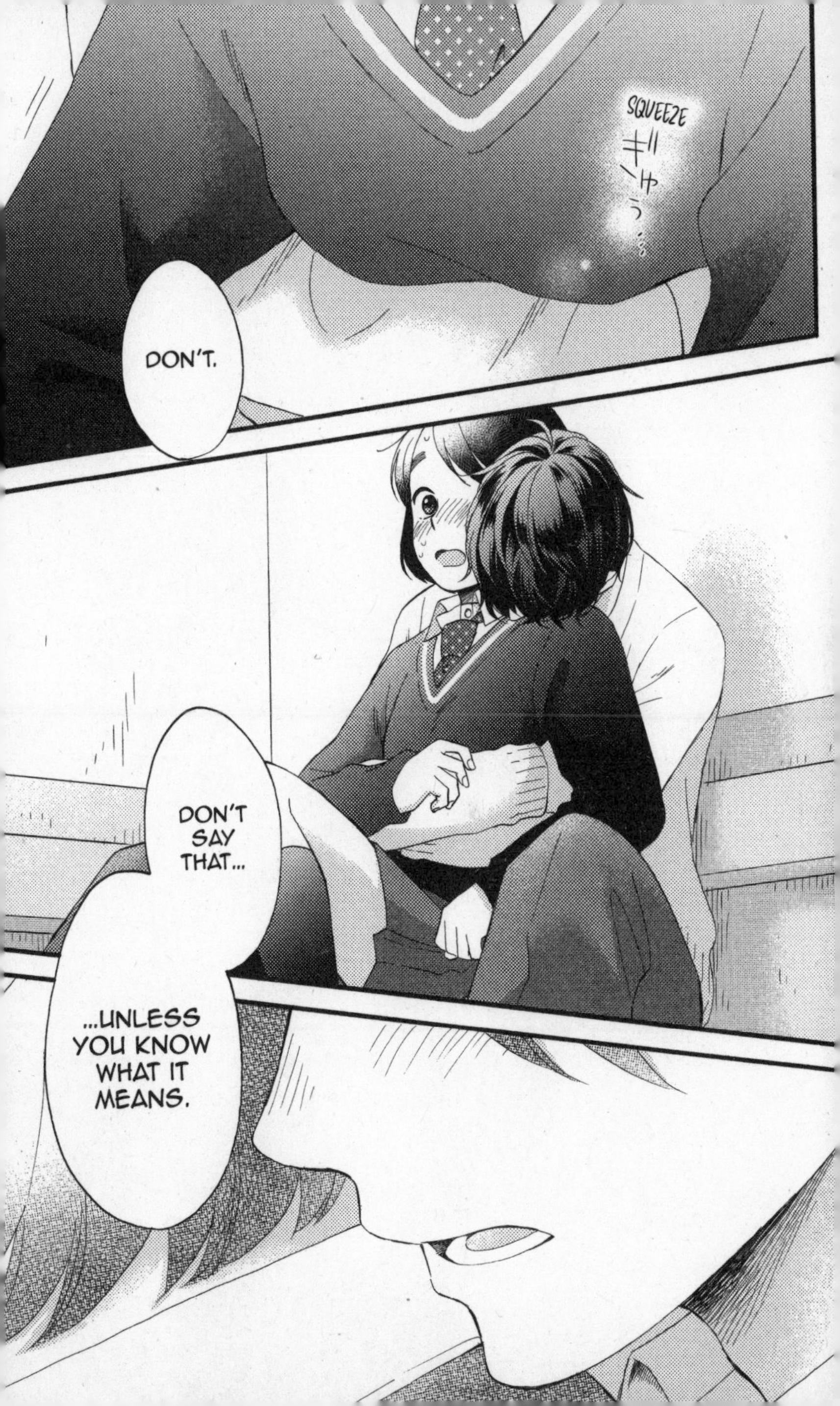
SQUEEZE
ギュう…
DON'T.
DON'T SAY THAT...
...UNLESS YOU KNOW WHAT IT MEANS.

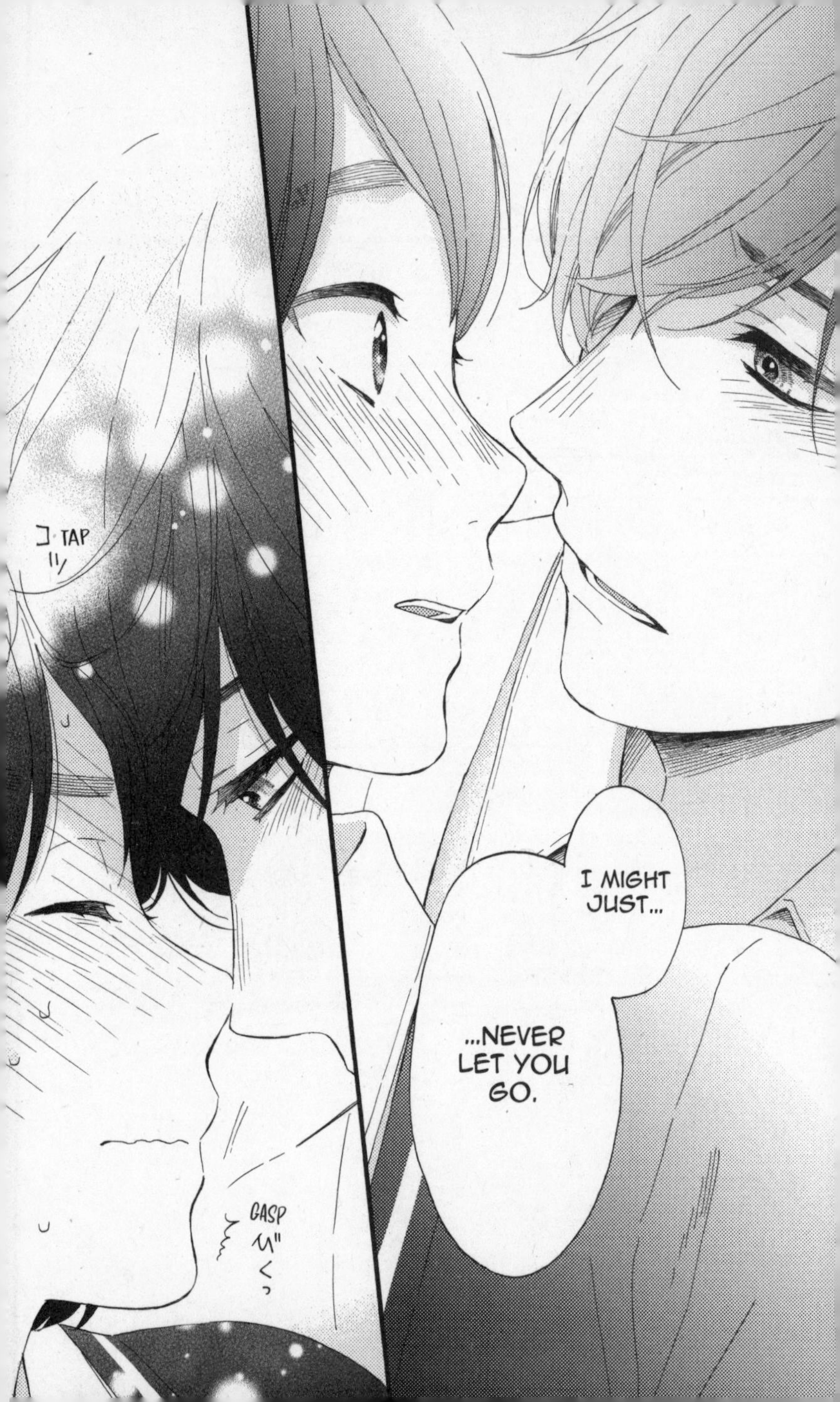
TAP
I MIGHT JUST...
...NEVER LET YOU GO.
GASP

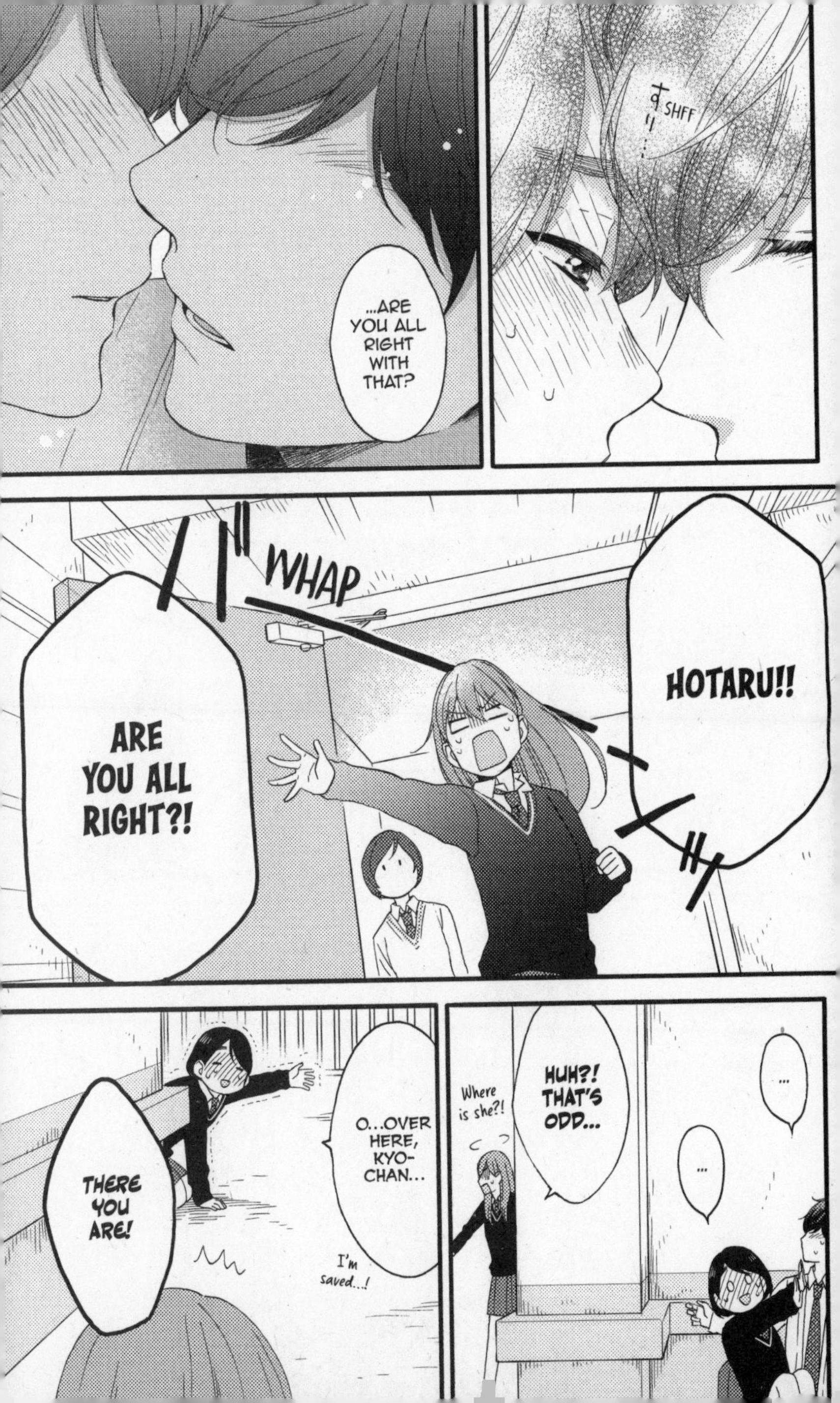

す
SHFF
...ARE YOU ALL RIGHT WITH THAT?
HOTARU!!
WHAP
ARE YOU ALL RIGHT?!
...
...
HUH?! THAT'S ODD...
Where is she?!
O...OVER HERE, KYO-CHAN...
I'm saved...!
THERE YOU ARE!

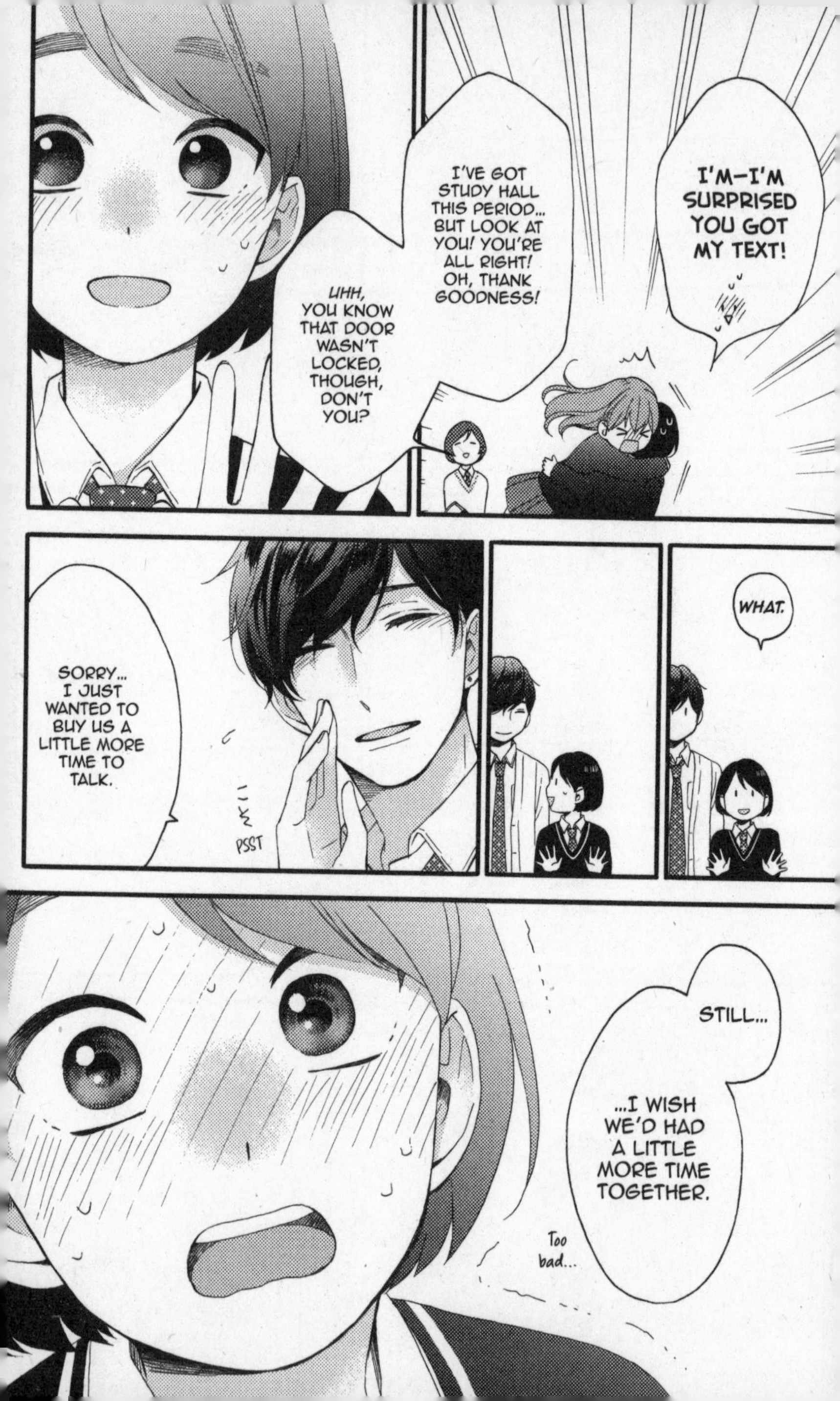
I'M—I'M SURPRISED YOU GOT MY TEXT!
I'VE GOT STUDY HALL THIS PERIOD... BUT LOOK AT YOU! YOU'RE ALL RIGHT! OH, THANK GOODNESS!
UHH, YOU KNOW THAT DOOR WASN'T LOCKED, THOUGH, DON'T YOU?
WHAT.
SORRY... I JUST WANTED TO BUY US A LITTLE MORE TIME TO TALK.
PSST
STILL...
...I WISH WE'D HAD A LITTLE MORE TIME TOGETHER.
Too bad...

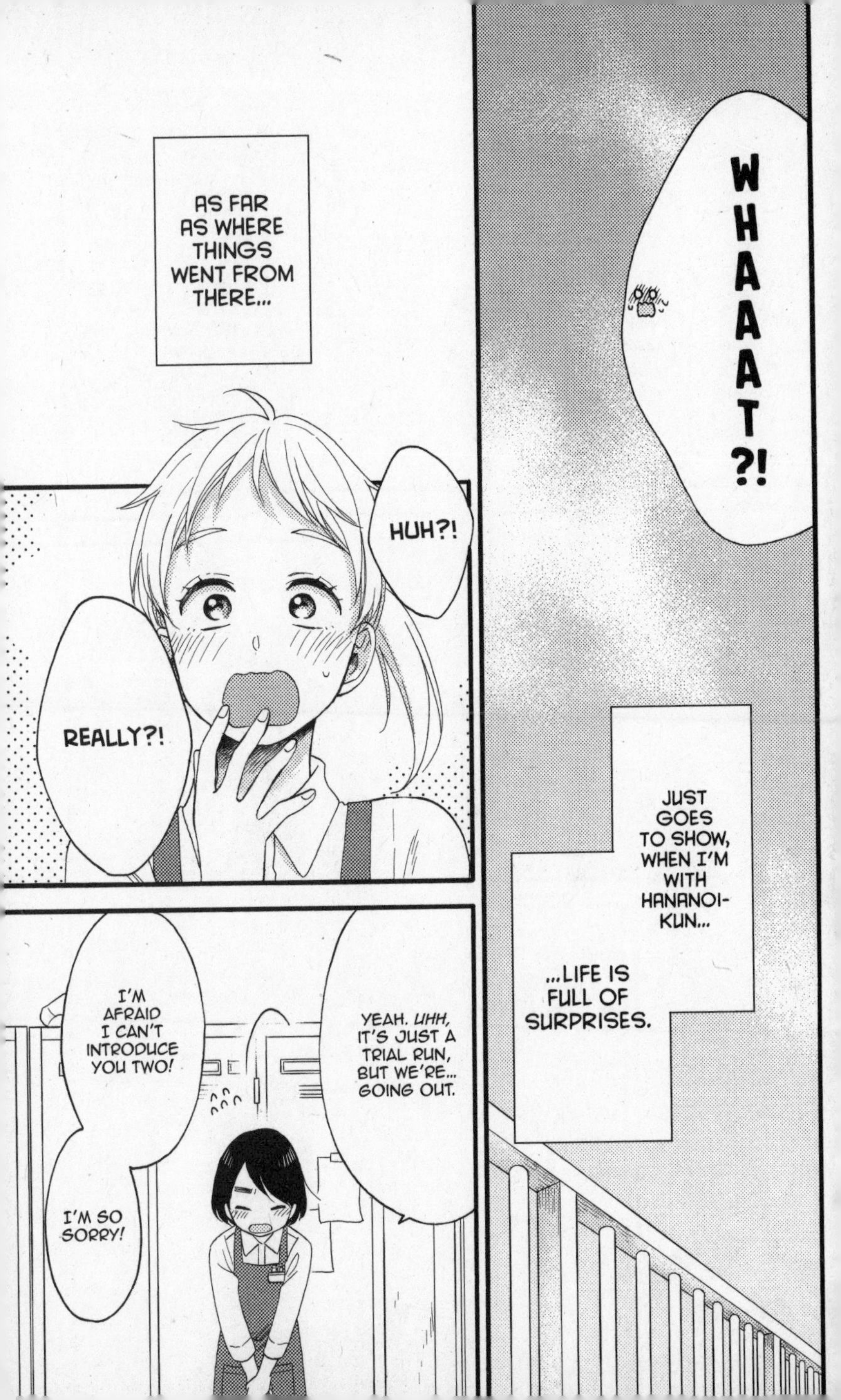
WHAAAT?!
JUST GOES TO SHOW, WHEN I'M WITH HANANOI-KUN...
...LIFE IS FULL OF SURPRISES.
AS FAR AS WHERE THINGS WENT FROM THERE...
HUH?!
REALLY?!
YEAH. *UHH,* IT'S JUST A TRIAL RUN, BUT WE'RE... GOING OUT.
I'M AFRAID I CAN'T INTRODUCE YOU TWO!
I'M SO SORRY!

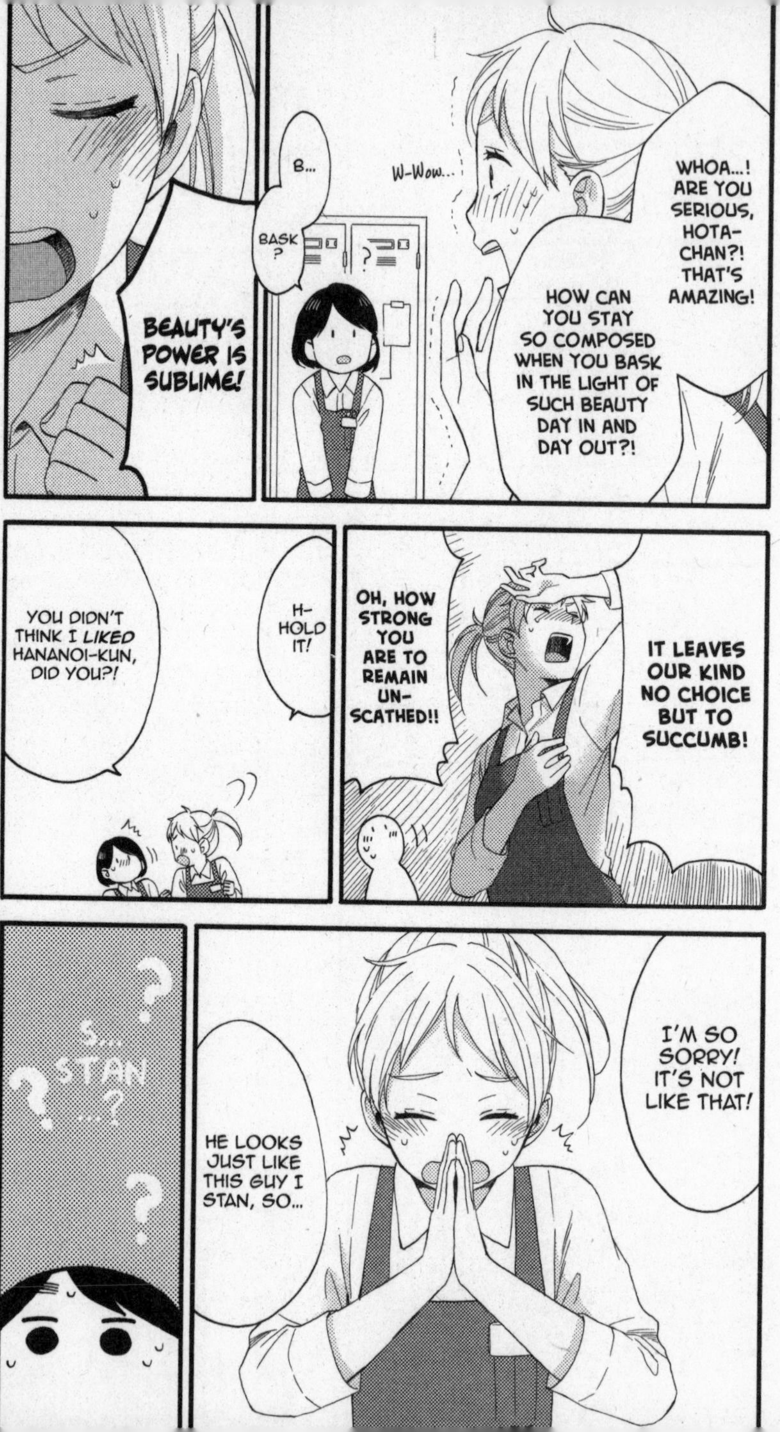
WHOA...! ARE YOU SERIOUS, HOTA-CHAN?! THAT'S AMAZING!
HOW CAN YOU STAY SO COMPOSED WHEN YOU BASK IN THE LIGHT OF SUCH BEAUTY DAY IN AND DAY OUT?!
W-Wow...
B...
BASK ?
BEAUTY'S POWER IS SUBLIME!
IT LEAVES OUR KIND NO CHOICE BUT TO SUCCUMB!
OH, HOW STRONG YOU ARE TO REMAIN UN-SCATHED!!
H-HOLD IT!
YOU DIDN'T THINK I *LIKED* HANANOI-KUN, DID YOU?!
I'M SO SORRY! IT'S NOT LIKE THAT!
HE LOOKS JUST LIKE THIS GUY I STAN, SO...
S... STAN ...?

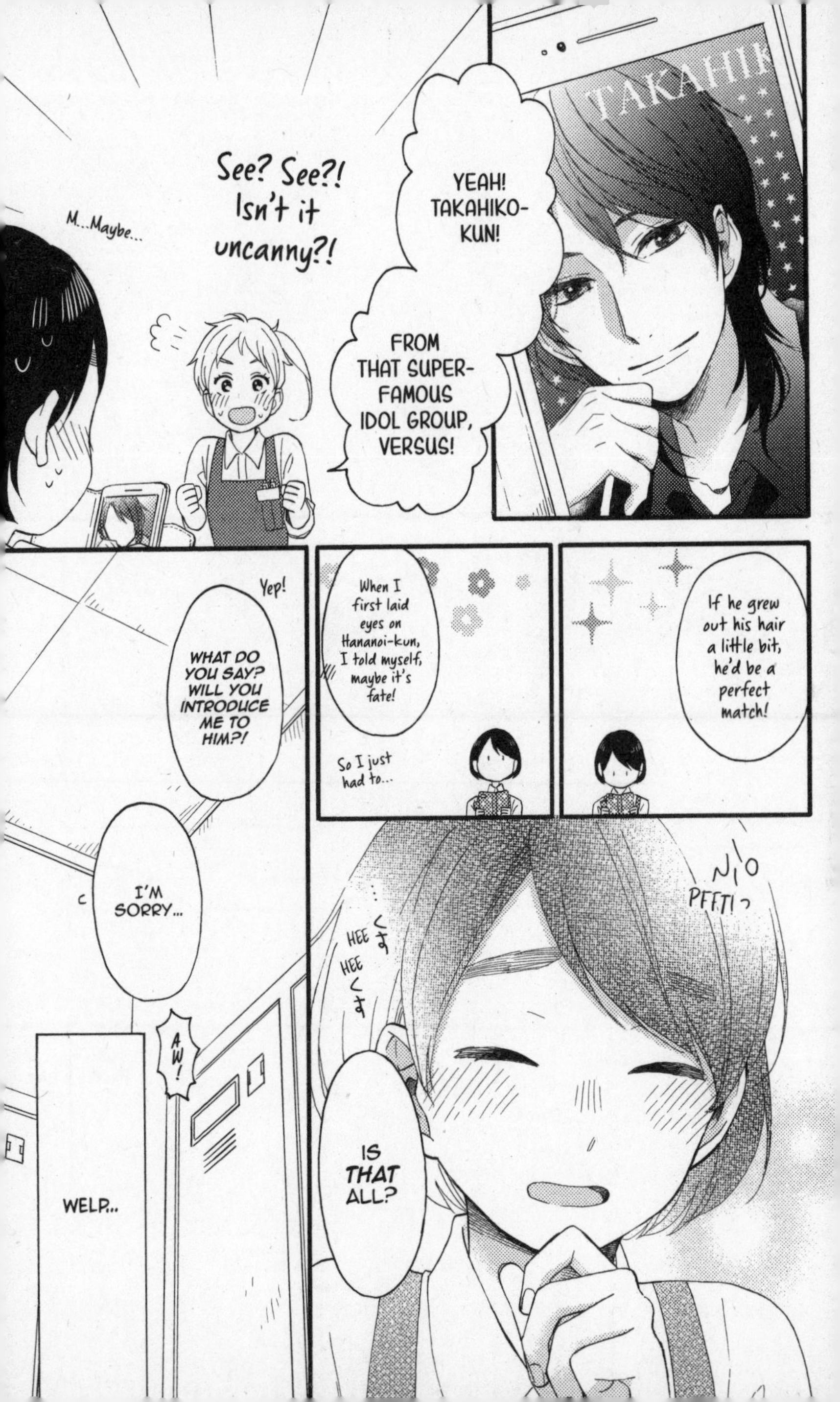
YEAH! TAKAHIKO-KUN!
FROM THAT SUPER-FAMOUS IDOL GROUP, VERSUS!
See? See?! Isn't it uncanny?!
M...Maybe...
If he grew out his hair a little bit, he'd be a perfect match!
When I first laid eyes on Hananoi-kun, I told myself, maybe it's fate!
So I just had to...
PFFT!
HEE
HEE
IS THAT ALL?
Yep!
WHAT DO YOU SAY? WILL YOU INTRODUCE ME TO HIM?!
I'M SORRY...
AW!
WELP...

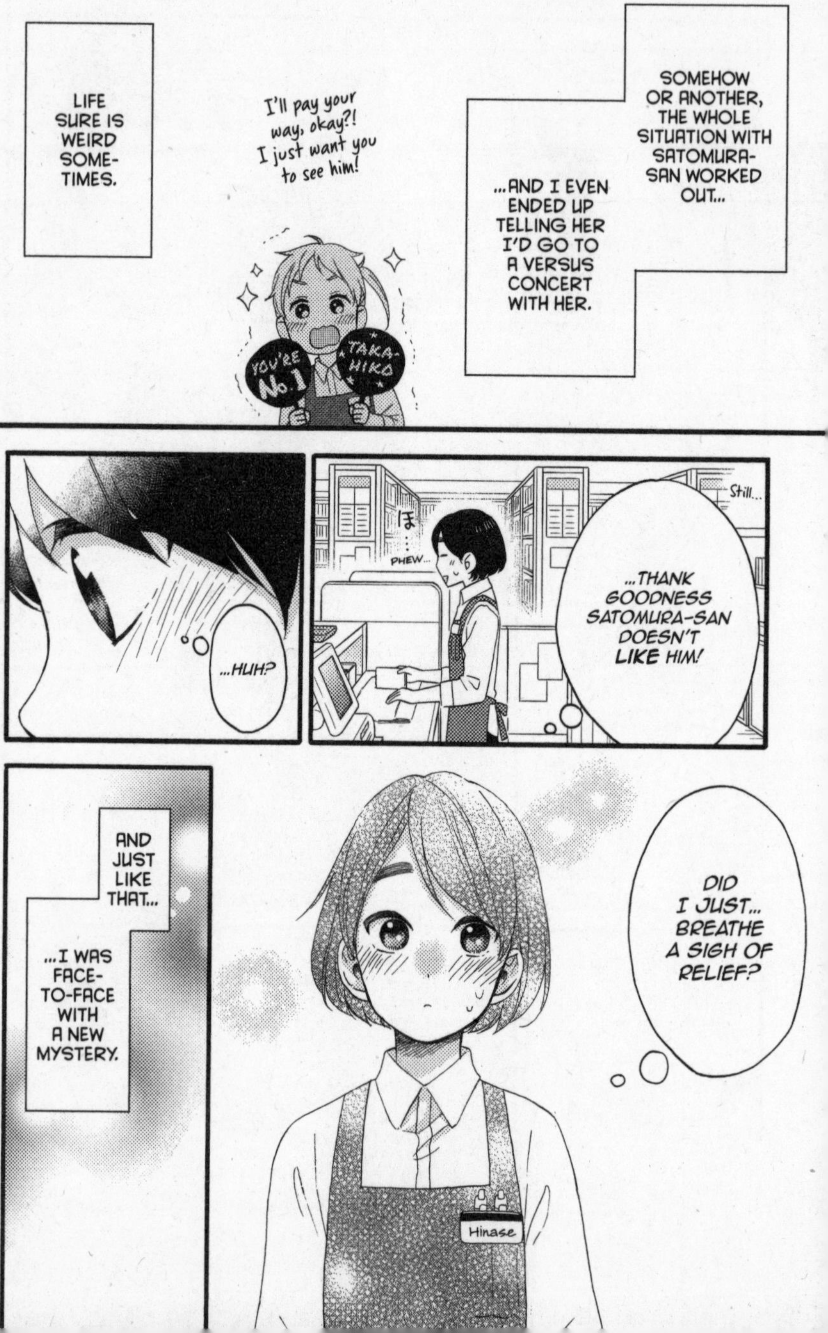
SOMEHOW OR ANOTHER, THE WHOLE SITUATION WITH SATOMURA-SAN WORKED OUT...
...AND I EVEN ENDED UP TELLING HER I'D GO TO A VERSUS CONCERT WITH HER.
I'll pay your way, okay?! I just want you to see him!
TAKA-HIKO
YOU'RE No.1
LIFE SURE IS WEIRD SOME-TIMES.
ほ…
PHEW...
Still...
...THANK GOODNESS SATOMURA-SAN DOESN'T **LIKE** HIM!
...HUH?
DID I JUST... BREATHE A SIGH OF RELIEF?
Hinase
AND JUST LIKE THAT...
...I WAS FACE-TO-FACE WITH A NEW MYSTERY.

Far, Far Away (1)

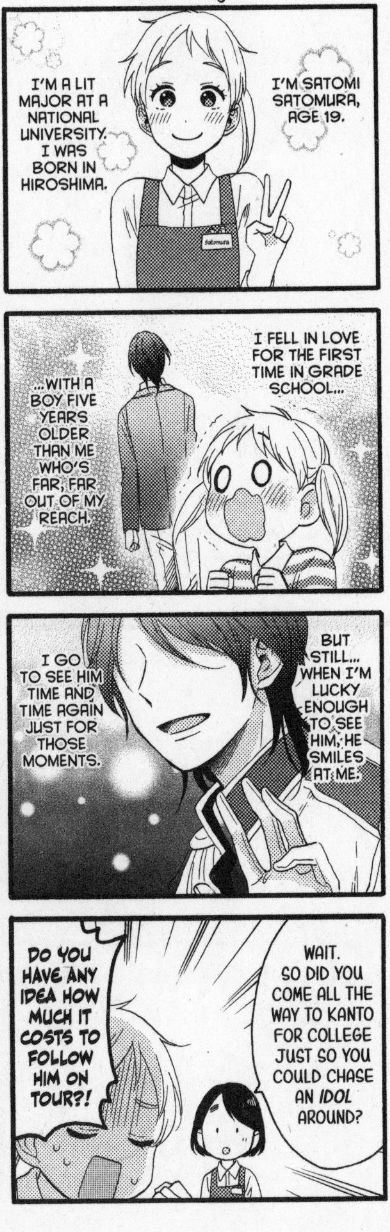

I'M SATOMI SATOMURA, AGE 19.
I'M A LIT MAJOR AT A NATIONAL UNIVERSITY. I WAS BORN IN HIROSHIMA.
Satomura
I FELL IN LOVE FOR THE FIRST TIME IN GRADE SCHOOL...
...WITH A BOY FIVE YEARS OLDER THAN ME WHO'S FAR, FAR OUT OF MY REACH.
BUT STILL... WHEN I'M LUCKY ENOUGH TO SEE HIM, HE SMILES AT ME.
I GO TO SEE HIM TIME AND TIME AGAIN JUST FOR THOSE MOMENTS.
WAIT. SO DID YOU COME ALL THE WAY TO KANTO FOR COLLEGE JUST SO YOU COULD CHASE AN *IDOL* AROUND?
DO YOU HAVE ANY IDEA HOW MUCH IT COSTS TO FOLLOW HIM ON TOUR?!

Far, Far Away (2)

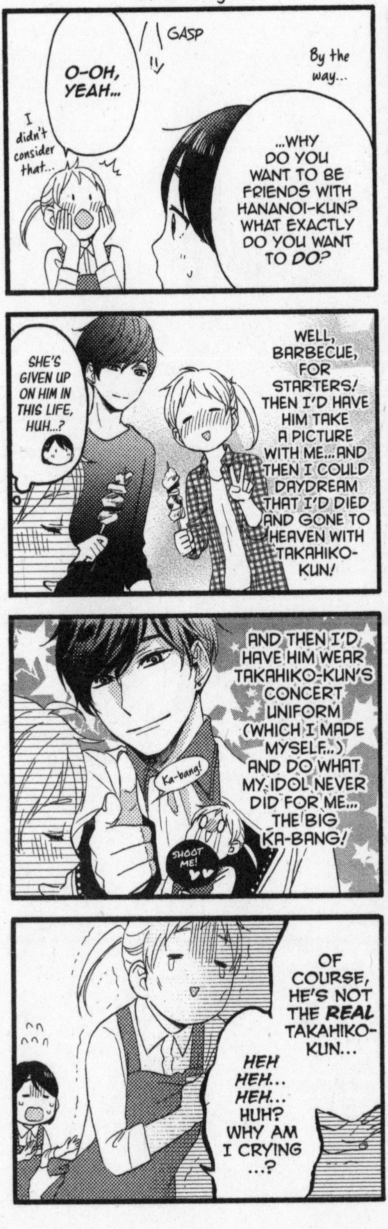

By the way...
...WHY DO YOU WANT TO BE FRIENDS WITH HANANOI-KUN? WHAT EXACTLY DO YOU WANT TO *DO*?
GASP
O-OH, YEAH...
I didn't consider that...
WELL, BARBECUE, FOR STARTERS! THEN I'D HAVE HIM TAKE A PICTURE WITH ME... AND THEN I COULD DAYDREAM THAT I'D DIED AND GONE TO HEAVEN WITH TAKAHIKO-KUN!
SHE'S GIVEN UP ON HIM IN THIS LIFE, HUH...?
AND THEN I'D HAVE HIM WEAR TAKAHIKO-KUN'S CONCERT UNIFORM (WHICH I MADE MYSELF...) AND DO WHAT MY IDOL NEVER DID FOR ME... THE BIG KA-BANG!
Ka-bang!
SHOOT ME!
OF COURSE, HE'S NOT THE ***REAL*** TAKAHIKO-KUN...
HEH HEH... HEH... HUH? WHY AM I CRYING ...?

How Was It?

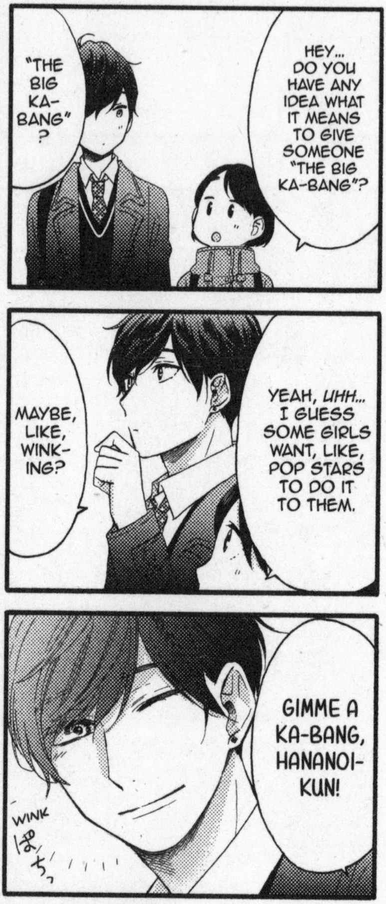
HEY... DO YOU HAVE ANY IDEA WHAT IT MEANS TO GIVE SOMEONE "THE BIG KA-BANG"?
"THE BIG KA-BANG" ?
YEAH, *UHH*... I GUESS SOME GIRLS WANT, LIKE, POP STARS TO DO IT TO THEM.
MAYBE, LIKE, WINKING?
GIMME A KA-BANG, HANANOI-KUN!
WINK
ぱちっ
WELL, HOTARU-CHAN? HOW WAS IT...?
GULP
きゅ…
THAT IS... PAINFULLY DIFFICULT TO PUT INTO WORDS.

How's This?

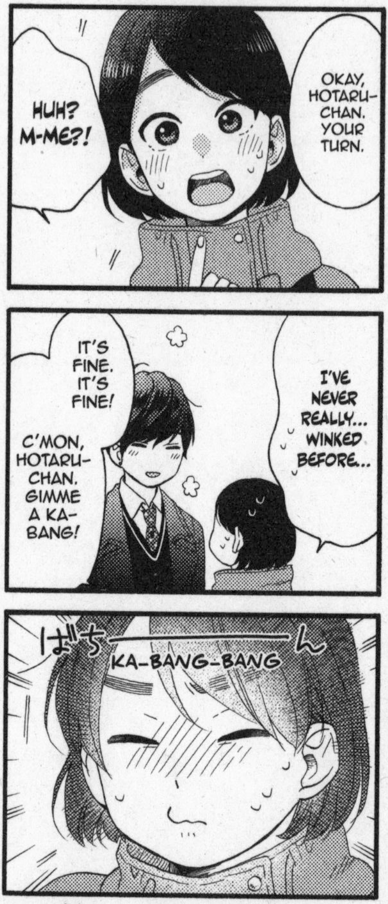
OKAY, HOTARU-CHAN. YOUR TURN.
HUH? M-ME?!
I'VE NEVER REALLY... WINKED BEFORE...
IT'S FINE. IT'S FINE!
C'MON, HOTARU-CHAN. GIMME A KA-BANG!
ばちーーーん
KA-BANG-BANG
CUTE!!
ズキュ
FWOOSH
HANA-NOI-KUN ?!

He couldn't hold back...

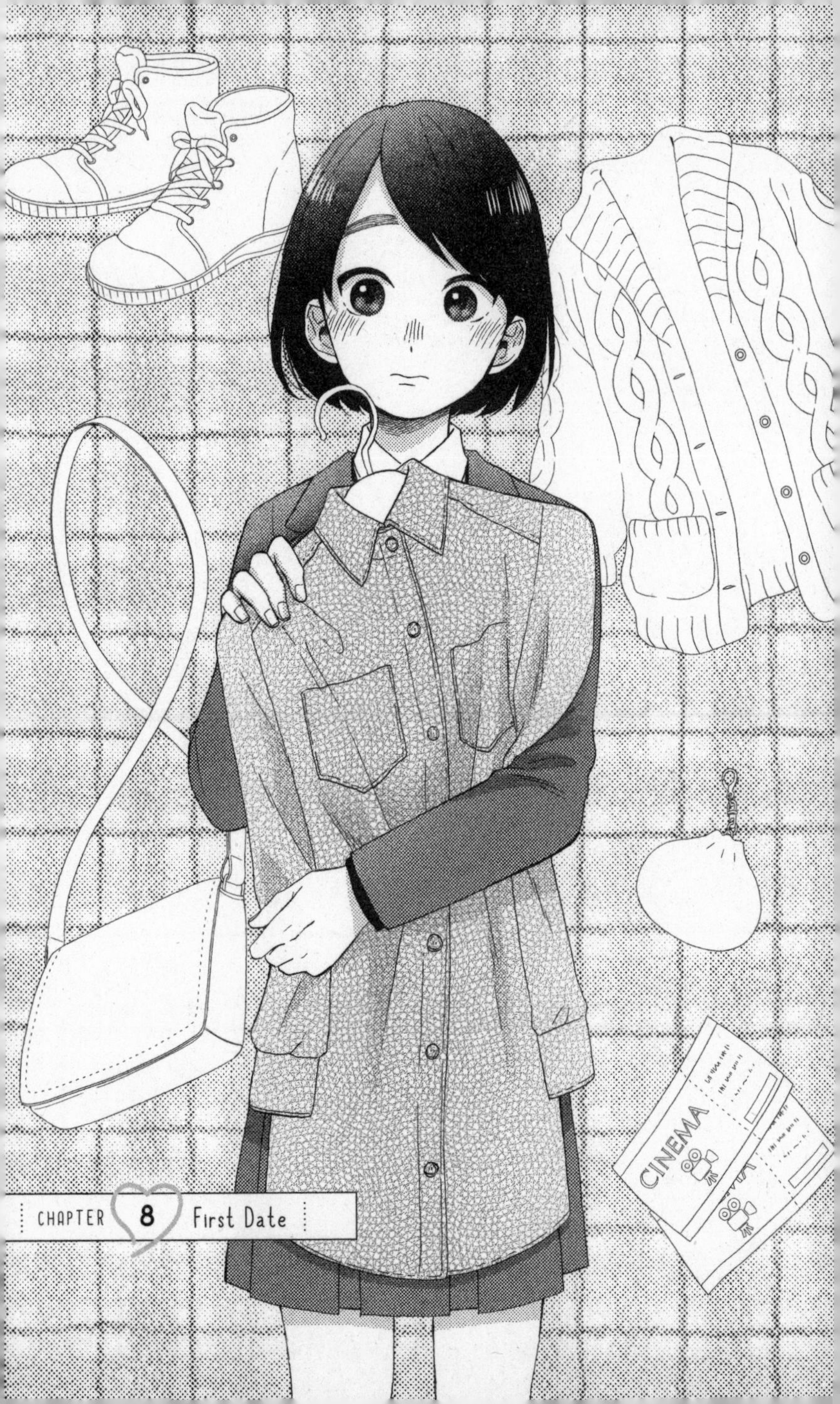
CHAPTER 8 First Date
CINEMA

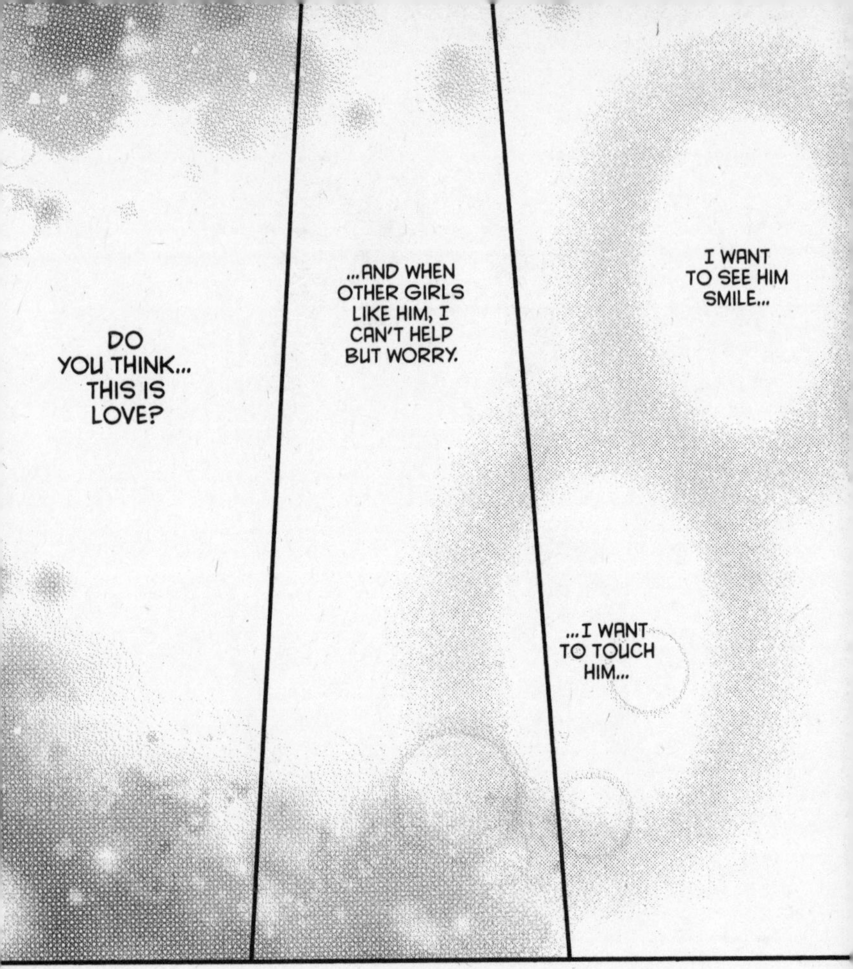
I WANT TO SEE HIM SMILE...
...I WANT TO TOUCH HIM...
...AND WHEN OTHER GIRLS LIKE HIM, I CAN'T HELP BUT WORRY.
DO YOU THINK... THIS IS LOVE?

A Condition Called Love

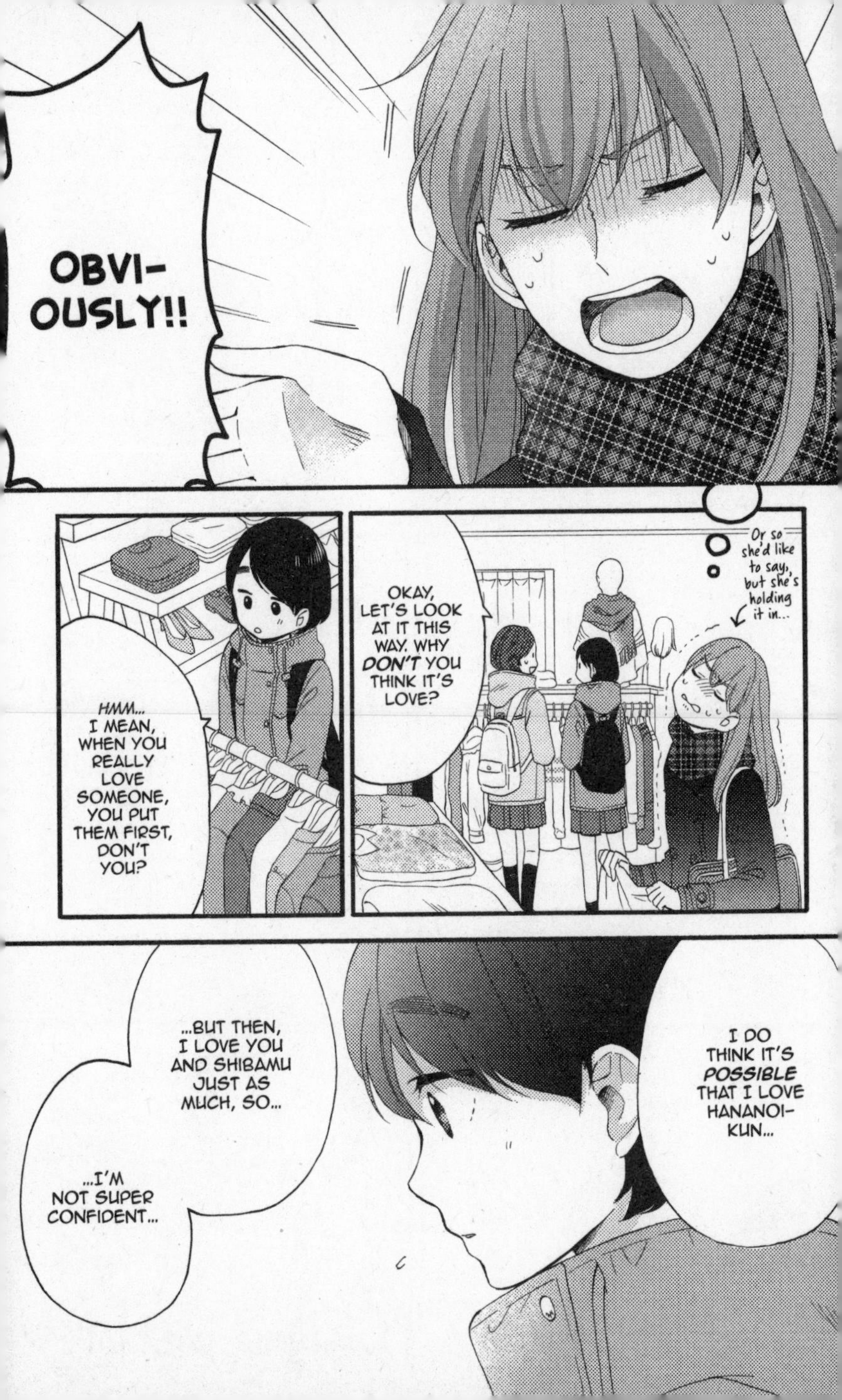
OBVI-OUSLY!!
Or so she'd like to say, but she's holding it in...
OKAY, LET'S LOOK AT IT THIS WAY. WHY *DON'T* YOU THINK IT'S LOVE?
HMM... I MEAN, WHEN YOU REALLY LOVE SOMEONE, YOU PUT THEM FIRST, DON'T YOU?
I DO THINK IT'S *POSSIBLE* THAT I LOVE HANANOI-KUN...
...BUT THEN, I LOVE YOU AND SHIBAMU JUST AS MUCH, SO...
...I'M NOT SUPER CONFIDENT...

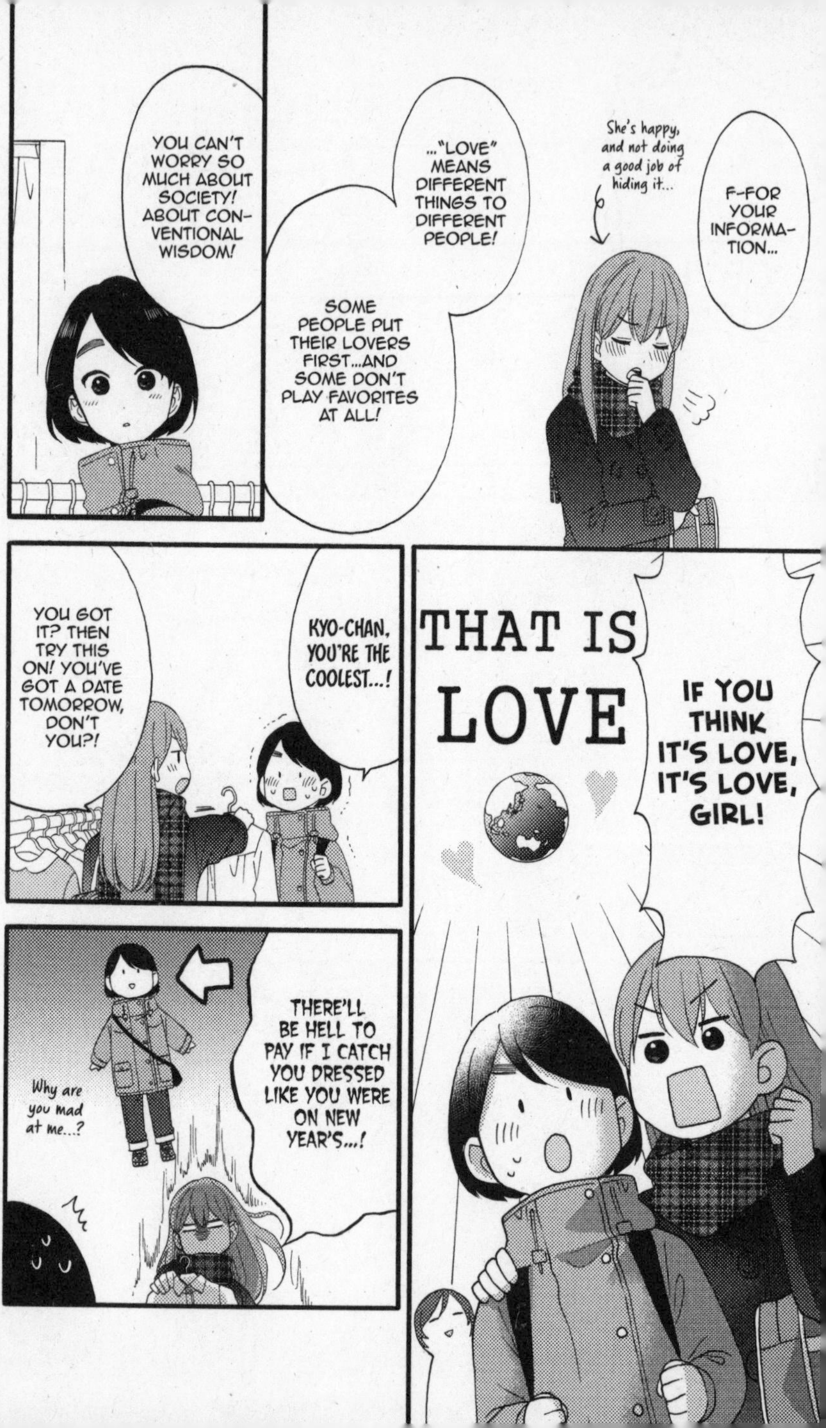
F-FOR YOUR INFORMATION...
She's happy, and not doing a good job of hiding it...
..."LOVE" MEANS DIFFERENT THINGS TO DIFFERENT PEOPLE!
SOME PEOPLE PUT THEIR LOVERS FIRST...AND SOME DON'T PLAY FAVORITES AT ALL!
YOU CAN'T WORRY SO MUCH ABOUT SOCIETY! ABOUT CON-VENTIONAL WISDOM!
THAT IS LOVE
IF YOU THINK IT'S LOVE, IT'S LOVE, GIRL!
KYO-CHAN, YOU'RE THE COOLEST...!
YOU GOT IT? THEN TRY THIS ON! YOU'VE GOT A DATE TOMORROW, DON'T YOU?!
THERE'LL BE HELL TO PAY IF I CATCH YOU DRESSED LIKE YOU WERE ON NEW YEAR'S...!
Why are you mad at me...?

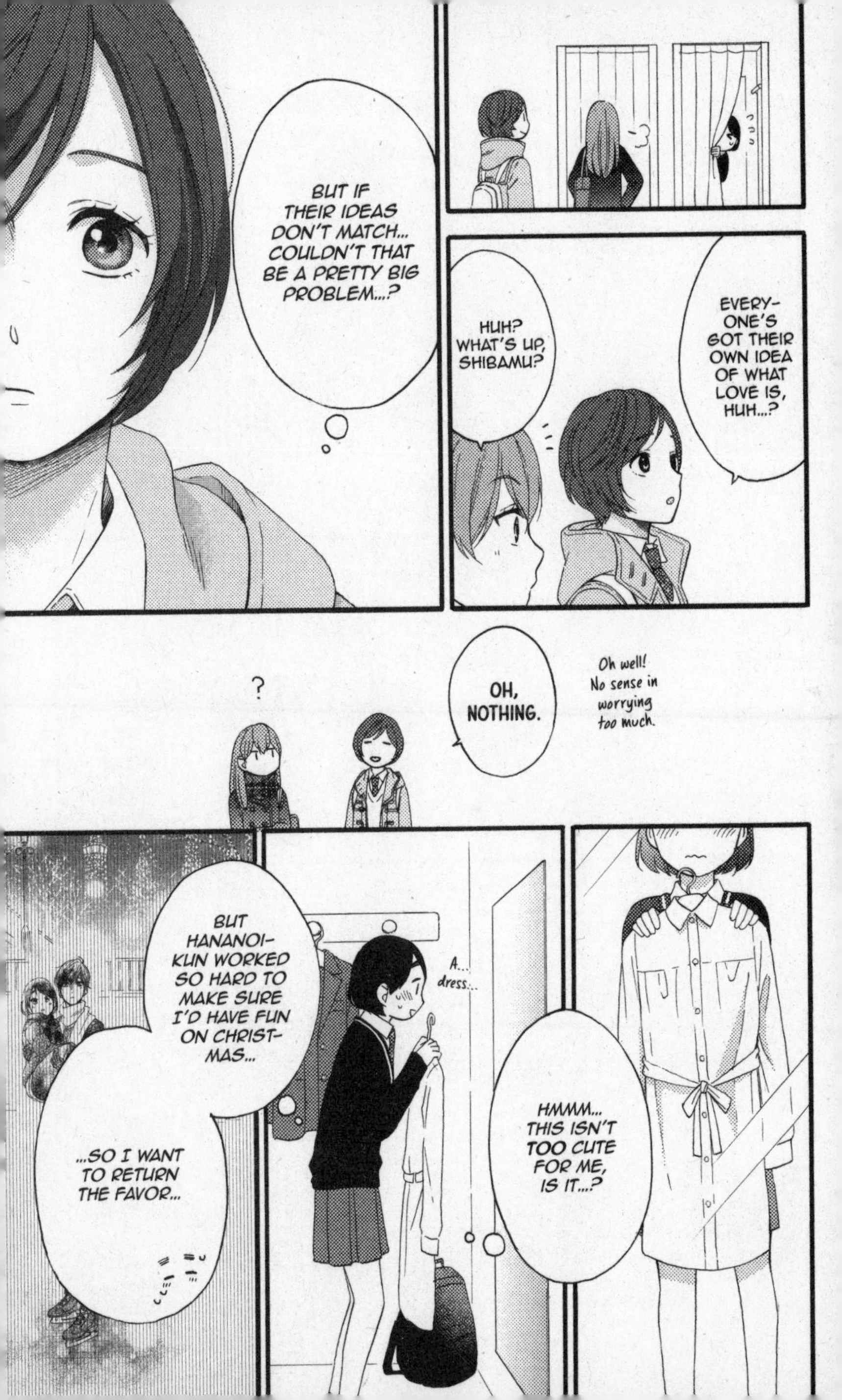
EVERYONE'S GOT THEIR OWN IDEA OF WHAT LOVE IS, HUH...?
HUH? WHAT'S UP, SHIBAMU?
BUT IF THEIR IDEAS DON'T MATCH... COULDN'T THAT BE A PRETTY BIG PROBLEM...?
Oh well! No sense in worrying too much.
OH, NOTHING.
?
HMMM... THIS ISN'T TOO CUTE FOR ME, IS IT...?
A... dress...
BUT HANANOI-KUN WORKED SO HARD TO MAKE SURE I'D HAVE FUN ON CHRISTMAS...
...SO I WANT TO RETURN THE FAVOR...

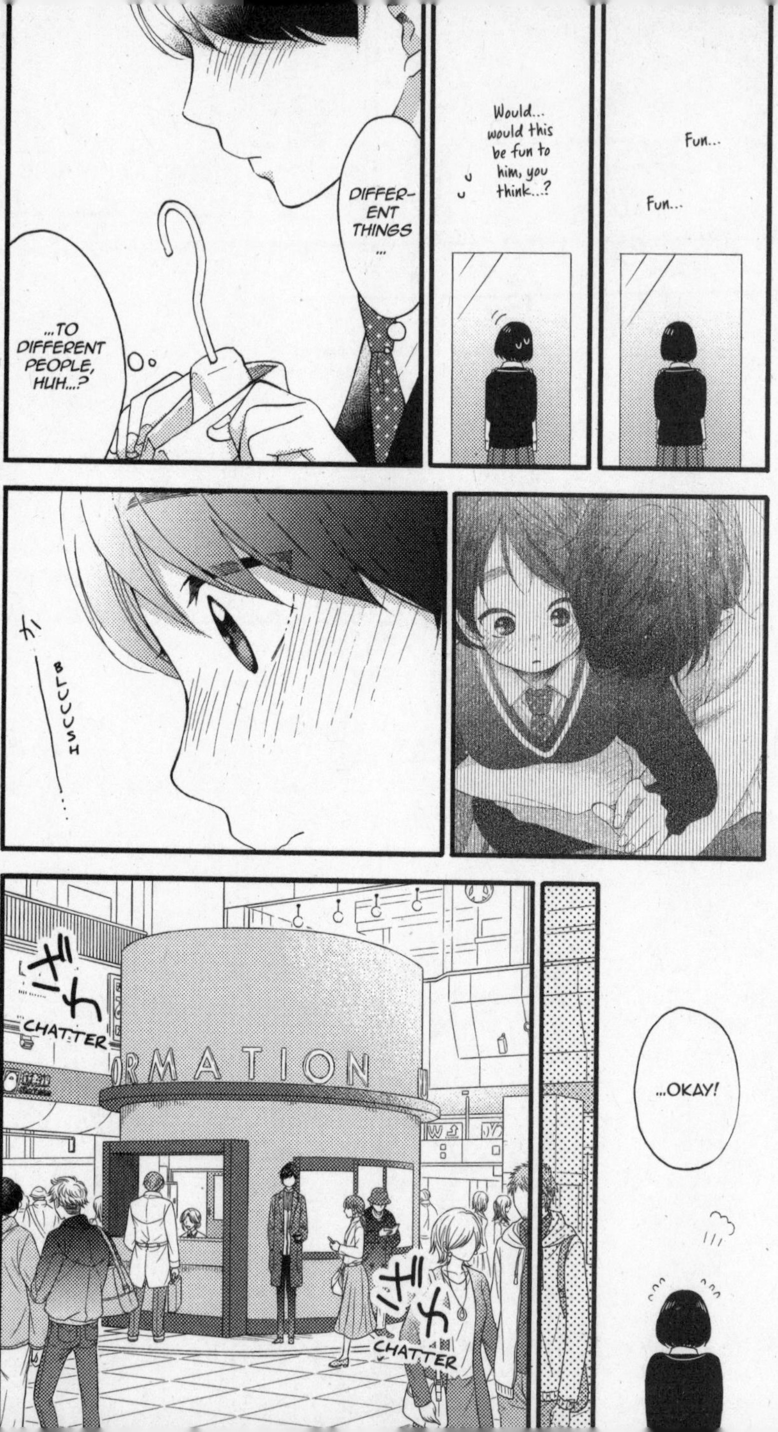

Fun...
Fun...
Would... would this be fun to him, you think...?
DIFFERENT THINGS...
...TO DIFFERENT PEOPLE, HUH...?
か
BLUUUSH
...OKAY!
ざわ
CHATTER
ざわ
CHATTER

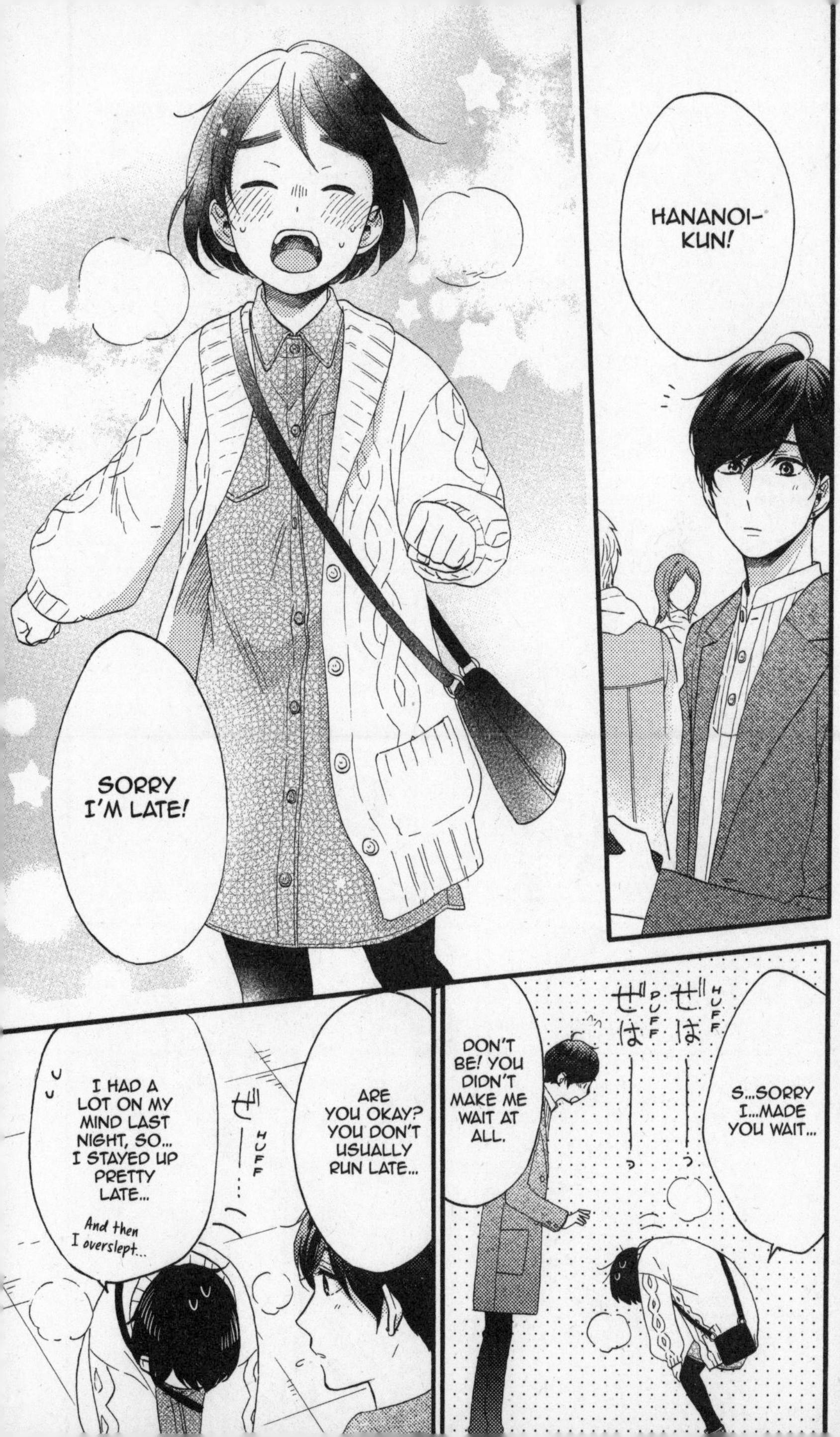
HANANOI-KUN!
SORRY I'M LATE!
ぜは──っ HUFF
ぜは──っ PUFF
S...SORRY I...MADE YOU WAIT...
DON'T BE! YOU DIDN'T MAKE ME WAIT AT ALL.
ARE YOU OKAY? YOU DON'T USUALLY RUN LATE...
ぜー… HUFF
I HAD A LOT ON MY MIND LAST NIGHT, SO... I STAYED UP PRETTY LATE...
And then I overslept...

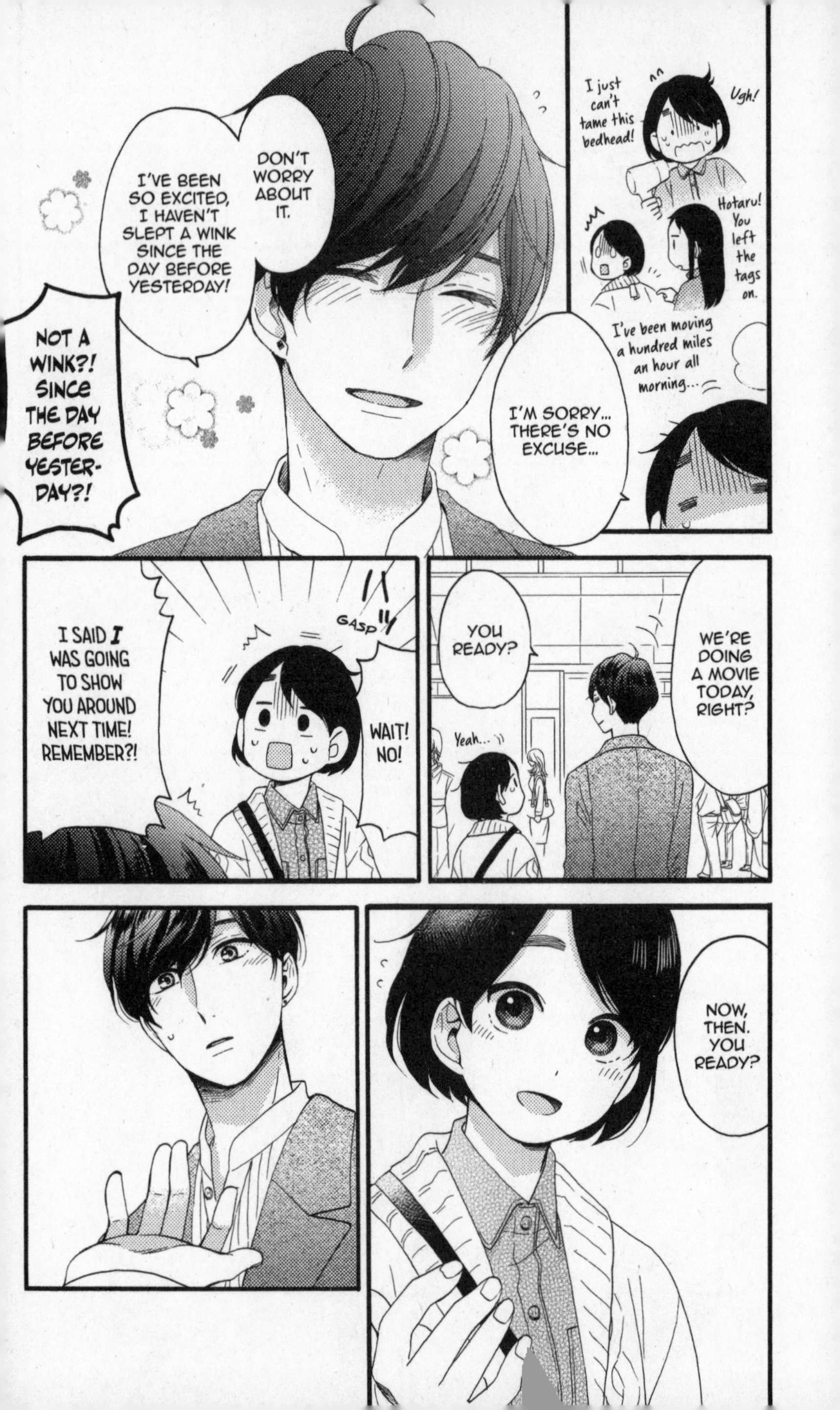
I just can't tame this bedhead!
Ugh!
Hotaru! You left the tags on.
I've been moving a hundred miles an hour all morning...
I'M SORRY... THERE'S NO EXCUSE...
DON'T WORRY ABOUT IT.
I'VE BEEN SO EXCITED, I HAVEN'T SLEPT A WINK SINCE THE DAY BEFORE YESTERDAY!
NOT A WINK?! SINCE THE DAY BEFORE YESTER-DAY?!
WE'RE DOING A MOVIE TODAY, RIGHT?
YOU READY?
Yeah...
GASP
WAIT! NO!
I SAID I WAS GOING TO SHOW YOU AROUND NEXT TIME! REMEMBER?!
NOW, THEN. YOU READY?

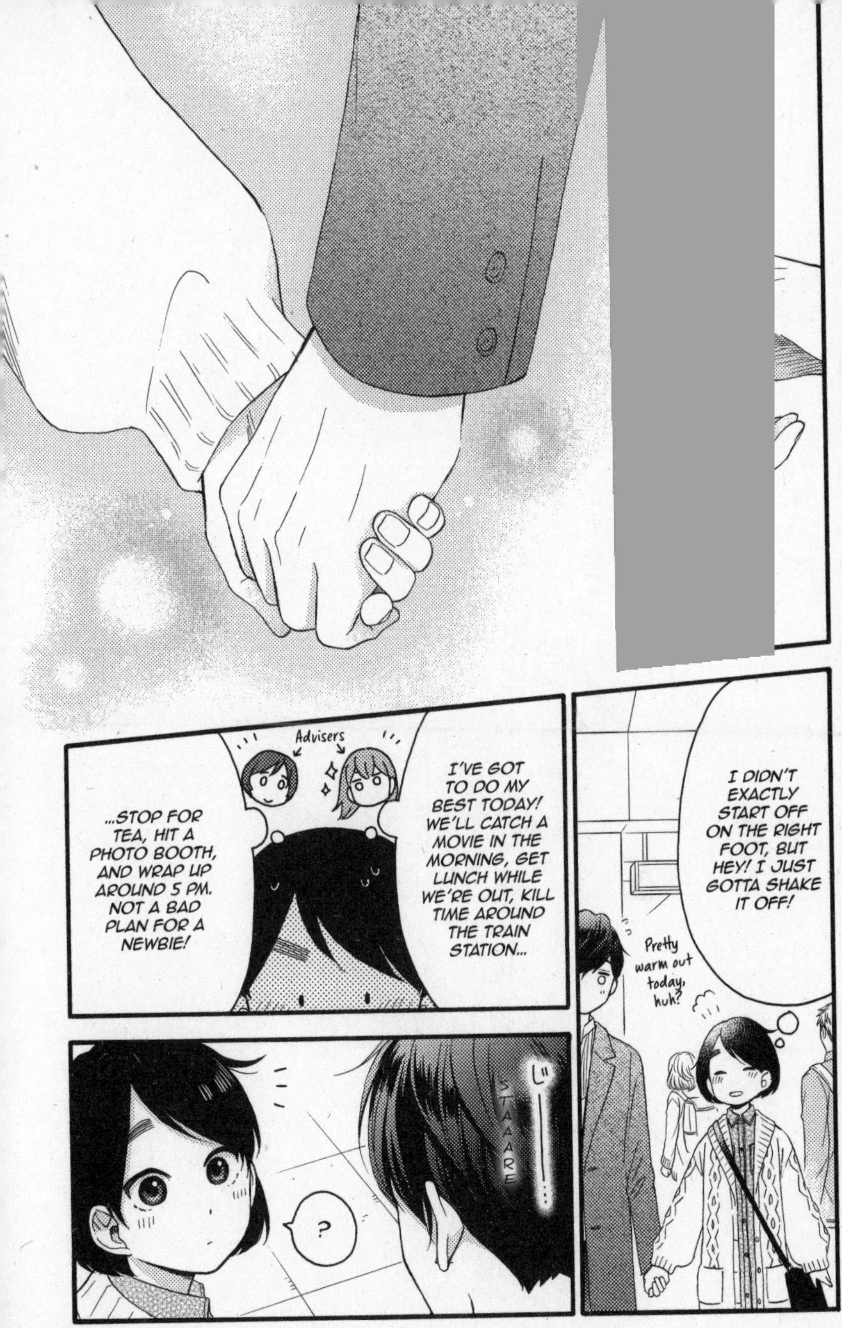

I DIDN'T EXACTLY START OFF ON THE RIGHT FOOT, BUT HEY! I JUST GOTTA SHAKE IT OFF!
Pretty warm out today, huh?
I'VE GOT TO DO MY BEST TODAY! WE'LL CATCH A MOVIE IN THE MORNING, GET LUNCH WHILE WE'RE OUT, KILL TIME AROUND THE TRAIN STATION...
Advisers
...STOP FOR TEA, HIT A PHOTO BOOTH, AND WRAP UP AROUND 5 PM. NOT A BAD PLAN FOR A NEWBIE!
じ
STAAARE
?

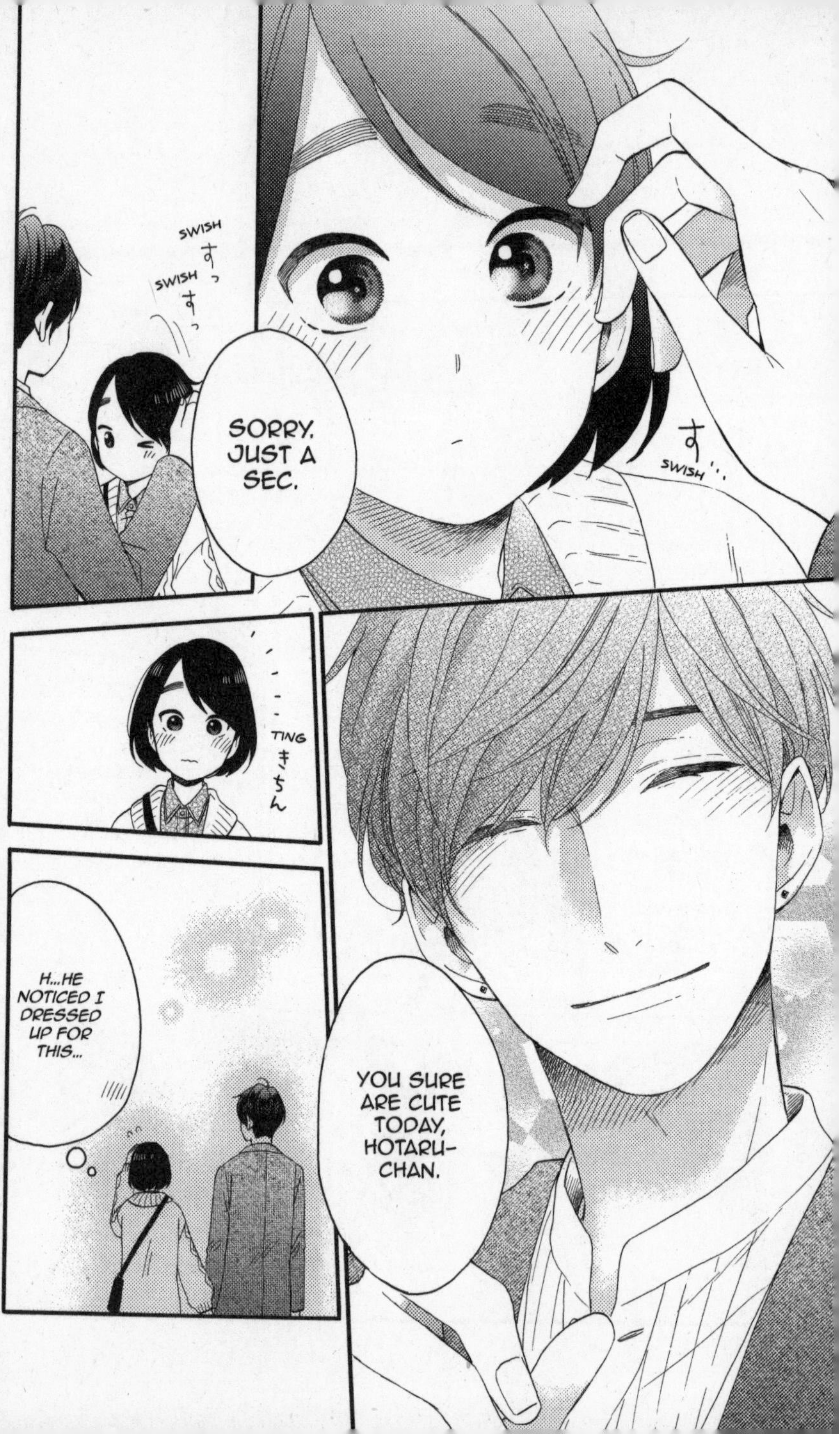
SORRY. JUST A SEC.
す SWISH
SWISH すっ
SWISH すっ
YOU SURE ARE CUTE TODAY, HOTARU-CHAN.
TING きちん
H...HE NOTICED I DRESSED UP FOR THIS...

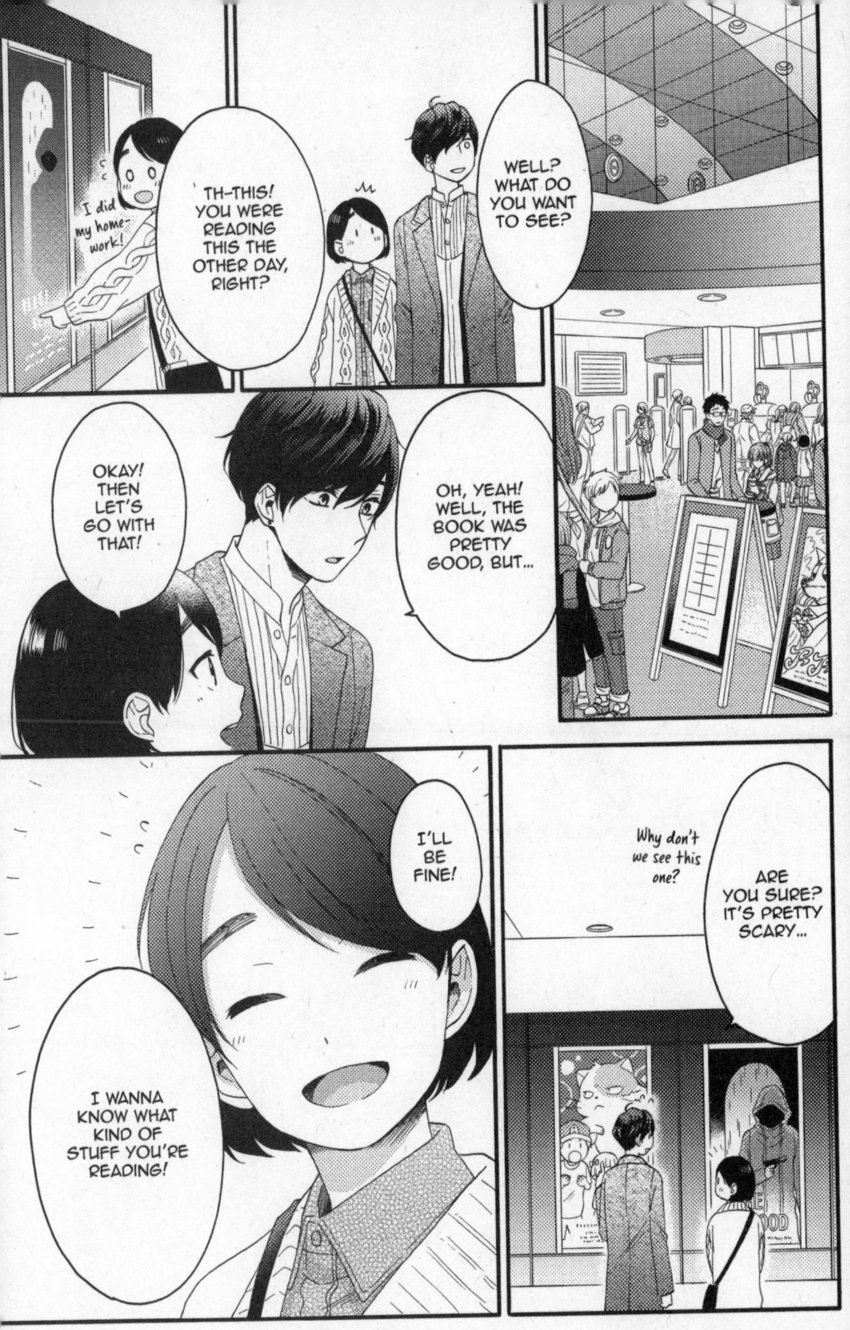
WELL? WHAT DO YOU WANT TO SEE?
TH-THIS! YOU WERE READING THIS THE OTHER DAY, RIGHT?
I did my home-work!
OH, YEAH! WELL, THE BOOK WAS PRETTY GOOD, BUT...
OKAY! THEN LET'S GO WITH THAT!
Why don't we see this one?
ARE YOU SURE? IT'S PRETTY SCARY...
I'LL BE FINE!
I WANNA KNOW WHAT KIND OF STUFF YOU'RE READING!

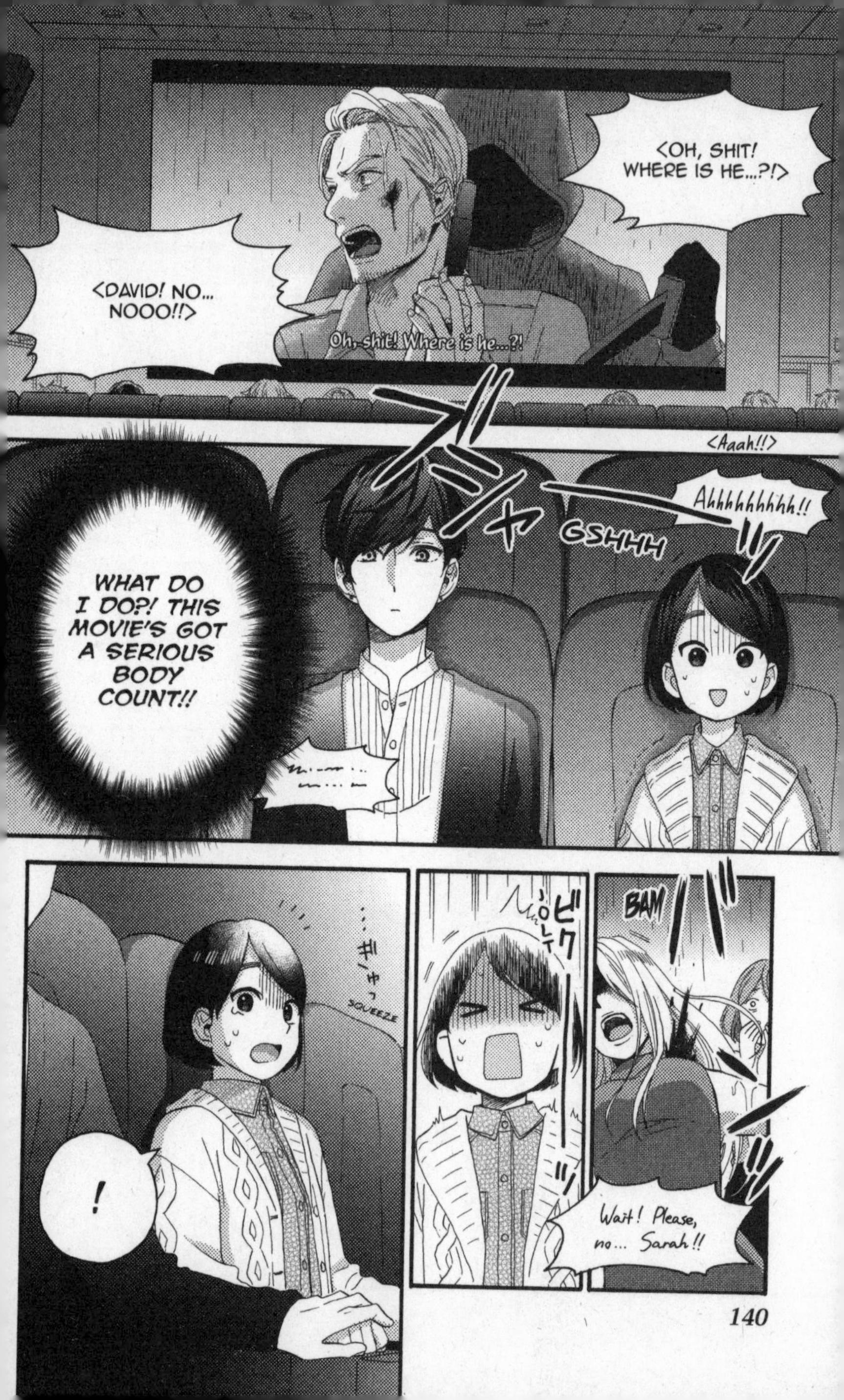
<OH, SHIT! WHERE IS HE...?!>
<DAVID! NO... NOOO!!>
Oh, shit! Where is he...?!
<Aaah!!>
Ahhhhhhhhh!!
GSHHH
WHAT DO I DO?! THIS MOVIE'S GOT A SERIOUS BODY COUNT!!
BAM
Wait! Please, no... Sarah!!
SQUEEZE
!

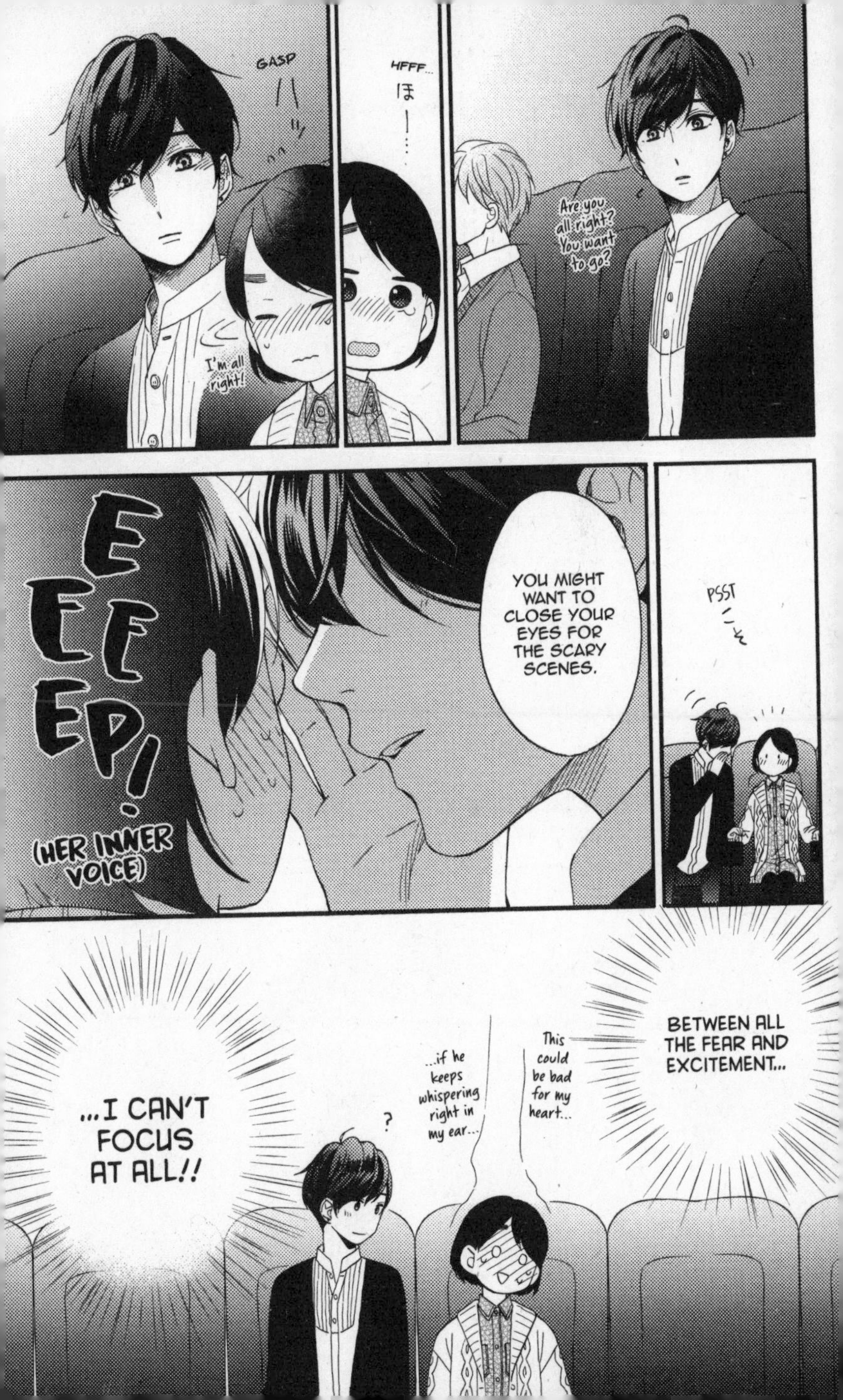
Are you all right? You want to go?
HFFF...
ほー…
GASP
ハッ
I'm all right!
PSST
こそ
YOU MIGHT WANT TO CLOSE YOUR EYES FOR THE SCARY SCENES.
EEEEP!
(HER INNER VOICE)
BETWEEN ALL THE FEAR AND EXCITEMENT...
This could be bad for my heart...
...if he keeps whispering right in my ear...
?
...I CAN'T FOCUS AT ALL!!

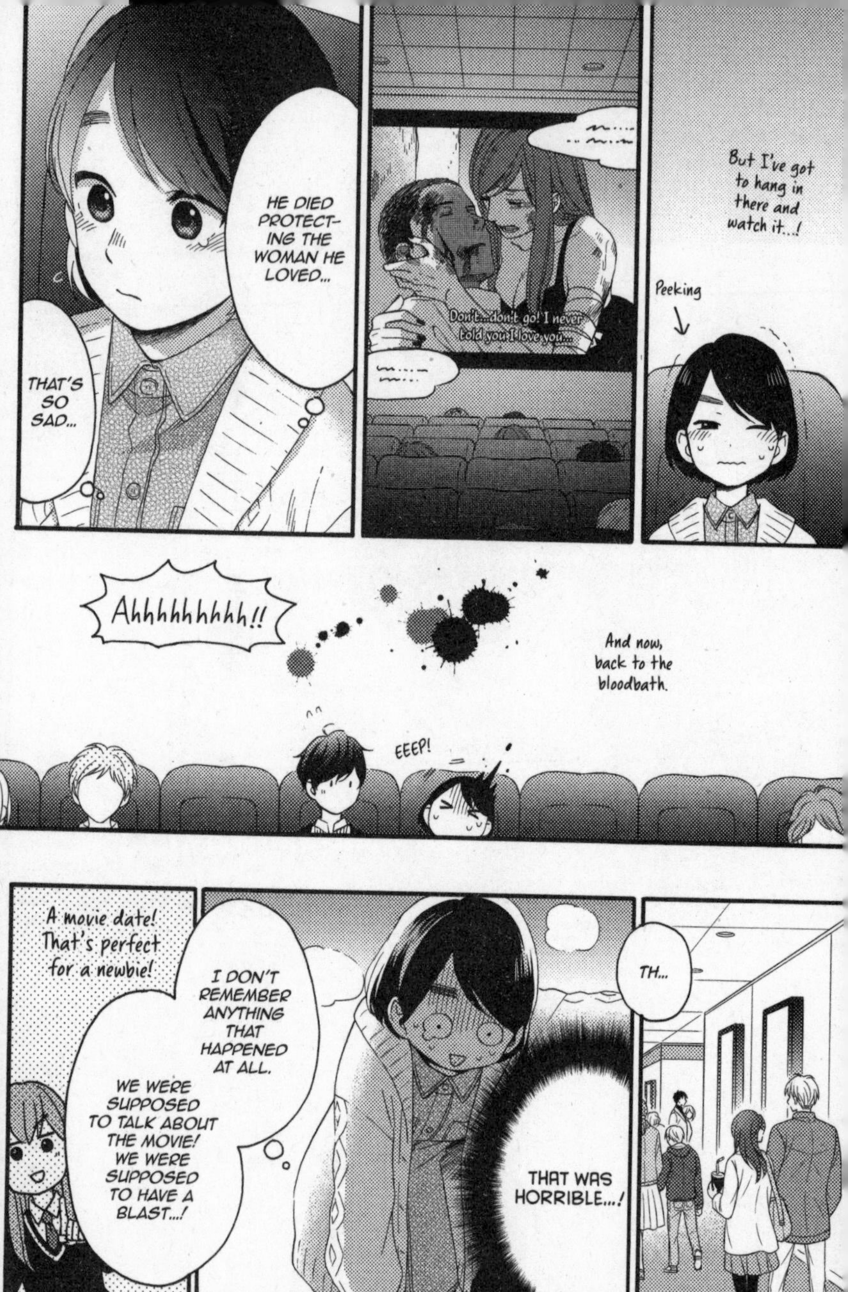

But I've got to hang in there and watch it...!
Peeking
Don't...don't go! I never told you I love you...
HE DIED PROTECTING THE WOMAN HE LOVED...
THAT'S SO SAD...
And now, back to the bloodbath.
Ahhhhhhhhh!!
EEEP!
TH...
THAT WAS HORRIBLE...!
I DON'T REMEMBER ANYTHING THAT HAPPENED AT ALL.
WE WERE SUPPOSED TO TALK ABOUT THE MOVIE! WE WERE SUPPOSED TO HAVE A BLAST...!
A movie date! That's perfect for a newbie!

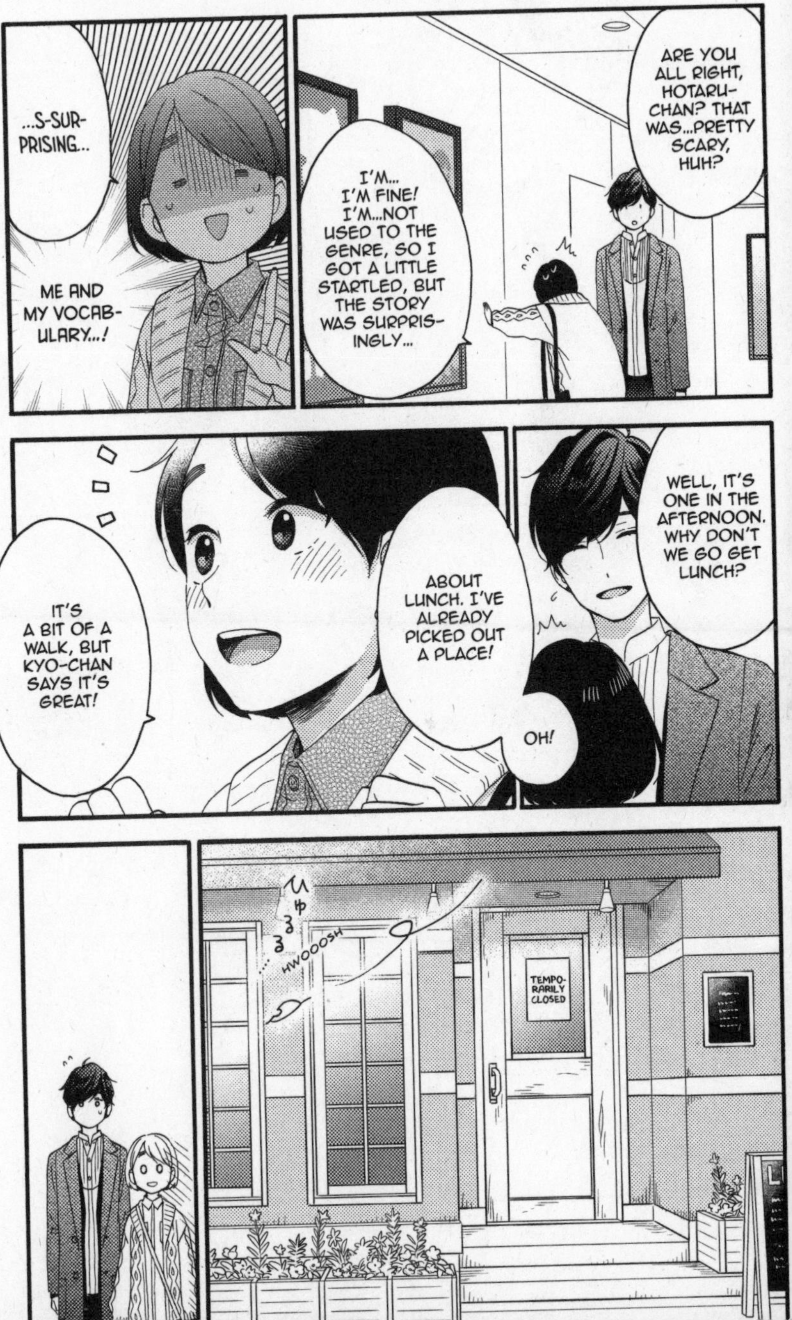
ARE YOU ALL RIGHT, HOTARU-CHAN? THAT WAS...PRETTY SCARY, HUH?
I'M... I'M FINE! I'M...NOT USED TO THE GENRE, SO I GOT A LITTLE STARTLED, BUT THE STORY WAS SURPRIS-INGLY...
...S-SUR-PRISING...
ME AND MY VOCAB-ULARY...!
WELL, IT'S ONE IN THE AFTERNOON. WHY DON'T WE GO GET LUNCH?
OH!
ABOUT LUNCH. I'VE ALREADY PICKED OUT A PLACE!
IT'S A BIT OF A WALK, BUT KYO-CHAN SAYS IT'S GREAT!
ひゅるる...
HWOOOSH
TEMPO-RARILY CLOSED

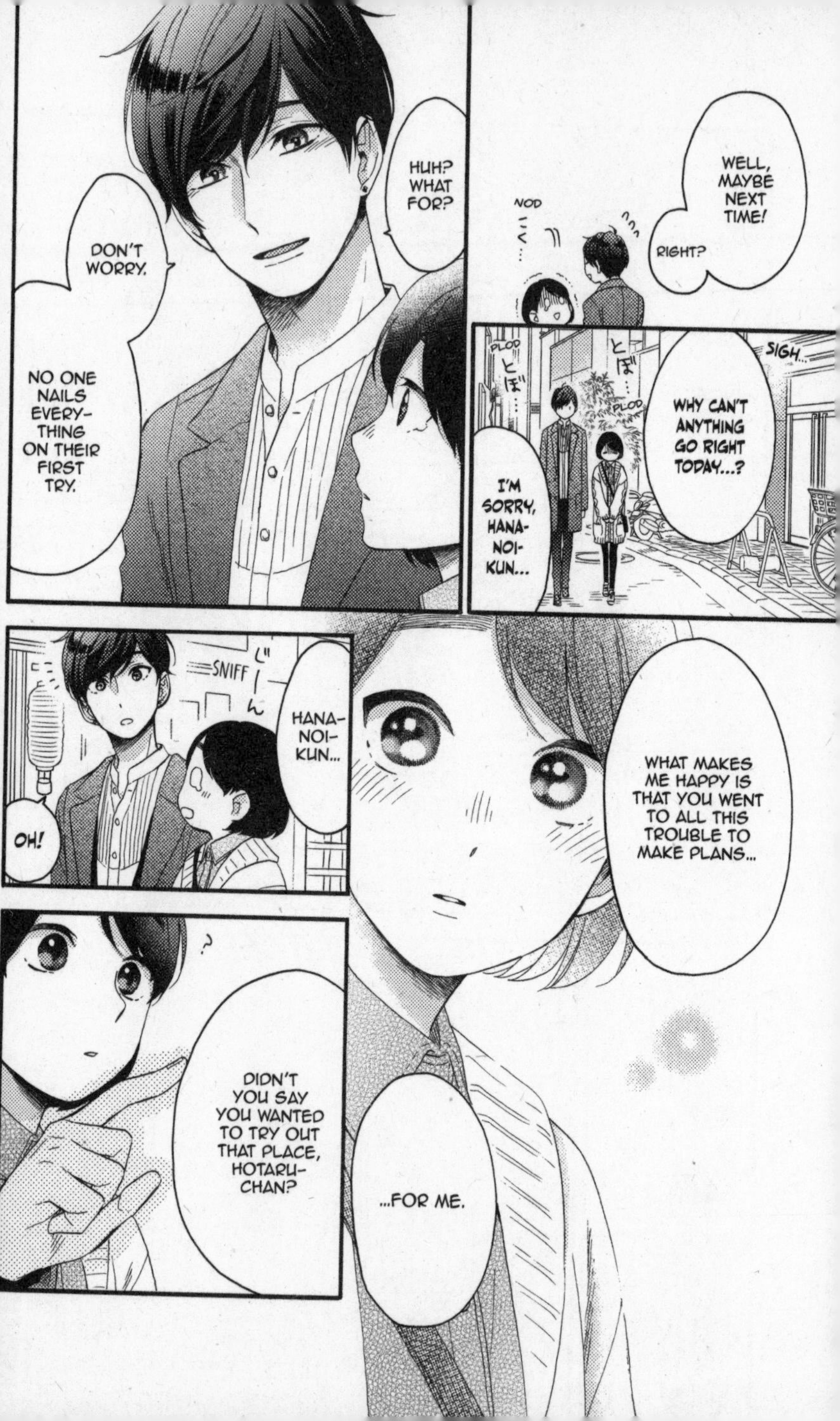

WELL, MAYBE NEXT TIME!
RIGHT?
NOD
こく…
SIGH...
WHY CAN'T ANYTHING GO RIGHT TODAY...?
PLOD
とぼ
PLOD
とぼ
I'M SORRY, HANA-NOI-KUN...
HUH? WHAT FOR?
DON'T WORRY.
NO ONE NAILS EVERY-THING ON THEIR FIRST TRY.
WHAT MAKES ME HAPPY IS THAT YOU WENT TO ALL THIS TROUBLE TO MAKE PLANS...
...FOR ME.
HANA-NOI-KUN...
SNIFF
じーん
OH!
?
DIDN'T YOU SAY YOU WANTED TO TRY OUT THAT PLACE, HOTARU-CHAN?

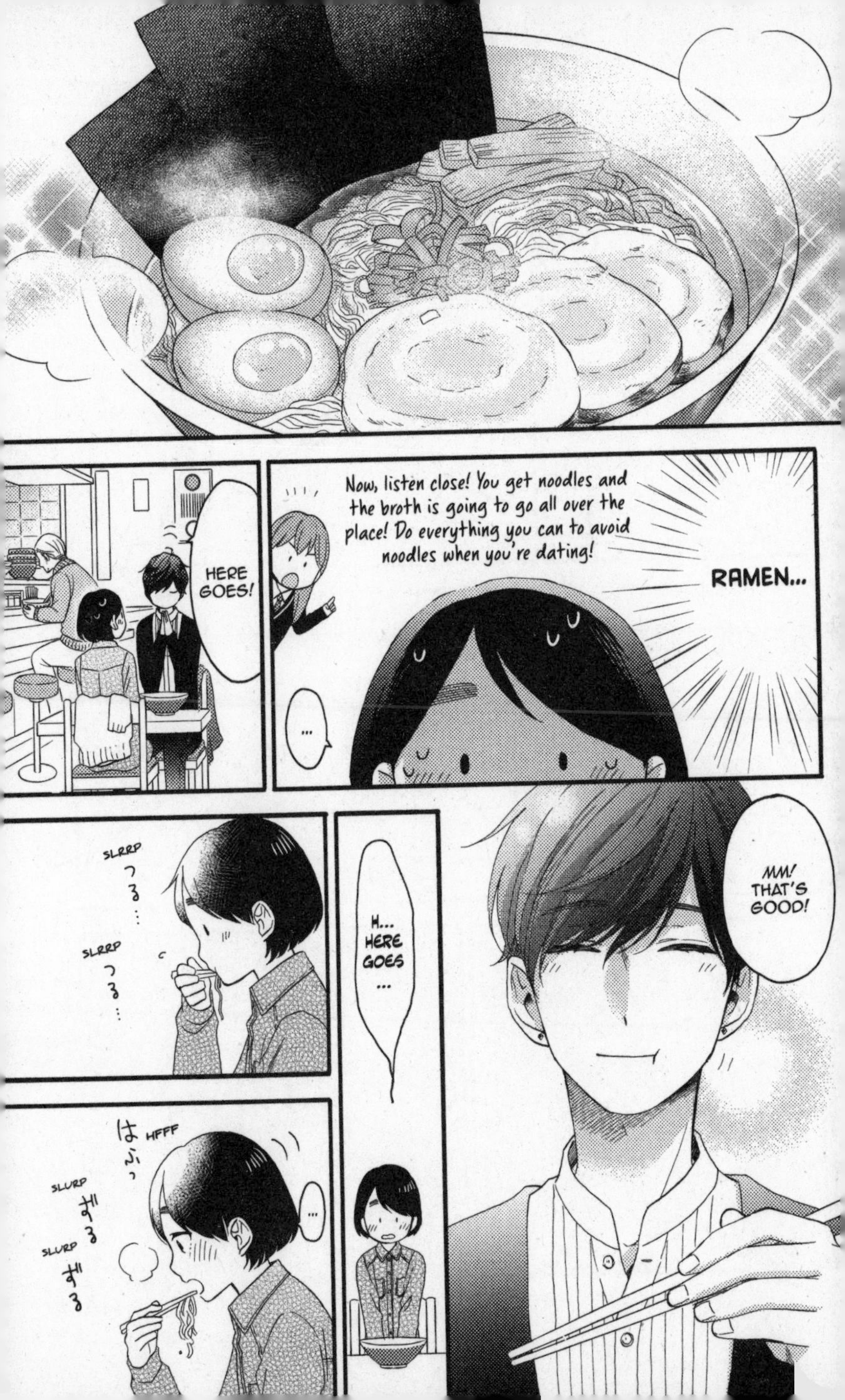
RAMEN...
Now, listen close! You get noodles and the broth is going to go all over the place! Do everything you can to avoid noodles when you're dating!
...
HERE GOES!
MM! THAT'S GOOD!
H... HERE GOES ...
SLRRP
つる…
SLRRP
つる…
HFFF
はふっ
...
SLURP
ずる
SLURP
ずる

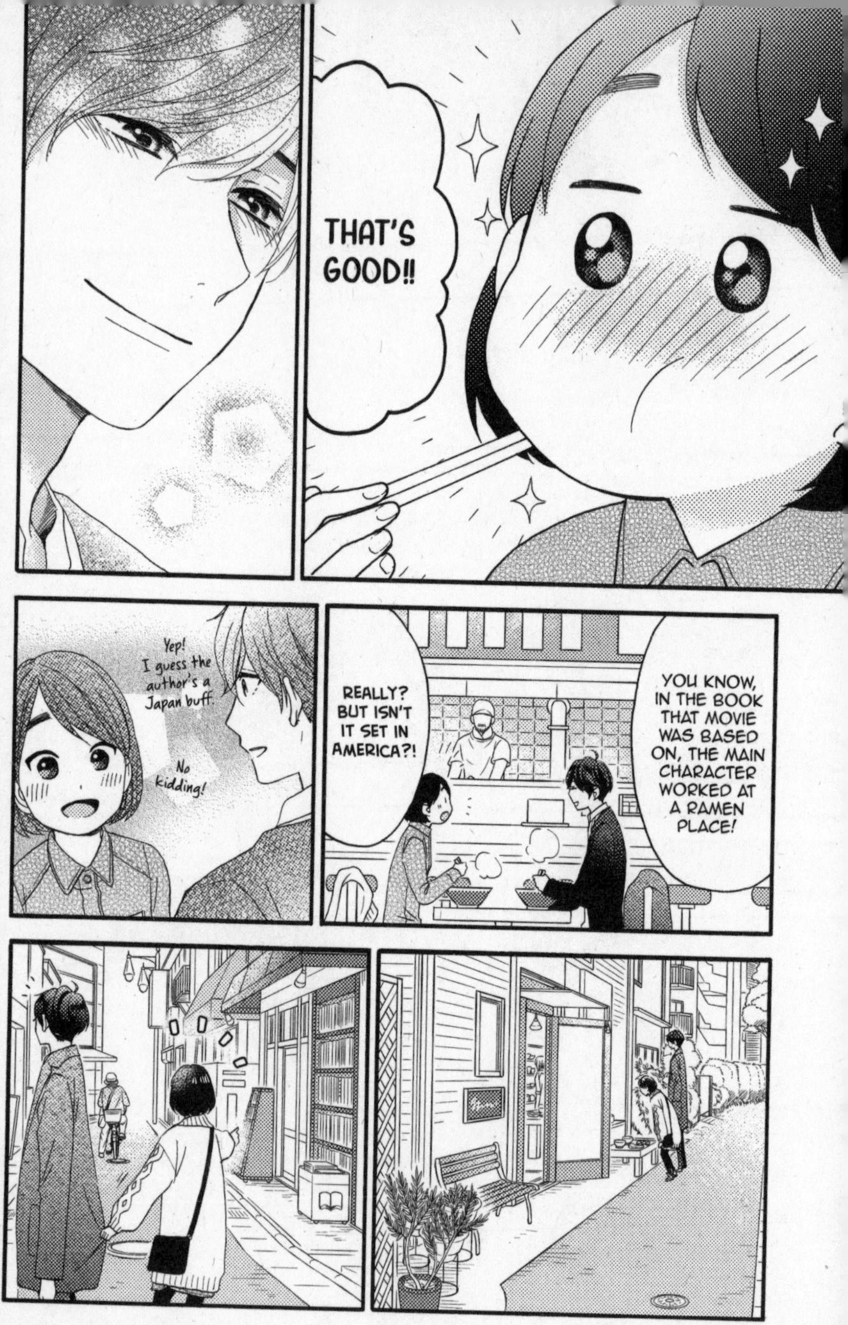
THAT'S GOOD!!
YOU KNOW, IN THE BOOK THAT MOVIE WAS BASED ON, THE MAIN CHARACTER WORKED AT A RAMEN PLACE!
REALLY? BUT ISN'T IT SET IN AMERICA?!
Yep! I guess the author's a Japan buff.
No kidding!

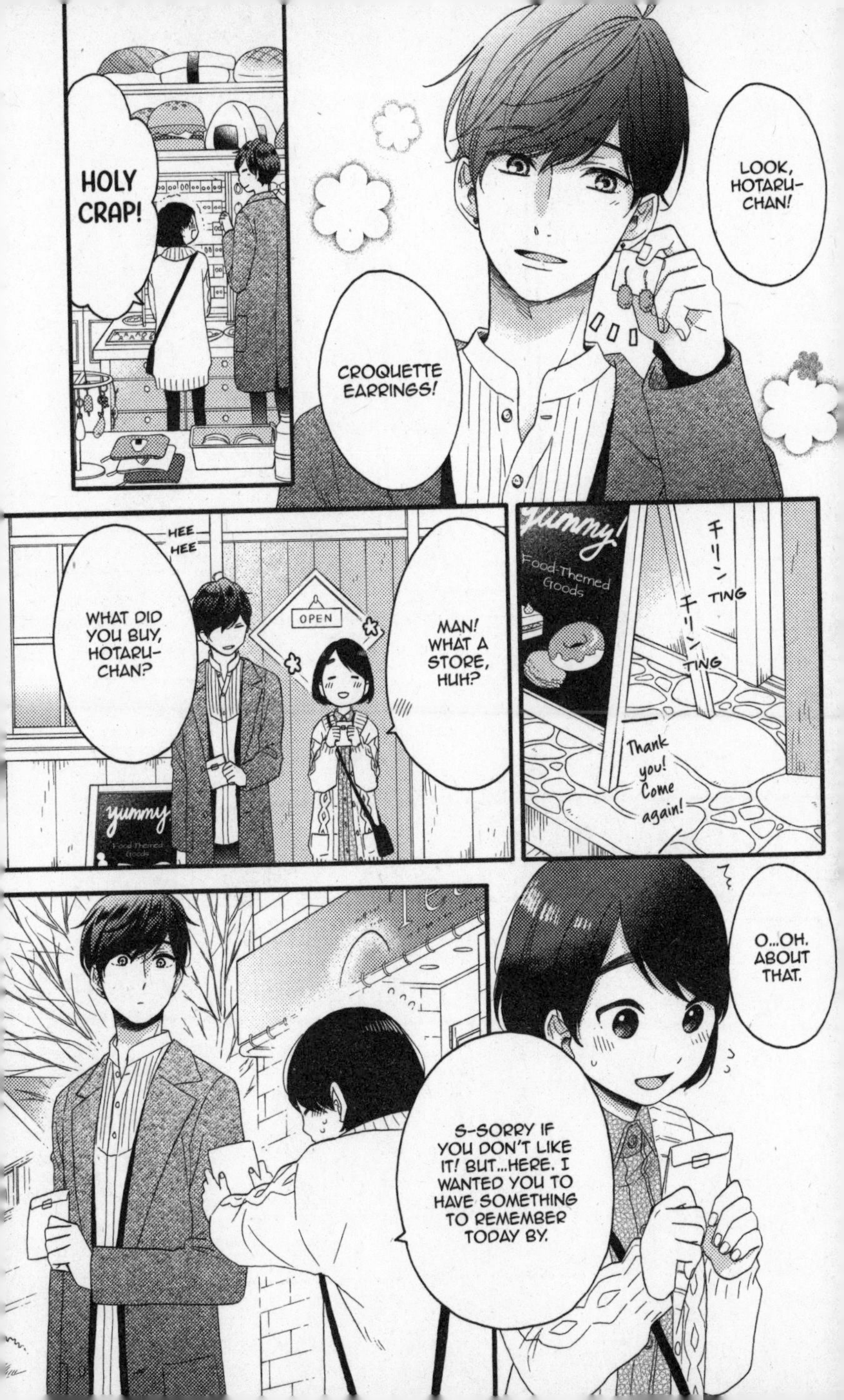
LOOK, HOTARU-CHAN!
CROQUETTE EARRINGS!
HOLY CRAP!
yummy! Food-Themed Goods
チリン TING
チリン TING
Thank you! Come again!
MAN! WHAT A STORE, HUH?
OPEN
HEE HEE
WHAT DID YOU BUY, HOTARU-CHAN?
yummy! Food-Themed Goods
O...OH. ABOUT THAT.
S-SORRY IF YOU DON'T LIKE IT! BUT...HERE. I WANTED YOU TO HAVE SOMETHING TO REMEMBER TODAY BY.

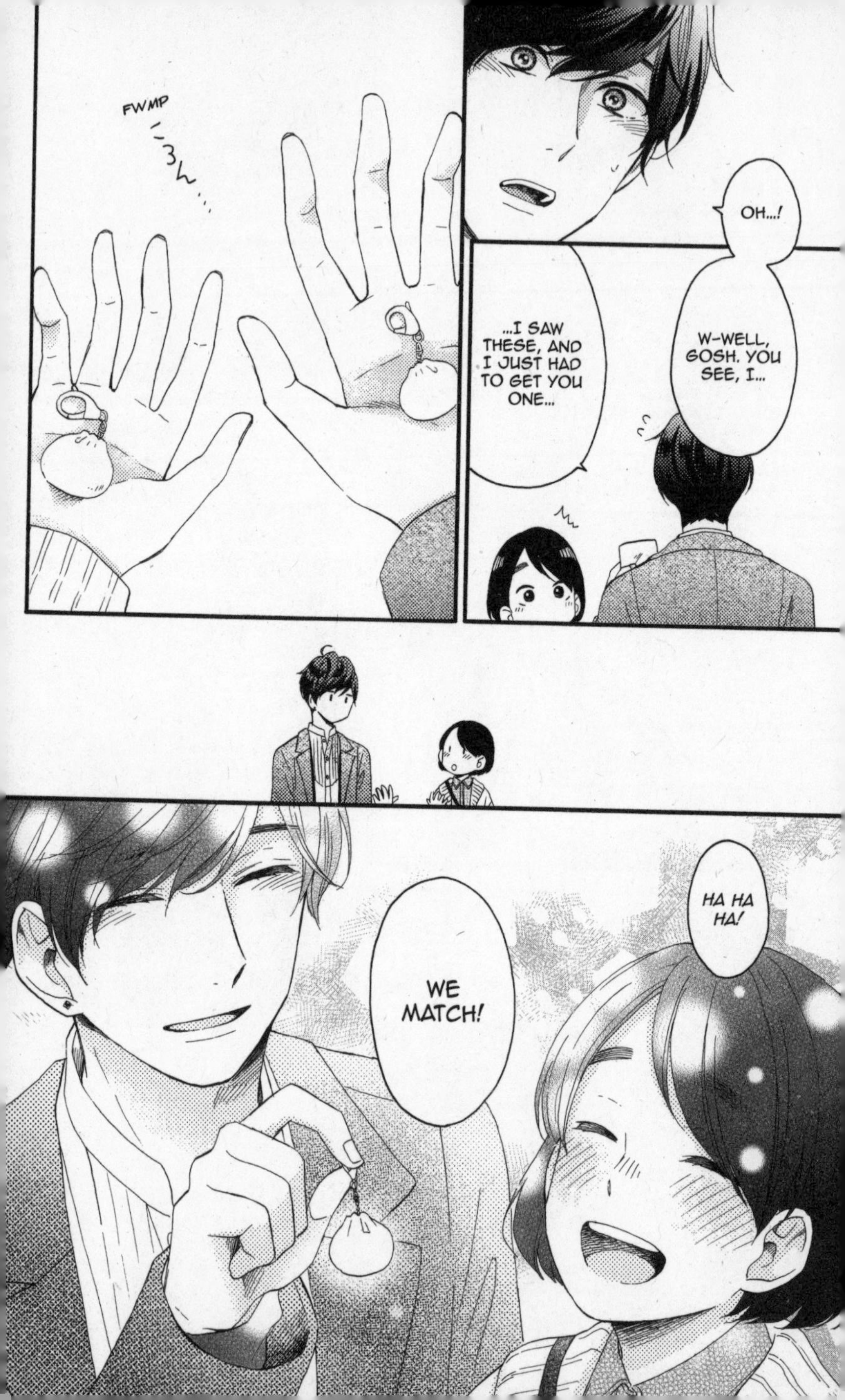
OH...!
W-WELL, GOSH. YOU SEE, I...
...I SAW THESE, AND I JUST HAD TO GET YOU ONE...
FWMP
HA HA HA!
WE MATCH!

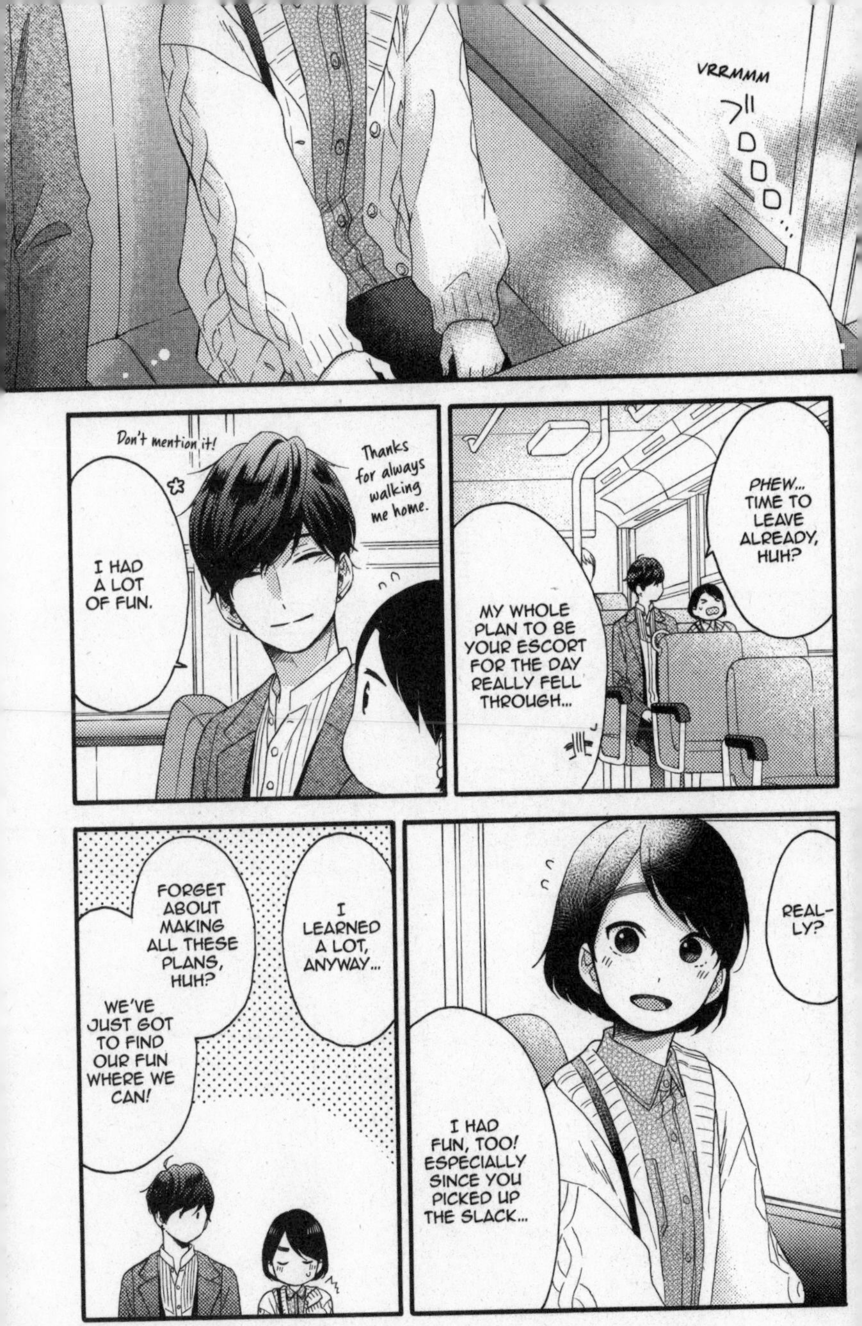
VRRMMM
PHEW... TIME TO LEAVE ALREADY, HUH?
MY WHOLE PLAN TO BE YOUR ESCORT FOR THE DAY REALLY FELL THROUGH...
Thanks for always walking me home.
Don't mention it!
I HAD A LOT OF FUN.
REAL-LY?
I HAD FUN, TOO! ESPECIALLY SINCE YOU PICKED UP THE SLACK...
I LEARNED A LOT, ANYWAY...
FORGET ABOUT MAKING ALL THESE PLANS, HUH?
WE'VE JUST GOT TO FIND OUR FUN WHERE WE CAN!

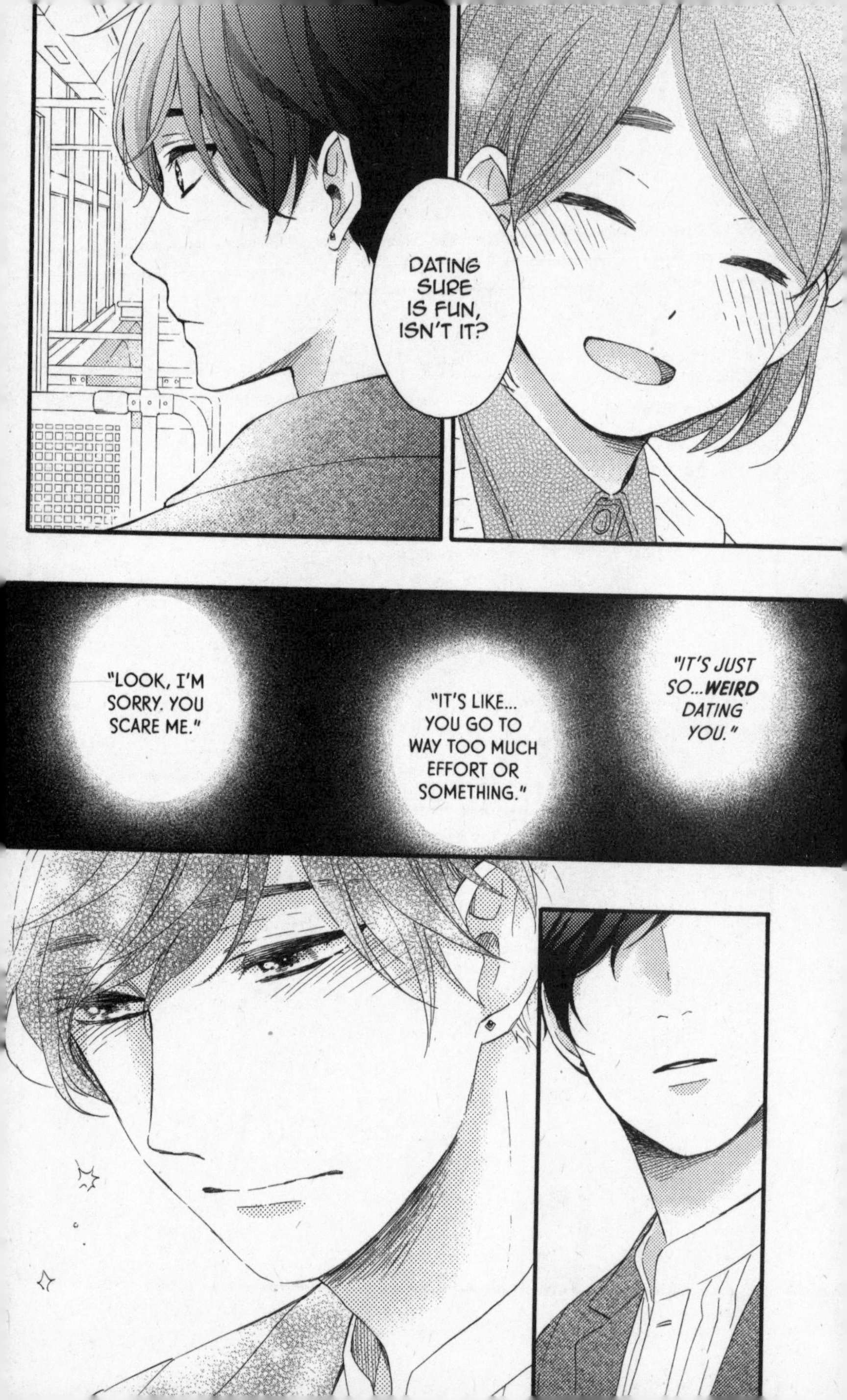
DATING SURE IS FUN, ISN'T IT?
"IT'S JUST SO...WEIRD DATING YOU."
"IT'S LIKE... YOU GO TO WAY TOO MUCH EFFORT OR SOMETHING."
"LOOK, I'M SORRY. YOU SCARE ME."

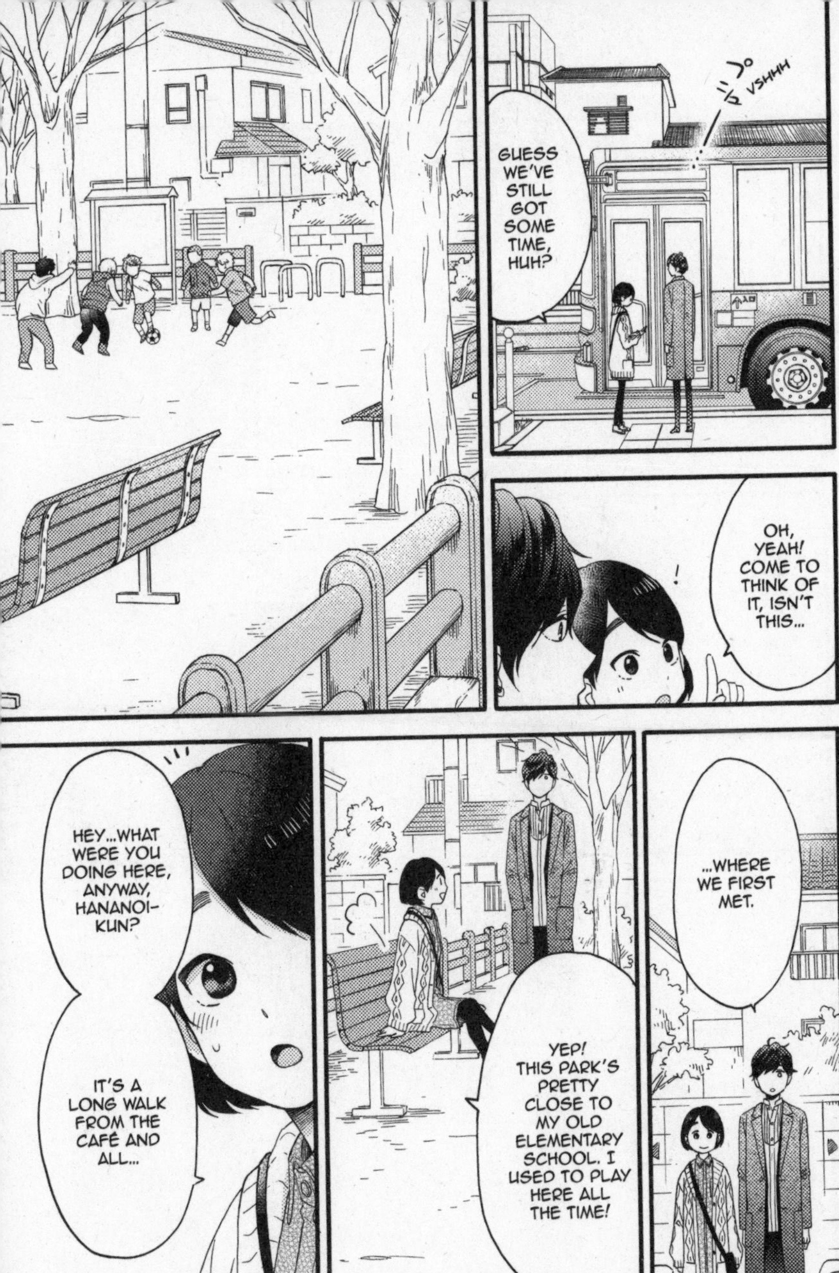
VSHHH
GUESS WE'VE STILL GOT SOME TIME, HUH?
OH, YEAH! COME TO THINK OF IT, ISN'T THIS...
...WHERE WE FIRST MET.
YEP! THIS PARK'S PRETTY CLOSE TO MY OLD ELEMENTARY SCHOOL. I USED TO PLAY HERE ALL THE TIME!
HEY...WHAT WERE YOU DOING HERE, ANYWAY, HANANOI-KUN?
IT'S A LONG WALK FROM THE CAFÉ AND ALL...

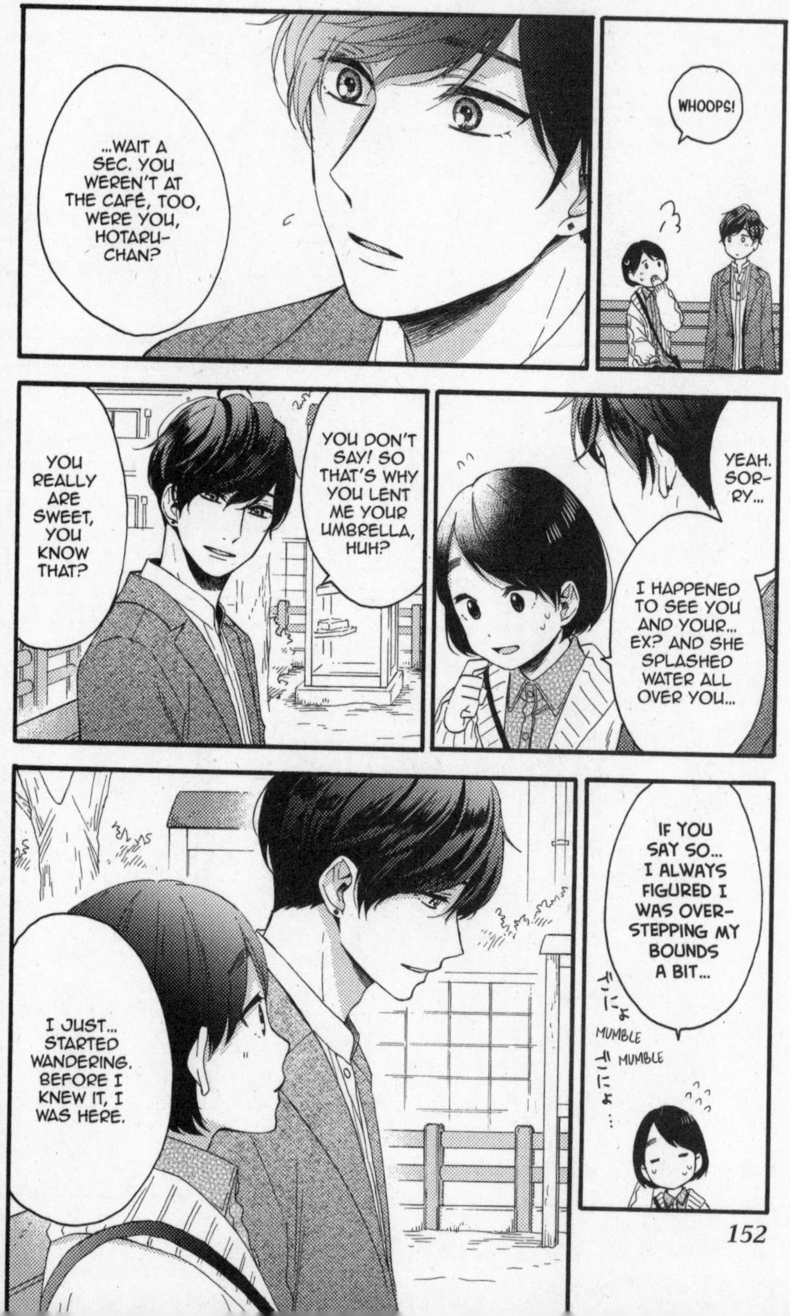
WHOOPS!
...WAIT A SEC. YOU WEREN'T AT THE CAFÉ, TOO, WERE YOU, HOTARU-CHAN?
YEAH. SORRY...
I HAPPENED TO SEE YOU AND YOUR... EX? AND SHE SPLASHED WATER ALL OVER YOU...
YOU DON'T SAY! SO THAT'S WHY YOU LENT ME YOUR UMBRELLA, HUH?
YOU REALLY ARE SWEET, YOU KNOW THAT?
IF YOU SAY SO... I ALWAYS FIGURED I WAS OVER-STEPPING MY BOUNDS A BIT...
MUMBLE
MUMBLE
I JUST... STARTED WANDERING. BEFORE I KNEW IT, I WAS HERE.

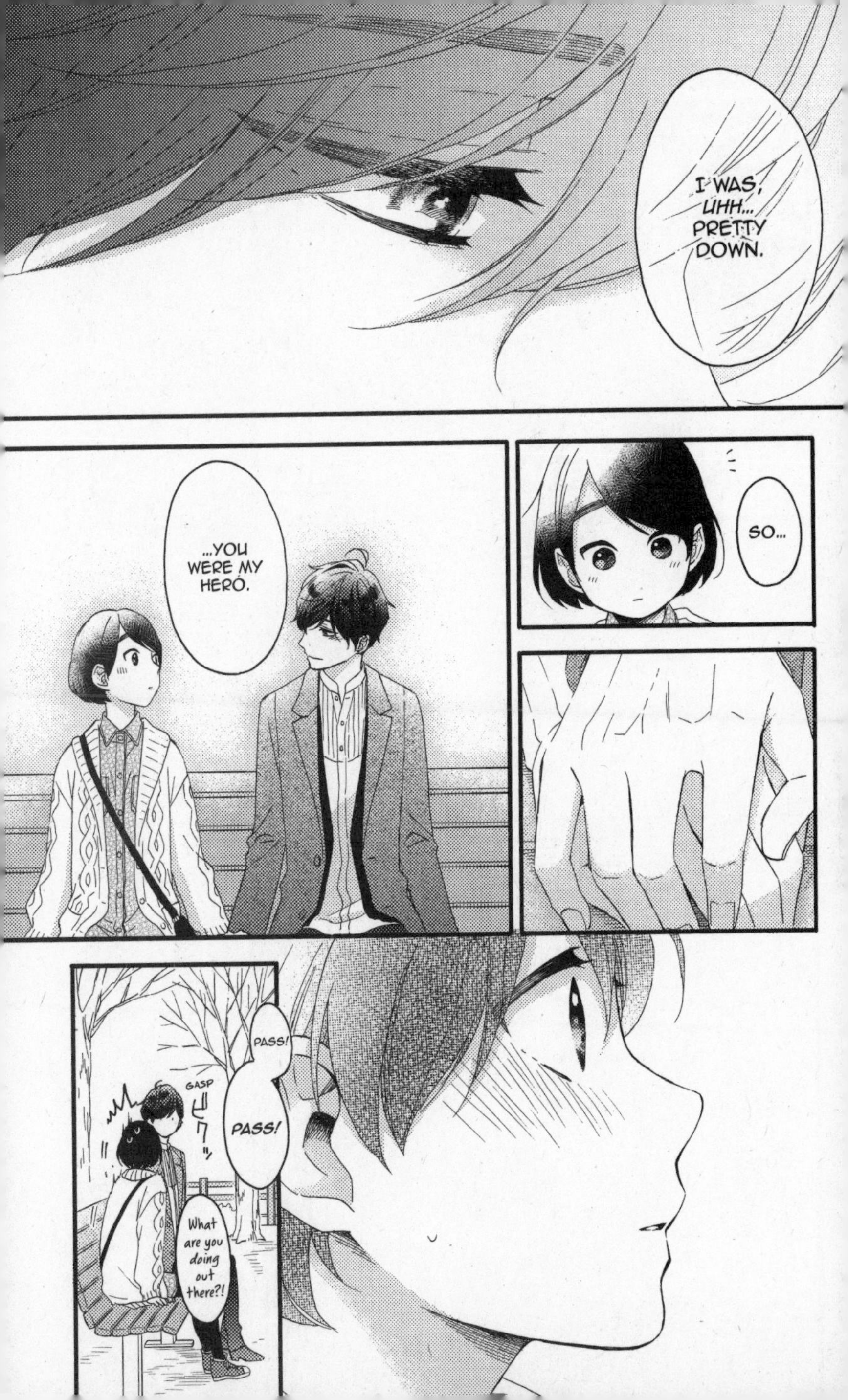
I WAS, UHH... PRETTY DOWN.
SO...
...YOU WERE MY HERO.
PASS!
PASS!
GASP
What are you doing out there?!

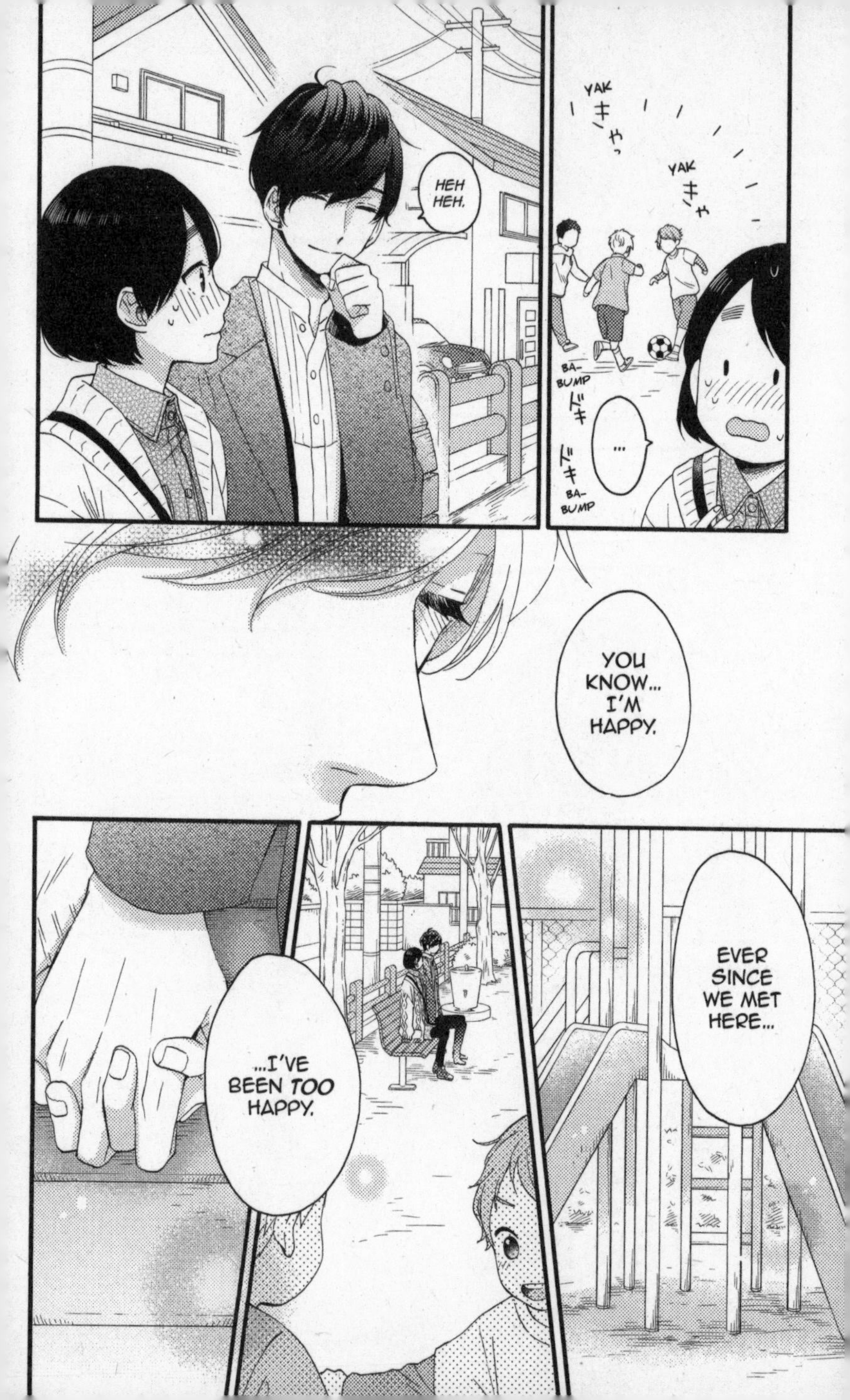
YAK
きゃっ
YAK
きゃ
BA-BUMP
ドキ
ドキ
BA-BUMP
...
HEH HEH.
YOU KNOW... I'M HAPPY.
EVER SINCE WE MET HERE...
...I'VE BEEN *TOO* HAPPY.

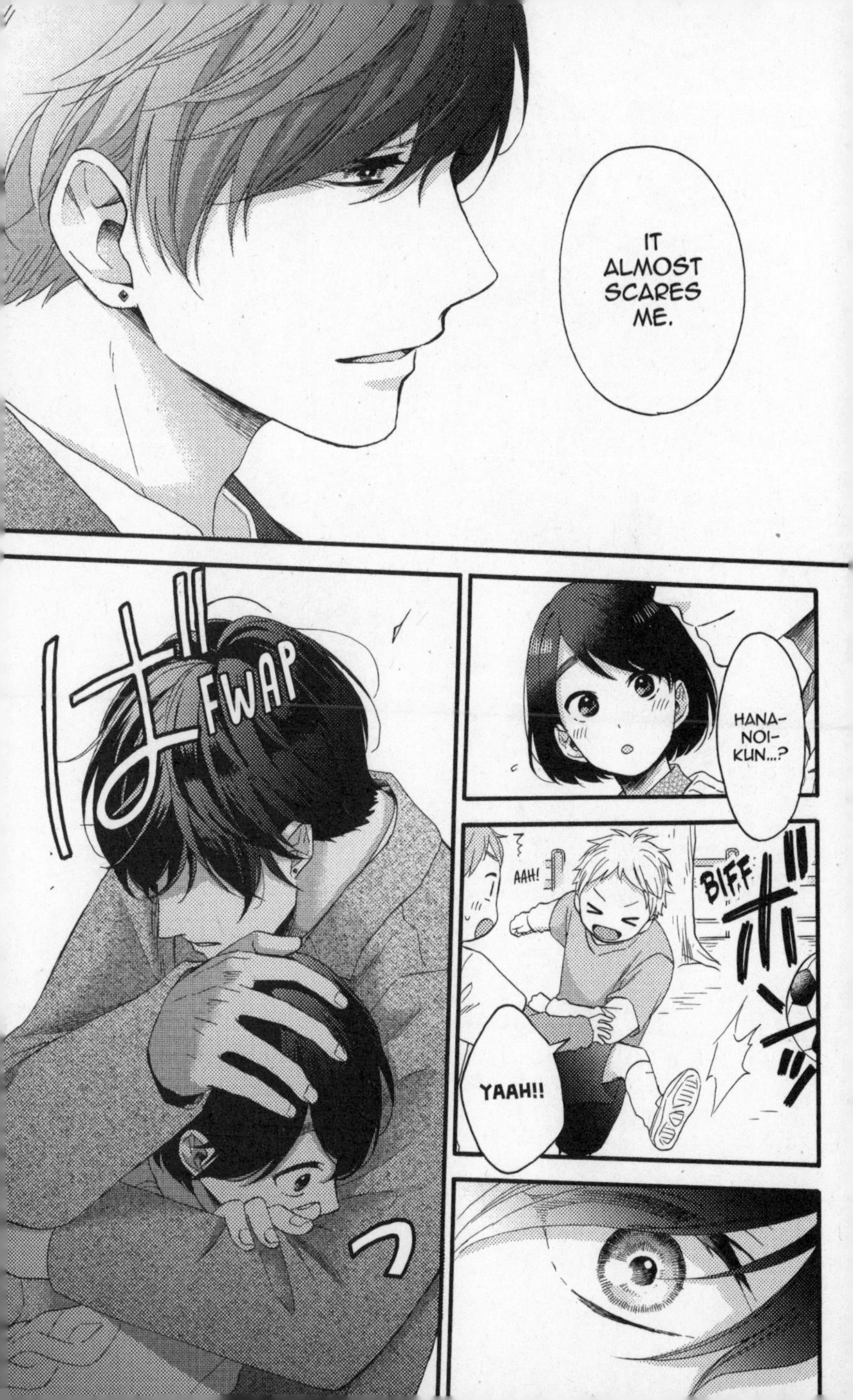
IT ALMOST SCARES ME.
HANA-NOI-KUN...?
BIFF
AAH!
YAAH!!
FWAP

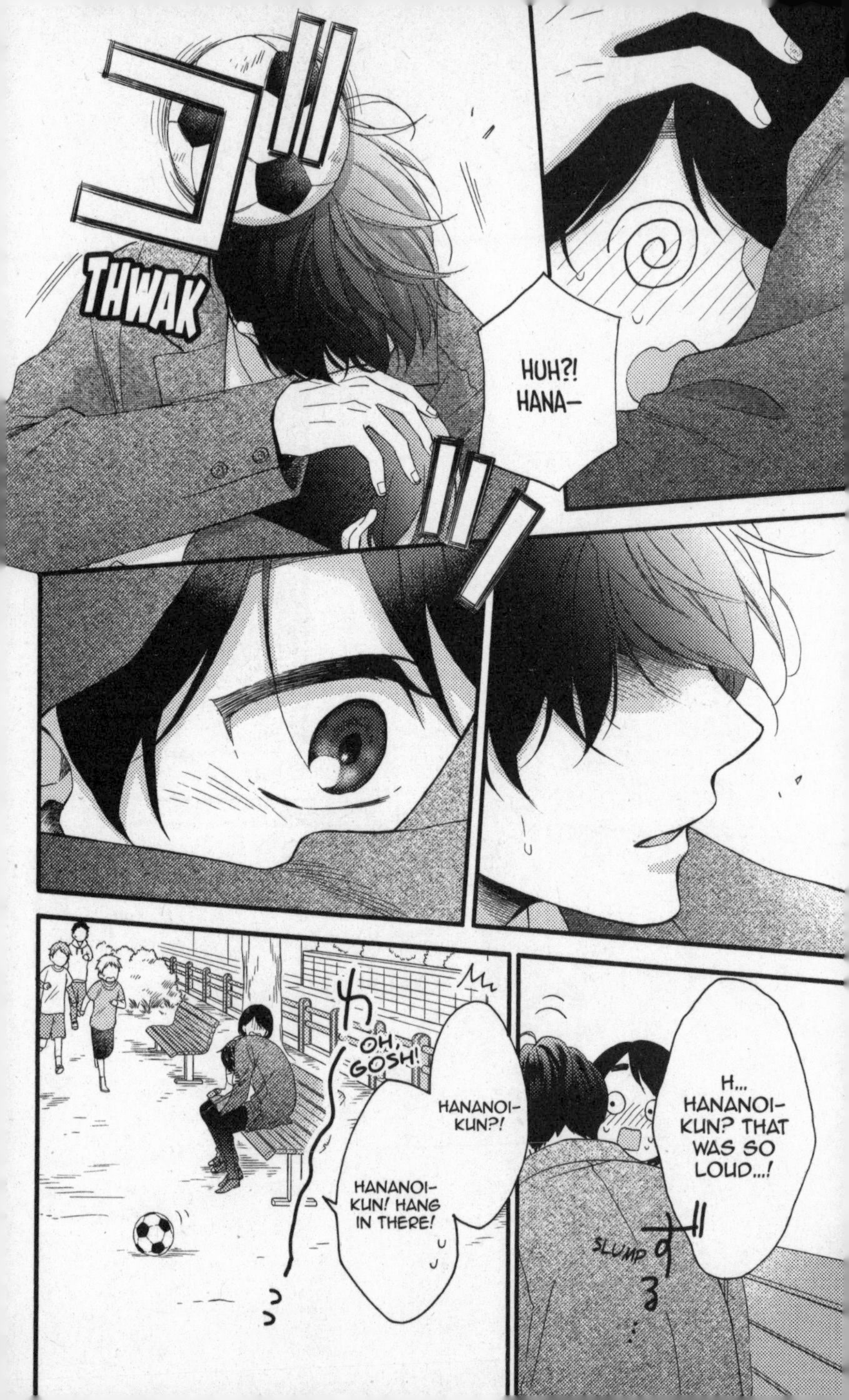
HUH?! HANA—
THWAK
H... HANANOI-KUN? THAT WAS SO LOUD...!
SLUMP
OH, GOSH!
HANANOI-KUN?!
HANANOI-KUN! HANG IN THERE!

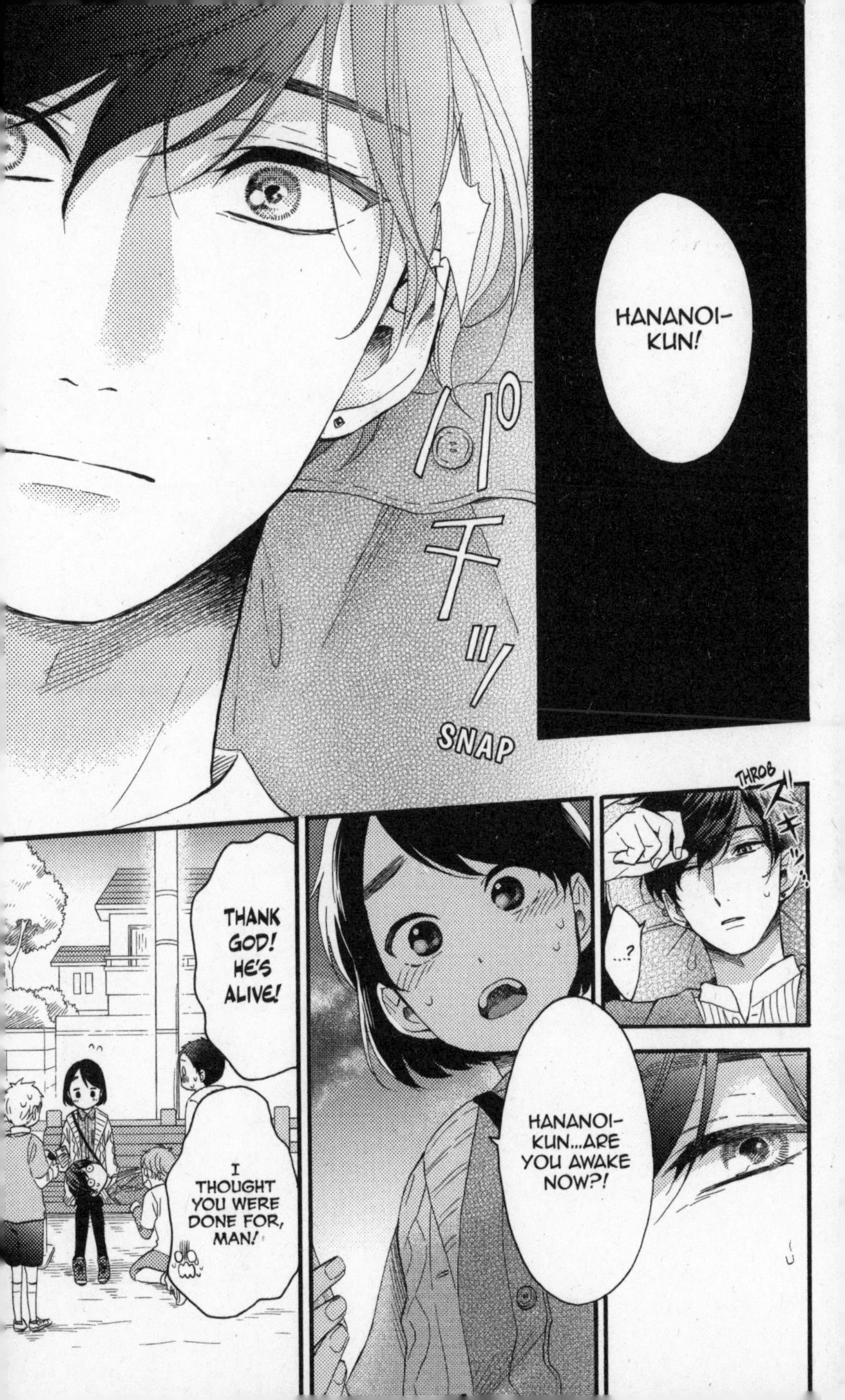
HANANOI-KUN!
パチッ
SNAP
THROB
...?
HANANOI-KUN...ARE YOU AWAKE NOW?!
THANK GOD! HE'S ALIVE!
I THOUGHT YOU WERE DONE FOR, MAN!

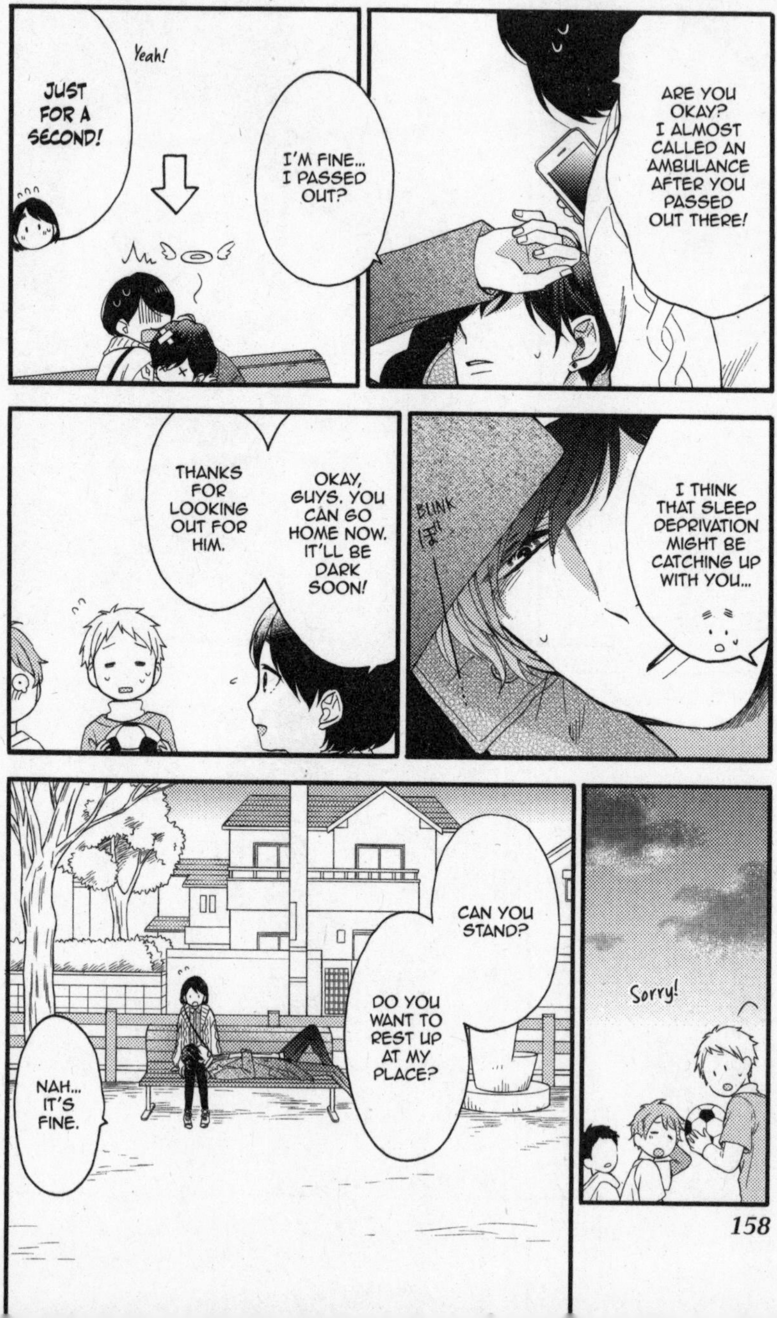

ARE YOU OKAY? I ALMOST CALLED AN AMBULANCE AFTER YOU PASSED OUT THERE!
I'M FINE... I PASSED OUT?
Yeah!
JUST FOR A SECOND!
BLINK
I THINK THAT SLEEP DEPRIVATION MIGHT BE CATCHING UP WITH YOU...
OKAY, GUYS. YOU CAN GO HOME NOW. IT'LL BE DARK SOON!
THANKS FOR LOOKING OUT FOR HIM.
Sorry!
CAN YOU STAND?
DO YOU WANT TO REST UP AT MY PLACE?
NAH... IT'S FINE.

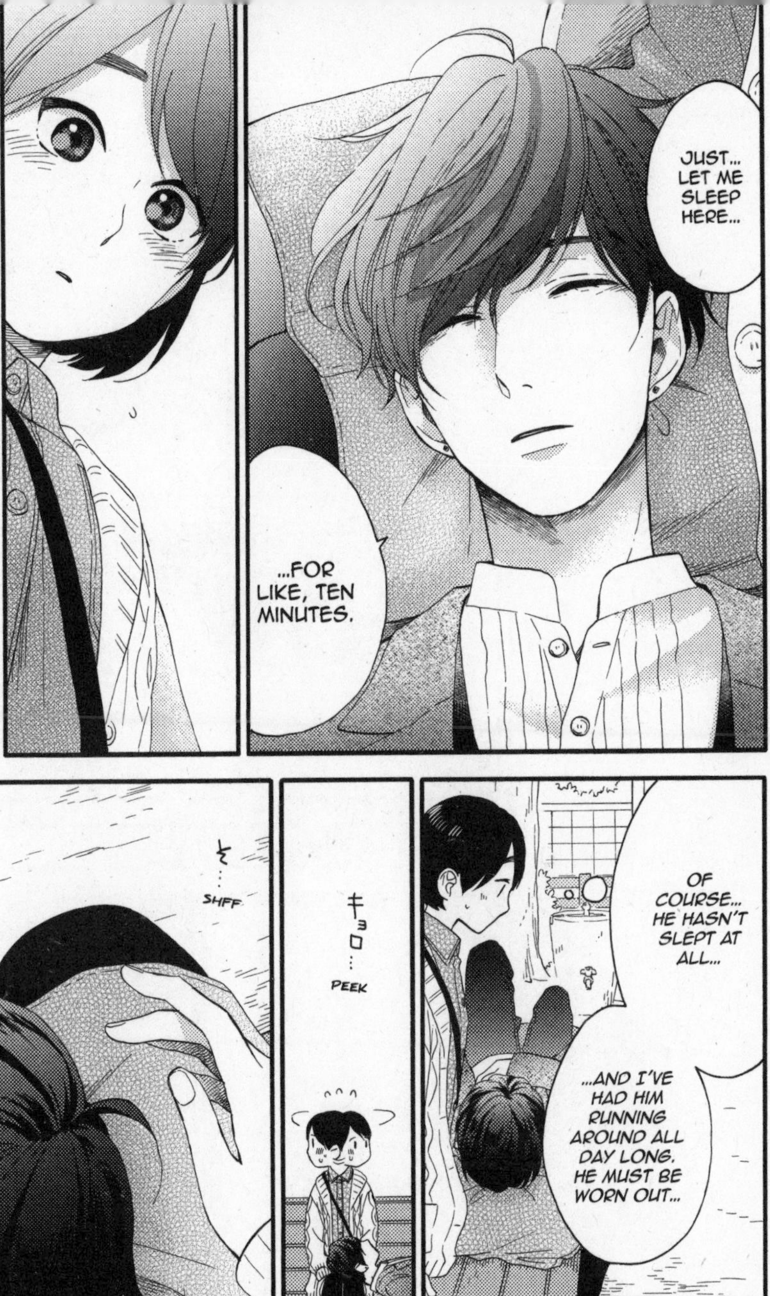
JUST... LET ME SLEEP HERE...
...FOR LIKE, TEN MINUTES.
OF COURSE... HE HASN'T SLEPT AT ALL...
...AND I'VE HAD HIM RUNNING AROUND ALL DAY LONG. HE MUST BE WORN OUT...
キョロ…
PEEK
SHFF

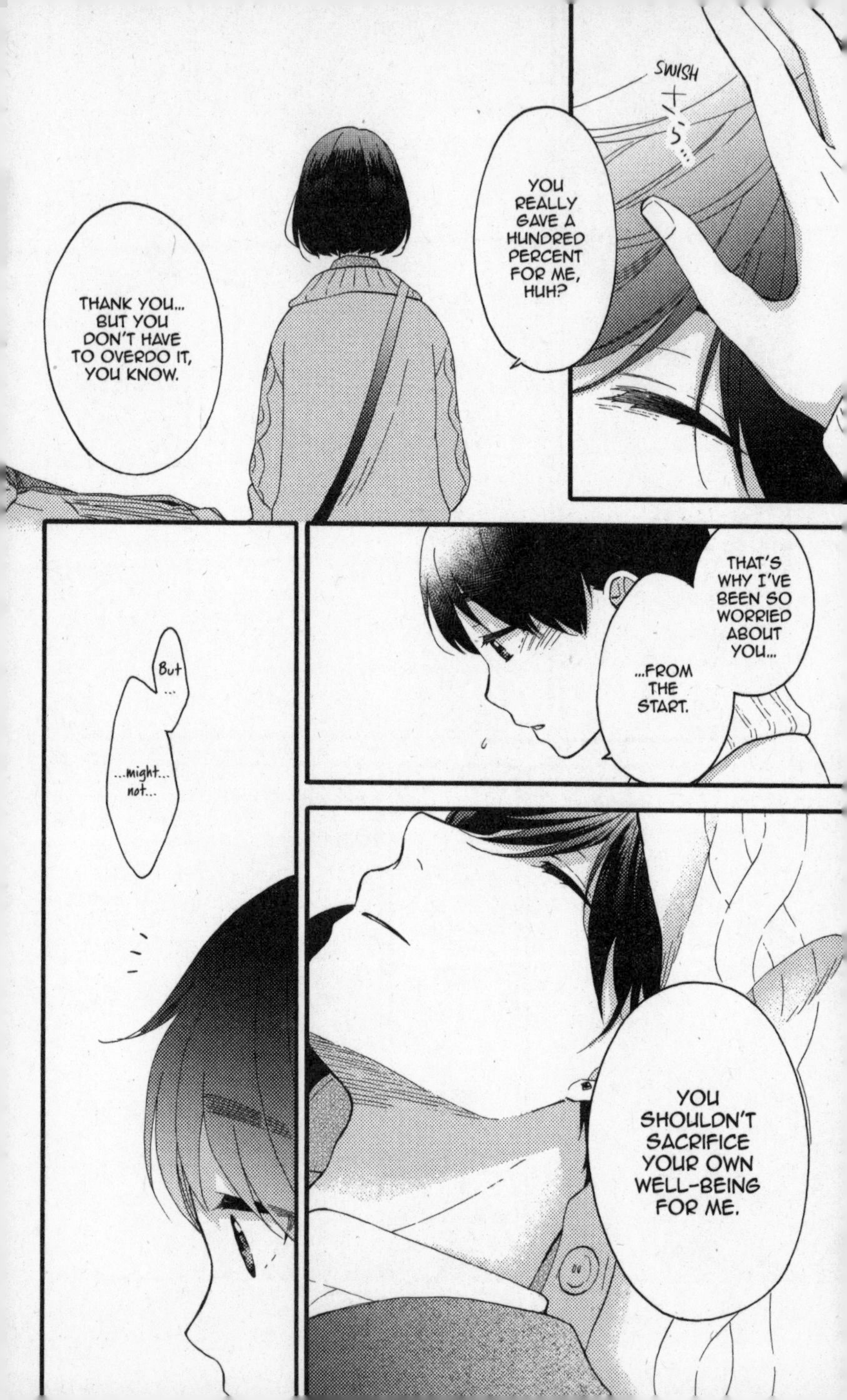
SWISH
YOU REALLY GAVE A HUNDRED PERCENT FOR ME, HUH?
THANK YOU... BUT YOU DON'T HAVE TO OVERDO IT, YOU KNOW.
THAT'S WHY I'VE BEEN SO WORRIED ABOUT YOU...
...FROM THE START.
YOU SHOULDN'T SACRIFICE YOUR OWN WELL-BEING FOR ME.
But...
...might... not...

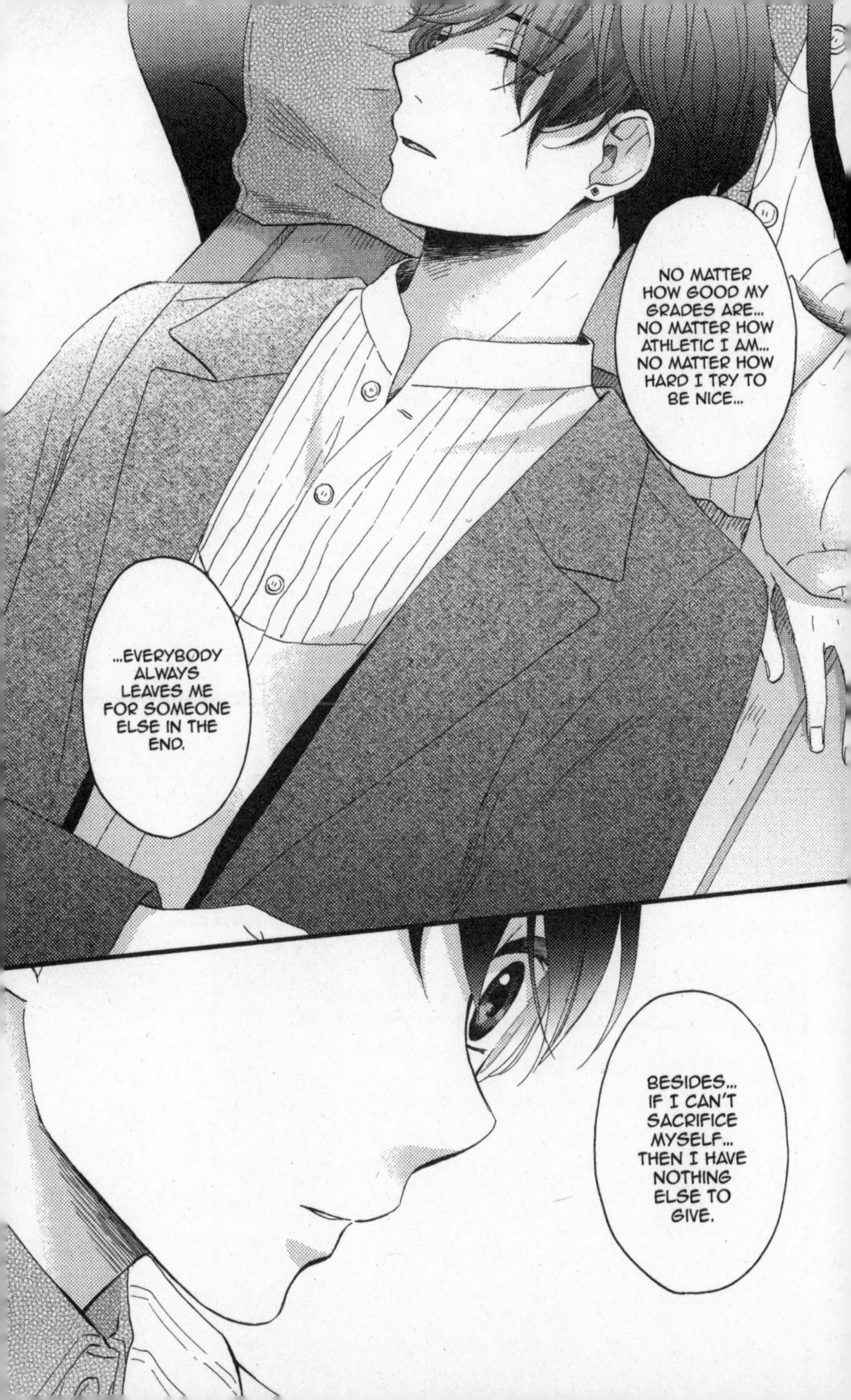
NO MATTER HOW GOOD MY GRADES ARE... NO MATTER HOW ATHLETIC I AM... NO MATTER HOW HARD I TRY TO BE NICE...
...EVERYBODY ALWAYS LEAVES ME FOR SOMEONE ELSE IN THE END.
BESIDES... IF I CAN'T SACRIFICE MYSELF... THEN I HAVE NOTHING ELSE TO GIVE.

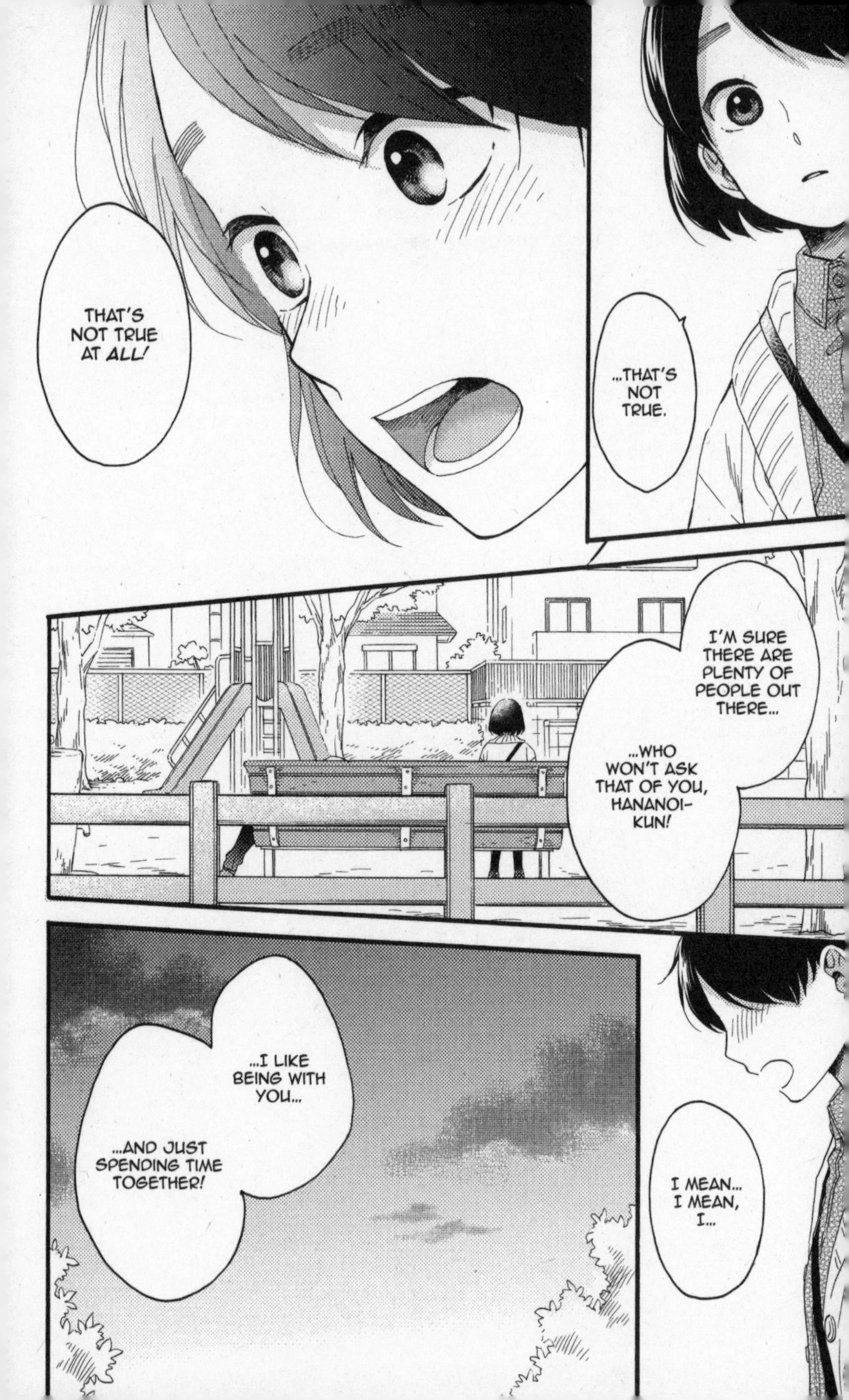
...THAT'S NOT TRUE.
THAT'S NOT TRUE AT ALL!
I'M SURE THERE ARE PLENTY OF PEOPLE OUT THERE...
...WHO WON'T ASK THAT OF YOU, HANANOI-KUN!
I MEAN... I MEAN, I...
...I LIKE BEING WITH YOU...
...AND JUST SPENDING TIME TOGETHER!

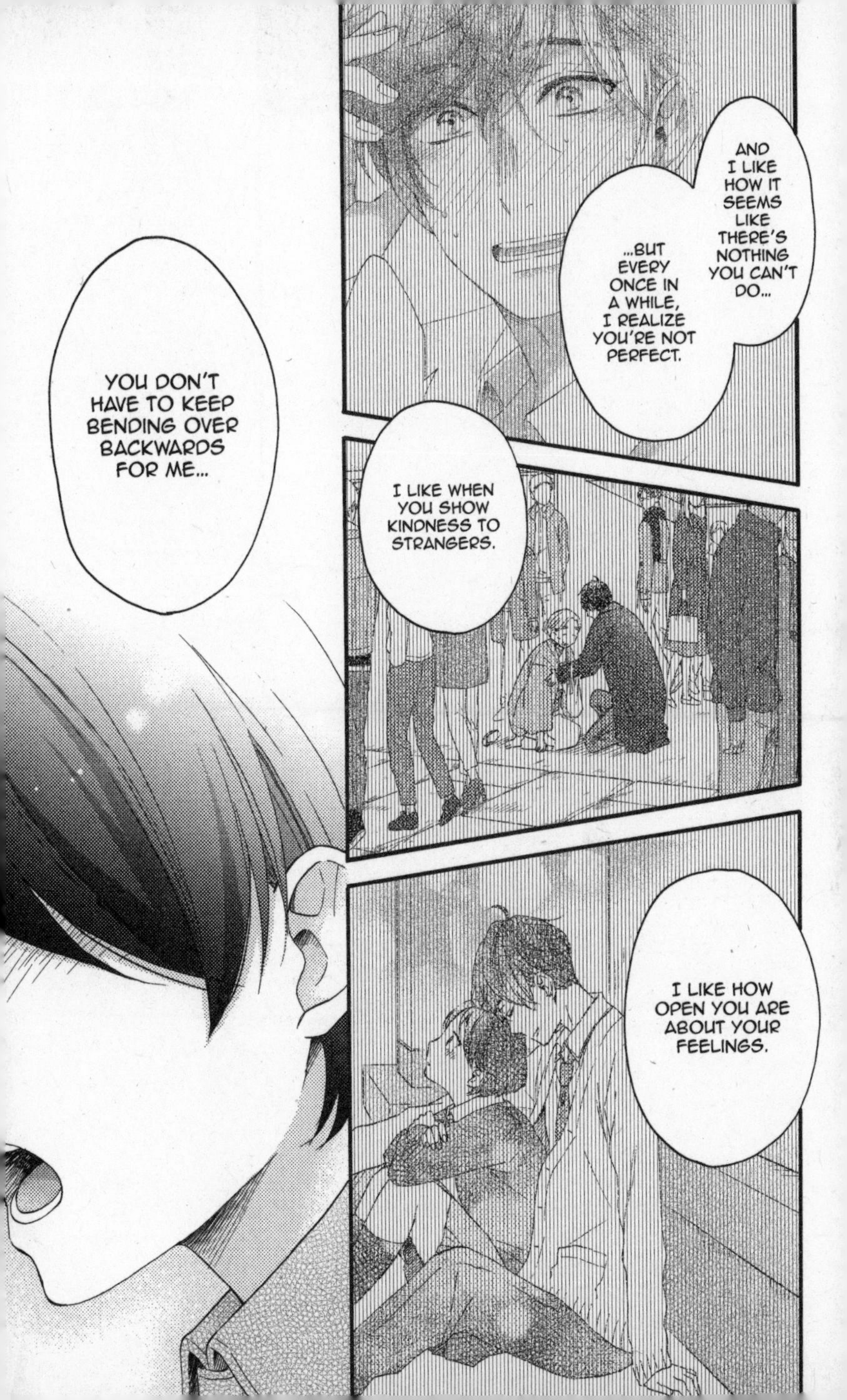
AND I LIKE HOW IT SEEMS LIKE THERE'S NOTHING YOU CAN'T DO...
...BUT EVERY ONCE IN A WHILE, I REALIZE YOU'RE NOT PERFECT.
I LIKE WHEN YOU SHOW KINDNESS TO STRANGERS.
I LIKE HOW OPEN YOU ARE ABOUT YOUR FEELINGS.
YOU DON'T HAVE TO KEEP BENDING OVER BACKWARDS FOR ME...

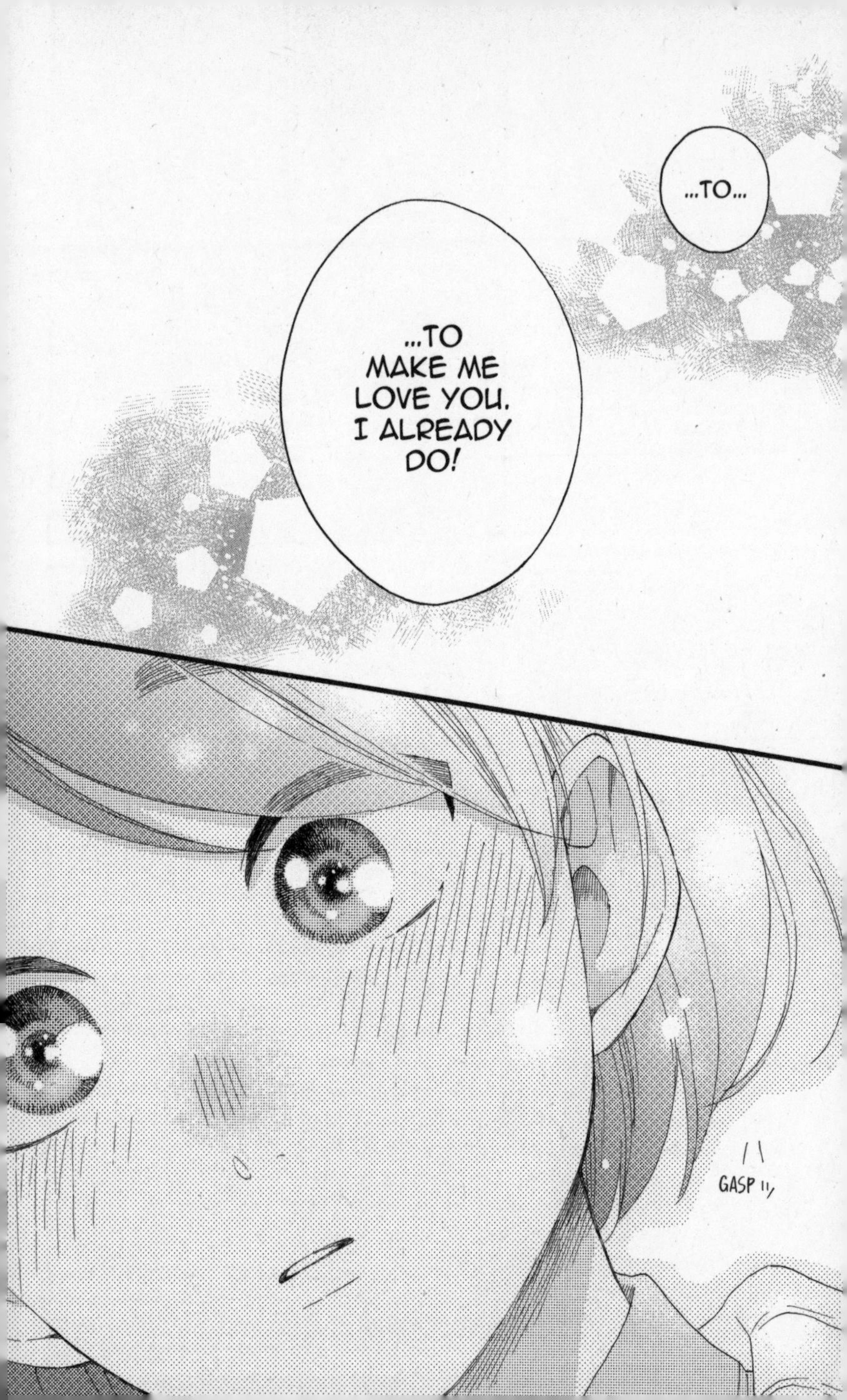
...TO...
...TO MAKE ME LOVE YOU. I ALREADY DO!
GASP

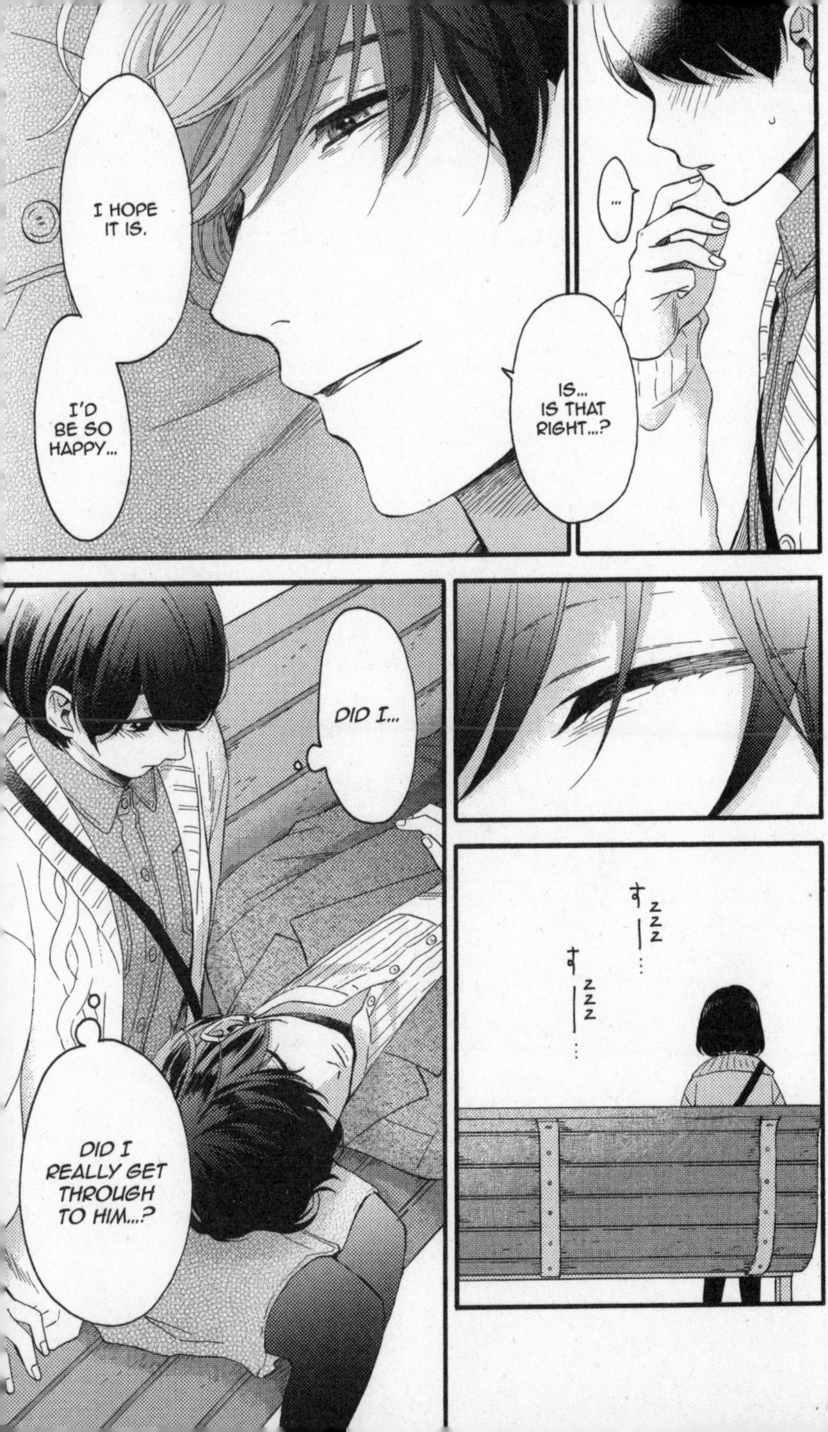
...
IS... IS THAT RIGHT...?
I HOPE IT IS.
I'D BE SO HAPPY...
すー… ZZZ
すー… ZZZ
DID I...
DID I REALLY GET THROUGH TO HIM...?

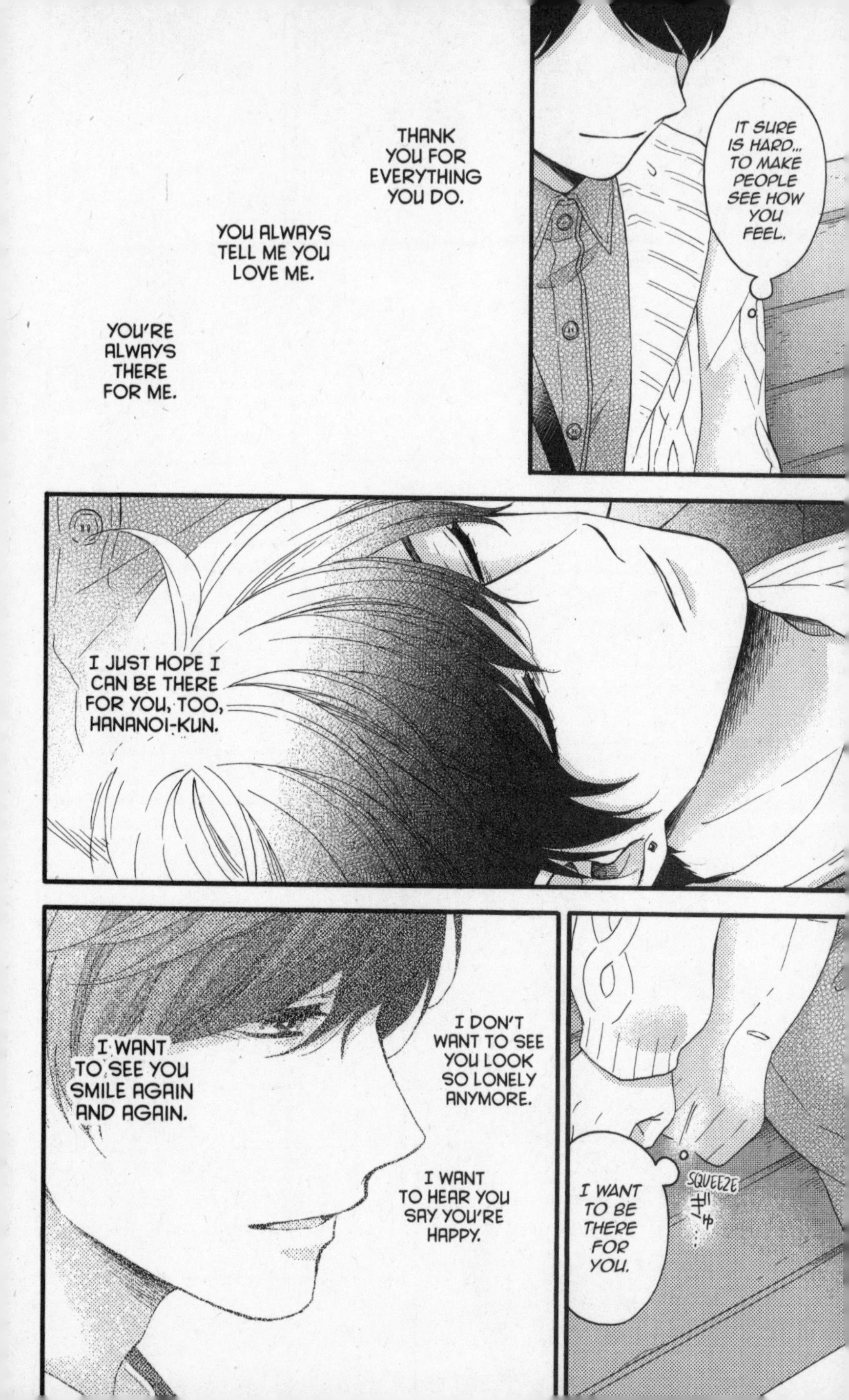
IT SURE IS HARD... TO MAKE PEOPLE SEE HOW YOU FEEL.
THANK YOU FOR EVERYTHING YOU DO.
YOU ALWAYS TELL ME YOU LOVE ME.
YOU'RE ALWAYS THERE FOR ME.
I JUST HOPE I CAN BE THERE FOR YOU, TOO, HANANOI-KUN.
SQUEEZE
I WANT TO BE THERE FOR YOU.
I DON'T WANT TO SEE YOU LOOK SO LONELY ANYMORE.
I WANT TO SEE YOU SMILE AGAIN AND AGAIN.
I WANT TO HEAR YOU SAY YOU'RE HAPPY.

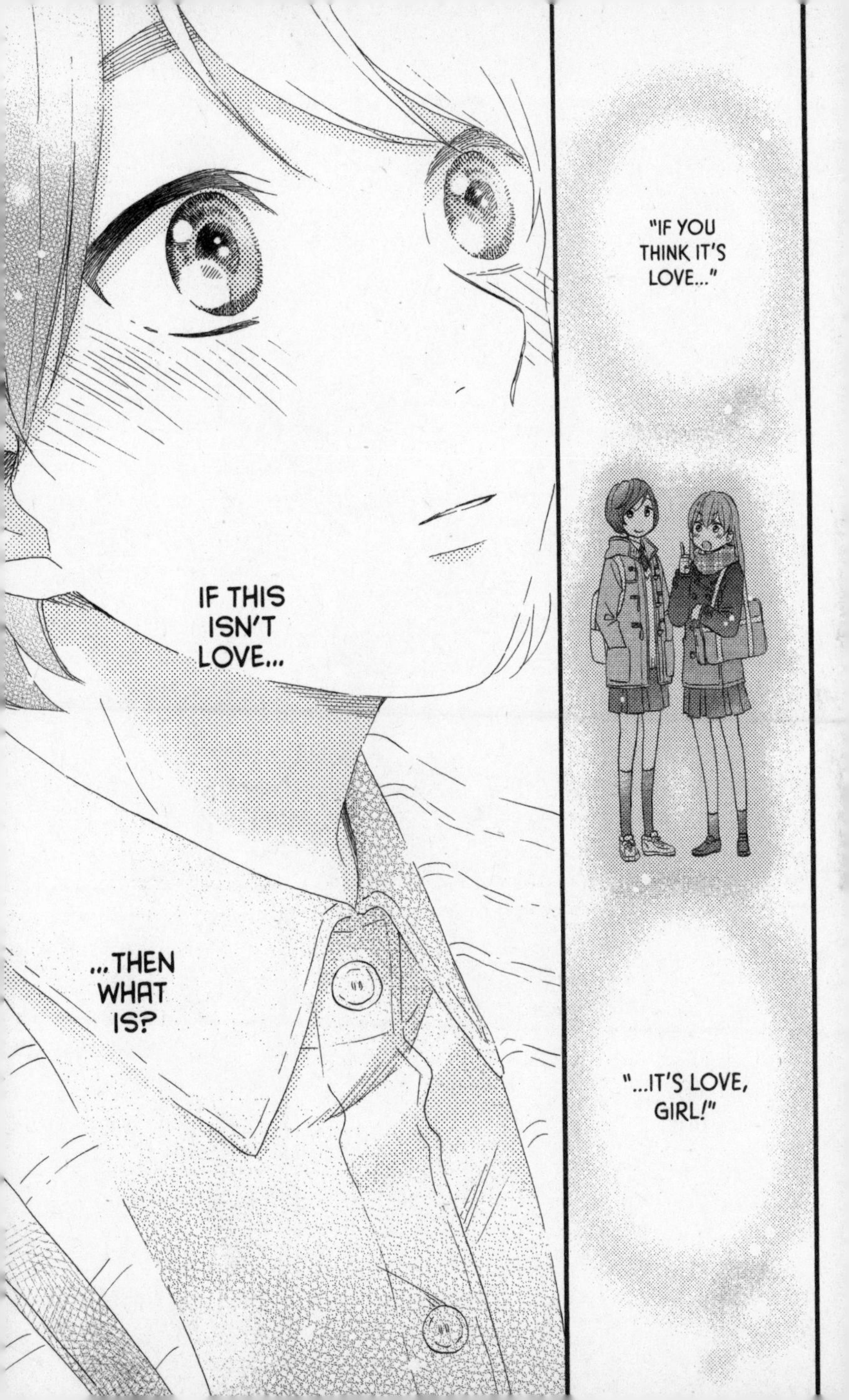
"IF YOU THINK IT'S LOVE..."
"...IT'S LOVE, GIRL!"
IF THIS ISN'T LOVE...
...THEN WHAT IS?

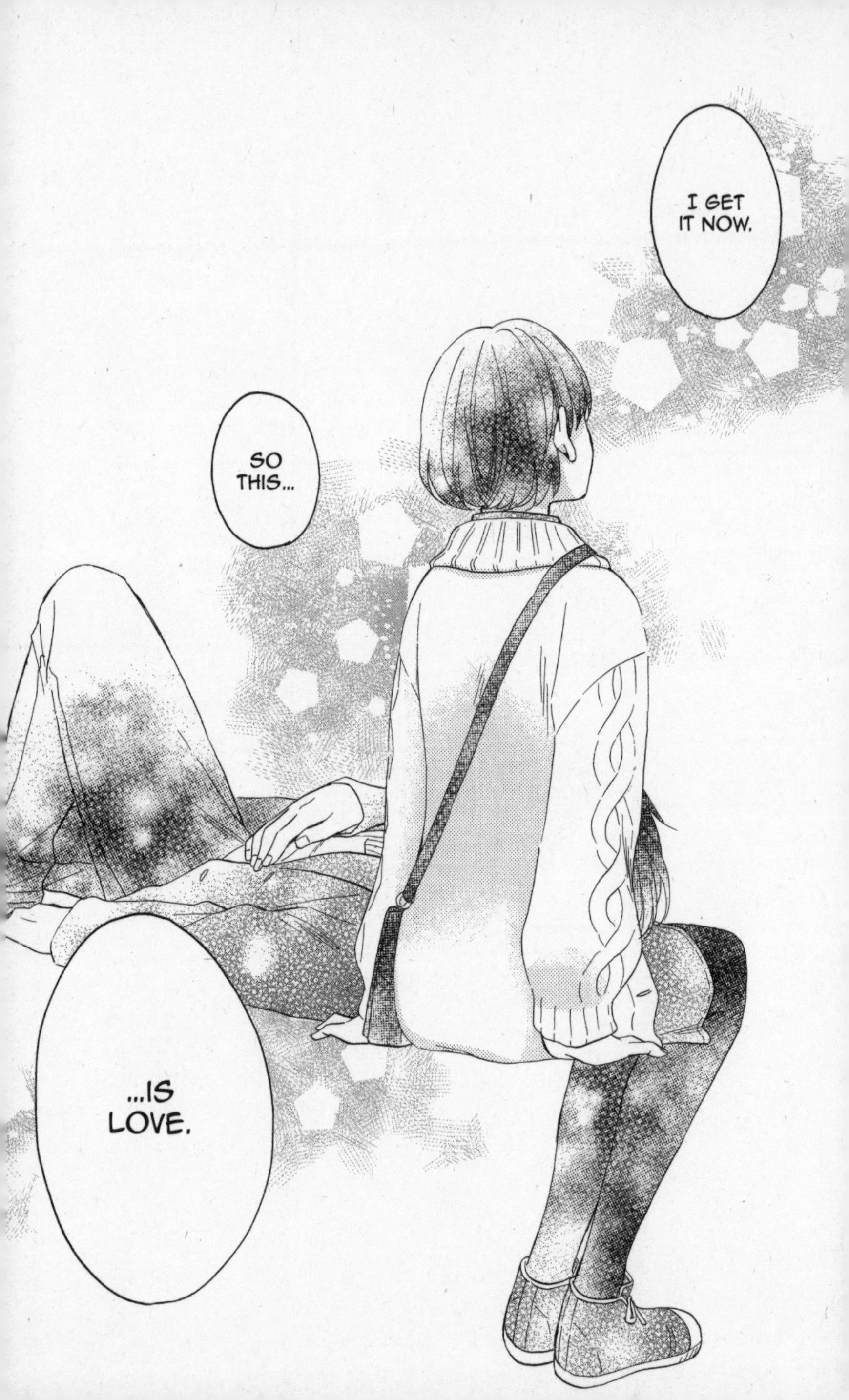
I GET IT NOW.
SO THIS...
...IS LOVE.

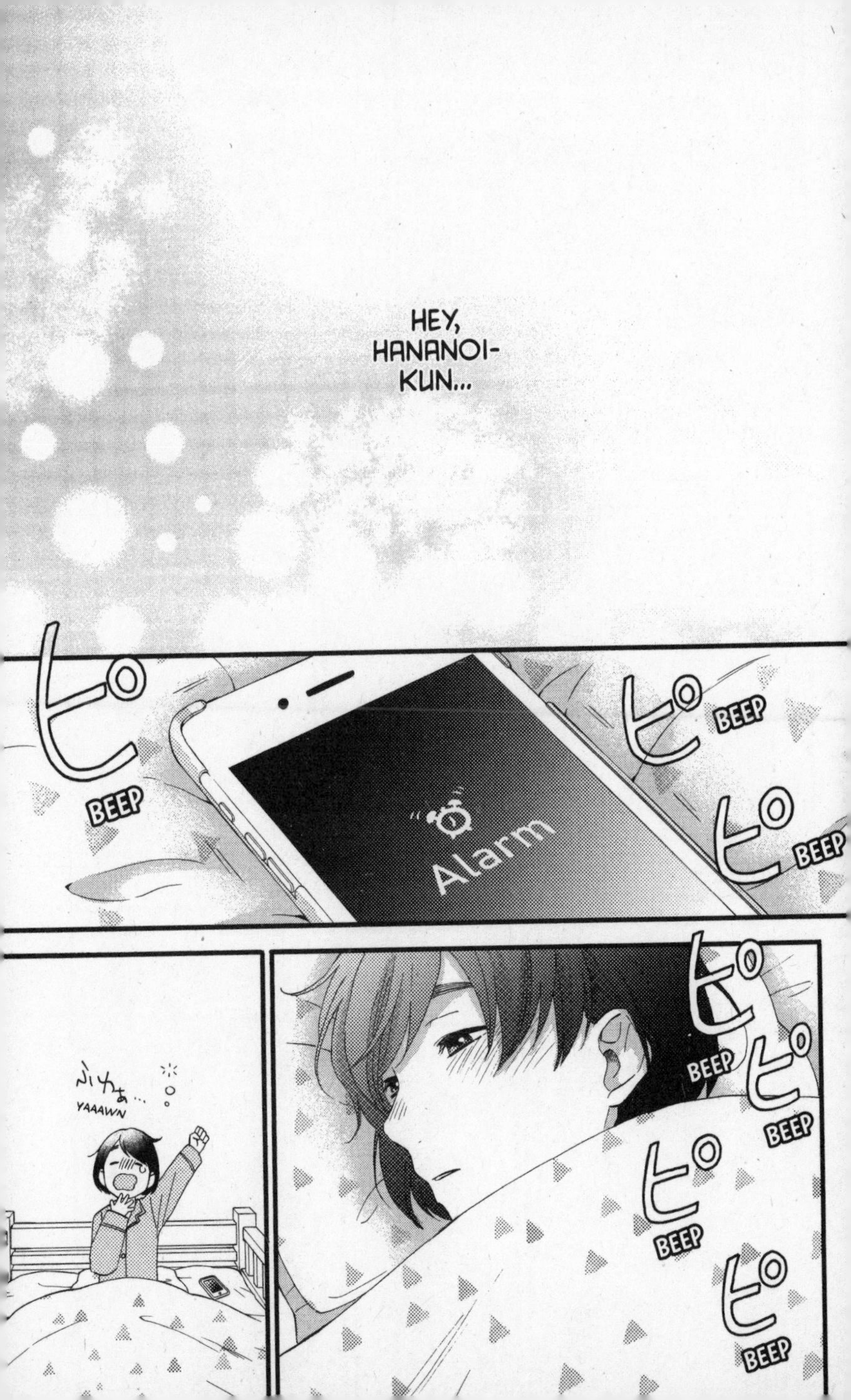
HEY, HANANOI-KUN...
ピ
BEEP
ピ
BEEP
Alarm
ピ
BEEP
ピ
BEEP
ピ
BEEP
ピ
BEEP
ピ
BEEP
ふわぁ...
YAAAWN

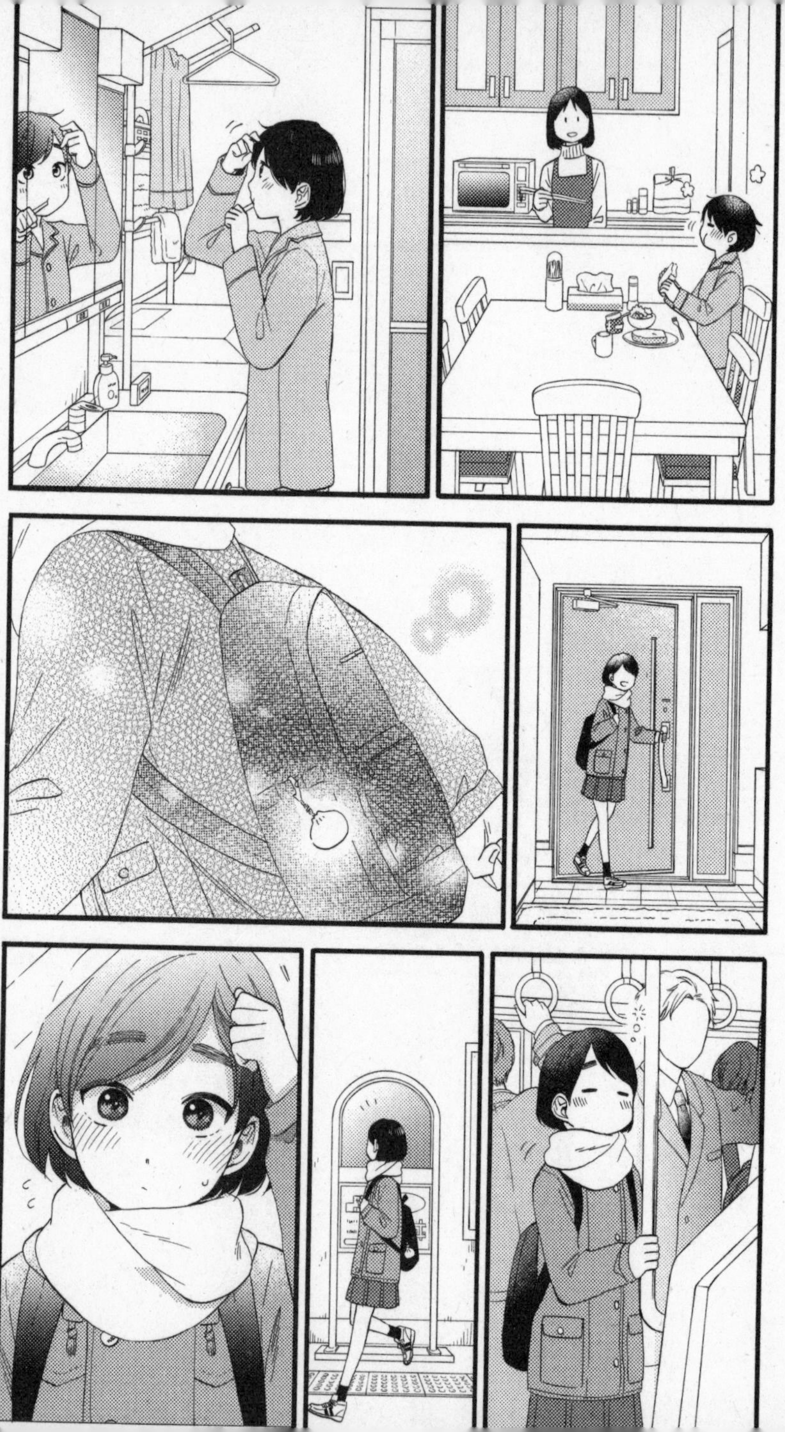

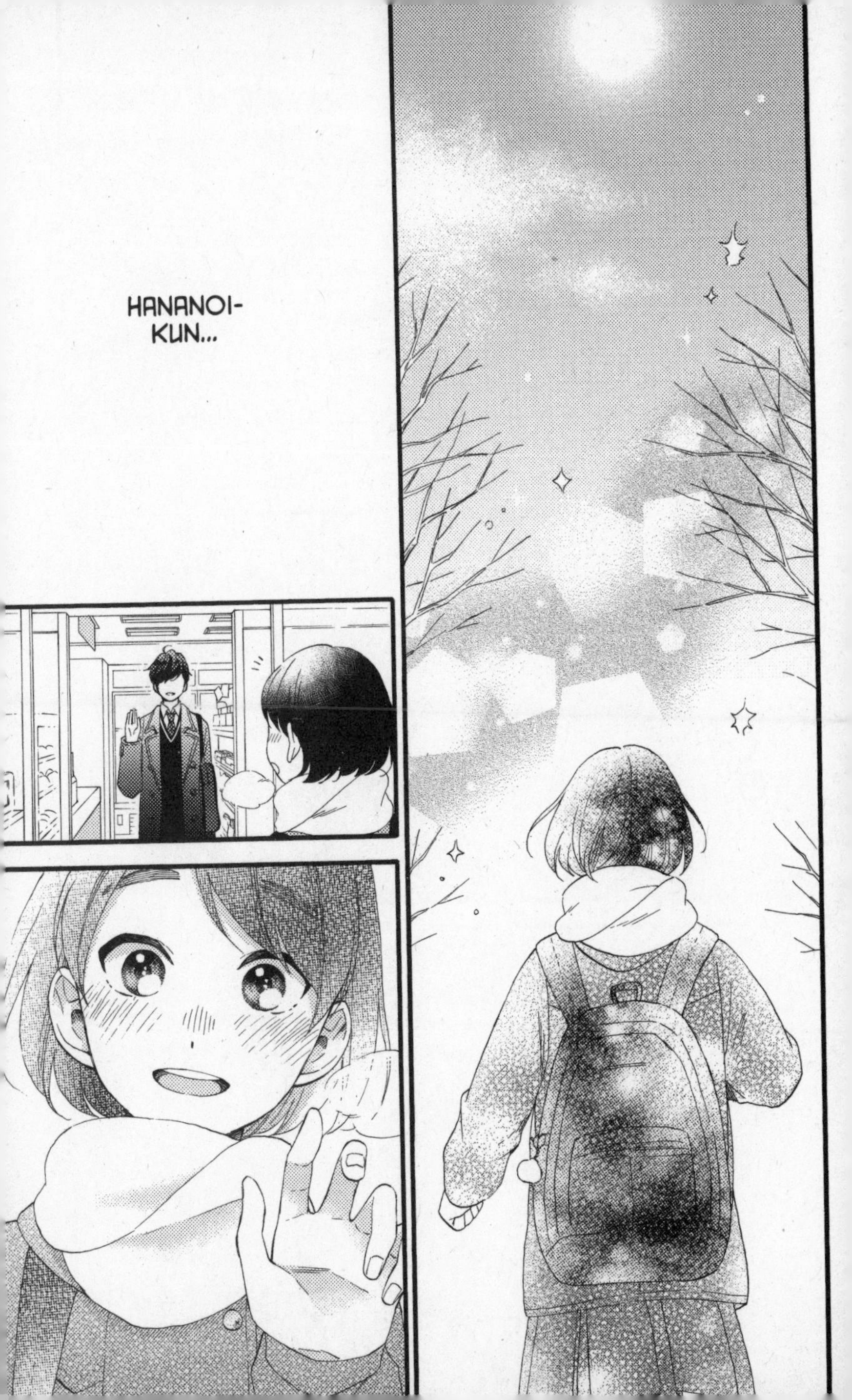
HANANOI-
KUN...

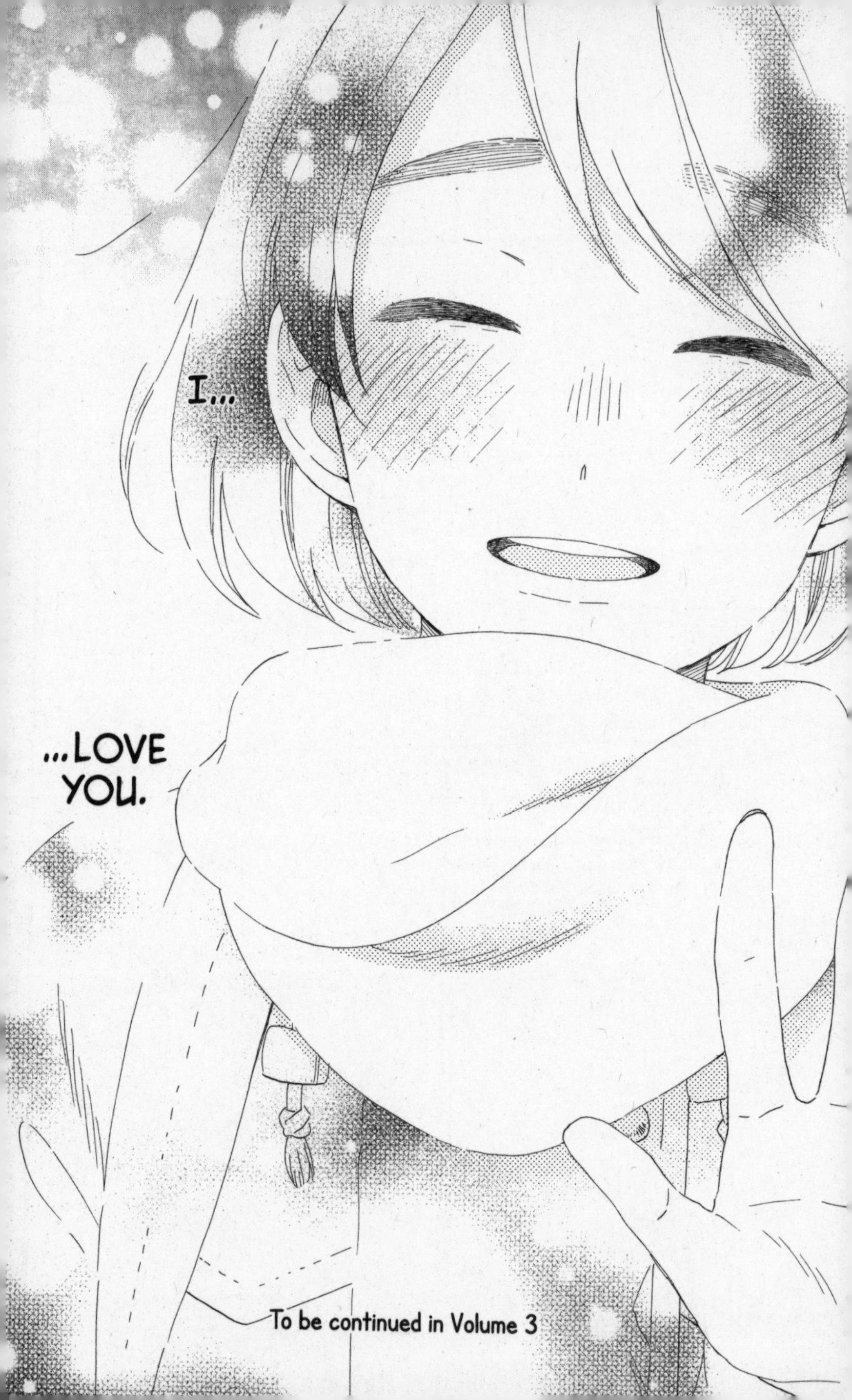
I...
...LOVE YOU.
To be continued in Volume 3

A Condition
Called Love💙

A Condition Called Love, Bonus Flashback

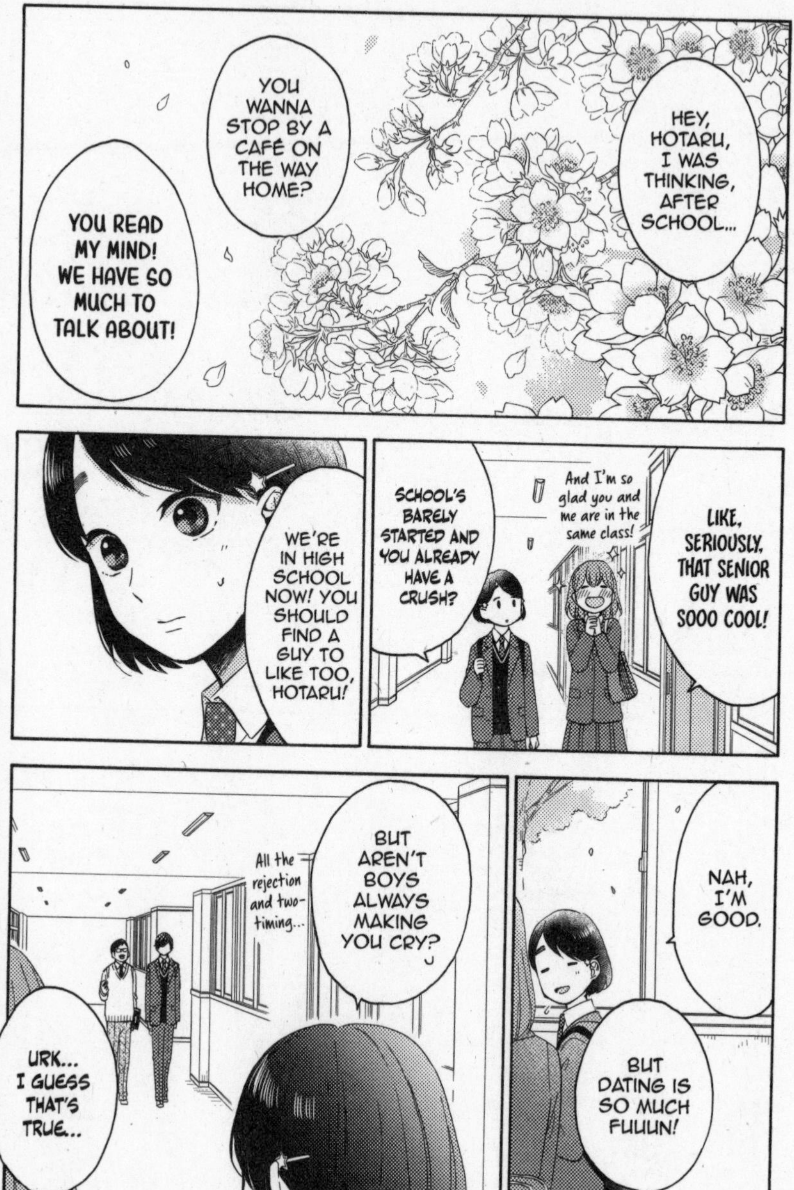
HEY, HOTARU, I WAS THINKING, AFTER SCHOOL...
YOU WANNA STOP BY A CAFÉ ON THE WAY HOME?
YOU READ MY MIND! WE HAVE SO MUCH TO TALK ABOUT!
LIKE, SERIOUSLY, THAT SENIOR GUY WAS SOOO COOL!
And I'm so glad you and me are in the same class!
SCHOOL'S BARELY STARTED AND YOU ALREADY HAVE A CRUSH?
WE'RE IN HIGH SCHOOL NOW! YOU SHOULD FIND A GUY TO LIKE TOO, HOTARU!
NAH, I'M GOOD.
BUT DATING IS SO MUCH FUUUN!
BUT AREN'T BOYS ALWAYS MAKING YOU CRY?
All the rejection and two-timing...
URK... I GUESS THAT'S TRUE...

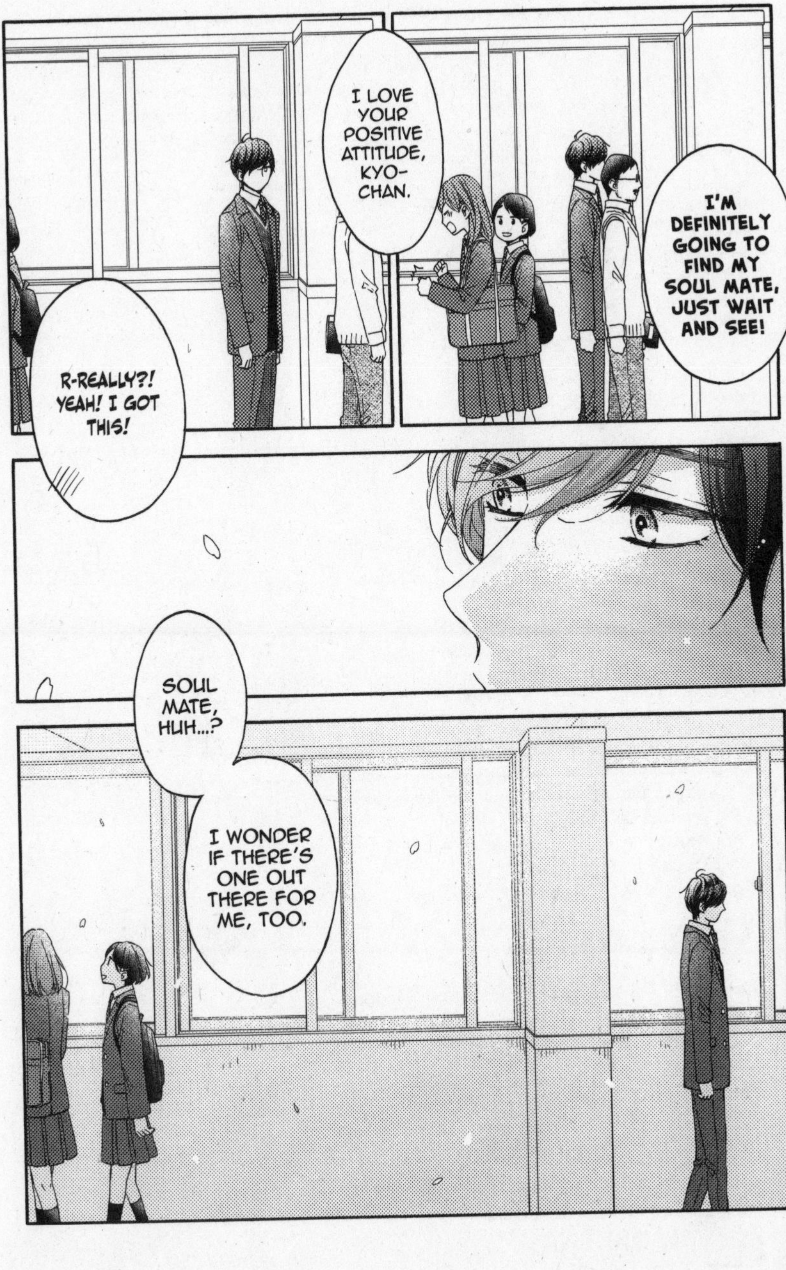
I'M DEFINITELY GOING TO FIND MY SOUL MATE, JUST WAIT AND SEE!
I LOVE YOUR POSITIVE ATTITUDE, KYO-CHAN.
R-REALLY?! YEAH! I GOT THIS!
SOUL MATE, HUH...?
I WONDER IF THERE'S ONE OUT THERE FOR ME, TOO.

A Kodansha Trade Paperback Original

A Condition Called Love 2 copyright © 2018 Megumi Morino
English translation copyright © 2023 Megumi Morino

Published in the United States by
Kodansha USA Publishing, LLC, New York.

Publication rights for this English edition arranged through
Kodansha Ltd., Tokyo.

First published in Japan in 2018 by Kodansha Ltd., Tokyo
as *Hananoi-kun to Koi no Yamai*, volume 2.

ISBN 978-1-64651-757-2

Printed in the United States of America.

9 8 7 6 5 4 3 2 1

Original Digital Edition Translation: Erin Procter
Original Digital Edition Lettering: Jacqueline Wee
Original Digital Edition Editing: Thalia Sutton
YKS Services LLC/SKY JAPAN, Inc.
Print Edition Lettering and Layout: Lys Blakeslee
Print Edition Editing: Aimee Zink
Kodansha USA Publishing edition cover design by Pekka Luhtala

Publisher: Kiichiro Sugawara

Director of Publishing Services: Ben Applegate
Director of Publishing Operations: Dave Barrett
Publishing Services Managing Editors: Alanna Ruse, Madison Salters,
with Grace Chen
Senior Production Manager: Angela Zurlo

KODANSHA.US

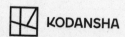

KODANSHA